JOHN MAYNARD KEYNES
AND INTERNATIONAL RELATIONS

John Maynard Keynes and International Relations

Economic Paths to War and Peace

DONALD MARKWELL

Warden of Trinity College
University of Melbourne

OXFORD
UNIVERSITY PRESS

OXFORD
UNIVERSITY PRESS

Great Clarendon Street, Oxford OX2 6DP

Oxford University Press is a department of the University of Oxford.
It furthers the University's objective of excellence in research, scholarship,
and education by publishing worldwide in

Oxford New York

Auckland Cape Town Dar es Salaam Hong Kong Karachi
Kuala Lumpur Madrid Melbourne Mexico City Nairobi
New Delhi Shanghai Taipei Toronto

With offices in

Argentina Austria Brazil Chile Czech Republic France Greece
Guatemala Hungary Italy Japan Poland Portugal Singapore
South Korea Switzerland Thailand Turkey Ukraine Vietnam

Oxford is a registered trade mark of Oxford University Press
in the UK and in certain other countries

Published in the United States
by Oxford University Press Inc., New York

British Library Cataloguing in Publication Data

Data available

Library of Congress Cataloguing in Publication Data

Data available

Typeset by SPI Publisher Services, Pondicherry, India
Printed in Great Britain
on acid-free paper by
Biddles Ltd., King's Lynn, Norfolk

ISBN 0-19-829236-8   978-0-19-829236-4

1 3 5 7 9 10 8 6 4 2

In memory of Hedley Bull, John Vincent, and my parents Dorothy and Noel Markwell.

A study of the history of opinion is a necessary preliminary to the emanci-
pation of the mind.

J. M. Keynes, *The End of Laissez-Faire*, 1924 and 1926[1]

Most of the valuable things in life have very little to do with international
affairs. But there is one necessary condition for everything good: peace.

J. M. Keynes, Hamburg, 26 August 1922[2]

In Washington Lord Halifax once whispered to Lord Keynes:
"It's true *they* have the money bags, but *we* have all the brains".

Doggerel from Anglo-American economic discussions
during World War II.[3]

The world has lost one of the very few with the imagination, courage and
leadership needed to... build a firm economic basis for peace...

Roy Harrod and Austin Robinson on Keynes, 1946[4]

---

[1] *The Collected Writings of John Maynard Keynes*, vol. 9, p. 277.
[2] Vol. 18, p. 26.
[3] R. N. Gardner, *Sterling-Dollar Diplomacy in Current Perspective* (New York, 1980) p. xiii.
[4] R. F. Harrod and E. A. G. Robinson, 'John Maynard Keynes', *The Economic Journal*, 56
   (1946), 171.

Contents

Acknowledgements

My debts are very many, and many are long-standing. My interest in Keynes was stimulated while studying economics at the University of Queensland in 1977–81. Colin Clark, who had worked closely with Keynes in the 1930s, was a consultant in the Department of Economics there.[1] Those who taught in it have contributed disproportionately to the study of Keynes.[2] In Oxford, Hedley Bull's long-standing interest in neglected thinkers about international relations was reflected in his encouragement to graduate students to study them.[3] I am grateful to him for suggesting this topic for my doctoral thesis, out of which this book has grown. He, Loukas Tsoukalis, John Darwin, and Martin Ceadel acted as supervisors. Their encouragement and advice was invaluable. I also owe a great debt to R. J. Vincent—who like Hedley Bull was 'untimely cut off'—for his friendship, and for his interest in this project.

Valuable advice has been received from many other people, and it is especially appropriate that I express my thanks to Chris Allsopp, Geoffrey Best, Vernon Bogdanor, Nigel Bowles, Mary Bull, Kathleen Burk, Edward Butchart, John Carey, W. M. Corden, Sir Zelman Cowen, John Coyne, Michael Freeden, R. D. Freeman, John Gray, Lord Hannay, Bryce Harland, Michael Hart, Sudhir Hazareesingh, Austin Holmes, Sir Michael Howard, Andrew Hurrell, G. John Ikenberry, Peter Jonson, Vijay Joshi, Bruce Lendon, David Leopold, I. M. D. Little, J. R. Lucas, Alex May, D. E. Moggridge, Patrick O'Brien, Robert O'Neill, Roger Opie, Terry O'Shaughnessy, R. A. C. Parker, L. J. Reeve, Sir Adam Roberts, Avi Shlaim, Lord Skidelsky, A. P. Thirlwall, Paula Thornhill, Jason Tomes, Michelle Totah, David Vines, Philip Waller, Ngaire Woods, Jonathan Wright, and Andrew Wyatt Walter.

I am grateful to the following for interviews: H. W. Arndt, D. G. Badger, T. J. Bartley, Judy Butlin, H. C. Coombs, Ernest Eyers, J. M. Garland, Lord Kahn, J. B. Kirkwood, Sir James Meade, Sir Leslie Melville, Sir John Philips, Lady Philips, Louis Rasminsky, W. B. Reddaway, and Sir Frederick Wheeler.

---

[1] On Clark, see, e.g. D. J. Markwell, *Keynes and Australia* (Sydney, 2000) pp. 40–3.

[2] e.g. A. Fitzgibbons, *Keynes's Vision: A New Political Economy* (Oxford, 1988); G. Mehta, *The Structure of the Keynesian Revolution* (London, 1977); B. Littleboy, *On Interpreting Keynes: A study in reconciliation* (London and New York, 1990); *History of Economics Review*, 25 (1996).

[3] See D. J. Markwell, 'Hedley Bull as a teacher', in R. J. O'Neill and D. N. Schwartz (eds.), *Hedley Bull on Arms Control* (Basingstoke & London, 1987) pp. 277–80.

I would like to express my appreciation to the various libraries and archives at which I have worked. My thanks go to the King's College Library, Cambridge, and especially Michael Halls, Jacqueline Cox, and Patricia McGuire; Marshall Library, Cambridge, and especially Judith Allen; Cambridge University Library; British Library, London; Public Records Office, now the National Archives, London; Bodleian Library, Oxford; Social Studies and History Faculty Libraries, Oxford; Institute of Economics and Statistics Library, Oxford; libraries of Trinity College, New College, and Merton College, Oxford; library and archives of the Reserve Bank of Australia, Sydney; National Library of Australia, Canberra; Seeley G. Mudd Library, Princeton; Houghton Library, Harvard; Massachusetts Historical Society, Boston; Sterling and Beinecke Libraries, Yale; Library of Congress, Washington, DC; George C. Marshall Research Library, Lexington, Va.; University of Virginia Library, Charlottesville; Columbia University Library, NY; Franklin D. Roosevelt Library, Hyde Park, NY; Hoover Institution Archives, Stanford; and the Public Archives of Canada, Ottawa. Research visits were made possible by the kind hospitality of Stewart and Jill Garrett, then in Washington, DC; Deborah Coyne and her family in Ottawa; Brian and Barbara Reddaway in Cambridge; and Geoffrey and June Markwell in Sydney.

I would like to thank the following for permission to reproduce published, or unpublished, material: Palgrave Publishers for permission to quote from the *Collected Writings of John Maynard Keynes*; The College Librarian of King's College, Cambridge, for permission to quote from unpublished writings of J. M. Keynes copyright The Provost and Scholars of King's College Cambridge 2006; Sir Edward Ford for permission to quote from the papers of Lord Brand held in the Bodleian Library, Oxford; Gillian B. Ingall for permission to quote from the Bryce Papers held in the Bodleian Library, Oxford; The Bodleian Library, Oxford, for their consent also to these quotations; British Library for permission to quote from the papers of Sir William Ashley; The Princeton University Library for permission to quote from the papers of Bernard Baruch, John Foster Dulles, Robert Lansing, Jacob Viner, and Harry Dexter White, held in the Seeley G. Mudd Manuscript Library, Princeton University Library; The George C. Marshall Foundation for permission to quote from Hervé Alphand; The University of Virginia Library for permission to quote from the Carter Glass Papers (#2913) and the Edward R. Stettinius Papers (#2723) held in the Albert and Shirley Small Special Collections Library, University of Virginia Library; The Massachusetts Historical Society for permission to quote from the Henry Cabot Lodge Papers; The National Library of Australia for permission to quote from a letter by W. M. Hughes, held in the Novar Papers; The Franklin D. Roosevelt Library, Herbert Hoover Presidential Library-Museum, and Yale University Library for their assistance with copyright matters. Every care has been taken to contact copyright owners, but this has not always been possible prior to publication. If notified, the publisher would be pleased to come to a suitable arrangement in each case.

Other assistance has been generously given by Humaira Ahmed, Don Amstad, Azeem Azhar, Henry Bannerman, Clare Bass, Laurence Claus, Guy Coughlan, Rob Crothers, L. Dalton, Pat Hall, Jeannette Hudson-Pudwell, Judith Kirby, Andrew Lewis, Malcolm Millar, Bill O'Chee, Cathy Ozkan, Alan Renwick, and Donald Strachan, to all of whom I am most appreciative.

This study was researched and written while I was a Rhodes Scholar and Junior Dean at Trinity College, Oxford; a visiting lecturer at the University of Western Australia; a Jane Eliza Procter Visiting Fellow at Princeton; a visiting scholar in the Research Department at the Reserve Bank of Australia; J. Arthur Rank Research Fellow at New College, Oxford; Fellow and Tutor in Politics at Merton College, Oxford; and Warden of Trinity College in the University of Melbourne, including during study leave back in Oxford. To all these institutions, I have much reason to be thankful.

At Trinity College, the University of Melbourne, I have especially benefited from the help and support of my research assistants, Geoffrey Browne, Jon Ritchie and Carolyn Daniel and my personal assistant, Kathryn McGrath, and express my profound thanks to them all. I owe special thanks, also, to Fay Dunlevy who completed the index. At Oxford University Press, Dominic Byatt has been patient and ever gracious. I thank him, and also Claire Abel, Sarah Argles, Tim Barton, Carol Bestley, Gwen Booth, Claire Gourlay, Lyndsey Rice, and Lizzy Suffling, and their colleagues at OUP for all they have done.

Sections of this study, or research related to it, have been presented as seminar papers in the University of Oxford (at least twice), the Reserve Bank of Australia, and the University of Keele. Parts of it have been published as 'J. M. Keynes, Idealism, and the Economic Basis of Peace', in David Long and Peter Wilson (eds.), *Thinkers of the Twenty Years Crisis* (Oxford, 1995), a chapter long superseded before it was published.

Last, but far from least, I must express my thanks to my late parents, and to my wife Kym, and children—Claire, Andrew, and Elizabeth.

Abbreviations

AR	*The Annual Register*
ARAPP	American Relief Administration—Paris papers, Hoover Institution Archives, Stanford
BBD	Bernard Baruch diary, unit IV, s. 4, BBP
BBP	Bernard Baruch papers, Princeton
BIS	Bank for International Settlements
BL	British Library, London
CGP	Carter Glass papers, University of Virginia
CU	Clearing Union
CW	*Collected Writings of John Maynard Keynes**
EAC	Economic Advisory Council
EJ	*The Economic Journal*
EMHP	E. M. House papers, Yale
FAK	Florence Ada Keynes, Keynes's mother
FDR	Franklin Delano Roosevelt
FRUS	*Foreign Relations of the United States*
FS	Finance Section of the Supreme Economic Council
GCMP	George C. Marshall papers, George C. Marshall Research Library, Lexington, Va.
HCLP	Henry Cabot Lodge papers, Massachusetts Historical Society, Boston
HDWP	Harry Dexter White papers, Princeton
HMD	Henry Morgenthau diaries, F. D. Roosevelt Library, Hyde Park, NY
IBRD	International Bank for Reconstruction and Development
IMF	International Monetary Fund
ITO	International Trade Organization
IWC	Imperial War Cabinet
JFDP	John Foster Dulles papers, Princeton

* References simply to 'Vol. *x*, p. *y*' are to *The Collected Writings of John Maynard Keynes*. The volumes are listed in the bibliography.

JNK	John Neville Keynes, Keynes's father
JVP	Jacob Viner papers, Princeton
KP	J. M. Keynes papers, King's College, Cambridge
LOC	Library of Congress, Washington, DC
LSE	London School of Economics and Political Science
NDP	Norman Davis papers, Library of Congress
NS	*New Statesman*
PAC	Public Archives of Canada, Ottawa
PMWP	Paul M. Warburg papers, Yale
PPC	Paris Peace Conference
PRO	Public Record Office (now the National Archives), Kew, London
RBAA	Reserve Bank of Australia Archives, Sydney
RHBP	R. H. Brand papers, Bodleian Library, Oxford
RLP	Robert Lansing Papers, Princeton
SEC	Supreme Economic Council
SWC	Supreme War Council
UNRRA	United Nations Relief and Rehabilitation Administration
VCMcCD	Vance C. McCormick diary, Sterling Library, Yale

John Maynard Keynes: A Chronology

1883	Born in Cambridge (6 June)
1902–5	Reading mathematics at King's College, Cambridge
1905–6	Preparing for Civil Service examinations
1906–8	Working in the India Office
1908	Returns to Cambridge to teach economics
1909	Fellow of King's College, Cambridge (to death)
1911–44	Editor of *The Economic Journal*
1913	*Indian Currency and Finance*
1915–19	Working in the Treasury, including at the Paris Peace Conference
1919	Resigns from Treasury, writes *The Economic Consequences of the Peace* (published December)
1921	*A Treatise on Probability*
1922	*A Revision of the Treaty* (January), at Genoa Conference for *The Manchester Guardian* (April)
1922–3	Editing *Manchester Guardian* supplements on 'Reconstruction in Europe'
1923	Chairman of *The Nation and Athenaeum*, *A Tract on Monetary Reform*
1924	Lectures on *The End of Laissez-Faire* (published 1926)
1925	*The Economic Consequences of Mr Churchill*, marries Lydia Lopokova, *Am I a Liberal?*, *A Short View of Russia*
1929	*Can Lloyd George Do It?* (with Hubert Henderson)
1929–31	Member, Macmillan Committee on Finance and Industry
1930–9	Member, Economic Advisory Council
1930	*A Treatise on Money* (October)
1931	Director of the merged *New Statesman and Nation*, urges revenue tariff (March), *Essays in Persuasion*
1933	*Essays in Biography*, *The Means to Prosperity*, 'National Self-Sufficiency'
1936	*The General Theory of Employment, Interest and Money*
1937	Major heart attack
1938	'A Positive Peace Programme' (March)
1940	*How to Pay for the War* (February), adviser to Chancellor of the Exchequer (July, until death), 'Proposals to Counter the German "New Order" '(November)
1941	US visit on Lend-Lease and post-war aims (May–July), first draft of Clearing Union plan (September)
1942	Becomes Lord Keynes

1

Introduction

In *The Economic Consequences of the Peace* in 1919, the Cambridge economist John Maynard Keynes (1883–1946) condemned the economic provisions of the Treaty of Versailles as a threat to the peace of Europe.[1] In 1936, his *General Theory of Employment, Interest and Money* expounded a new economic system which, it emphasized, 'might be more favourable to peace than the old has been'.[2] During the Second World War, Keynes was the principal British negotiator in the creation of the International Monetary Fund (IMF) and World Bank. Though most famous for his contribution to economic theory and domestic economic policies, Keynes was, in these and other ways, an important writer on, and participant in, international relations.

Yet, though their writings in many cases touch on international issues, students of Keynes have not in any systematic or thorough way studied his thinking from the perspective of international relations. This is despite voluminous literature about him, including several major biographical studies: Robinson's superb memoir,[3] Harrod's *Life*,[4] Moggridge's short *Keynes*[5] and his substantial *Maynard Keynes: An Economist's Biography*,[6] three volumes of Skidelsky's rounded biography,[7] Hession's psychological study,[8] and Cairncross' essay.[9] The literature on Keynes's economics and the development of his economic thinking,[10] and on other aspects of his life and

---

[1] Vol. 2, e.g. pp. 157, 169–70.

[2] Vol. 7, p. 381.

[3] E. A. G. Robinson, 'John Maynard Keynes', *EJ*, 57 (1947), 1–68.

[4] R. F. Harrod, *The Life of John Maynard Keynes* (London, 1972 [1951]).

[5] D. E. Moggridge, *Keynes* (London and Basingstoke, 2nd edn., 1980).

[6] D. E. Moggridge, (ed.), *Maynard Keynes: An Economist's Biography* (London and New York, 1992).

[7] R. Skidelsky, *John Maynard Keynes: Hopes Betrayed, 1883–1920*, vol. 1 (London, 1983); *The Economist as Saviour, 1920–1937*, vol. 2 (London, 1992); *Fighting for Britain, 1937–1946*, vol. 3 (London, 2000).

[8] C. H. Hession, *John Maynard Keynes: A Personal Biography* (New York, 1984).

[9] Alec Cairncross, 'John Maynard Keynes', *Oxford Dictionary of National Biography*, vol. 31 (Oxford, 2004), pp. 483–98.

[10] For example, P. Clarke, *The Keynesian Revolution in the Making, 1924–1936* (Oxford, 1988).

thought,[11] has mushroomed. But little of this literature has been specifically concerned with Keynes and international relations. That Keynes gave considerable attention to the economic causes of war and economic means of promoting peace has been generally neglected. Although invaluable, the thirty volumes of *The Collected Writings of John Maynard Keynes*[12] are concerned with Keynes as an economist,[13] and, for the student of international relations, require supplementing with further archival and other research.

This book seeks to explain the thinking about international relations which underlay Keynes's writings and actions. It does so through a systematic exegesis of Keynes's thinking on international relations as it evolved from his undergraduate days until his death. This exegesis is necessarily selective. Keynes's writings and actions in the field of international relations were so extensive that it has not been possible to give detailed coverage of all. For example, less attention is given to his role in war finance, and in discussing war debts and reparations after 1922, than to many other topics.

The exegesis is, moreover, supplemented by some evaluative and interpretative judgements. There is some discussion of both the context and the influence of his thought, though full assessments of these subjects are not attempted. It is not possible in a volume of this nature and scope to evaluate fully his views on all issues—even on major topics of continuing or renewed controversy such as his attitude to the Paris Peace Conference (PPC) and reparations demands against Germany.[14]

The exegesis, though proceeding chronologically, develops a particular interpretation of Keynes's thought. It argues that Keynes was an idealist thinker about international relations in the sense identified by Hedley Bull in his discussion of the idealist or progressivist doctrines that predominated in the 1920s and early 1930s:[15]

---

[11] For example, D. Crabtree and A. P. Thirlwall (eds.), *Keynes and the Bloomsbury Group* (London and Basingstoke, 1980); Thirlwall (ed.), *Keynes as a Policy Adviser* (London and Basingstoke, 1982); R. M. O'Donnell, *Keynes: Philosophy, Economics and Politics: The Philosophical Foundations of Keynes's Thought and Their Influence on his Economics and Politics* (Basingstoke and London, 1989).

[12] London and Basingstoke, 1971–89.

[13] From the 'General Introduction' to most volumes: e.g. vol. 1, p. viii. 'Keynes as a working economist and participant in public affairs', vol. 30, pp. xi, xiv.

[14] Renewed disagreement with Keynes on this is reflected in, e.g. M. F. Boemeke, G. D. Feldman, and E. Glaser (ed.), *The Treaty of Versailles: A Reassessment after 75 Years* (Washington, DC, and Cambridge, UK, 1998); N. Ferguson, *The Pity of War* (London, 1998); M. MacMillan, *Peacemakers: The Paris Conference of 1919 and Its Attempt to End War* (London, 2001); see also, e.g. Z. Steiner, *The Lights that Failed: European International History, 1919–1933* (Oxford, 2005).

[15] 'The Theory of International Politics, 1919–1969', in B. Porter (ed.), *The Aberystwyth Papers: International Politics, 1919–1969* (London, 1972) pp. 33–4.

By the 'idealists' we have in mind writers such as Sir Alfred Zimmern, S. H. Bailey, Philip Noel-Baker, and David Mitrany in the United Kingdom, and James T. Shotwell, Pitman Potter, and Parker T. Moon in the United States....The distinctive characteristic of these writers was their belief in progress: the belief, in particular, that the system of international relations that had given rise to the First World War was capable of being transformed into a fundamentally more peaceful and just world order; that under the impact of the awakening of democracy, the growth of 'the international mind', the development of the League of Nations, the good works of men of peace or the enlightenment spread by their own teaching, it was in fact being transformed; and that their responsibility as students of international relations was to assist this march of progress to overcome the ignorance, the prejudices, the ill-will, and the sinister interests that stood in its way.

We shall see that Keynes believed that it was possible to replace the conflictual international politics of the past with greater harmony and peace; that important in his particular form of idealism was the belief (not mentioned by Bull) that there are major economic causes of war, and that peace could be promoted by economic means; and that his evolving ideas about the economic determinants of war and peace were central to his contributions to planning and debating post-war reconstruction during and after both world wars. In identifying Keynes as an idealist, this volume also helps to differentiate him from other idealists, reflecting the diversity of progressivist or liberal internationalist thinking which recent authors have been keen to stress.[16]

This book identifies in Keynes's writings several economic factors which he believed could cause war, including impoverishment, population pressure, penetration by foreign capital, and the 'competitive struggle for markets'.[17] Although Keynes was consistent over many years in his Malthusian pessimism on population pressure, his views on the other factors evolved. In particular, we trace the evolution of his thought through four positions, identified here as classical liberal, early liberal institutionalist, protectionist, and mature liberal institutionalist. First, Keynes was (in his phrase) brought up with the classical liberal notion that free trade promotes peace, and he believed this through to the very early 1930s. Second, however, by 1919 he had concluded that internationally agreed state action was necessary to reconstruct and manage the international economy so that economic interdependence could work. This early liberal institutionalism foreshadowed both his search for a middle way between laissez-faire and Marxian socialism, and

---

[16] For example, P. Wilson, 'The myth of the "First Great Debate"', *Review of International Studies*, 24 (1998) special edition, 1–15.

[17] Vol. 7, p. 381.

his mature liberal institutionalism of 1936–46. Before then, however, reflecting the protectionist and autarkic ideas of the Depression years, Keynes came temporarily to believe that a higher degree of economic isolation and national self-sufficiency might be more conducive to peace than economic internationalism was. This third view culminated in articles he wrote in 1933. Fourth, Keynes came to think that, if there were an international monetary system that did not pit the interests of countries against each other, and if states could and did pursue economic policies to promote full employment, then there would be no economic causes of war (other perhaps than population pressure). A high degree of freedom of trade would then be compatible with, and might promote, peace. This mature liberal institutionalism found expression in *The General Theory*, and underlay Keynes's attempts during the Second World War to build a suitable international monetary system and to promote the pursuit of Keynesian policies internationally.

By studying Keynes's thought about international relations, we gain a fuller picture of the history of ideas concerning economic aspects of international order, especially in post-war reconstruction. As a case study in idealist thought, examining Keynes's thinking gives us further insight into the liberal-idealist tradition in international relations, including reminding us that some of the preoccupations of later theorists—such as interdepend- ence,[18] and the need (or otherwise) for a leader or hegemon in the international economy[19]—were not new. In his study of British liberalism from 1914 to 1939, *Liberalism Divided*, Freeden wrote that liberal attitudes to international relations deserve a study on their own.[20] The growing literature on inter-war idealism partly provides this, both demonstrating an idealist tradition and reflecting the important diversity within it.[21] This book aims to

[18] For example, R. N. Cooper, *The Economics of Interdependence* (New York, 1968); R. Keohane and J. Nye, *Power and Interdependence* (Boston, 1977).

[19] For example, C. P. Kindleberger, *The World in Depression* (Berkeley, 1973); R. Keohane, *After Hegemony* (Princeton, 1984).

[20] M. Freeden, *Liberalism Divided* (Oxford, 1986), p. 14. See also pp. 363–5.

[21] For example, D. Long and P. Wilson (eds.), *Thinkers of the Twenty Years Crisis* (Oxford, 1995); D. J. Markwell, 'Sir Alfred Zimmern Revisited: fifty years on', *Review of International Studies*, 12 (1986), 279–92; M. E. Ceadel, *Semi-Detached Idealists: the British Peace Movement and International Relations, 1854–1945* (Oxford, 2000); Wilson, 'The myth of the "First Great Debate"'; id, *The International Theory of Leonard Woolf: A Study in Twentieth Century Idealism* (New York and Basingstoke, 2003); C. Sylvest, 'Continuity and change in British liberal internationalism, c. 1900–1930', *Review of International Studies*, 31 (2005), 263–83; A. Osiander, 'Rereading Early Twentieth-Century IR Theory: Idealism Revisited', *International Studies Quarterly*, 42 (1998), 409–32; B. C. Schmidt, 'Lessons from the Past: Reassessing the Interwar Disciplinary History of International Relations', *International Studies Quarterly*, 42 (1998), 433–59; L. M. Ashworth, *Creating International Studies: Angell, Mitrany and the Liberal Tradition* (Aldershot, 1999); see also, e.g. D. Drinkwater, *Sir Harold Nicolson and International Relations: The Practitioner as Theorist* (Oxford, 2005).

help fill the gap further. We also gain a fuller picture of the events in which Keynes was involved, such as the Paris Peace Conference and the origins of the Bretton Woods institutions. Much of what he wrote or said (e.g. *The Economic Consequences*) had a major impact on events. By examining the international relations dimension of his thought, for example in *The General Theory*, we can better understand the evolution of Keynes's economic thinking, which has had a profound impact: the evolution described in this book is part of the story of his paradigm shift from classical to Keynesian economics. It is hoped that this study will also facilitate the assessment, from time to time, of the contemporary relevance of Keynes's ideas to evolving circumstances.

2

Keynes as a Classical Liberal

[W]e suffer from the habit of interpreting the great ones of the past by reference to what came after or, at the best, what was prevailing in their maturity and old-age, instead of interpreting them in the light of what came before and what they were imbibing in their youth.

J. M. Keynes, 1943[1]

Keynes was, in a phrase he frequently used, brought up[2] to accept certain ideas that were central to the classical liberalism of the late nineteenth and early twentieth centuries. He worked in the British Treasury during the First World War to finance a war effort towards which he was increasingly hostile. He also contributed during and immediately after the war to British government thinking about how to treat the defeated enemy. But his ideas on this faced fierce resistance.

This chapter traces the evolution of Keynes's thinking on these and other issues to the end of 1918. It outlines aspects of Keynes's thought on international issues before the First World War, especially how he was brought up to think that free trade promoted peace, and his attitudes to the Empire and to population pressure; his approach to the First World War, conscription, and (briefly) war finance; and, in some detail, the evolution of his thought on reparations to the end of 1918. We see repeatedly Keynes's hostility to economic nationalism—his belief before the First World War that it would lead to conflict, his belief that it had contributed to the outbreak of the war, and his desire not to see a return to it afterwards.

[1] Keynes to E. Tillyard, 25 June 1943, L/43/88–9, KP.
[2] This expression is used of Keynes or of others at, e.g. vol. 7, pp. xxiii, xxv, xxix, xxxi, 175, 177, 335, 339, 351, 364, 366.

2.1 'BROUGHT UP' A FREE TRADER: 'THE SPIRIT OF BURKE AND ADAM SMITH'[3]

Keynes was born in 1883, the son of a Cambridge logician and economist, J. N. Keynes, and of F. A. Keynes (née Brown). He went up from Eton to King's College, Cambridge, in 1902 to read mathematics, and stayed on to study economics, political science, and other subjects for the civil service examination in 1906. He worked in the India Office for two years before returning to Cambridge in 1908 to lecture in economics. Keynes's work in the India Office generated an interest in Indian financial arrangements that led to his first book, *Indian Currency and Finance* (1913).[4] A dissertation on probability won Keynes a Fellowship at King's in 1909, and after revision was published in 1921 as *A Treatise on Probability*.[5]

In 1938, Keynes claimed that it was part of his pre-1914 beliefs, influenced by an incomplete reading of G. E. Moore's *Principia Ethica* (1903), and shared by the friends who later formed the core of 'Bloomsbury', that good states of mind (consisting in communion with objects of love, beauty, and truth) were far more important than social action or even 'the life of action generally'. This, Keynes said, was 'our Ideal'. But 'in practice, of course, at least so far as I was concerned, the outside world was not forgotten or forsworn'.[6]

The Edwardian Keynes repudiated any obligation on the individual to obey general rules, especially of morality.[7] This insistence on the right of the individual to decide his or her own conduct, though earlier perhaps most important in sexual matters, was important during the First World War in leading Keynes to oppose conscription. Keynes and his friends were, he wrote, 'among the last of the Utopians, . . . who believe in a continuing moral progress by virtue of which the human race already consists of reliable, rational, decent people, influenced by truth and objective standards, who can be safely released from the outward restraints of convention and traditional standards and inflexible rules of conduct, and left, from now onwards, to their own sensible devices, pure motives and reliable intuitions of the good.'[8] By 1938, when

---

[3] D. H. Robertson told Keynes in 1941 that his Clearing Union proposals gave 'a growing hope that the spirit of Burke and Adam Smith is on earth again': vol. 25, p. 67; see ch. 6, this volume; Robertson, too, had been 'brought up in the liberal tradition': D. H. Robertson, *Britain in the World Economy* (London, 1954), p. 81.

[4] Vol. 1.

[5] Vol. 8. See, e.g. vol. 10, p. 445.

[6] See vol. 10, pp. 436, 438, 445. Cf. B. Russell, *The Autobiography of Bertrand Russell*, i, *1872–1914* (London, 1967), pp. 70–1; see also A. J. Ayer, *Russell and Moore: The Analytical Heritage* (London, 1971), p. 137.

[7] Vol. 10, p. 446.   [8] Vol. 10, p. 447.

he wrote his memoir 'My Early Beliefs', Keynes was to regard this view as misunderstanding human nature, which was subject to vulgar passions,[9] and as ignoring the need to preserve those social institutions which create order.

'My Early Beliefs' portrayed only part of Keynes's early philosophy, not least exaggerating his detachment from 'real life'.[10] While at Eton, Keynes had also developed an interest in Edmund Burke.[11] In 1904 he wrote a lengthy, sophisticated, sympathetic but not uncritical essay on Burke's political principles.[12] Keynes endorsed Burke's 'timidity in introducing present evil for the sake of future benefits', emphasizing that our 'power of prediction is so slight' that 'it is seldom wise to sacrifice a present benefit for a doubtful advantage in the future'.[13] The theme of uncertainty, which some regard as the core of Keynes's economics, recurs in his discussions of international relations over subsequent decades. Keynes's endorsement of Burke's objection to violent methods of progress stressed that what the state sought must not only be better than the status quo, but sufficiently better to make up for the evils of the transition:[14] a view evident in Keynes's later approach to Marxism, and indeed all revolutionary change.[15] Keynes continued:[16]

It is upon this principle that Burke's attitude towards war is mainly based; there are occasions, he maintains, when it is a necessary means, and never can such occasions altogether cease, but it is a means that brings innumerable evils in its train. It is not sufficient that a nation's legal claims should have been infringed. Only great causes justify it; with much prudence, reverence, and calculation must it be approached.

This, as we shall see, was Keynes's view also. In notes on reading Burke, Keynes had quoted him as attacking 'the jingo', and as describing war for profit as criminal, and calculation of profit in war as false.[17]

Keynes saw Burke as a free trader: it was, *inter alia*, 'as one of the earliest exponents of Laisser Faire' that 'he is most important in the history of opinion'. Burke had much in common with the Manchester school of the nineteenth century, and with Adam Smith.[18] Quoting Burke's 1778 letters to

---

[9] Vol. 10, p. 450.   [10] See UA/22/7, KP.

[11] Harrod, *Life*, pp. 56, 58; Skidelsky, *Hopes*, p. 98 n. 101. He acquired Burke's *Complete Works* as a prize.

[12] See UA/20/1, UA/20/2, and UA/20/3, KP; Moggridge, *Biography*, pp. 74, 124–7; Skidelsky, *Hopes*, pp. 154–7; *Saviour*, pp. 61–4; Fitzgibbons, *Vision*, ch. 4; B. W. Bateman and J. B. Davis (eds.), *Keynes and Philosophy* (Aldershot, 1991), ch. 3; O'Donnell, *Philosophy*, pp. 276–85.

[13] UA/20/3/13, 17, KP; see also UA/20/3/85.

[14] UA/20/3/18, KP; Skidelsky, *Hopes*, p. 156; *Saviour*, p. 62.

[15] See, e.g. vol. 21, p. 245; Fitzgibbons, *Vision*, p. 59. But Keynes thought Burke too timid: UA/20/3/43–4, KP.

[16] UA/20/3/18, KP.   [17] UA/20/1/80, 82, KP.

[18] UA/20/3/21, 23, 33, KP.

Bristol on Irish trade, which implied that free trade promoted peace,[19] Keynes described Burke as the earliest advocate of the principles of *The Wealth of Nations* in the House of Commons.[20] (Both Smith[21] and, more unreservedly, the Manchester school of Cobden and Bright[22] believed that free trade would promote peace.)

Skidelsky is surely right to see in Keynes's attitude to Burke in 1904 'the political temper of the Middle Way which Keynes espoused in the inter-war years'.[23] Some writers have seen Burke's clemency as evident in Keynes's approach to the Treaty of Versailles.[24] The clemency to which Keynes's 1904 essay referred was treating one's own people with moderation and kindness: there was no reference to a defeated enemy.[25] However, in 1920, Keynes, writing on Versailles, quoted Burke on the unwisdom of indicting a whole people.[26]

Keynes in his undergraduate days was 'a keen Liberal'.[27] In May 1903, the Colonial Secretary, Joseph Chamberlain, reignited the controversy between free trade and imperial preference that was to divide Balfour's Government and reunite the Liberals (who were almost unanimously for free trade), helping them to power in 1905.[28] Keynes played his own enthusiastic, if minor, part in this great controversy.

In August 1903, what Keynes later referred to as 'the famous manifesto of the professors'[29] appeared as a letter to *The Times*.[30] In the letter, most leading economists, including F. Y. Edgeworth, Alfred Marshall, J. S. Nicholson, A. C. Pigou, and W. R. Scott, opposed tariff reform on the grounds that it would not consolidate the Empire but engender 'irritating controversies' between members of it, and 'by leading to the revival of Protection', injure

---

[19] See Burke's letters to the gentlemen of Bristol on the Trade of Ireland, 1778, *The Works of the Right Honourable Edmund Burke*, iii (London, 1815) at (e.g.) p. 218; J. Prior, *Memoir of the Life and Character of the Right Hon. Edmund Burke*, i (London, 1826), pp. 341–2.

[20] UA/20/3/35, KP. On Keynes in the 1920s associating Burke with 'individualism and *laissez-faire*', see vol. 9, pp. 274, 276–7; cf. p. 288.

[21] A. Smith, *The Wealth of Nations* (ed. Edwin Cannan, London, 1904) at, e.g. pp. 457–8. See D. Winch, *Adam Smith's Politics* (Cambridge, 1978), p. 81; E. Brose, 'Adam Smith's View of International Relations', M.Phil. thesis (Oxford, 1983). Some doubt that Smith believed this. He was widely thought in the 19th century to have done so.

[22] H. Bull, 'Richard Cobden and International Relations', seminar paper, LSE, 1956; H. L. Nathan, *Free Trade To-Day* (London, 1929), p. 128.

[23] Skidelsky, *Saviour*, p. 64.

[24] Moggridge, *Biography*, p. 126; Bateman and Davis, *Philosophy*, pp. 44–5; Fitzgibbons, *Vision*, p. 71.

[25] UA/20/3/42, KP.

[26] Vol. 17, p. 77.

[27] G. Mander to Keynes, 9 Nov. 1904, PP/45/209, KP; see also, e.g. PS/1/15, KP.

[28] See A. Sykes, *Tariff Reform in British Politics, 1903–1913* (Oxford, 1979).

[29] Vol. 10, p. 271.

[30] *The Times*, 15 Aug. 1903. For some of the reaction, see *The Times*, 18, 20, 21, 22 Aug.

material well-being and 'political purity' at home. Among the economists repudiating the manifesto were London professors H. S. Foxwell and W. A. S. Hewins, and Archdeacon William Cunningham (Cambridge).[31] Most support for tariff reform came from economic historians, and theoreticians (especially of the 'Marshallian' orthodoxy) were overwhelmingly for free trade.[32] Pigou elaborated the arguments of the manifesto, and treated free trade as the policy of peace, in two books, *The Riddle of the Tariff* (1903)[33] and *Protective and Preferential Import Duties* (1906).[34] Alfred Marshall in August 1903 prepared a 'Memorandum on the Fiscal Policy of International Trade', which, after revision in 1908, was published at the instigation of the Chancellor of the Exchequer, Lloyd George. The published version argued that schemes for imperial preference 'if approached in a spirit of greed, rather than of self-sacrifice' were 'likely to arouse animosity in other lands, and to postpone the day at which it may be possible to work towards a federated Anglo-Saxondom, which seems to be an even higher ideal than Imperial Unity'.[35] (A letter from Marshall to Sir Frederick Pollock in 1898 reflected Marshall's devotion to Adam Smith, whom he described as 'my Lord and Master', his greater interest in Anglo-American relations than the Empire, and his recognition of the shift of economic power from Britain to the USA.)[36]

In September 1903, a pamphlet by Prime Minister A. J. Balfour, entitled *Some Economic Notes on Insular Free Trade*, argued that British negotiators needed to be free 'to use fiscal inducements' to respond to the hostile tariffs of other powers.[37] In the autumn of 1903, Joseph Chamberlain and the Duke of Devonshire both left Balfour's Cabinet, Chamberlain to crusade for imperial preference, Devonshire to oppose it. The Duke was Chancellor of Cambridge University, and his advocacy of free trade was applauded there.

That Keynes followed these events with keen interest is evident from his later writings, and from his speeches and letters at the time. He referred in 1924 to Marshall's 'admirable Memorandum';[38] in 1936, to Foxwell's 'mild protectionism in the nineteen-hundreds (refusing to sign the famous manifesto of the professors)';[39] and in 1930, to Balfour's *Notes* as 'the most

[31] *AR*, 1903, p. 188; Foxwell and Hewins letters, *The Times*, 20 Aug. 1903.
[32] A. Kadish, *Historians, Economists, and Economic History* (London, 1989), p. 217.
[33] (London), pp. 27–8, 60, 88, 106.
[34] (London), pp. 80–2, 109–10, 114–17.
[35] A. Marshall, *Memorandum on the Fiscal Policy of International Trade*, Aug. 1903, revised Aug. 1908, published as Parliamentary Paper 321 (London, 11 Nov. 1908). See L/M/14–15, KP.
[36] Marshall to Pollock, 7 June 1898, MS Bryce 120, fol. 52, Bodleian; see also fol. 51.
[37] *AR*, 1903, p. 196.
[38] Vol. 10, p. 218.
[39] Vol. 10, p. 271; see pp. 267 ff, 275, 292. Although a Professor in London, Foxwell lived at 1 Harvey Road, Cambridge, near the Keynes's: p. 282.

"academic" memorandum which a Prime Minister ever circulated to his Cabinet', which 'bears re-reading'.[40] As a young man Keynes's view was clear: he advocated free trade in 1903 (with Pigou), 1904, and 1905 in the Cambridge Union and elsewhere,[41] in support of Liberals in the 1906 election,[42] in 1909,[43] and in 1910.[44]

Keynes's earliest Cambridge debating speeches preceded Chamberlain's call for tariff reform. In January 1903, Keynes spoke in the Cambridge Union against the motion 'That this House heartily approves the policy of joint action with Germany in the Venezuelan dispute'.[45] In May 1903, he proposed 'That this House sincerely hopes that Home Rule for Ireland is beyond the sphere of practical politics.'[46] When the fiscal controversy got underway, Keynes was inexhaustible in his advocacy of free trade. Amongst several speeches was one, on 21 November, 1903, in the St John's College Debating Society, moving '[t]hat the Spirit of Nationalism is, at the present time, one of the most considerable hindrances to the progress of Civilisation.'[47] Three days later, in the Cambridge Union, he spoke against the motion '[t]hat in the Opinion of this House a Policy of Retaliatory Tariffs is essential to the Prosperity of the Empire.'[48] Amongst a number of other speeches was one with which in January 1905, with a brilliant portrayal of a languid Balfour, he proposed '[t]hat this House regrets the capture of the Conservative Party by the Tariff Reform League.'[49]

Keynes's undergraduate debating speeches lucidly expressed a reasonably coherent view of international relations. Whilst acknowledging 'that there may be cases in which war is justifiable',[50] he had a strong preference for 'peace, international amity and reciprocity'.[51] These he associated with his ideal world of universal free trade and a few great groups of self-governing states, loosely linked in the manner of the British Empire, with relations between these groups as 'friendly [and] as free from jealousy as there really seems some hope that the American Empire and the British Empire may become'. This ideal contrasted sharply with a world of 'four vast empires . . . in hatred and jealousy'. Keynes connected peace and prosperity with 'the interdependence and connexion of material well-being throughout the world', and with avoiding 'the expense and the degradation of huge armaments'. Nationalism, seeking to 'make one bit [of the world] independent of the rest', would almost necessarily make it 'an object of jealousy and hostility'.[52]

[40] Vol. 10, pp. 43–5; see also p. 271.
[41] See below, and Kadish, *Historians*, pp. 217, 291 n.
[42] Skidelsky, *Hopes*, pp. 166–7; Mander to Keynes, 25 Dec. 1905, PP/45/209, KP.
[43] See below, and vol. 15, pp. 18–19.   [44] See below, and vol. 15, pp. 39–43.
[45] OC/5/4 ff, KP.   [46] OC/5/34 ff, KP.   [47] OC/2/137–42, KP.
[48] OC/5/53 ff, KP.   [49] OC/5/125 ff, KP.   [50] OC/5/69, KP.
[51] OC/2/137–42, KP.   [52] OC/2/137–42, KP.

As previously in a school essay,[53] Keynes defended patriotism—positive spirit about one's country. He distinguished it from nationalism, which he associated with antipathy to others, including a 'feeling that anyone else's prosperity is your damage'. He mentioned the Pan-Celtic, Pan-German, Pan-Slav, and Zionist movements, with their 'love of isolation' and 'tenacious jealousy', as amongst the forces leading 'to war and to protection'. Keynes saw 'the spirit of Germany moulded by militarism', and clearly thought that Chamberlain's 'ideal', as he put it, of a 'self-sufficient and isolated Empire' would provoke rivalry between empires.[54] Chamberlain's Empire would be 'a menace to the world's peace, and a challenge to foreign powers, with ports closed against all the nations'.[55] He continued: 'If once we allow our rival empires to grow up in jealousy, nothing but an Armageddon, and Universal war can prelude the dawn of everlasting peace.' It was necessary to 'think of the foreigner as a neighbour, not as a potential murderer'.[56] This, it seems, was the thrust of Keynes's answer to the tariff reform argument that imperial consolidation, by strengthening the Empire, would promote peace.[57] He also rejected the argument for imperial preference that it would give Britain a means of retaliating against foreign discrimination against those parts of the Empire giving preference to Britain (German action against Canada was a prominent issue). Such tariff wars were, Keynes said, not 'worth the candle'.[58]

In one speech, Keynes explicitly rejected Little Englandism, and continued:

We, who are Imperialists, believe, on the whole, in the beneficence of these [Imperial] ambitions; we think that British rule brings with it an increase of justice, liberty, and prosperity; and we administer our Empire not with a view to our own pecuniary aggrandisement, and to the monopolisation of the trade of one fifth of the world, but looking rather towards the fortunes of those who are fellow citizens and to their prosperity.

He drew a sharp contrast between British and German imperialism. Germany's aims and 'ways are not our ways'; and Germany—envious of 'our possessions', 'restless', 'Machiavellian', and with 'far reaching' ambitions—'considers us her natural antagonist'.[59]

Chamberlain would, Keynes said, change the British Empire, replacing freedom by uniformity, and encouraging 'the secession now of this and now of that colony, as each in turn felt itself "bested" in the bitter market strife of conflicting interests'.[60] Amongst the reasons Keynes opposed the complete

---

[53] PP/31/9/1–3, KP.   [54] OC/2/137–42, KP.   [55] OC/5/56, KP.
[56] OC/2/137–42, KP.   [57] OC/5/54, 58, KP.
[58] OC/5/118, KP; see Nathan, *Free Trade To-Day*, pp. 113–14.
[59] OC/5/23–4, KP.   [60] OC/5/56–7, KP.

separation of Britain and Ireland was 'trade connection'.[61] He acknowledged that Ireland had been greatly wronged by Britain, and deserved relief by the British taxpayer; but Ireland under Home Rule could neither share in imperial expenses without representation in the House of Commons, nor be permitted such a voice in the internal affairs of Britain.

An important difference between British and German policy was that, unlike Britain, Germany was willing to use force to obtain, for example, arrears of unpaid interest on the Great Venezuelan Railway. Keynes said that British policy had rightly been, and was, that British investors abroad knew the precariousness of their investments, obtained higher rates of interest to compensate them for that risk, and could not expect the British government to support their demands with gunboats. (There were, however, other Venezuelan outrages against British subjects and ships which Keynes thought did justify fighting her.)[62]

We see, then, in Keynes's debating speeches of 1903–5 a strong desire for peace, notwithstanding a preparedness to go to war, and a belief that enduring peace was possible; a belief that free trade promotes peace, and that economic isolationism, protection, and rival empires were likely to lead to political conflict and war; a belief that the British Empire advanced the well-being of its peoples, but was of its essence a loose association of free peoples; an alarm at German militarism, and a particular desire for Anglo-American harmony; and a belief that, though a state such as Germany might, Britain did not and should not use force abroad to protect the investments of its nationals.

This view of international relations clearly belongs in the liberal-idealistic tradition of thought. As we have seen, idealism in international relations, as understood here, is the belief that it is possible to progress from the conflictual international politics of the past to a fundamentally more harmonious, peaceful, and just future. Such idealism is most commonly associated with reformist domestic ideologies such as liberalism and socialism. By contrast, 'realism', which sees recurrent conflict as inevitable, is often, though not exclusively, associated with conservatism. Although the term 'idealism' is most frequently used to refer to inter-war thought, the classical liberal idea that free trade promotes peace was clearly a form of idealism.[63]

Keynes remained a vigorous advocate of free trade. His first known letter to a newspaper[64] was to *The Economist* in February 1909, asserting free trade's contribution to the centralization in London of the world's banking, and the

---

[61] OC/5/40, KP.   [62] OC/5/4–24, KP.

[63] See, e.g. Bull, 'Theory', p. 34; E. H. Carr, *The Twenty Years' Crisis* (2nd edn., 1946; London and Basingstoke, 1983), pp. 5–6, 43–6, 50 ff.

[64] Vol. 15, p. 17.

danger of tariff reform to shipping, banking, and broking.[65] In the two general elections of 1910, Keynes spoke and wrote against tariff reform and for free trade Liberal candidates. He was secretary of the Cambridge University Free Trade Association, and addressed Indian undergraduates on 'India and Protection'.[66] He wrote to the *Cambridge Daily News* in December 1909, saying that he attached unusual importance to a Liberal victory in the forthcoming election because only a decisive defeat could make the Conservative party repent of tariff reform.[67]

In January 1910, Keynes spoke again in the Cambridge Union against tariff reform. 'Protection is a flower which grows in rank soil. Depressions must come, and depressions which are the signal for movements towards [free trade] abroad are here incitements to' protectionism. Amongst the positive arguments for free trade, Keynes mentioned 'International relations' and the 'Internal corruption' protection would produce.[68] In 1910, Keynes made several other speeches, including at least one other in the Cambridge Union,[69] in favour of free trade.[70] A letter from him in the *Cambridge Daily News* in January attacked Archdeacon Cunningham's advocacy of protection. He defended from Cunningham's misinterpretation J. S. Nicholson's *Project of Empire*, 'whose object is the development on free trade lines of Adam Smith's imperial ideas'. Nicholson, said Keynes, showed that protection has no tendency to retain capital at home. Keynes cited Nicholson as showing 'that this aspect of the matter was fully dealt with by Adam Smith in some chapters of his famous work, which are not known so well as they should be'.[71] How well they were known to Keynes himself in January 1910, is not certain: he wrote on an Aegean holiday in March that he had read 'nearly half of Adam Smith. It is a wonderful book'.[72] By 18 May, Keynes had lectured on Adam Smith.[73] Pre-war lecture notes[74] and writings in 1914–15 suggest familiarity with *The Wealth of Nations*, including Smith's 'celebrated campaign against the mercantilists'.[75]

Where had Keynes acquired the view that free trade promoted peace? His own answer was that he was brought up with it, that he 'imbibed' it in his youth. As he put it in 1933, he 'was brought up, like most Englishmen, to respect free trade not only as an economic doctrine which a rational and

---

[65] Vol. 15, pp. 18–19.   [66] Vol. 15, p. 39. OC/2/13, KP.
[67] Vol. 15, pp. 40–1.   [68] OC/5/182–208, KP.   [69] *The Granta*, 12 Nov. 1910, p. 90.
[70] See PS/1/18–21, KP.   [71] Vol. 15, p. 43.
[72] Keynes to JNK, 22 Mar. 1910, PP/45/168/7/21–2, KP. Presumably 'it' is *The Wealth of Nations*.
[73] Keynes to JNK, 18 May 1910, PP/45/168/7/38, KP.
[74] Vol. 12, pp. 692, 699–700, 723, 752–3.
[75] Vol. 11, p. 325; see also pp. 315–16, 530, 537–8.

instructed person could not doubt but almost as a part of the moral law'. He shared, in this respect, 'the mental habits of the pre-war nineteenth-century world'. The 'nineteenth-century free traders, who were amongst the most idealistic and disinterested of men', believed 'they were the friends and assurers of peace and international concord and economic justice between nations'. Keynes implied that he, too, had regarded these claims as fundamental truths.[76] Keynes believed that each century has an outlook, an approach of mind;[77] that he had grown up with a nineteenth-century outlook and was slowly developing, and helping to shape, a twentieth century one; and that a central tenet of that nineteenth-century outlook was free trade.[78] The evolution from the nineteenth century to twentieth-century conditions, and the need for thought to change to suit the new circumstances, were central to Keynes's thinking.[79] An undated pre-1914 paper on 'Modern Civilisation' depicted unparalleled social and economic change, by which 'many of the boundaries between nations are being broken down', and which was liable to change 'our duties'.[80]

The idea that free trade promotes peace was a central tenet of the liberal economic orthodoxy on which Keynes frequently said he was brought up, and accepted with 'no reserves at all'.[81] Smith and Burke, for both of whom he developed great admiration, have been mentioned as early proponents of this idea. Partly under their influence, it was very widely shared among British liberal economists, philosophers, and others throughout the nineteenth century.[82] John Stuart Mill's *Principles of Political Economy*, published in several editions from 1848, declared the extent and increase of international trade as 'the principal guarantee of the peace of the world'.[83] Mill was described by Keynes, writing of Sidgwick and Marshall in the 1860s, as 'the greatest intellectual influence on the youth of the age'.[84] Belief in the pacific effects of free trade was prevalent in the work of classical liberal economists from the mid-nineteenth century to the early twentieth century, such as F. W. Newman,[85] Henry Fawcett,[86] Charles Gide,[87] Henry

---

[76] Vol. 21, pp. 233–5.   [77] See vol. 10, pp. 93–4; vol. 21, p. 234.

[78] Vol. 21, p. 234.   [79] For example, vol. 14, p. 124; vol. 17, p. 442.

[80] (Dating from 1905?) UA/22/1–10, KP; see also OC/5/103 ff, KP.

[81] Vol. 7, p. 334; see also, e.g. vol. 20, p. 505.

[82] See, e.g. M. Ceadel, *Thinking about Peace and War* (Oxford, 1987), p. 179; M. Howard, *War and the Liberal Conscience* (Oxford, 1981) esp. ch. 2; Prior, *Burke*, i, pp. 341–2.

[83] J. S. Mill, *Principles of Political Economy* (Toronto, 1965 [1848]), p. 594.

[84] See vol. 10, pp. 135, 168, 171; see also, pp. 204–5, 280, 289; see J. N. Keynes, *The Scope and Method of Political Economy* (3rd edn., London, 1904), p. 77.

[85] F. W. Newman, *Lectures on Political Economy* (London, 1851), p. 25.

[86] H. Fawcett, *Manual of Political Economy* (6th edn., London, 1883), p. 391; see also H. Fawcett, *Free Trade and Protection* (4th edn., London, 1881).

[87] C. Gide, *Principles of Political Economy* (London, 1909), p. 345.

Sidgwick,[88] Alfred Marshall,[89] J. S. Nicholson,[90] and A. C. Pigou.[91] This belief was shared by such thinkers as Goldsworthy Lowes Dickinson,[92] Bertrand Russell,[93] and Norman Angell[94] before the First World War. This liberal-idealist tradition was thus dominant (though not universal) among the Cambridge economists and moral philosophers of the late nineteenth and early twentieth centuries. Keynes was self-consciously a part of this Cambridge intellectual tradition, referring to its influence upon himself.[95] For example, in 1922, his introduction to Cambridge Economic Handbooks said the authors 'believe themselves to be orthodox members of the Cambridge School of Economics', whose ideas 'and even their prejudices' were traceable to contact with Marshall and Pigou.[96] Especially through his essays on several Cambridge economists, Keynes became one of the historians of Cambridge economics.[97]

Although, studying under Marshall and Pigou, Keynes read, wrote essays, and attended lectures on international trade during 1905–6,[98] we have seen that his belief in the pacific effects of free trade preceded that tuition in economics. The explanation for this early belief appears to lie in his exposure to such ideas through his family circumstances. Keynes's 'Lives of Economists' shows a particular interest in ancestry[99] and 'the intellectual atmosphere...at home and at Cambridge' in which the economists 'grew up'.[100] It is likely that this interest reflected Keynes's own experience. More than once, Keynes referred to what he learnt of Fawcett, Marshall, Jevons, and others as a boy

---

[88] H. Sidgwick, *The Elements of Politics* (London, 1891), pp. 293–4, defending Cobden's 'ideal of universal peace brought about by universal free trade.'

[89] See above. A. Marshall, *Industry and Trade* (London, 1919), p. 4; Marshall to Edgeworth, 1911, L/M/25, KP.

[90] J. S. Nicholson, *Principles of Political Economy,* iii (London, 1901 and 1908), p. 363: 'the best guarantee for peace is the extension of commerce'.

[91] See above.

[92] G. L. Dickinson, *The Choice Before Us* (London, 1918 [1917]), ch. 7 (e.g. p. 129: trade 'a potent influence making for peace'); *The International Anarchy, 1904–1914* (London, 1926), p. 19.

[93] Russell, *Autobiography,* i, p. 153.

[94] N. Angell, *The Great Illusion* (3rd edn., London, 1911); see also, e.g. Angell, *The Foundations of International Polity* (London, 1914), pp. 210–11.

[95] For example, vol. 8, p. xxiv; vol. 10, pp. 434–5.

[96] Vol. 12, pp. 856–7. In 1928 (Marshall having died in 1924) this was replaced with reference to the questioning of 'traditional treatments': 'In the end this activity of research should clear up controversy. But for the moment controversy and doubt are increased', vol. 12, p. 860.

[97] See *Essays in Biography,* vol. 10, esp. part II.

[98] UA/3/1/14ff, UA/3/2/5–8, 46 ff, KP; vol. 10, pp. 190 n, 215–16.

[99] Vol. 10, pp. 61, 162; see J. A. Schumpeter, *Ten Great Economists* (London, 1952), p. 260.

[100] Vol. 10, p. 72 n; see also, e.g. pp. 109–11, 251, 351.

from his father, John Neville Keynes.[101] Thus he wrote, after Marshall's death in 1924, of Cambridge in the 1880s and 1890s:[102]

In that first age of married society in Cambridge, ... several of the most notable dons, particularly in the School of Moral Science, married students of Newnham.[103] The double link between husbands and wives bound together a small cultured society of great simplicity and distinction. This circle was at its full strength in my boyhood, and, when I was first old enough to be asked out to luncheon or to dinner, it was to these houses that I went. I remember a homely, intellectual atmosphere which it is harder to find in the swollen, heterogeneous Cambridge of today. The entertainments at the Marshalls' were generally occasioned, in later days, by the visit of some fellow-economist, often an eminent foreigner, and the small luncheon party would usually include a couple of undergraduates and a student or a young lecturer from Newnham. I particularly remember meeting in this way Adolph Wagner and N. G. Pierson, representatives of a generation of economists which is now almost past.

Keynes had close connections with many of those listed above as advocates of the view that free trade promotes peace. Henry Fawcett (1833–84) was 'the most important non-family influence' on Keynes's father.[104] Henry Sidgwick (1838–1900)[105] and Alfred Marshall (1842–1924)[106] were, as close colleagues of Keynes's father, known to Maynard Keynes since boyhood: in 1944, he wrote of them as 'familiar Cambridge figures of my youth'.[107] Keynes proof-read Sidgwick's *Principles of Political Economy*, of which J. N. Keynes edited a posthumous edition in 1901.[108] In 1904, Keynes cited Sidgwick's *Elements of Politics* in his essay on Burke.[109] Keynes came to know Goldsworthy Lowes Dickinson (1862–1932) very well in his undergraduate years at King's, if not earlier.[110] Bertrand Russell (1872–1970) recorded that he 'first knew Keynes

---

[101] See vol. 10, pp. 109, 138, 199, 268 n.   [102] Vol. 10, pp. 213–14; see also pp. 249–50.

[103] This describes the marriage of Keynes's parents.

[104] Skidelsky, *Hopes*, p. 6; see pp. 8, 10, 13n; Robinson says Fawcett was connected by marriage to the Keynes family: 'Keynes', 3, vol. 10, pp. 176, 268 n.

[105] Vol. 10, pp. 168, 176, 220, 222–3, 236–8, 267–8; Kadish, *Historians*, p. 154. For JNK's admiration for Sidgwick: e.g. JNK to Col. Higginson, 3 Nov. 1878: bMS Am 1162.10 (512–13), Houghton Library, Harvard.

[106] Vol. 10, chs. 14, 15; see also, e.g. vol. 7, pp. xxv, xxix; see, e.g. L/M, PP/45/168/10/73 ff, PP/45/168/13/117, KP; cf. Moggridge, *Biography*, pp. 18, 20.

[107] Vol. 10, p. 237. See also J. N. Keynes, *Scope*, p. vii; L/43/78, KP; *John Maynard Keynes, 1883–1946, Fellow and Bursar*, A Memoir prepared by direction of the Council of King's College, Cambridge, 1949, pp. 9, 13–14; G. Keynes, *The Gates of Memory* (Oxford, 1983), p. 19; R. F. Kahn, *The Making of Keynes' General Theory* (Cambridge, 1984), p. 190.

[108] Hession, *Keynes*, p. 26; Harrod, *Life*, p. 55; Sidgwick, *The Principles of Political Economy* (3rd edn., London, 1901), p. viii.

[109] UA/20/3/49, KP.

[110] E. M. Forster, *Goldsworthy Lowes Dickinson* (London, 1962 [1934]); Harrod, *Life*, p. 129; Skidelsky, *Hopes*, pp. 112, 116, 181; see, e.g. 25 Dec. 1905, pp/45/174; Keynes to A. D. Knox, 25 Dec. 1905, PP/45/174; Keynes to A. Hobhouse, 14 Sept. 1905, PP/45/149; see also, e.g. PP/45/168/13/76, KP. For Dickinson annotating *The Economic Consequences*, see EC/10/4, KP.

through his father'. They clearly knew each other well in the 1900s.[111]
A. C. Pigou (1877–1959) became a Fellow of King's in 1902, the year Keynes
entered it as an undergraduate. 'They became friends, and remained friends,
for the whole of Keynes's life'[112]—despite later intellectual disagreements. As
well as debating alongside Pigou in 1903, Keynes became familiar with his
writings on free trade.[113]

Keynes's contact with Norman Angell started somewhat later. Angell
(1872–1967) was the most prominent of the liberal pacificist[114] writers in
the years immediately preceding the First World War. His *The Great Illusion*
(previously *Europe's Optical Illusion*) had a spectacular impact after 1909.[115]
Angell claimed in his memoirs that Keynes encouraged and approved the
Norman Angell movement, though perhaps doubted Angell's argument on
the futility of an indemnity.[116] Keynes chaired a meeting of the Political
Economy Club at which Angell spoke in 1912. Although Angell referred
later to being 'on several points taken unawares', he was comforted that the
'only people who can pick holes in' his ideas 'are those who believe in them'.[117]
Angell probably heard Keynes's paper in Oxford in May 1914 on population
pressure.[118] In October 1914, Keynes wrote to F. M. (Freddie) Hardman, a
former pupil serving with the British Expeditionary Force: 'There are various
pamphlets by Angell, Gilbert Murray, etc. which I'll send you along from time
to time.'[119] Gilbert Murray's *Thoughts on the War* was published in October
1914.[120] The work of Angell's to which Keynes referred could be *The Foundations of International Polity* (1914), *Prussianism and its Destruction* (1914),
or perhaps 'The Case against Inaction', published in the Angell movement
monthly *War and Peace* in October 1914. Chapter 4, this volume, examines
various connections between Angell and Keynes after the Great War.

---

[111] Russell, *Autobiography*, i, p. 71; PP/45/277, PP/45/168/13/69, KP.

[112] Kahn, *Making*, p. 189; see PP/45/254, L/M/8–10, PP/45/168/13/16, 21–2, and other
letters, KP; cf. S. Howson and D. Winch, *The Economic Advisory Council, 1930–1939* (Cambridge,
1977), p. 64.

[113] Keynes to JNK, 22 May 1908, PP/45/168/13/27, KP.

[114] Following Taylor and Ceadel, the distinction is made between a pacifist, who believes that
'all war is *always wrong*', and a pacificist, who believes 'that war, though *sometimes necessary*, is
always an irrational and inhumane way to solve disputes, and that its prevention should always be
an overriding political priority': M. Ceadel, *Pacifism in Britain 1914–1945* (Oxford, 1980), p. 3.

[115] See, e.g. J. D. B. Miller, *Norman Angell and the Futility of War* (London, 1986), p. 6 ff.

[116] N. Angell, *After All* (London, 1951), p. 169; cf. 153.

[117] Angell to Keynes, 19 Feb. 1912, OC/2/86, KP; see Angell, *After All*, p. 310; Skidelsky,
Hopes, p. 213.

[118] See below.

[119] Keynes to F. M. Hardman, 25 Oct. 1914, PP/45/131, KP.

[120] D. Wilson, *Gilbert Murray OM, 1866–1957* (Oxford, 1987), pp. 220–1. While supporting
the war, Murray urged 'a generous settlement with Germany'.

In *The General Theory*, discussing the controversy between free trade and protection, Keynes referred to himself as being 'so lately as 1923,... a faithful pupil of the classical school who did not at that time doubt what he had been taught and entertained on this matter no reserves at all'.[121] The inclination of some 'new liberals' before the First World War to be more sceptical of the irenic effects of capitalism[122] seems to have passed Keynes by. As Freeden says, Keynes was, even in the mid-1920s, '[c]uriously indifferent to or uninformed about the development of liberalism since the 1890s'.[123]

2.2 THE EMPIRE

Keynes's approach to the Empire may best be studied by elaborating his views before the First World War, and briefly considering how they developed in later years.

In the Cambridge Union in 1903, Keynes declared that Britain's 'Imperial Mission' was not her own pride or magnificence 'but to provide facilities for the growth under freedom and justice and without molestation from abroad of these young nations... when a country becomes part of the Empire it is free to pursue its own destiny, in its own way. Because our ideal is democratic.'[124] As a schoolboy, Keynes had written of Britain's only realizing under Queen Victoria 'the responsibilities of Empire and... our duties to subject races'.[125] Yet also as a schoolboy, during the Boer War, he was unmoved by imperial jingoism.[126] It may be that Keynes's approach to the Empire is best described as Burkean. In his 1904 essay on Burke, Keynes seemingly endorsed Burke's distinction between 'the jingo's love of supremacy' and 'the true imperial spirit of liberty'.[127] Setting out Burke's view of Empire, Keynes wrote: '[T]here is, in truth, very little to criticise.'[128] Keynes also endorsed Burke's commitment to 'the duties... of nations to their neighbours'.[129]

As we have seen, Keynes also opposed the development of the Empire into a trading bloc, believing that this would be a menace to the world's peace.[130] His notion of the Empire was as a loose grouping of self-governing states, which

---

[121] Vol. 7, pp. 334–5; see also p. 348.

[122] For example, Hobson, a free trader, linked capitalism with militarism: see Freeden, *Liberalism*, pp. 150, 219.

[123] Freeden, *Liberalism*, p. 157, see also 159; O'Donnell, *Philosophy*, 313–21. Cf. OC/5/103 ff, KP.

[124] OC/5/54, KP.   [125] PP/31/7/3, KP.

[126] Moggridge, *Biography*, pp. 41–3; Skidelsky, *Hopes*, p. 89 ff.

[127] UA/20/3/65, KP.   [128] UA/20/3/66–7, KP.   [129] UA/20/3/80, KP.

[130] OC/5/56, KP.

grouping (it seems) such states were free to leave. Though such associates as Robert Brand and Philip Kerr (later Lord Lothian)[131] were long active in the Round Table, founded in 1910 to work for imperial unity, there is no evidence that Keynes had any interest in such projects.[132] He believed at times between the wars that concern for the Empire perverted British foreign policy.[133]

John Strachey's scintillating Marxist critique of Keynes in 1932 stressed his naïveté on imperialism: his failure, as Strachey saw it, to see it as an enduring cause of war.[134] However, writing in 1920, Keynes did suggest that 'the universally practised policies of economic imperialism' helped shape the state of affairs out of which the First World War arose.[135] Keynes nowhere defined 'economic imperialism', nor explained how it helped cause the war. But he probably meant, as other free traders did,[136] the adoption of exclusionist policies by imperial powers in various territories, seeking to monopolize markets or sources of raw materials for themselves. He may also have meant to include that 'peaceful penetration' of south-eastern Europe to which he had referred in *The Economic Consequences*.[137] In 1919, he sharply contrasted his own proposal for a free trade union across most of Europe and beyond with 'the former German dream of Mittel-Europa', 'an avowedly imperialistic scheme of exclusion'. This contrast was the standard free traders' dichotomy between projects of imperial economic unity that promote international conflict, and free trade, which promotes harmony. Keynes lamented that the breakup of the old multinational empires of Europe created new frontiers 'between greedy, jealous, immature, and economically incomplete, nationalist states'.[138] He showed little or no interest in the principle of national self-determination.[139] It seems that Keynes's quiescence about the British Empire was partly because (until 1932) Britain stood for free trade, and against economic nationalism.

At least before the First World War, Keynes broadly approved of British policy in India. After working in the India Office, he was an 'apologist of our Indian administration'.[140] He wrote in 1909 that 'British rule in India has little

---

[131] Amongst other links, Keynes, Brand, and Kerr were together at Paris and in the 1920s Liberal Summer Schools, including the Liberal Industrial Inquiry, 1926–8. For Keynes-Kerr letters not in *CW*, see Freeden, *Liberalism*, pp. 116–18.

[132] On the Round Table: Alexander May, 'The Round Table, 1910–66', D.Phil. thesis (Oxford, 1995). Dr May confirms this point. Cecil and Zimmern were also members of the Round Table before or during the First World War, but not for long after, when their interests were much more engaged by the League.

[133] See below.

[134] E. J. St L. Strachey, *The Coming Struggle for Power* (London, 1932), pp. 203–4; see H. Thomas, *John Strachey* (London, 1973), p. 277.

[135] Vol. 17, p. 52.

[136] For example, Nathan, *Free Trade To-Day*, p. 131 ff.   [137] Vol. 2, pp. 10–11.

[138] Vol. 2, p. 169.   [139] See, e.g. vol. 3, p. 8; cf. vol. 2, p. 39.   [140] Vol. 15, p. 36.

to fear from free criticism'.[141] He believed it benefited India economically.[142] His 1914 paper on population, discussed in Section 2.3, spoke of India and Egypt receiving 'the advantages of settled, humane and intelligent government' (though these 'have been very nearly counterbalanced by the tendency of population to increase').[143] Keynes's contributions to discussion of Indian finance included various pre-war articles;[144] *Indian Currency and Finance* (1913);[145] his active membership of the 1913–14 Royal Commission on Indian Finance and Currency, chaired by Austen Chamberlain;[146] his evidence to the Indian Exchange and Currency Committee in July 1919;[147] and his evidence to the second Royal Commission on Indian Currency and Finance in 1926.[148] Keynes was to have served as vice-chairman of the Indian Fiscal Commission in 1921, but was too busy.[149] He welcomed this Commission as 'a last effort, almost certainly doomed to futility, to save India for modified free trade'.[150]

Although Keynes in his pre-1914 writings made various criticisms of the details of British policy in India, and various proposals for reform, he respected the beneficence of the India Office.[151] This was notwithstanding his cynicism about bureaucracy, including the India Office.[152] He defended the honour of government of India officials who were attacked in the House of Commons and elsewhere over silver purchases in 1912. During this scandal, Keynes observed wryly, 'the question of Indian currency became almost interesting'. Such phoney scandals would arise 'so long as the relations of the House of Commons to India combine in a high degree responsibility with ignorance'.[153]

Repeatedly, Keynes lauded India's gold-exchange standard of 1893–1914: it was 'the best currency system then existing in the world'.[154] It made gold available at a fixed price for international transactions, but used a non-gold internal currency.[155] Keynes declared in 1911 that 'the ideal currency of the future' would evolve from it.[156] He believed that the gold resources of a country must be centralized, rather than in circulation, because 'gold in the

---

[141] Vol. 15, p. 33.   [142] Vol. 15, p. 36.   [143] SS/1/22, KP.
[144] Vol. 11, ch. 1.
[145] Vol. 1; see also A. Chandavarkar, *Keynes and India* (London, 1989); R. S. Sayers, 'The Young Keynes', *EJ*, 82 (1972), 592–4.
[146] Vol. 15, chs. 2–4.   [147] Vol. 15, pp. 272–301.   [148] Vol. 19, pp. 476–524.
[149] Vol. 15, p. 301; vol. 17, pp. 317–20, 326, 331–3.   [150] Vol. 17, p. 319.
[151] See, e.g. vol. 1, pp. 97, 167–8.   [152] See, e.g. vol. 1, pp. 101, 165–6.
[153] Vol. 1, pp. 101–2; vol. 15, pp. 90–5; Chandavarkar, *India*, pp. 63–5.
[154] Vol. 19, p. 521; see, e.g. vol. 11, pp. 275–6.
[155] See vol. 1, ch. 2, esp. pp. 21–2; vol. 15, pp. 70–1.
[156] Vol. 15, p. 69; see pp. 61–2, 69–79; vol. 1, p. 25.

pockets of the people is not in the least available at a time of crisis or to meet a foreign drain'.[157]

Keynes encapsulated the argument of *Indian Currency*: 'I urge that, in her gold-exchange standard, and in the mechanisms by which this is supported, India, so far from being anomalous, is in the forefront of monetary progress. But in her banking arrangements, in the management of her note issue, and in the relations of her government to the money market, her position *is* anomalous; and she has much to learn from what is done elsewhere.'[158] Keynes urged that the government of India look beyond British experience for guidance[159] (e.g. in creating a state bank)[160]. The notion that ideas should know no national boundaries recurs in Keynes's writings. But he also urged giving careful attention to local conditions when applying experience elsewhere.[161]

Indian Currency attacked the gold standard in passing:[162]

The time may not be far distant when Europe, having perfected her mechanism of exchange on the basis of a gold standard, will find it possible to regulate her standard of value on a more rational and stable basis. It is not likely that we shall leave permanently the most intimate adjustments of our economic organism at the mercy of a lucky prospector, a new chemical process, or a change of ideas in Asia.

Keynes had been referring to the process whereby the high level of demand in India for gold meant, 'at a time of plentiful gold supply like the present', that gold was drawn from the Western nations, thus helping them fight inflation. Keynes several times stressed that the high level of demand for gold in India was the product of primitive prejudice. India's love of the precious metals harmed her economy but benefited Western economies. By bringing her hoarded gold back into active circulation, India could have the money markets of the world at her mercy, with the danger of 'a very great inflation of gold prices'.[163] Thus, the gold standard meant that the Western economies, whose money supplies and interest rates were determined by gold, were at the mercy of irrational and unstable forces. Keynes's writings on Indian currency make clear that he valued internal price stability above exchange rate fixity.[164] These became recurring themes, with Keynes coming to stress international control of the more rational and stable standard he wanted.[165]

---

[157] Vol. 15, p. 78.   [158] Vol. 1, p. 182.

[159] See, e.g. vol. 1, pp. 36, 142 n 1, 163, 168, 182.

[160] Vol. 15, pp. 151–211 *passim*, esp. pp. 202–11.

[161] On local conditions, see, e.g. vol. 1, p. 36; vol. 15, pp. 150, 158, 161, 188, 202.

[162] Vol. 1, p. 71; see also vol. 19, p. 506; vol. 20, pp. 157–65.

[163] Vol. 1, pp. 70–1; see also, e.g. vol. 15, p. 295.

[164] For example, in 1919: vol. 15, pp. 273–6, 279, 281, 293, 298. In 1926: vol. 19, esp. pp. 479, 499–501.

[165] Vol. 1, p. 71; see, e.g. vol. 19, pp. 507–8.

In the inter-war years, Keynes frequently argued for a deliberate reduction in British investment abroad.[166] But writing in 1909–10, to rebut the arguments of tariff reformers that free trade drove capital abroad to the detriment of British enterprise and labour,[167] Keynes argued that to reduce foreign investment would hurt both the British economy and those countries in which Britain had invested. Countries such as India, Argentina, and Canada required more money, not less, 'if we are to gain the full fruit of our enterprise'. Investment in them made possible their buying, on credit, an important share of British exports. Reversing this would involve the slow decline of London as the financial centre of the world.[168] Keynes thus thought that the Empire and investments abroad benefited Britain, and were not the drain Hobson and others claimed.[169] In describing 'Europe Before the War', *The Economic Consequences* (based on Keynes's talk in Oxford in May 1914) referred to the relation of the Old World to the New:

Of the surplus capital goods accumulated by Europe a substantial part was exported abroad, where its investment made possible the development of the new resources of food, materials, and transport, and at the same time enabled the Old World to stake out a claim in the natural wealth and virgin potentialities of the New: even before the war ... the equilibrium thus established between old civilisations and new resources was being threatened.[170]

During the Second World War, Keynes again saw the advantage of the colonies to Britain as sources of food and raw materials.[171]

Keynes certainly saw Britain's role as being to assist, not to exploit, her colonies. Thus, for example, India's accumulation of precious metals retarded her development, and the government ought to counteract this.[172] In 1909, Keynes wrote that Indians should be helped to get higher education in England, to enable greater participation in their own administration.[173] (In 1943, he wrote that 'since the Indianisation of the Viceroy's Council, the once prized efficiency of the [Indian Civil Service] and the Government, at any rate on the administrative side, has largely disappeared, which is a sad forecast of what will happen when we have entirely withdrawn our hands'.)[174] Other writings during the Second World War stressed that British colonial possessions involved real responsibility by Britain: for the USA to buy British capital assets (e.g. tin and rubber investments in Malaya) without accepting the

---

[166] See ch. 5, this volume.   [167] Vol. 15, p. 44.   [168] Vol. 15, pp. 54–5.
[169] For example, J. A. Hobson, *Imperialism* (London, 1938 [1902]).
[170] Vol. 2, pp. 13–15.
[171] See, e.g. Thirlwall, *Policy Adviser*, p. 74.
[172] Vol. 15, p. 81; see also, e.g. pp. 69–70, 84, 87, 125–6, 229, 231–3, 295; Vol. 19, pp. 490, 515, 519–20.
[173] Vol. 15, p. 32.   [174] Vol. 28, p. 188.

responsibility for these 'intensely living and personal enterprises' would constitute 'unadulterated (and, in the end, grossly inefficient) exploitation'.[175]

Keynes shared the common presupposition that there were important gradations between degrees of civilization, and that some peoples could legitimately be classified as 'barbarous and primitive'.[176] When studying for the civil service examination in 1906, he had learned the classical doctrine that the family of nations included only the Christian nations of Europe, their offshoots, and those nations (the Ottoman Empire, Japan) which they admitted.[177] He regarded censorship of political discussion in India as defensible (unlike in an English university) because 'an ignorant populace may be excited' by 'distortions of fact'.[178] British rule extended to India the advantages of civilized experience.[179]

In 1923, Keynes considered how 'the general principle of pacifism' applied to Britain's colonies:

> [We] must do what we can in the interests of good government, but with the unalterable determination that in no circumstances will we hold our position by force. If our position becomes untenable without force, then we must leave quietly, glad to be quit of a dangerous responsibility.[180]

After Britain went off the gold standard in 1931, Keynes advocated a currency bloc based on Sterling; but he did not welcome the adoption of imperial preference at Ottawa in 1932.[181] Later in the 1930s, when resistance to 'the brigand powers' (Germany, Italy, and Japan) was crucial, Keynes scorned those who identified Britain's interest as simply retaining her Empire and who would give the brigand powers a free hand 'so long as they agree not to lay hands, for the time being, on any of our own imperial interests'.[182] 'Civilisation and liberty' were 'a fairer cause than the integrity of our possessions'.[183] Keynes did not share the enthusiasm of some 1930s idealists for the Empire and Commonwealth as a nucleus of peace-loving states whose joint action could provide a major building block for world order. He urged instead the solidarity of the peace-loving European powers.[184]

As we have seen, Keynes argued in 1940 that major sales of capital assets in the colonies to the USA should be accompanied by the transfer of political responsibility.[185] In 1943, his inclination, as he was 'so fed up with India', was

---

[175] Vol. 23, p. 15; see Harrod, *Life*, p. 591.

[176] Vol. 8, p. 273. Keynes nonetheless defended the *rationality* of such peoples.

[177] UA/4/4/73, KP. See H. Bull and A. Watson (eds.), *The Expansion of International Society* (Oxford, 1984).

[178] Vol. 15, pp. 32–3.   [179] Vol. 15, p. 197.   [180] Vol. 17, p. 451.

[181] See ch. 5, this volume.   [182] Vol. 28, p. 48. See also pp. 110–11, 125–6.

[183] Vol. 28, p. 110.   [184] See ch. 5, this volume.   [185] Supra; vol. 23, pp. 15–16.

to 'clear out' of India on any terms and at the earliest possible moment; 'few can have a lower opinion of the Government of India today than I have'.[186] He rejected post-First World War commercial and currency proposals centred on the Empire. But in the 1945 negotiations on the US loan to Britain, he 'protested vehemently against any reference to matters which were primarily the concern of the Commonwealth and Empire'.[187]

2.3 POPULATION PRESSURE, AND THE SPIRIT OF MALTHUS

Given the attention that population questions received from economists on whom Keynes was 'brought up', it is not surprising that he developed a keen interest in them.[188] What is more surprising is that Keynes rejected the optimism of late Victorian liberal economists, and became, and long remained, a Malthusian pessimist. In 1905–6, he was taught by Marshall that, though Malthus was right on a good deal in his own time, so much had changed since then, for example in the transportation of food supplies, that, apart from wars, there was now a safe and stable system balancing world food supply and population.[189] Yet, if persuaded then, Keynes did not stay persuaded. In 1912, he wrote of China's overpopulation of recent centuries as an obstacle to her recovering her 'Golden Age'.[190] In May 1914, he presented a paper on population pressure to the Political Philosophy and Science Club, meeting in Oxford.[191] It appears that participants in the discussion included J. A. Hobson, Gilbert Murray, Graham Wallas, W. H. Beveridge, and W. T. Layton.[192] Part of Keynes's paper formed the basis for his post-war writings on Malthus. Keynes said that Malthusian pessimism was justified, and action to control population growth was necessary. Citing overpopulation in India, Egypt, and China, he said: 'Three quarters of the world have never ceased to live under Malthusian conditions.' The opening up of new sources of food supply gave Western countries only a temporary postponement of the problem of feeding a growing population. With the last fifty years being 'a period of economic transition, probably unexampled in the history of the

---

[186] Vol. 28, p. 188.   [187] Harrod, *Life*, p. 718.

[188] For example, Sidgwick, *Elements*, p. 295 ff; A. Marshall, *Principles of Economics* (5th edn., London, 1907), pp. 173 ff, 320–2.

[189] UA/3/2/15 ff, KP.

[190] Vol. 11, pp. 526–7.

[191] SS/1/1–37, KP; see J. Toye, 'Keynes on population and economic growth', *Cambridge Journal of Economics* 21 (1997), 1–26; J. Toye, *Keynes on Population* (Oxford, 2000).

[192] SS/1/37, KP.

world', that postponement was possibly coming to an end. Since 1900, the terms of trade between agricultural and industrial products had been moving against manufactures; the USA now consumed all the food produced there, rather than exporting it. The dependence of Western countries not on their own food supply but on the world's meant that there was no point in reducing the population of one country alone. 'It is no longer possible to have a *national* policy for the population question.' Keynes clearly favoured birth control. Referring to the tension between 'cosmopolitan humanitarianism' and the need for a race to protect itself, Keynes said:

> Almost any measures seem to me to be justified in order to protect our standard of life from injury at the hands of more prolific races. Some definite parcelling out of the world may well become necessary, and I suppose that this may not improbably provoke racial wars. At any rate, such wars will be about a substantial issue.[193] Countries in the position of British Columbia are entirely justified in protecting themselves from the fecundity of the East by very rigorous immigration laws and other restriction measures. I can imagine a time when it may be the right policy even to regulate the international trade in food supplies, though there are economic reasons... for thinking this improbable.

Keynes expressed the hope that the West could attain equilibrium in its population.[194]

Keynes's 1914 paper invoked the spirit of Malthus, whom Keynes was frequently to salute as 'the first of the Cambridge economists'.[195] As Keynes probably knew from reading James Bonar on Malthus, Malthus had predicted the dangers Keynes now claimed were arising from population growth in the countries from which Britain imported food.[196] Similar claims were also sometimes derived from Ricardo's theory of the rising price of food;[197] and Marshall was amongst the economists believing that the rate of exchange between British manufactures and American food and raw materials was turning against Britain.[198]

Liberal writers such as Sidgwick who, like Keynes, had seen a tension between the 'cosmopolitan' and 'national ideals' and generally favoured free

---

[193] This is probably by contrast with 'patriotic or militarist arguments' he had just mentioned: SS/1/34, KP.

[194] SS/1/36, KP.

[195] For example, vol. 10, pp. 71, 78, 101, 107; but see p. 79n.

[196] J. Bonar, *Malthus and His Work* (London, 1885) pp. 246–7. Keynes cited Bonar in interwar works: e.g. vol. 10, p. 71n. Keynes probably used Bonar's work in writing on Malthus in 1914. Bonar was a friend of his father, and Keynes described him later as, since 1885, 'the leading authority' on Malthus: Keynes to D. Macmillan, 1 Jan. 1931, CO/1/93–4, KP.

[197] E. Roll, *A History of Economic Thought* (4th edn., London, 1973), p. 187.

[198] Marshall, *Principles*, p. 674.

admission of immigrants, had recognized arguments for immigration restrictions.[199] Keynes's father had also presented the contrast between cosmopolitan and national standpoints as important in discussing migration and tariff policy.[200] There was alarm in British Columbia in 1914 about 'unassimilable material' from Asia; and such concerns were strong in all the Dominions.[201] The possibility of war caused by population pressure in Asia or elsewhere was taken seriously by liberals other than Keynes, such as Dickinson, even if they believed that the means (such as birth control) existed to prevent that pressure.[202] Keynes in 1914 regarded these concerns as urgent. It is possible that his views on racial wars, overpopulation generally, and eugenics, were influenced by reading H. G. Wells.[203]

2.4 FIRST WORLD WAR

Skidelsky paints a more accurate picture than Harrod of Keynes's approach to the First World War: after initial acquiesence in the war, he came to loathe it, and to support moves to bring it to an early end; was a conscientious objector; and was embroiled in bitter arguments within the British government over the direction of the war effort.[204]

Although on Friday, 31 July 1914, Keynes wrote of being 'in a fever of excitement' over international developments, he described *The Times* as very bellicose, and commended as exceedingly good a leader in *The Manchester Guardian* which opposed British intervention in any general European war arising from the Austro-Serbian crisis unless for a clear 'cause with which most of us at least can sympathise'. *The Manchester Guardian* stressed the need for the interests which the mass of the community had in peace to prevail, not least through Parliamentary scrutiny, over those 'strong influences, social and bureaucratic, which are anxious for war': Britain should 'keep out of this quarrel, which is none of [our business]', but act 'as counsellors of peace among other nations'.[205] (It appears that Keynes had not expected Russia and

---

[199] Sidgwick, *Elements*, pp. 295–7.

[200] J. N. Keynes, *Scope*, pp. 76–8.

[201] May, 'Round Table', pp. 131–7.

[202] Dickinson, *Choice*, ch. 6 (e.g. pp. 116–17).

[203] Harrod, *Life*, pp. 124, 171. In 1905, Keynes read H. G. Wells, *A Modern Utopia* (London, 1905); see p. 180 ff. See Chs. 4 and 5, this volume.

[204] Skidelsky, *Hopes*, chs. 12–14; cf. Harrod, *Life*, ch. 6.

[205] Keynes to JNK, 31 July 1914, PP/45/168/7/248–9, KP. Leaders headed 'The Nation's Danger', 'Parliament and the Crisis', 'The Tension of the Money Market', *The Manchester Guardian*, 31 July 1914.

Germany to join an Austro-Serbian war.)[206] By late Sunday, 2 August, Keynes (who had advised Basil Blackett in the Treasury in June 1914) had responded urgently to Blackett's request for his help in the financial crisis the international tensions had provoked.[207] It appears that in early August Keynes hoped to be offered a post in the Treasury.[208] He later described the German invasion of Belgium as 'a breach of engagements and of international morality'.[209] It is likely that this persuaded him that Britain should go to war. It may be that, though Bertrand Russell responded adversely,[210] Keynes was influenced by admiration for Sir Edward Grey,[211] whose exposition of the British position so influenced men such as Gilbert Murray and George Trevelyan, both of whom Keynes admired.[212] Alfred Marshall thought that Germany 'engineered the war'.[213] Keynes blamed the war on the ambitions of German leaders unchecked by an indoctrinated people,[214] though he thought in 1915 that 'Germany and Germans are not so different from the rest of the world as our daily press would hypnotise us into believing'.[215]

Keynes thought, initially with some enthusiasm, that having gone to war, it was essential that Britain win.[216] He wanted a total effort on the financial front, and was deeply critical of banks which put self-interest before this, 'when all should have been thinking of the state'.[217] But, the war turning out not to be the short war he expected,[218] his commitment to the war effort was soon to collide with grief at the deaths of men he knew. This duality of feeling was to bedevil him for the rest of the war. Of the death of Freddie Hardman, Keynes wrote on 4 November 1914: 'It makes one bitterly miserable and long that the war should stop quickly on almost any terms.'[219] This sentiment did not prevent Keynes from working in the Treasury from January 1915, with crucial responsibility for war finance. His grief and anger at the slaughter led

---

[206] Ferguson, *Pity*, p. 192.

[207] See Skidelsky, *Hopes*, p. 289; Harrod, *Life*, p. 229 ff.

[208] Blackett to Keynes, 13 Aug. 1914, L/14/42–3, KP. On chafing at being an observer in October 1914, see Skidelsky, *Hopes*, p. 294.

[209] On the invasion, see vol. 2, p. 40; see also p. 91.

[210] A. Ryan, *Bertrand Russell: A Political Life* (New York, 1988) ch. 3.

[211] Harrod, *Life*, pp. 110, 252. On the importance of Grey's opinions: vol. 18, p. 132.

[212] See, e.g. Wilson, *Murray*, pp. 218–19; G. M. Trevelyan, *Grey of Fallodon* (London, 1937) p. 263 ff. On Trevelyan-Keynes links, see Moggridge, *Biography*, pp. 82, 169, 173n., 174; Harrod, *Life*, pp. 116, 681; vol. 10, pp. 61, 351; vol. 22, p. 135.

[213] Marshall to Keynes, 21 Feb. 1915, L/M/50–1, KP.

[214] Vol. 2, p. 79; see p. 1; cf. vol. 16, p. 182; Vol. 17, p. 52.

[215] Vol. 11, p. 344.

[216] See Skidelsky, *Hopes*, p. 295; Harrod, *Life*, p. 252; vol. 16, p. 143. For Germany: vol. 11, p. 340.

[217] Vol. 11, p. 328; see p. 251 ff for fierce attack.

[218] C. Bell, *Old Friends* (London, 1956), p. 45; Ferguson, *Pity*, p. 319.

[219] Skidelsky, *Hopes*, p. 296.

him to come to regard the war as futile and criminal and, from early 1916 on, to advocate (and at times expect)[220] an early end to it.[221] He appears to have welcomed Lord Lansdowne's letter to *The Daily Telegraph* in November 1917 advocating peace negotiations.[222] Though he continued at his post, Keynes's emotions and personal relationships were strained by his continuing to work on the finance of a war to which he was increasingly hostile.[223] It is not known whether he shared Alfred Marshall's view that using the blockade of Germany to cut her food supplies was likely to lay the seeds of another war with Germany.[224] In August 1924, Keynes said that he did not know what the world gained through the Great War.[225]

In May 1920, Keynes presented the background causes of the war as:[226] first, 'the essential character of international politics and rivalries' in the late nineteenth century, with (as he later put it)[227] opposing 'groupings of great powers, with expanding ambitions and expanding armaments'; second, 'militarism everywhere (certainly in Russia as well as in Germany and Austria-Hungary)'; and third, 'the universally practised policies of economic imperialism'. Thus, 'it is not possible to lay the entire responsibility for the state of affairs out of which the war arose on any single nation'. However, Keynes believed:

Germany bears a special and peculiar responsibility for the war itself, for its universal and devastating character, and for its final development into a conflict without quarter for mastery or defeat. A criminal may be the outcome of his environment, but he is none the less a criminal. The evidence which has become public in the past year has convinced me that, during the weeks preceding August 1914, persons in power in Germany deliberately provoked the war and intended that it should commence when it did.

The war drove Keynes to an increasing passion for peace. In 1916, he rejected the 'false ideas of the inevitability and glory of war' which 'bellicose mystics' had spread in Germany. He believed that 'deep-rooted hatred of war' evident in all belligerent countries meant, for example, 'that the German people will

[220] For example, vol. 16, p. 186; but Keynes in Mar.–Apr. 1916 saw a good chance of war continuing for over a year: vol. 16, pp. 184, 186; cf. Skidelsky, *Hopes*, pp. 325, 336; E. Bishop, *A Virginia Woolf Chronology* (Basingstoke and London, 1989), p. 36.

[221] Skidelsky, *Hopes*, p. 302. On 'Politicus': vol. 16, p. 179.

[222] Skidelsky, *Hopes*, pp. 346–7.

[223] Ibid., pp. 335, 345, and *passim*; M. Keynes (ed.), *Essays on John Maynard Keynes* (Cambridge, 1975), p. 67; see, e.g. letters from David Garnett, PP/45/116, KP.

[224] Marshall to Keynes, 21 Feb. 1915, L/M/50–1, KP.

[225] *Birmingham Evening Dispatch*, 20 Aug. 1924.

[226] Vol. 17, p. 52.   [227] Vol. 18, p. 126.

be cured for a generation at least of warlike actions and pan-Germanic dreams'.[228]

Keynes took a detailed interest in Russian events (as he was to do for the rest of his life).[229] He shared the common liberal and intellectual antipathy towards Czarist Russia, and seemed pleased when the Czar was overthrown.[230] After the Bolshevik revolution, Keynes joked to his mother that 'the only course open to me is to be buoyantly bolshevik':[231]

[A] further prolongation of the war, with the turn things have taken [i.e. the Bolshevik Revolution], probably means the disappearance of the social order we have known hitherto. With some regrets I think I am on the whole not sorry. The abolition of the rich will be rather a comfort and serve them right anyhow. What frightens me more is the prospect of *general* impoverishment. In another year's time we shall have forfeited the claim we had staked out in the New World and in exchange this country will be mortgaged to America.... I reflect with a good deal of satisfaction that, because our rulers are as incompetent as they are mad and wicked, one particular era of a particular kind of civilisation is very nearly over.

Keynes's desire for radical social change, and his concerns about impoverishment and about the balance of resources and power between Britain and the USA, were to be themes central to his post-war thinking—though, as we shall see, he suppressed the first in *The Economic Consequences*.

2.5 CONSCIENTIOUS OBJECTION

The conscription debates during the First World War were important in the evolution of British liberalism;[232] and Keynes's attitude helps explain the nature of his liberal beliefs. There has been a long-running debate on whether Keynes was a conscientious objector, and, if so, on what grounds. Harrod's *Life* denied that Keynes was an objector.[233] In 1956, Clive Bell wrote that Keynes was a conscientious objector of a 'peculiar' and 'most reasonable kind': 'He was not a pacificist; he did not object to fighting in any circumstances; he objected to being made to fight.'[234] Harrod's review of Bell rejected this claim.[235]

[228] Vol. 16, pp. 182–4.

[229] For references to 1905 revolution, e.g. see OC/5/125 ff, KP.

[230] Vol. 16, p. 187. Keynes to FAK, 30 Mar. 1917, PP/45/168/9/8–9; see also 10–11, KP. For 1922 criticism of Czarism, see vol. 17, pp. 435–6.

[231] Vol. 16, pp. 265–6. Cf. Keynes to Kahn, 27 May 1940, L/K/125, KP.

[232] Freeden, *Liberalism*, pp. 20–6.   [233] Harrod, *Life*, pp. 251–2.

[234] Bell, *Old Friends*, pp. 46–7. Bell used the word 'pacificist' as we use 'pacifist'.

[235] R. F. Harrod, 'Clive Bell on Keynes', *EJ*, 67 (1957), 692–9.

Elizabeth Johnson, citing letters in Keynes's papers, argued that Bell's interpretation was correct,[236] and Harrod went some way to admitting this.[237] Skidelsky agrees that Keynes was an objector, but interprets his reasons differently.[238]

Keynes's draft exemption application, addressed from King's College on 28 February 1916, reads:[239]

I claim complete exemption because I have a conscientious objection to surrendering my liberty of judgment on so vital a question as undertaking military service. I do not say that there are not conceivable circumstances in which I should voluntarily offer myself for military service. But after having regard to all the actually existing circumstances, I am certain that it is not my duty so to offer myself; and I solemnly assert to the Tribunal that my objection to submit to authority in this matter is truly conscientious. I am not prepared on such an issue as this to surrender my right of decision, as to what is or is not my duty, to any other person, and I should think it morally wrong to do so.

Skidelsky suggests, *contra* Johnson, that Keynes's claim of exemption was not based on 'the classical liberal ground that the state had no right to compel its citizens to fight'. Rather, 'he was making a political point about the war'; that is, 'he objected to being drafted for a war whose continuation he believed to be wrong'. Skidelsky writes that it 'is quite out of character for Keynes to take a stand on abstract right. He was too much of a political utilitarian to deny that government had the right to do anything which would increase the social advantage.'[240] This seems directly contrary to the natural meaning of Keynes's own words, which do take a stand on the right of individual decision on military service. Keynes did not acknowledge that the state had a right to conscript individuals.

Johnson seems right to argue that Keynes's claim for exemption was on grounds of refusal to surrender a personal right of decision as to whether to fight; that this was consistent with the philosophy described in 'My Early Beliefs'; and that it was shared by many liberals of the time, such as Sir John Simon.[241] It was also shared by, for example, Gilbert Murray[242] and

---

[236] E. S. Johnson, 'Keynes' Attitude to Compulsory Military Service', *EJ*, 70 (1960), 160–5. Adapted version in E. S. and H. G. Johnson, *The Shadow of Keynes* (Oxford, 1978), pp. 38–44.

[237] R. F. Harrod, 'A Comment', *EJ*, 70 (1960), 166–7.

[238] Skidelsky, *Hopes*, p. 316 ff.

[239] Vol. 16, p. 178.

[240] Skidelsky, *Hopes*, p. 318.

[241] Johnson, *Shadow*, p. 44. For 'My Early Beliefs': vol. 10, pp. 446–7. For Simon: vol. 16, p. 157. Simon was 'convinced that forcing anyone [to bear arms] is wrong': T. Wilson, *The Myriad Faces of War* (Cambridge, 1986), p. 213.

[242] Wilson, *Murray*, p. 237; F. West, *Gilbert Murray: A Life* (London and Canberra, 1984), pp. 153, 160.

L. T. Hobhouse.[243] It is compatible with Keynes's stress on other occasions on 'the right and duty of fearless individual judgment'.[244] Keynes's 1904 essay on Burke had said that utilitarianism provided a good basis for a political philosophy, but seemingly endorsed Burke's view that 'there is a certain minimum of personal freedom which should never be infringed'.[245] Keynes's mother seems also to have supported 'the voluntary principle'.[246]

Johnson argues convincingly that Keynes, in acknowledging that there might be 'conceivable circumstances in which I should voluntarily offer myself for military service', was making clear that he was not a pacifist. Some of his friends, such as Bertrand Russell and Gerald Shove, were. Nor was Keynes saying that he opposed conscription because of his attitude to this particular war, though his desire to take a stand on liberty of judgment may have been fortified by that. The possibility that Keynes gave voluntarist grounds because he thought these would be more acceptable than a policy objection may be doubted, if only because both were equally outside the legal terms for exemption (e.g. 'a conscientious objection', not to surrendering one's right of decision nor to *this* war, but 'to the undertaking of combatant service').[247]

Keynes's statement that, in the actually existing circumstances, he saw no duty to volunteer, may have been, as Skidelsky suggests, because he opposed the continuation of the war. But it may have been (additionally, or alternatively) because he believed that the best contribution he could make was to continue his Treasury work, including fighting to have a war effort run on tight financial lines. In 1915–16, Keynes argued that the diversion of manpower from industry to fighting was wasteful when it was more important for British labour to supply food and equipment for the Allies than to add to Britain's own armed forces: British conscription would help Germany.[248]

Johnson and Skidelsky show that in December–January 1915–16, Keynes (like the Cabinet ministers Reginald McKenna and Walter Runciman, who did not resign) was considering resigning from the Treasury in opposition to conscription, but by 28 January, his mother no longer feared 'his throwing everything up in consequence of the Compulsion Bill'.[249] There is no firm evidence that he contemplated resignation after that, though Skidelsky speculates that he did.[250] Keynes reluctantly admitted to Lytton Strachey on

---

[243] Freeden, *Liberalism*, pp. 22–3, 270–1.   [244] Vol. 10, p. 360; see also vol. 28, p. 77.

[245] UA/20/3/86, KP; see also A/20/3/10–11, 23, KP.

[246] FAK to Keynes, 29 Mar. 1916, PP/45/168/8/126, KP; see also Marshall to Keynes, 29 Dec. 1915, L/M/59–60, KP.

[247] Military Service Act (1916), Section 2 (1) (d), quoted from Johnson, *Shadow*, p. 40.

[248] See, e.g. vol. 16, pp. 110–15, 157–61; see also p. 187.

[249] Johnson, *Shadow*, pp. 39–40; Skidelsky, *Hopes*, p. 321.

[250] Skidelsky, *Hopes*, pp. 320, 325.

20 February, 'that there *was* a point at which he *would* think it necessary to leave—but what that point was he couldn't say'.[251] This implies, *contra* Skidelsky, that Keynes was not then contemplating resignation. The next day, Keynes sent £50 to the National Council against Conscription.[252] Having in this and other ways sought to help various conscientious objectors during the war, including testifying for friends,[253] Keynes was one of many signatories of a memorandum to Lloyd George on 1 January 1919 urging the speedy release of the 1,500 conscientious objectors still in prison.[254]

2.6 WAR FINANCE DURING THE FIRST WORLD WAR[255]

During both world wars, Keynes's work was crucial in financing the war efforts. His greater practical contribution during both wars was in external war finance; his greater theoretical contribution was on internal finance during the Second World War, reflecting his shift to Keynesian economics. Keynes believed that victory depended on efficient economic organization: as he put it in 1916, to 'go on giving the army what they want longer than the Germans can do to theirs'.[256]

2.6.1 External War Finance[257]

Despite some complacency about Britain's position, Keynes was, early in the Great War, discussing the use of gold reserves to purchase urgent necessities abroad at 'the later stages of a war', and the danger of inflation resulting.[258] He came to emphasize the importance to belligerents of foreign financial resources, and expressed surprise at German—and more general—underestimation of financial influences in war.[259] Countries needed to buy from abroad, perhaps because of the diminution of industrial production due to the scarcity of essential raw materials, or due to the diversion of labour to

---

[251] Skidelsky, *Hopes*, p. 324. Original emphasis.

[252] See bundle 30.12 (box 30), KP.

[253] See, e.g. Keynes to FAK, 26 Mar. 1916, PP/45/168/8/123–4; Johnson, *Shadow*, pp. 43–4.

[254] Wilson, *Murray*, p. 240.

[255] See vol. 16, chs. 1–3.

[256] Vol. 16, p. 187; see also pp. 141, 159, 271, 306; vol. 9, p. 372.

[257] See K. Burk, *Britain, America and the Sinews of War, 1914–1918* (Boston, 1985); K. Burk (ed.), *War and the State* (London, 1982), ch. 4.

[258] For example, vol. 11, pp. 315–16, 319, 322–3, 328.   [259] Vol. 20, pp. 339–41.

fighting.[260] A crucial part of Britain's war effort was to give her allies purchasing power in various parts of the world.[261]

As early as September 1915, Keynes noted that only Britain's financing important food and munitions imports enabled France and Italy to maintain 'their methods of warfare'.[262] In 1919, Keynes wrote that without lavish American financial assistance, both before and after they entered the war, the Allies could never have won.[263] Only one-seventh of British war finance was borrowed from abroad, but Keynes described it as 'indispensable'.[264] Reflecting his earlier experience, Keynes wrote in 1940 that an 'important source of our war strength' lay in 'our capacity to finance an adverse balance of trade' from resources accumulated before the war in gold and foreign investments.[265] He had written in 1910 of this factor in the Boer War.[266]

Having been since 1915 involved, as a member of the Treasury's Finance Division, in inter-allied purchasing and British borrowing and lending, Keynes headed the new division created early in 1917 to deal with external finance.[267] In 1923, Keynes declared that 'all the money we either lent or borrowed passed through my hands'.[268] He was deeply involved in Anglo-American financial relations, including the real difficulties in their relations preceding US entry to the war,[269] and after, including as a member in September 1917 of the Reading mission to the USA to sort out financial arrangements and survey the state of British representation.[270] He encouraged tapping all segments of the US loan market, including the public, with a 'variety of wares'.[271] Borrowing depended on good war news, and British credit being unquestioned.[272] Keynes was greatly concerned at the extent of Britain's indebtedness to the USA,[273] at what he took to be American 'satisfaction in reducing us to a position of complete financial helplessness and

---

[260] Vol. 11, p. 316.

[261] Vol. 16, p. 218.

[262] Vol. 16, p. 123. Two memoranda by Keynes in 1915–16, not in *CW*, are at MS Asquith 133, fols. 31–4, 65–6, Bodleian Library.

[263] Vol. 2, pp. 173–4; see vol. 9, p. 48; vol. 18, p. 265.

[264] Vol. 20, pp. 339–40; see also p. 11; vol. 16, pp. 125, 140, 224, 250, 279.

[265] Vol. 9, p. 432; see vol. 21, p. 515; vol. 22, p. 29.

[266] Vol. 15, p. 59.

[267] See, e.g. Keynes to FAK, 11 Feb. 1917, PP/45/168/9/4–5; Burk, *Sinews*, p. 7; Burk, *War*, pp. 91–2.

[268] Vol. 16, p. 3; see M. Keynes, *Essays*, pp. 142–61.

[269] See T/14, KP; vol. 16, pp. 197–8 (e.g.).

[270] See, e.g. PP/45/168/9/40ff; correspondence with Blackett and others, T /1, KP; Burk, *Sinews*, pp. 167–82.

[271] Vol. 16, pp. 70–1, 120, 208; see also pp. 197–8, 274–85.

[272] Vol. 16, pp. 185, 209.

[273] Vol. 16, p. 265. See also pp. 432–3. Ferguson believes Keynes's concerns were exaggerated: *Pity*, p. 327.

dependence',[274] and at the consequent 'power of the United States to dictate to us'.[275] He concluded later that Britain should have refused to carry the financial burden she did in the First World War.[276]

Keynes insisted on British control of allied expenditures financed through British credits to prevent wasteful competition.[277] He saw British financial aid to the allies as buying their support in the war, and British 'financial methods' as keeping 'the war popular, much too popular in my view', by making 'life relatively tolerable' for the people.[278] Despite exchange crises, such as in December 1916, which strained Britain's finances, Keynes opposed the suggestion that Britain go off the gold standard, and opposed exchange controls.[279] But, as Burk has established, in the exchange crisis of July 1917 he 'made the heretofore heretical suggestion' that 'in a choice between the rate of exchange and [Britain's] remaining gold, the rate would have to give way'. The British threat to let this happen resulted in the USA advancing funds to meet the exchange situation.[280] This crisis may have 'increased Keynes's doubts about the efficacy of orthodox arguments in favour of rigid parities'.[281]

Conversation with Norman Davis of the US Treasury in October 1918 left Keynes hopeful of working with Davis for a 'pro-British financial policy', and Anglo-American financial partnership from which France would be excluded.[282] He soon heard of a deal, which Davis opposed, between the USA and France whereby France, if she received an indemnity from Germany, would use it to repay her debts to the USA.[283] Keynes was involved in discussion in August–November 1918, under the auspices of the Political Intelligence Department of the Foreign Office, on future inter-ally economic organization.[284] This included participating in a meeting at Balliol College, Oxford, in late September, at which Alfred Zimmern and Lord Eustace Percy promoted a proposal for developing the wartime inter-Allied organization into a more elaborate international economic organization. They proposed a General Economic Board to deal with credits to countries needing assistance, and to control commodities, and urged that Britain and the USA cancel French and Italian debts to them, with the USA to cancel at least a large

---

[274] Vol. 16, p. 287; for context, see Burk, *Sinews*, p. 214 ff.
[275] Vol. 16, p. 199; see also p. 418.
[276] Vol. 18, p. 349.
[277] M. Keynes, *Essays*, p. 150; Burk, *Sinews*, pp. 45–9; Vol. 16, pp. 213, 231, 235–7.
[278] Vol. 16, p. 187; see also pp. 159, 200; vol. 4, p. 26.
[279] See, e.g. vol. 16, pp. 209–12, 215–22; vol. 22, pp. 9–11; K. Burk, *Sinews*, pp. 86–7.
[280] K. Burk, 'J. M. Keynes and the Exchange Rate Crisis of July 1917', *Economic History Review*, 32 (1979), 412–13; see also Burk, *Sinews*, p. 203 ff; vol. 16, pp. 243–63.
[281] Burk, 'Crisis of July 1917', p. 415.
[282] T/32/1–9, KP. On Anglo-French financial conferences in Oct. 1918, see T/34, KP.
[283] Keynes to Bradbury, 29 Oct. 1918, T/32/10, KP.   [284] PT/2, KP.

part of Britain's debt to her. These ideas were further expounded in a detailed memorandum circulated in various departments in October.[285] It referred, *inter alia*, to the danger of 'a recrudescence of Bolshevism'.[286] But the USA, suspicious that it would mean the buyers of their produce dictating the terms of supply, rejected the scheme for a General Economic Board.[287] It was not until February 1919 that the Supreme Economic Council was created at the peace conference; and, as we shall see, the USA repeatedly made clear that war debts would not be cancelled.

In November 1918 Keynes proposed in the Treasury that Britain seek complete cancellation of inter-Allied war debt, with Britain forgoing her share of reparations, which would go to assist newly created states (or as otherwise decided by the peace conference). Bonar Law dismissed the proposal as 'too altruistic'.[288] Despite American refusals, Keynes repeated the proposal of cancellation of war debts at Paris, in *The Economic Consequences*,[289] and later. Keynes's proposals would have involved Britain's forgiving the debts owed to her as well being forgiven her debt to the USA, and were partly aimed at making possible lower reparations demands. Through the 1920s, Keynes was concerned at the great burden of British war debts to the USA.[290] In 1940, influenced by his experience a generation before, he warned against 'establishing financial relations between the Allied and Associated powers on a pseudo-commercial basis'.[291]

2.6.2 Internal War Finance

Keynes favoured Asquith's rather than Lloyd George's approach to wartime resource allocation. He envisaged that Britain, observing her external financial constraint (which, it was hoped, would limit her war commitment), would provide the money and the Allies the armies, as against Lloyd George's notion of a war of great armies unconstrained by finance.[292] Seeing efficient economic organization as crucial to victory, Keynes stressed resource constraints from early in the war.[293] There needed to be tight central control on

---

[285] 'Memorandum on the Future Development of the Existing Inter-Allied Organisation', 21 Oct. 1918, copy at PT/2/3–10, KP; see also, e.g. Alfred Zimmern, *Nationality and Government* (London, 1918), pp. 293–7; *Europe in Convalescence* (London, 1922), pp. 82–3, 204–6; *The Third British Empire* (London, 1926) lecture 4; and esp. *The League of Nations and the Rule of Law* (London, 1936), pp. 151–9.

[286] PT/2/35, KP.   [287] Zimmern, *League*, pp. 157–8.

[288] Vol. 16, pp. 418–19; see PT/7/11–23, KP.   [289] Vol. 2, p. 171.

[290] Vol. 9, pp. 49–51; vol. 18, pp. 194, 267–8.   [291] Vol. 22, p. 176.

[292] Thirlwall, *Policy Adviser*, pp. 110–11; see vol. 16, p. 294.

[293] Vol. 16, pp. 110–11, 155–6, 157–61, 187; Ferguson, *Pity*, p. 319.

spending.[294] Private consumption needed to be constrained—by higher taxation and savings—if 'a considerably increased army and a continuance of subsidies to allies' were to be feasible.[295] But, as we have seen, Keynes opposed conscription partly because he believed that it was more important for British labour to supply food and equipment for the Allies than to add to her own armed forces.

Keynes accepted that where insufficient real resources could be gained in taxes and loans,[296] recourse would be needed to increasing the money supply. No harm followed if this money were hoarded. If it were 'spent on a government loan, the proceeds...can be used to cancel the inflationism'.[297] But if the money were spent on goods, imports would rise and the trade balance worsen. 'The scope for inflationist methods was therefore limited by the need to maintain gold payments and to finance the allies.'[298] Shortages of shipping and labour had the blessing that they constrained spending.[299]

In *The Economic Consequences*, Keynes advocated a capital levy as a means of helping defray the national debt caused by the war.[300] Many other liberals and socialists also advocated a levy.[301] Not least, it would shift part of the tax burden from 'the active elements of society' to 'idle old-won wealth'.[302] By late 1922, though he thought many European countries should impose a levy as an alternative to inflation and currency depreciation, Keynes did not favour introducing a levy 'in this country at this moment'. It had not been demonstrated beyond controversy that the burden of taxation arising from the national debt was unsupportable without a levy.[303] Keynes came to think that many people exaggerated how useful a capital levy could be in reducing national debt.[304] In evidence to the Colwyn Committee on National Debt and Taxation in 1925, he presented the arguments for and against a capital levy in a way balanced somewhat against one in present circumstances.[305] He long regretted that such a levy had not been used soon after the war,[306] and was later to advocate one for use after the Second World War.[307]

[294] Vol. 16, pp. 300–2.

[295] Vol. 16, pp. 115, 118, 142, 147, 185; see also M. Keynes, *Essays*, pp. 145–7.

[296] Vol. 16, p. 117.   [297] Vol. 16, pp. 122–3, 126.

[298] M. Keynes, *Essays*, p. 146.

[299] Vol. 22, p. 11.

[300] Vol. 2, p. 178; see also, e.g. L/20/122–3, KP.

[301] See Freeden, *Liberalism*, pp. 151–4.

[302] Vol. 17, p. 271; cf. vol. 19, pp. 313, 840–1.

[303] Vol. 19, pp. 3–4, 48–9, 62–4; vol. 4, pp. 53–60; for France: vol. 19, pp. 565–6; vol. 9, p. 77.

[304] Vol. 19, pp. 217, 688.

[305] Vol. 19, pp. 313, 839–55.

[306] For example, vol. 19, pp. 787–8; vol. 6, p. 156.

[307] For example, vol. 9, p. 404 ff. For other inter-war discussions, see, e.g. vol. 17, pp. 187–9, 359. Vol. 18, pp. 72, 349. For undated letters on a capital levy [?1943], PP/45/254/57–60, KP.

2.7 REPARATIONS, 1916–18

Until the autumn of 1916, Keynes gave little thought to post-war reconstruction issues. This was changed, slowly, by his involvement in discussions on
reparations. Other than incidental thoughts,[308] this began with his role in
drafting, with Sir William Ashley, a memorandum completed in January
1917.[309]

2.7.1 The Ashley-Keynes Memorandum

The significance of this memorandum—including its importance as a repudiation of Norman Angell's view that an indemnity necessarily harmed the
recipient—has been insufficiently recognized. It originated with the appointment by Asquith in March 1916 of a Cabinet Committee on Reconstruction.[310] In May 1916, its Secretary sought from the Board of Trade a
memorandum on 'the probable economic effect on our trade and industry
of an indemnity (whether in money or in kind) paid by the enemy at the
conclusion of the War or within a reasonable time afterwards to make good
damage in the territories overrun'.[311] Sir William Ashley, an economic histor-
ian and tariff reformer,[312] was asked to write it.[313] Ashley asked for Keynes to
help him.[314] Keynes agreed,[315] with considerable qualms: 'I am so absolutely
occupied in *bellum* questions, that I believe I shall be better advised to leave
post-bellum questions alone altogether.'[316]

Keynes was so busy that they had little contact before October, when the
Board of Trade sought urgently from Ashley the draft memorandum.[317]

---

[308] For example, vol. 11, pp. 275, 280, 319 (Sept.–Dec. 1914).

[309] Vol. 16, pp. 313–34. It was misdated '2 January 1916' when completed in Jan. 1917.
Keynes, in 1938, said it was prepared 'early in 1916': vol. 16, p. 335. The error seems to have been
generally repeated until vol. 30, p. 175, and Moggridge, *Biography*, p. 289, despite references in
the memorandum to articles and events in 1916.

[310] See CAB 37/144/44, PRO; see also RECO 1/664, PRO. T1/11977/28199, PRO.

[311] V. Nash to Sir H. Llewellyn Smith, 16 May 1916, [Sir W. Ashley papers] Add. MS 42246,
fol. 4, BL. Except where indicated, letters below are from this source.

[312] See Kadish, *Historians*, pp. 228, 234, 240.

[313] W. Carter to W. Ashley, 22 May 1916, fol. 5; Ashley to Llewellyn Smith, 27 May 1916, fols. 6–7.

[314] On former dealings, see (e.g.) Ashley to Keynes, 15 Apr. 1913, PP/45 [Ashley], EJ/6/6, EJ/
1/2, KP.

[315] Llewellyn Smith to Ashley, 4 June 1916, fols. 9–10; 9 June, fol. 10. Ashley to Keynes,
15 June 1916, T/1/26–7, KP.

[316] Keynes to Ashley, 16 June 1916, fol. 12.

[317] P. Ashley to W. Ashley, 9 Oct. 1916, fol. 37. The only sign of contact: Keynes to Ashley,
31 July 1916, fol. 13.

Ashley supplied one bearing only his name.[318] The Board of Trade printed Ashley's translation of Adolph Wagner's account of 'The Indemnity of 1871 and its Effects' as a departmental paper.[319] On 27 October, Keynes sent Ashley comments on his memorandum, saying his criticisms were of details and not fundamental.[320] A second draft of the memorandum was prepared[321] and, after further delay,[322] Keynes sent Ashley further suggestions on 31 December, 'mainly directed to bringing the memorandum more closely in connection with our exact terms of reference'.[323] On 2 January, Ashley sent the Board of Trade the 'Memorandum some sections of which Keynes has drafted, and to the whole of which we now both assent. . . . it does not differ in substance from the draft originally prepared.'[324] The memorandum was printed and circulated to various departments. Ashley received letters from the Board of Trade,[325] the Reconstruction Committee,[326] and the Treasury[327] expressing great interest in it.

The memorandum argued that the payment of an indemnity was, in general, harmful to the paying, and beneficial to the receiving, country.[328] For example, the memorandum rejected the notion that an indemnity would give 'stimulus to the trade of the defeated enemy and a corresponding hindrance to the trade of the victorious Alliance'.[329] That an indemnity could be beneficial was an important proposition to establish because many people, attributing Germany's 1873 financial crisis to the French indemnity after the Franco-Prussian war, believed that an indemnity was bound to do more harm than good.[330] This argument had gained prominence from such writers as Norman Angell[331] and Robert Brand.[332] Ashley–Keynes argued, however, that the overall influence of the indemnity on Germany was

---

[318] Ashley's 12 Oct. draft: fols. 38–75; Llewellyn Smith to Ashley, 13 Oct., fol. 76; 16 Oct., fol. 77.

[319] See P. Ashley at Board of Trade to W. Ashley, 10 Nov. 1916, fol. 79; Llewellyn Smith to Ashley, 2 Jan. 1917, fol. 83.

[320] Fol. 78. Keynes's comments of 27 Oct. 1916: fols. 131–7.

[321] Ashley's second draft: fols. 138–66 and 100–25.

[322] Keynes to Ashley, 11 Dec. 1916, fol. 80; 28 Dec. 1916, fol. 81.

[323] Keynes to Ashley, 31 Dec. 1916, fol. 82.

[324] W. Ashley to Llewellyn Smith, 3 Jan. 1917, fol. 84; see Llewellyn Smith to Ashley, 2 Jan., fol. 85; P. Ashley to W. Ashley, 9 Jan., p. 86; Keynes to W. Ashley, 10 Jan., fol. 87; Llewellyn Smith to W. Ashley, 15 Jan., fol. 88. The printed version is at: fols. 182–90.

[325] Llewellyn Smith to Ashley, 15 Jan. 1917, fol. 88.

[326] Nash to Ashley, 16 Jan. 1917, fols. 89–90; 14 Feb. 1917, fol. 91.

[327] Sydney Armitage Smith to Ashley, 3 Mar. 1917, fol. 95.

[328] Vol. 16, p. 314.

[329] Vol. 16, p. 334; see also p. 330.

[330] Vol. 16, p. 314.

[331] Angell, *The Great Illusion*, p. 87.

[332] R. H. Brand, 'Lombard Street and War', *The Round Table*, 2 (1912), pp. 246–84; Keynes to Ashley, 31 July 1916, fol. 13.

favourable in the 1870s, though it 'did also hasten and intensify the speculative movement which brought about the [financial] crisis of 1873'.[333]

Ashley–Keynes argued that such adverse effects could be reduced or eliminated, depending on (*inter alia*) the duration of payments; and that
prolonged payment was *alternative* to large immediate transfers. They quoted
Wagner on the adverse effects of the 1871–3 indemnity:

These effects could, to a certain extent, have been avoided by spreading the payment
of the indemnity over a *longer* period, by investing to a larger amount and for a longer
period in *foreign* securities, and by enforcing payment to a larger extent in the form of
concrete use-values and things other than money (e.g. navy, payments in kind, cession
of colonies).[334]

The memorandum considered transfers in the form either '(1) of a quantity
of existing property; or (2) of a sum of immediate cash; or (3) of a promise to
transfer property or cash over a series of years'.[335] Under (1), it saw very
considerable and instructive benefits.[336] Under (2), it suggested that if, 'when
the war ends, there are still at least £100 millions of gold in the vaults of the
Reichsbank, there seems no conclusive reason why a considerable part of this
should not be parted with'; and that, if Germany could raise loans in neutral
countries (such as the USA, Holland, and Scandinavia), 'the proceeds could
be used to discharge the short-period obligations of the allies in these
countries'. The memorandum presented the methods of immediate and
prolonged payment as being in a sense alternatives, or, if the indemnity
demand is 'too large to be covered by the transference of immediately
available wealth', complementary. It cited Wagner's contention 'that it is
wise to spread the reception of an indemnity over a longer period than that
of 1871–3': 'For it might be only by means of a prolongation of the period that
Germany (and Austria) would be able to accumulate considerable fresh
quantities of wealth for indemnity purposes. It will be especially necessary
to pay regard to this consideration if the productive capacity of Germany is
seriously weakened by immediate transfers of property…' Enforcing prolonged payment 'depends on the assumption that the allies will retain in their
hands during that protracted period adequate guarantees'.[337]

The memorandum also stressed that its terms of reference 'limit the
character of the indemnity contemplated to that of an indemnity designed
"to make good damage in the territories overrun"'.[338] The indemnity was for
Belgium and France (the priority of Belgium was then widely accepted, as the
war against her was wholly illegal). Britain was not to be a recipient. The
memorandum said:

---

[333] Vol. 16, pp. 315, 318.   [334] Vol. 16, p. 321.   [335] Vol. 16, p. 313.
[336] Vol. 16, pp. 324–6.   [337] Vol. 16, pp. 327–30.   [338] Vol. 16, p. 333.

With an indemnity restricted to the restoration of the economic life of the occupied territories, the economic advantage to Great Britain would chiefly consist in the avoidance of that further taxation which will be necessary if Great Britain is to assist in the restoration of the ravaged countries without an adequate contribution to that purpose from the enemy.

It is clear that the memorandum was prepared mainly by Ashley, with Keynes suggesting changes, and doing so under great pressure of other work. In his comments of 27 October 1916 on Ashley's draft of 12 October, Keynes doubted that Germany had either done as much shipbuilding or acquired such large stocks of raw materials as Ashley considered possible and 'wartime fairy stories' suggested: 'I doubt if Germany has acquired even the minimum necessary for the preservation of her economic life. And if we are considering methods of raising wealth proper rather than of spreading starvation and unemployment in Germany, I should have thought there was little in this particular source.'[339]

Keynes also thought Ashley's estimates of Germany's gold stock[340] and holdings of foreign securities[341] too high. The confiscation of foreign securities in German ownership was contrary to international law, international propriety, and international morality.[342] Keynes stressed that 'We cannot both deprive Germany of her sources of wealth and also expect her to save on her pre-war standards for the purpose of paying a tribute.'[343]

Keynes's comments reflected his antipathy to protectionism.[344] He wished to conclude the memorandum by saying that it 'has been directed to nothing except the immediate economic consequences of a sudden transfer of wealth between nations; that no regard has been paid to political wisdom, international morality or to the best way of preserving peace for the future'.[345] Keynes also said that 'on its political side the problem depends' greatly on 'the magnitude of the transfer of wealth in contemplation. If no more is desired than the re-institution of the economic life of occupied territory', it would be easier to use methods without injurious side effects 'than if it is desired to extract the maximum possible money value'. Keynes clearly did not regard the memorandum as advocating large-scale reparations.

In his comments of 31 December 1916 on Ashley's second draft,[346] Keynes emphasized 'the danger of indirect ill-effects' from 'an immediate transfer of

[339] Fols. 131–2; see vol. 16, p. 324, para. 17.
[340] Fols. 132–3; Ashley at fol. 63; Keynes at fol. 133.
[341] Compare fols. 61–3 with vol. 16, pp. 325–6, para. 20; see Keynes at fol. 113.
[342] Fol. 132.
[343] Fol. 133.
[344] See fols. 135–6 and 70; see fol. 124 for Keynes's slight adjustment to the next draft.
[345] Fol. 137.
[346] See fols. 100–25 for Ashley's draft, with Keynes's proposed changes. Fols. 126–8 have Keynes's proposed addition of a final section (paras. 27–9 of final memorandum).

cash' (even though this could be beneficial to the recipient). He said that 'the transferance of wealth over a series of years' 'in special circumstances... might involve a reduction of exports' for the recipient country.[347] Keynes made changes to stress that Britain would not be a recipient of 'an indemnity of reparation for territories overrun'.[348] He also played down the indirect benefits to Britain of an indemnity paid to overrun territories.[349] Keynes deleted the reference to 'territorial' guarantees of 'payment spread over a term of years', simply wanting 'adequate guarantees'[350] (the final version suggested 'the retention of some German colony which it is intended ultim-ately to restore').[351] Keynes suggested the words: 'If an indemnity were sought to an amount, for example, of £100,000,000...'[352] This figure was deleted from the final version;[353] but it suggests the order of magnitude Keynes had in mind at the end of 1916.

Given Keynes's role, it is paradoxical that in 1938 Lloyd George depicted him as having been, through the Ashley–Keynes memorandum, 'the sole patentee and promoter' of exactions from Germany 'over a long period of years'.[354] In reply to that charge, Keynes stressed that the memorandum made no recommendations, and was 'based throughout on the assumption that [Britain] would make *no* claim for reparation'.[355] He might have added that the memorandum was written when there was little pressure for a large-scale indemnity,[356] and it was based on the assumption that an indemnity would be relatively small. Keynes never repudiated the idea, which Ashley-Keynes argued, that some indemnity could be beneficially received. In a different climate, his writings of late 1918 and beyond were concerned to show the limits necessary on an indemnity, and the harm it could do.

2.7.2 The Board of Trade Memorandum and the Milner Committee

On 24 January 1917, a Board of Trade memorandum on 'Economic Desid-erata in the Terms of Peace' was circulated to the Imperial War Cabinet (IWC).[357] It was dated 27 October 1916, but part was updated at the

[347] Fol. 101.
[348] See fols. 113, 121, 125 (para. beginning 'But if the indemnity is not so limited'). Cf. fols. 124–5, 126–8.
[349] Fols. 124–5.
[350] Compare fols. 67 and 120.
[351] Vol. 16, p. 330.
[352] Fols. 126–8.
[353] Para. 28: vol. 16, p. 334.
[354] See D. Lloyd George, *The Truth About the Peace Treaties* (London, 1938), pp. 445–9.
[355] Vol. 16, pp. 311–12, 333–6.   [356] B. Kent, *The Spoils of War* (Oxford, 1989), p. 28 ff.
[357] CAB 29/1, fols. 36 ff, PRO.

beginning of January 1917. It was concerned with a negotiated peace, not directed to 'the permanent crushing of the commercial and industrial power of Germany'.[358] The Memorandum said:[359]

Assuming a complete victory, the Board of Trade see no reason to doubt the expediency of exacting an indemnity, though the proceeds of any indemnity which the Central Powers could pay will necessarily go but a short way towards meeting the cost of the war.... The Board of Trade have obtained from Professor Ashley and Mr. J. M. Keynes a valuable memorandum on the probable effects of an indemnity on our trade. Briefly, the result is to show that, from an economic point of view, indemnity in kind is to be preferred, so far as practicable, to indemnity in money, and that any cash payments should be spread over a considerable period. This memorandum is circulated with this paper.

It is not clear why the Board of Trade memorandum should have made either of these claims about the Ashley–Keynes memorandum: though there is some support for them there, neither is clearly stated as a conclusion. Ashley and Keynes were not so much saying that any cash payment should be prolonged, as that this might be the only way to get a considerable payment. Though moderate in tone, the Board of Trade memorandum was turning a discussion of the effects on Britain of an indemnity paid to Belgium and France into prescriptions for an indemnity in which Britain would share. In interpreting the Ashley–Keynes memorandum this way, the authors of the Board of Trade memorandum may have been more influenced by Ashley's draft of 12 October 1916, than by the final document of 2 January 1917.[360] The Board memorandum also referred to Wagner's argument about avoiding the 'pernicious effects' after the Franco-Prussian war 'by spreading the payment over a longer period, and by enforcing payment to a larger extent in things other than money'.[361] Ashley's translation of Wagner was appended.[362]

American entry to the war on 6 April 1917 contributed to a flurry of activity on possible peace terms. Copies of the Ashley–Keynes memorandum and the translation of Wagner were sought for immediate circulation to members of the Imperial War Cabinet (IWC)[363] which, at meetings on 12 and 13 April, 'appointed a Committee to consider the economic and other non-territorial desiderata in the terms of Peace',[364] chaired by Lord Milner. On 20 April, Milner submitted to his committee a form of draft report,[365] which said:

[358] CAB 29/1, fol. 36.
[359] CAB 29/1, fol. 37. The Ashley–Keynes memorandum is at fols. 63–71.
[360] See Llewellyn Smith to Ashley, 13 Oct. 1916: fol. 76.
[361] CAB 29/1, fol. 37.   [362] CAB 29/1, fols. 47–61.
[363] P. Ashley to W. Ashley, 11 April 1917: fol. 96.   [364] CAB 21/71, fol. 24, PRO.
[365] CAB 21/71, fol. 16.

Obviously our [indemnity] demands [in peace negotiations] must take account of the then existing conditions of the enemy countries, the state of their resources and their ability to pay any indemnity, whether in money or kind. . . . For the reasons ably stated in two memoranda submitted by the Board of Trade, it appears to the Committee that an indemnity in kind is both more practicable and in every way preferable to an indemnity in money, though the latter, which could in any case only cover a small proportion of the losses to be made good, might also be resorted to in a certain measure.

This passage is similar to the exposition in the Board of Trade's memorandum,[366] which itself was in part based on the Ashley–Keynes memorandum. These appear to be the two memoranda Milner mentioned.

The report of the Milner Commitee, dated 24 April 1917, though based on Milner's draft, was less lukewarm about a money indemnity than his draft, and somewhat more ambitious in its hopes for an indemnity.[367] It recommended, however, that protracted payments, in kind or of money, 'should be spread over a *short* term of years':[368] Milner's draft had said 'over a term of years'.[369] The 'strong opinion' was expressed in the Milner committee 'that it is undesirable to attempt to hold the enemy countries to the payment of a tribute, whether in money or in kind, for a prolonged period. Anything like complete reparation for the losses caused by the war, was manifestly impossible'.[370] The Ashley–Keynes point that adequate guarantees would be necessary for prolonged payments was used as an argument *against* prolonged payments: they would lead to many difficulties and 'retard the gradual re-establishment of a pacific spirit throughout the world'. Ashley was assured that his and Keynes's memorandum 'had very much influence' on Milner's committee.[371]

The Milner Report was too mild for some members of the IWC, who thought 'that insufficient stress had perhaps been laid on the idea of indemnity in cash': 'It was pointed out that a cash indemnity would certainly be required for Belgium, and that such a form of indemnity, though perhaps not most useful from the point of view of the Allies, would be very effective in crippling Germany. It was pointed out, however, that the amount of pecuniary indemnity payable by Germany was relatively small...'[372] The Ashley–Keynes proposal of holding some German colonies as a guarantee for an indemnity was opposed because Lord Curzon's committee on territorial desiderata was likely to oppose restoring any German colonies.

---

[366] CAB 29/1, fol. 37.   [367] CAB 21/71 fols. 24–7, at fol. 25.
[368] CAB 21/71, fol. 25; emphasis added.   [369] CAB 21/71, fol. 16.
[370] CAB 21/71, fol. 16.   [371] P. Ashley to W. Ashley, 29 April 1917, fols. 97–8.
[372] CAB 23/40, IWC, 26 April 1917, p. 6, PRO.

2.7.3 Discussions in Anticipation of the Armistice

Further intense consideration of the indemnity/reparations question took place in October–December 1918. During the Allied discussions leading to the Armistice, Keynes hastily finished on 31 October 1918 'Notes on an Indemnity' giving a preliminary estimate of Germany's capacity to pay.[373] He drew a distinction between amounts that would and would not crush her. Crushing Germany's credit and recuperative power 'might defeat its object by leading to a condition in which the allies would have to give her a loan to save her from starvation and general anarchy'. In all, '(say) £1,000 million could be obtained without crushing Germany, half of it immediately' as ships, assets in ceded territory, and other immediately transferable property, and half as payments in cash or kind 'over a period of years'.[374] Keynes also argued that the return of 'Alsace-Lorraine ought to go far to compensate France for damage done'.[375]

In November and December, Keynes spent much time on reparations (and spent some days in early November in Belgium and northern France surveying the devastation).[376] It seems that he participated in writing a Board of Trade memorandum finalized on 26 November.[377] He appeared before the Hughes Committee in late November and early December. He was the principal author of a Treasury memorandum circulated to the IWC before their meeting on 23 December.[378]

2.7.4 Another Board of Trade Memorandum

On 17 October, the Board of Trade was asked by the IWC for 'a Memorandum on the economic considerations' in Allied preparations for 'an eventual peace conference' with the defeated powers.[379] The memorandum seems to have been largely completed before the Armistice; a brief addendum was dated 26 November.[380] The memorandum was prepared 'in semi-official

[373] Vol. 16, pp. 338–43; for signs of the Ashley–Keynes memorandum, see, e.g. p. 338 n 1.
[374] Vol. 16, pp. 341–2.   [375] Vol. 16, p. 339.
[376] Moggridge, *Biography*, pp. 285–6; vol. 17, p. 348; vol. 2, pp. 75–6; cf. vol. 26, p. 100.
[377] *Memorandum by the Board of Trade on Economic Considerations Affecting the Terms of Peace*, CAB 29/1, fol. 283 ff, PRO; see, esp., fol. 289.
[378] Keynes to FAK, 16 Dec. 1918, PP/45/168/9/139–40, KP: 'my Indemnity memo'. Vol. 16, p. 311; see also pp. 337, 344; M. Keynes, *Essays*, pp. 156–7, 163. The memorandum is at CAB 29/2, fol. 68 ff, PRO, and vol. 16, pp. 344–83.
[379] CAB 29/1, fol. 283.
[380] CAB 29/1, fol. 291; L. Woodward, *Great Britain and the War of 1914–1918* (London, 1967), p. 548. T1 12323/20212, Hughes Committee, 29 Nov. 1918, p. 5, PRO.

consultation with the Treasury' and other departments.[381] References to it by Llewellyn Smith and Keynes imply that Keynes was a member of the Committee which prepared it.[382] As we shall see, it proposed a payment comparable to Keynes's figure of 31 October (£1,000 million), though perhaps as high as £2,000 million.

The Board memorandum drew a distinction between indemnity (payment 'towards "the Allies" expenditure on the war'), and reparation (payment 'towards the cost of making good the injuries which the enemy has inflicted on the Allied populations and their property by devastation, destruction, spoliation, and exactions of various kinds').[383] This distinction was widely accepted, including by the members of the later Hughes Committee in their deliberations,[384] but not in their report.[385] The Board of Trade memorandum said that reparation claims, which would take precedence over an indemnity, would be so colossal that 'the limit of the sum to be demanded will be fixed rather by the capacity of the Central Powers to pay'. The figure should be fixed 'now rather than leaving the amount to be haggled over for years after the war'. It was thought unsafe 'to put the total claims for reparation ... at less than [£]2,000,000,000', and this was unlikely to be retrievable 'unless payment is spread over so long a time that a long period of occupation of German territory would be necessary to enforce it'. The memorandum also referred to the danger of adverse commercial and financial repercussions on the Allies from seeking to exact even legitimate reparation claims.

The memorandum referred to Wagner's monograph on the 1871–3 indemnity, and appended the 'very valuable memorandum' by Ashley and Keynes.[386] It pointed 'strongly to the superiority of an indemnity in kind, including securities, over an indemnity in cash'.[387] The memorandum concluded that reparations could and should be taken in various kinds— such as ships, *matériel* for reconstruction, potash, coal, gold, and external investments held in the Central Powers. A lump sum of £1,000 million in this form was suggested as realistic. Given the difficulties involved in raising, say, £2,000 million (which would 'include no contribution towards ordinary war expenses'), 'the determination of the total amount demanded is clearly one ... of high policy'.[388]

[381] CAB 29/1, fol. 283.
[382] T1 12323/20212, Hughes Ctee, 29 Nov., p. 5.
[383] CAB 29/1, fol. 289.
[384] For example, T1 12323/20212, Hughes Ctee, 29 Nov., p. 4.
[385] CAB 27/43, fol. 92.   [386] CAB 29/1, fol. 289.
[387] CAB 29/1, fol. 290.   [388] CAB 29/1, fol. 293.

2.7.5 Keynes and the Hughes Committee

With William Morris Hughes and others pressing for Germany to pay the full cost of the war, and the Board of Trade reporting that this was impossible, the IWC on 26 November 1918 appointed a Committee on Indemnity, chaired by Hughes. In the IWC meeting Hughes recognized that 'a fair reading of President Wilson's proposals would show that they did not include any suggestion as to a war indemnity'.[389] But, as he wrote later, he was determined to 'argue stoutly that we can ask for an Indemnity under the Reparation clause'.[390] Lloyd George reacted cautiously to Hughes's desire for large payments from Germany: 'the only way in which Germany could pay a large indemnity would be by manufacturing cheaper than other nations and by selling to them'. At this point, Bonar Law, the Chancellor, referred to a Treasury Committee which had concluded that £2,000 million was the maximum amount which Germany could pay. It is not clear whether Bonar Law was referring to Keynes and any others working on the Treasury memorandum, which was not then complete, or to those who had worked on the Board of Trade memorandum, dated that day, which had used the figure £2,000 million as a maximum.[391] In any case, 'Mr. Bonar Law did not agree with this view. The debt of the British Government would be [£]8,000,000,000..., of which [£]1,000,000,000...was owed to the United States.'[392]

Lloyd George proposed a Cabinet committee 'to find out...whether we could get an indemnity out of Germany without doing ourselves harm'.[393] The committee, chaired by Hughes, included Lord Cunliffe, a former governor of the Bank of England; Herbert Gibbs, chairman of the City of London Conservative Association;[394] W. A. S. Hewins, the tariff reform economist, now a junior minister; a Canadian minister, Sir George Foster; and Walter Long. Keynes attended the early sittings.[395]

The Committee's report said that the Board of Trade memorandum of November and the Ashley-Keynes memorandum 'proved of great value'.[396] The Committee were made aware by Keynes and Llewellyn Smith that a more

[389] CAB 23/42, IWC, 26 Nov. 1918, minute 12, PRO; see vol. 2, p. 87 n.
[390] Hughes to Sir R. Munro Ferguson, 14 Dec. 1918, Novar papers, MS 696/2748–9, Australian National Library.
[391] For example, Kent, *Spoils*, pp. 36–7, refers to the unfinished memo.
[392] CAB 23/42, IWC, 26 Nov. 1918, minute 12.
[393] CAB 23/42, IWC, 26 Nov. 1918, minute 12.
[394] Kent, *Spoils*, p. 37.
[395] T1 12323/20212, Hughes Ctee. He attended at least the meetings of 28 and 29 Nov., and of the afternoon of 2 Dec.
[396] CAB 29/2, fol. 26, PRO.

elaborate report was being prepared,[397] but the Committee did not see the Treasury memorandum.[398] Keynes told the Committee that the Treasury were investigating, as separate issues, 'what we guess the reparation bill will be and what the maximum Germany can pay will be'. It looked 'very probable that the amount of reparation is larger than the amount Germany can pay'.[399] Keynes rejected the figure of £20,000 million which Lord Cunliffe had already mentioned.[400] Keynes argued that the starting point of consideration should be Germany's capacity to pay; Hughes insisted on first deciding what Germany ought to pay. Keynes gave £1,000 million as the maximum Germany could pay in immediately movable property, with £600 million or £700 million payable over thirty years; 'you can only get larger sums than that if you stimulate her exports', for example by wage reductions, or by giving German goods preference in foreign markets. The effect of attempting to enforce payments was unpredictable: 'The extent to which you can press down the level of life of the population without producing revolution and Bolshevism turns on the force of the [German] Government.'[401] Later that day, Keynes increased his estimate to '1,000 millions of movable property, and something under another 1,000 millions in the form of tribute [over thirty years]; that is to say, altogether something about 2,000 millions'.[402] But the tenor of the Committee was against moderation, with Hughes declaring 'He would be a very rash man, in view of what has happened, to prophesy what Germany could not do.'[403]

By 2 December, the Committee had a report which its members were prepared to submit to the Cabinet.[404] It recommended:[405]

1. The Allies cost of the war is the measure of the Indemnity which Germany and the Powers associated with her should in justice pay.
2. Although it is not possible to estimate the capacity of the Enemy Powers to pay, the full amount should be demanded and the Committee have no reasons to suppose that this claim cannot be met.
3. The Indemnity should be payable in cash, kind, securities, and by means of a funding loan.

[397] T1 12323/20212, Hughes Ctee, 29 Nov., p. 5.
[398] Cf. Woodward, *War*, p. 549. Kent, *Spoils*, p. 37.
[399] T1 12323/20212, Hughes Ctee, 29 Nov., p. 6. See p. 8.
[400] Ibid., pp. 2, 6.
[401] Ibid., p. 8.
[402] Ibid., p. 11.
[403] Ibid., p. 12.
[404] CAB 29/2, fols. 26–34. Dated 2 Dec. 1918, this is what emerged at the end of the meeting on 2 Dec. See T1 12323/20212, Hughes Ctee, 2 Dec., p. 30.
[405] CAB 29/2, fol. 34: p. 8 of report.

4. The fear of economic ill-effects from the receipt of an indemnity is not well founded.

5. Our economic position without an Indemnity will be undeniably worse than it would be with an Indemnity.

6. The enforcement of an Indemnity will operate as a deterrent to a future aggression and be a substantial guarantee of the world's peace.

In arguing point 4, the Committee relied almost solely on the Wagner–Ashley–Keynes analysis of the 1871–73 indemnity, and the Report borrowed passages from the Ashley–Keynes memorandum.[406] This was despite Keynes's insisting before the Committee that it had been written on the assumption of a much smaller indemnity than Hughes envisaged, and 'that it was written, at any rate by me, on the free-trade hypothesis that it was not injurious if this country was flooded with cheap German goods'.[407] Keynes's request for an explanatory rider to the references to the memorandum was rejected. Hughes was passionate: 'on behalf of Australia, I hope you will not prevent us from getting an indemnity; we want it very badly'.[408]

The Report of 2 December 1918, was, however, not submitted to the Cabinet. On 2 December, a conference of Allied leaders in London established an Inter-Allied Commission on Reparation and Indemnity.[409] There was a tussle between the USA and the Allies on whether indemnities should be included, or only reparations, as the USA wanted.[410] Hughes, Cunliffe, and Lord Sumner were appointed the British delegates to the Inter-Allied Commission. Lloyd George stressed in the IWC on 3 December that, both for the Inter-Allied Commission and the Hughes Committee, 'it was not enough to decide how much Germany could pay, but it was also necessary to say how she could pay'.[411] Instead of submitting its report to the IWC, the Hughes Committee set to work again.[412] Under pressure from Lloyd George, Hughes promised him a report by the evening of 10 December, and that day the Committee agreed and signed its conclusions.[413] Although Gibbs recognized that 'the evidence so far as it went was rather against us' on Germany's capacity to pay, the Committee, especially under Cunliffe's and Hughes's prompting, specified at £24,000 million the full cost of the war, and said it had no reason to believe Germany could not pay this.

---

[406] CAB 29/2, fol. 30 ff; see, e.g. T1 12323/20212, Hughes Ctee, 2 Dec., pp. 18, 21.

[407] T1 12323/20212, Hughes Ctee, 2 Dec., p. 21.

[408] Ibid., p. 25. See vol. 2, p. 87 n; Keynes secured another change: 2 Dec., p. 30.

[409] CAB 23/42, IWC, 3 Dec. 1918, minute 2; Kent, *Spoils*, p. 39.

[410] Woodward, *War*, p. 550 n.; CAB 23/42, IWC, 3 Dec., minute 2.

[411] CAB 23/42, IWC, 3 Dec., minute 2. See Kent, *Spoils*, p. 39.

[412] See, esp., T1 12323/20212, Hughes Ctee, 9 Dec., p. 1; see Hewins at Hughes Ctee, 10 Dec., p. 5.

[413] T1 12323/20212, Hughes Ctee, 10 Dec., pp. 15–16.

Lloyd George's urgency was at least partly because the election campaign was nearing its climax, and he felt pressed by mounting demands that Germany bear the full cost of the war. Keynes described these events graphically in *The Economic Consequences*.[414] Lloyd George had previously referred to the Central Powers 'paying the cost of the war up to the limit of their capacity', and not so 'as to wreck our industries'. He sought to avoid further commitment by referring to 'a strong committee of experts' appointed to advise on how much, and how, Germany should pay. But as others promised to 'squeeze [Germany] until you can hear the pips squeak', Lloyd George 'capitulated'. In Bristol, on 11 December, he promised 'fullest indemnities from Germany', and asserted Britain's right and intention 'to demand the whole cost of the war', saying that a Committee appointed by the IWC advised that it could be done.

The next day, Paul Cravath, an American official in London who had worked closely with Keynes, wrote to him to stress that Britain could not collect more than the damages defined in the Armistice undertaking, and that Lloyd George's Bristol speech did not give the true situation. This letter, shown to Bonar Law, gave Keynes an opportunity to reiterate the American insistence 'that we were honourably engaged not to ask for the general costs of the war'.[415] Cravath, who believed that US Treasury officials in Washington did not understand 'the situation over here', also promised Keynes to work on his return to the US for 'a satisfactory arrangement between the British and American Treasuries'.[416]

2.7.6 The Treasury Memorandum

It was in this climate that Keynes, and perhaps others, completed the Treasury memorandum on which much work had been done in November. The undated memorandum is sometimes said to date from or before 26 November,[417] but it was clearly not completed until mid-December.[418] This memorandum

---

[414] See vol. 2, pp. 88–91; Kent, *Spoils*, p. 40; on 'hearing the pips squeak', see FAK to Keynes, 11 Dec. 1918, PP/45/168/9/137; Keynes to FAK, 12 Nov. 1919, PP/45/168/10/21–2, KP; cf. vol. 28, p. 163.

[415] Cravath to Keynes, 12 Dec. 1918, with annotations, RT/1/3, KP. For their close links, see also RT/1/4–10, KP.

[416] Cravath to Keynes, 20 Dec. 1918, RT/1/8, KP; cf. D. H. Miller, *My Diary at the Conference of Paris*, i (New York, 1924), pp. 33–4.

[417] For example, Skidelsky, *Hopes*, p. 355; Kent, *Spoils*, pp. 36–7, esp. 37 n.

[418] Reference to Dec. in it: vol. 16, p. 377; see also T1 12323/20212, Hughes Ctee, 29 Nov. pp. 5–6. It was 'substantially complete' by 6 Dec. Miller, *Diary*, i, pp. 36–7. Keynes to FAK, 16 Dec. 1918, PP/45/168/139–40, KP.

was essentially Keynes's. He gave it much sustained attention. Its circulation prior to the IWC meeting on 23 December was a powerful counterattack against the Hughes report. The memorandum set out in full Keynes's position on reparations for the first time, including the major arguments he was to use in *The Economic Consequences*. Indeed, some sections were reproduced verbatim there.[419]

It is likely that, in preparing this memorandum, Keynes saw one by Alfred Zimmern in the Foreign Office, dated 3 December, distinguishing reparation from indemnity, and worrying that more might be asked of Germany than legitimately could.[420] The Treasury memorandum cited the Armistice undertakings, under which compensation could be claimed from Germany 'for all damage done to the civilian population of the Allies and to their property by the aggression of Germany by land, by sea, and from the air'.[421] As Zimmern and Cravath had done, it argued that this excluded any claim for repayment of the general cost of the war,[422] though something like this might be justified for Belgium.[423] The Allies' preliminary reparation claim was, very roughly, around £4,000 million. By contrast, the cost of the war to the Allies, including war pensions and demobilization costs, made a grand total of £24,350 million.[424] Germany's capacity to pay was far less than that: 'an actual payment of £2,000 million, if effected without evil indirect consequences, would be a very satisfactory achievement'; £3,000 million is 'in excess of what could in fact be obtained'.[425] '[T]ribute over a period of years is, broadly, alternative to, and not additional to, the exaction of the maximum amount' of transferable property, raw materials, and territory. Payments over a series of years required Germany to reduce her imports and increase her exports, to increase the balance available for making payments abroad. This would mean substantial harm to British export trade and British home industries.[426] This meant that 'the limit of what we can safely exact, having regard to our own selfish interests only, may therefore be as low as £2,000 million'.[427] There was, however, 'no reason...why less than the full cost of reparation should be asked of the enemy in the first instance, and the burden of proving incapacity should be thrown on them'. As the Ashley–Keynes memorandum had said, the Franco-Prussian experience did not prove that indemnities were harmful: 'it must be advantageous to a country to receive imports without having to work

---

[419] Vol. 2, pp. 106–31.

[420] Memo. from Zimmern to Headlam Morley, 3 Dec. 1918, PT/10/4–5, KP; see also PT/10/2–3; G. L. Dickinson asked Keynes, 'How much are you going to rob Germany?': Dickinson to Keynes, 4 Dec. 1918, PP/45/86/6, KP.

[421] Vol. 16, p. 347.   [422] Vol. 16, p. 348.   [423] Vol. 16, p. 350.

[424] Vol. 16, pp. 357–8.   [425] Vol. 16, pp. 378, 358.

[426] Vol. 16, pp. 369–71, 375, 380–1.   [427] Vol. 16, p. 381.

or pay for them, and the process is correspondingly disadvantageous to the country paying the indemnity'.[428] The choice was either (*a*) to take ruthlessly *all* quickly transferable property, and then to ask 'only a small tribute over a term of years', or (*b*) 'to levy less ruthlessly in the immediate future, and to supply Germany with considerable quantities of raw material', and 'having thus nursed [Germany] back into a condition of high productivity, to compel her to exploit this productivity under conditions of servitude for a long period of years'. The memorandum favoured the first alternative.[429]

2.7.7 The Imperial War Cabinet, 23 and 24 December 1918

The Treasury memorandum was distributed to the IWC, and referred to in their meeting on 23 December. When 'it was pointed out that it controverted the conclusions of Mr. Hughes' Committee', Bonar Law explained that it had been sought 'before the appointment of Mr. Hughes' Committee ... and was not intended as a criticism of the work of the Committee'.[430] Discussion was deferred a day to Christmas Eve, when a long discussion of the Hughes report took place.[431] Keynes was present.[432] The Treasury Memorandum had clearly placed Hughes on the defensive. He stressed his Committee's belief that 'no just distinction could really be drawn between' indemnity and reparation. He rested his argument on the economic effects of indemnity solely on the Ashley–Keynes 'investigations'. But among those expressing scepticism, Bonar Law, clearly influenced by the Treasury, could not 'see a way of our getting more than reparation without being damaged ourselves'. When Lloyd George said that Hughes's figure of £24,000 million could not be obtained, Hughes 'agreed that it might[433] not be possible to get that sum. But it was not for us to limit our demand, but for Germany to prove ... that she could not pay all that she ought to do'.

Though Hughes thought Germany would have a stable Government and was safe from Bolshevism, Lord Milner 'suggested that the most certain way of "bolshevising" Germany would be to put an excessive burden on her'.[434] Churchill considered the burden of Hughes's proposal upon the ordinary working-class household in Germany excessive. Bonar Law, Sir Robert Borden,

---

[428] Vol. 16, pp. 378–9.   [429] Vol. 16, pp. 382–3.

[430] CAB 23/42, IWC, 23 Dec. 1918, minute 3; cf. Kent, *Spoils*, pp. 39–40, with Woodward, *War*, p. 550.

[431] CAB 23/42, IWC, 24 Dec. 1918, minute 3.

[432] Vol. 16, p. 337; see also PT/9, KP.

[433] Not that it 'would not be possible': vol. 16, p. 337.

[434] Keynes had expressed this worry: T1 12323/20212, Hughes Ctee, 29 Nov., p. 8; Vol. 16, pp. 381–2.

and C. Barnes (Labour) suggested that claiming an indemnity was not compatible with Wilson's declared principles; Lloyd George insisted that it was. Barnes's speech reflected the fact that, prior to the Armistice, there had been few demands for Germany to pay the full cost of the war: 'the insistence on an indemnity was an afterthought' since the Armistice.[435] But strong reference was also made to the strength of feeling in the country in favour of a large indemnity.

Clearly, as far as many members of the IWC were concerned, the Hughes Report was an unreliable guide. Nonetheless, the IWC agreed with Lloyd George's proposal to instruct the British delegates to the Inter-Allied Commission to 'endeavour to secure from Germany the greatest possible indemnity she can pay consistently with the economic well-being of the British Empire and the peace of the world, and without involving an army of occupation in Germany for its collection'.[436] However, Lloyd George reported to the IWC on 30 December that Wilson was stiffer in opposing indemnity in addition to reparation than on any other question.[437] As Keynes saw it, Wilson's resolve was not to survive the 'bamboozlement' of Paris.

2.8 CONCLUSION

At the end of 1918, Keynes had a clear view of some of the elements of the post-war order he wished to see. His liberal-idealist faith in free trade, on which he had been brought up, was unshaken. He had urged the abandonment of inter-Allied debt, and Britain's forgoing her share of reparations, which he hoped would go to assist the new states.[438] He had urged a moderate approach to reparations; and clearly wished the defeated powers to be treated so that they would not need assistance to avoid starvation, unemployment, anarchy, or perhaps Bolshevism. The fundamental views which underlay his actions at the peace conference, and which were to be expounded in *The Economic Consequences*, were already formed, and were shared by many others. But these views of the honourable, prudent, and practicable treatment of the defeated enemy, and what post-war arrangements would conduce to peace, were under fierce challenge within the British government. Which view would prevail would now be determined both by continuing struggle within the British government, and by the attitudes of the other powers, especially the USA, at Paris and after.

---

[435] But for Keynes's contempt for Barnes, see vol. 2, p. 89.
[436] CAB 23/42, IWC, 24 Dec. 1918, minute 3.
[437] Ibid. 30 Dec. 1918, p. 5.
[438] Vol. 16, pp. 418–19; see ch. 3, this volume.

3

The Paris Peace Conference and the Need for International Action

From January to June 1919, Keynes was the principal British Treasury representative at the Paris Peace Conference (PPC).[1] He was the Chancellor of the Exchequer's representative on the Supreme Economic Council (SEC) from its creation in February, and a member of its Finance Section (FS), and of various other committees. Keynes became an important, but by no means lone, advocate at Paris of the need for concerted international action to restart the European economy. He argued that relief must be provided to prevent starvation. War debts should, if possible, be forgiven. Reparations should be kept within Germany's moral obligation and capacity to pay. But the European economy, which was dependent on Germany, would not resume working if private enterprise were left unaided. Guarantees of credit, especially from the USA, were necessary. So, while Keynes wished there to be free trade and private enterprise, laissez-faire was not enough. He and others fought hard against those whose vision of the peace was more punitive than their own, especially those who saw continuing conflict with Germany as unavoidable and harmony impossible. In the event, Keynes so opposed the Treaty of Versailles that, in early June, he resigned from the Treasury in anger and exhaustion, and subsequently launched a great public assault on the Treaty.

For Keynes, the most important international relationship at Paris was the Anglo-American. He thought that the USA could forgive war debts, and lend to restart the European economy, and offered the greatest hope of moderating the reparation demands. Keynes believed that, in general, there were no necessary conflicts of policy between the USA and Britain, and strove to ensure Anglo-American cooperation at Paris.[2] He worked closely with the US financial and economic experts, some of whom believed that US 'leadership' on such issues as relief was essential.[3] But American power was not used

---

[1] For general background on the conference, see, e.g. MacMillan, *Peacemakers*. Boemeke et al., *Treaty of Versailles* (e.g. ch. 15).

[2] See, e.g. vol. 16, pp. 388–9.

[3] For example, Col. House, assuming Wilson's agreement, 27 Nov. 1918: *FRUS, PPC, 1919*, ii, pp. 636–7.

as Keynes, and those American officials, believed necessary for European reconstruction. As Wilson and McAdoo had done during the war, some other US officials saw the economic dependence of Allied powers on the USA as creating the opportunity for the USA to exercise power over them.[4]

This chapter deals in turn with Keynes's activities during the peace conference concerning food supplies for Germany and Austria; seeking cancellation of war debts, and promoting a credit scheme for the rehabilitation of Europe; and concerning reparations, including his attempt to modify the draft Treaty. For brevity, the Allied and Associated Powers are referred to here as the Allies.

3.1 FEEDING GERMANY AND AUSTRIA

In the early months of 1919 Keynes was actively engaged in negotiations on relief to Germany and Austria, which, in the case of Germany, initially arose in the context of Armistice renewal talks.[5] The blockade of Germany, imposed during the war, had been continued under the Armistice agreement. In January 1919, this agreement was due for renewal. Like many others, especially in the US team at Paris (including Wilson, Hoover, and others),[6] Keynes feared the spread of Bolshevism in Germany unless relief were given immediately.[7] Although Keynes had in late 1918 recognized the danger of Bolshevism in Germany, and was to do so repeatedly at Paris and after, he later wondered if some British anxiety over German food supplies had been exaggerated.[8]

In January, Keynes was involved in discussing the 'financial constitution' of the Inter-Ally Supreme Council for Supply and Relief, including the shares that each state would carry of the financial burden of relief. Keynes favoured Britain's taking a 25 per cent share, more than Bonar Law wished, making an obligation of £12,500,000 (which Britain assumed).[9] Britain was still both

---

[4] *FRUS, PPC, 1919*, ii, pp. 727–31 (per McFadden); for Wilson and McAdoo, see Burk, 'Crisis of July 1917', pp. 409, 417.

[5] For background, see Foreign Office paper of 20 Aug. 1943, 'The Administration of the German Armistice and the Political–Economic Direction of the Rhineland Occupation, 1918–1919': copy at L/43/128–42 (see also 127), KP.

[6] See, e.g. vol. 10, p. 398; *FRUS, PPC, 1919*, ii, pp. 554, 680–1, 698–9, 704–7, 710–11; Davis to House, 10 Jan., folder 2/46, box 186, EMHP; 'From Davis for Glass', 19 Jan., para. 9, box 130, CGP; H. White (Paris) to H. C. Lodge, 14 Jan., 7 Mar., box 53, HCLP; R. Lansing to R. J. Buck, 4 Mar.; Lansing to E. N. Smith, 23 Mar., box 5, RLP; V. C. McCormick diary (VCMcCD), 3 Apr. (group no. 478, box 15, folder 2, McCormick papers, Yale).

[7] See, e.g. vol. 10, p. 397; A. J. Mayer, *Politics and Diplomacy of Peacemaking* (London, 1968) stresses the fear of Bolshevism at Paris.

[8] Vol. 10, pp. 401–2.

[9] Vol. 16, pp. 390–1. Keynes to Hoover, 29 Jan., box 81, ARAPP.

borrowing from the USA, and lending to other states. Keynes sought further British borrowing from the USA, arguing that without it Britain would not be able to take its part in the relief operation. The Treasury in Washington was strongly opposed to further lending, but Keynes found US Treasury officials in Paris, such as Norman Davis, more receptive.[10] Britain's need for American help to provide relief was a recurrent issue (arising also, e.g., in Austrian relief).

3.1.1 Food for Germany

The Supreme Council for Supply and Relief, on which Keynes served under Lord Reading, decided on 12 January to supply the Germans with 270,000 tons of food (cereal, fats, and condensed milk).[11] But the problem of how Germany would pay for these supplies divided the victorious powers (especially pitting France against Britain and the USA) and dominated a series of conferences between delegates of the Allies, including Keynes, and Germany: on 15–16 January,[12] and again on 14–16 February[13] at Treves; on 4–5 March at Spa;[14] and on 13–14 March in Brussels.[15] The food supplies agreed in January did not begin until after Brussels.

Dr Carl Melchior was a German spokesman in these and later meetings. Keynes was over time to develop a friendship with him that included correspondence and contact, intermittently, over many years.[16] In 1921, Keynes wrote a moving, though incomplete and not invariably accurate, account of his dealings with Melchior.[17] Ferguson has suggested that Keynes's approach to Germany in 1919 was significantly influenced by a homosexual infatuation with Melchior.[18] Even if that is an accurate depiction of Keynes's attitude to

---

[10] Vol. 16, pp. 387–9; see, e.g. *FRUS, PPC, 1919*, ii, p. 571; 'For Glass from Davis', 16 Jan., box 130, CGP; 'For Davis from Glass', 20 Jan., box 101–2, CGP; Davis to Keynes, 30 Jan., box 81, ARAPP.

[11] Skidelsky, *Hopes*, p. 358.

[12] Minutes of the meetings at Treves are at, e.g. folder 2/644, box 203, EMHP; box 60, NDP. It appears that Keynes's report (vol. 16, pp. 394–404) was based in part on these minutes. Some material is at RT/1/36 ff, KP.

[13] See vol. 10, p. 405 ff. Minutes, with appendices, box 60, NDP.

[14] For Keynes's account, see vol. 10, p. 409 ff. Papers from the conference are in box 1, NDP. A report on Spa, submitted to the SEC, is at *FRUS, PPC, 1919*, x, pp. 49–53.

[15] Vol. 10, pp. 423–6. 'Memorandum of the Conference ...', and appendices, folder 2/663, box 203, EMHP; Minutes and other papers, box 43, NDP.

[16] See FI/2, and PS/5, KP, for correspondence 1919–32, esp. 1922–3.

[17] Vol. 10, pp. 389–429; for date, see vol. 30, p. 165.

[18] N. Ferguson, 'Let Germany Keep Its Nerve', *The Spectator*, 22 Apr. 1995, 21. Cf. N. Ferguson, *Paper and Iron* (Cambridge, 1995), pp. 211 ff, 226–8, 448, where some of the points made below are acknowledged. See also Ferguson, *Pity*, p. 400; Ferguson, 'Keynes and German Inflation', 369. Cf. MacMillan's robust approach (*Peacemakers*, p. 193) with Keylor (in Boemeke et al., *Treaty of Versailles*, p. 486) and Marks (ibid, p. 339 n. 6).

Melchior, which is not certain, it is clear that Keynes, having been thinking about reparations since 1916, had formed his own views before any dealings with the Germans. Others in the British and American teams had formed the same views. Admiration for Melchior, far from being an idiosyncrasy of Keynes's, was expressed in April by Lloyd George and in May by Woodrow Wilson.[19]

At the first Treves conference, Keynes saw as a very important concession that the Supreme War Council (SWC) had (as he had wished) authorized Germany to use her liquid resources to buy food, rather than keeping those resources to be taken as reparations.[20] But the central practical problems for the British and the Americans, who wished to facilitate the supply of food to Germany, remained getting French agreement to Germany's paying with gold, and getting German agreement to hand over her shipping, all the while making clear to Germany that there could be no credits for food.[21] Tensions between Britain and the USA, on one side, and France on the other, and between civilian and military authorities, were evident in Keynes's and Davis's recurrent tensions with Foch.[22]

It has been suggested that 'the attraction Keynes felt for' Melchior in their first meetings on relief 'strongly influenced his judgment'.[23] If by this it is implied that the way Keynes handled the relief question reflected an infatuation with Melchior, or a bias in favour of Germany regardless of the merits of the case, then three points may be made against the claim. First, there were good reasons for Keynes to favour food relief in Germany: humanitarian concern, and the desire to avoid Bolshevism (or reaction) bred of hunger. At the time of the second Treves conference, for example, the situation was, or appeared to Keynes to be, that if Bolshevism were to be staved off, Germany's need for food supplies was urgent; the Germans insisted that their food supply should be assured before they surrendered their ships; the French refused to allow German gold to be used to buy food; the Germans did not have adequate other liquid resources; and no loan would be forthcoming from the Allies. After this February conference, Keynes was more than ever convinced that the only possible solution lay in allowing Germany to use her gold to buy food.[24] Immediately after the Brussels conference, Keynes's mother

---

[19] *FRUS, PPC, 1919*, v, pp. 151, 801.

[20] Minutes of meeting, 11 a.m., 15 Jan., 9, folder 2/644, box 203, EMHP; box 60, NDP; see also vol. 16, pp. 392–3.

[21] See, e.g. vol. 10, p. 401; vol. 16, p. 397; minutes of meeting, 11 a.m., 15 Jan., 5–6, 9, 11–12. Minutes, 11.30 a.m., 16 Jan., 3–4; minutes, 3 p.m., 16 Jan., 1–2.

[22] In Jan.: vol. 10, pp. 391, 399. Vol. 16, pp. 399, 403–4; see minutes of meeting, 3 p.m., 16 Jan., 3. In Apr.–May, there were tensions with Foch over the taking of securities from Germany; see, e.g. *FRUS, PPC, 1919*, x, pp. 230, 235.

[23] Ferguson, 'Nerve', p. 21.   [24] Vol. 10, p. 408.

expressed the hope 'that you will be able to get some food into those hungry mouths before it is too late'.[25]

Second, Keynes's concern, and impatience with what he perceived as French obstruction, was shared by others who (unlike many Frenchmen) had no reason to seek maximum reparations: most importantly, American officials such as Herbert Hoover[26] and Norman Davis. On 19 January, Davis told Carter Glass, the US Treasury Secretary, that Treves had persuaded him that the German 'condition is graver than we thought'.[27] Of course German officials sought to encourage this perception: but it was shared by British and American officials able to make independent judgements. On 20 January, Keynes sent Davis copies of two telegrams he had received on growing anarchy in Germany.[28] At the time of the Spa conference in early March, Robert Lansing, the US Secretary of State, wrote that Germany was on the verge of 'Soviet Government', and that the situation could have been averted with food and raw materials two months before:[29]

We were ready to have the blockade lifted and the food and raw materials go in, but the Allies, particularly the military chiefs, opposed. Great Britain finally saw the menace and favored sending the articles in. France has now come to the same view, but demands that we give Germany credit and that the Germans must not actually pay us as it would deplete the power of Germany to pay an indemnity. France says, 'You supply the goods and we will take the pay for them.' Of course we will do no such thing. Meanwhile the whole social structure of Germany is in flames and we sit and watch the conflagration.

Lansing feared Bolshevism from the Pacific to the Rhine—and perhaps beyond. But the US refusal to agree to credit for Germany to buy food was clear.[30]

Third, Keynes's dealings with the German officials showed a capacity for firmness as well as sympathy. At the first Treves meetings, Keynes insisted that, if Germany persisted in refusing to use her cash resources to pay for food, the world would see that it was Germany's fault that 'the offer to revictual Germany' had failed.[31] Both then, and at the second Treves conference, when the Germans again insisted on their need for a credit for food, Keynes

---

[25] FAK to Keynes, 16 Mar. 1919, PP/45/168/9/159, KP.
[26] See, e.g. *FRUS, PPC, 1919*, x, pp. 297–8, 322–3.
[27] 'From Davis for Glass', 19 Jan., para. 6, box 130, CGP.
[28] Keynes to Davis, 20 Jan., encl. two telegrams from Sir H. Rumbold, Berne, box 43, NDP.
[29] Lansing to Buck, 4 Mar., box 5, RLP.
[30] See also, e.g. 'For Davis from [Albert] Rathbone', 14 Mar., para. 4, box 43, NDP. See minutes, Treves, 16 Jan., 3 p.m., 1–2, folder 2/644, box 203, EMHP. 'Neutral Finance Commission', minutes, 8 Apr., 4, boxes 47 and 58, NDP.
[31] Minutes, 11.30 a.m., 16 Jan., 3–4, folder 2/644, box 203, EMHP.

made the impossibility of this very clear.[32] At the second meeting, the head of the German delegation, von Braun, replied with a formal statement, stressing the Armistice commitments to provide food for Germany, the need to lift the blockade so Germany could buy food from neutral powers such as Argentina, her need to keep her shipping so as to get food if she were not given credit, and the certainty of 'the inundation of all Europe by Bolshevism' if 'the means of assuring the nourishment of Germany' were not guaranteed immediately.[33] The minutes record that 'By reason of its general character the Associated Delegates declared themselves unable to discuss the [von Braun] declaration, which would be submitted to their Governments.'[34] Keynes wrote: 'we turned our trains towards Paris.'[35]

In 'Dr Melchior', Keynes described the stand-off between Germany and the associated powers at the Spa conference, his private interview with Melchior to seek to resolve it, and the deliberately dramatic rupture of the conference.[36] On 4 March, Keynes declared on behalf of the Allies that 'until the ships have been handed over it is not possible to consider additional supplies beyond 270,000 tons'.[37] When von Braun reiterated that Germany would not hand over the ships until food supplies up to the harvest were assured,[38] Rear-Admiral Hope took Keynes's advice to abandon the conference, and advised the Germans that 'the Allied and Associated Delegates are leaving for Paris immediately to report to their Governments'—in the middle of the night of 5–6 March.[39] This tactic was, in part, to bring to a head the division between the French and Anglo-American positions. The SEC on 7 March received resolutions proposed by the British, American, and French delegates, and, unable to agree, decided to submit them to the SWC.[40] The British proposal involved releasing some food for some ships, not unlike the German suggestion at Spa. The American draft, stressing that 'Germany will collapse and peace be impossible if... assurance of food and productivity is not immediately given', made proposals in similar spirit. The French proposed

[32] Vol. 10, pp. 401, 404, 406; see also p. 408; minutes, 3 p.m., 16 Jan., 2, folder 2/644, box 203, EMHP; minutes, 14–16 Feb., par. 4(V), and Annex 8, box 60, NDP.

[33] Annex 9, minutes, 14–16 Feb., box 60, NDP; vol. 10, pp. 406–8.

[34] Minutes, 14–16 Feb., par. 4(V), box 60, NDP.

[35] Vol. 10, p. 407.

[36] Vol. 10, p. 416.

[37] 'Declaration des Gouvernements Allies', 4 Mar., box 1, NDP; vol. 10, p. 410.

[38] 'Declaration du President de la Delegation allemande', 5 Mar., box 1, NDP. *FRUS, PPC, 1919*, x, pp. 52–3.

[39] 'Response des Gouvernements Allies a la Delegation Allemande', from Spa, 5 March, box 1, NDP. *FRUS, PPC, 1919*, x, p. 53; iv, pp. 266–7.

[40] Ibid., pp. 48–55. Ibid., iv, pp. 252–93.

delivering 'the 270,000 tons of food already agreed on' when Germany showed a 'genuine intention' to hand over 'the whole of her mercantile fleet forthwith'.

The SWC meeting on 8 March was colourfully depicted by Keynes in 'Dr Melchior'.[41] The central problem was, as Clementel told the SWC, that 'on the advice of Mr. Hoover, 270,000 tons had been fixed as the amount of the first instalment of food-stuffs: But difficulties had arisen as regards the payment, so that nothing had as yet been sent.'[42] Keynes encapsulated Lord Robert Cecil's proposals on behalf of the SEC:[43]

[T]hat Germany be informed that she is bound to deliver the ships, that we categorically undertake to furnish the food as soon as she begins to deliver the ships, that she be permitted to use her liquid assets, including gold, to pay for the food, and that the Blockade be raised to the extent of allowing Germany to export goods (with some exceptions) and to purchase food in neutral countries. He had to add that his French colleagues had not yet agreed to the use of the gold.

This SWC debate gives a sharp contrast between those who believed that Germany was at risk of revolution and needed to be helped, and those who believed that this threat was exaggerated, that Germany must be shown 'no signs of weakness',[44] and that reparation to France must take priority over payment for food for Germany.[45] As Keynes said, 'everything turned on the gold',[46] which the French did not want used for food payment but for reparations. Keynes recounted how Lloyd George humiliated Klotz, and how, the threat of starvation and hence Bolshevism being stressed by Cecil, Hoover, and Lloyd George,[47] it was agreed that 'the gold was to be used after all'.[48] Keynes and Loucheur drafted the agreed text to provide the basis for negotiations with Germany in Brussels. Keynes also worked closely with US officials on how to mobilize other German resources, such as foreign securities, to pay for food.[49]

At the Brussels conference of 13–14 March, Keynes (at Admiral Wemyss' instigation) saw Melchior privately, successfully seeking to ensure that the Germans made the declaration on surrendering their ships which, at French

[41] Vol. 10, pp. 416–23.

[42] *FRUS, PPC, 1919*, iv, p. 277.

[43] Vol. 10, p. 418; see *FRUS, PPC, 1919*, iv, pp. 254–5, 275–7.

[44] Ibid., p. 283.

[45] There were some who thought Bolshevism would weaken Germany, and this was to be welcomed: S. P. Tillman, *Anglo-American Relations at the Paris Peace Conference of 1919* (Princeton, 1961), p. 242.

[46] Vol. 10, p. 418.

[47] *FRUS, PPC, 1919*, iv, pp. 275, 279, 280 ff, 286, 288 ff, esp. p. 290; vol. 10, p. 421.

[48] Vol. 10, p. 423. Cf. *FRUS, PPC, 1919*, iv, p. 290; re Keynes on Klotz, see MacMillan, *Peacemakers*, p. 201.

[49] Davis to Rathbone, 8 Mar., p. 3, box 43, NDP.

insistence, was necessary '*before* they were told our intentions about feeding them'.[50] The German declaration made, Wemyss stated (in terms only slightly elaborating on what was agreed in the SWC on 8 March) the Allies' intentions on 'the revictualling of Germany'. Von Braun accepted them in principle, and technical details were sorted out in subcommittees on finance, food, and shipping.[51] Brussels had concluded 'the arrangements for taking over the German merchant shipping and laying out a program for Germany's food supply until next harvest'.[52] After Brussels, 'the food trains started for Germany'.[53]

Some detailed business remained to be done with the German financial experts. So, as chairman of the Inter-Allied Financial Delegates in Armistice Negotiation with Germany,[54] Keynes initiated the SEC's inviting Melchior and other German officials (unbeknownst to Foch) to France, where they stayed in Compiègne and then at Versailles.[55] At Keynes's instigation, the SEC also approved invitations to neutral financiers for discussions regarding the future financial relations between Germany and neutral countries. Keynes boasted to his father: 'My latest deed has been to summon six Germans and also representatives of the Neutrals to Paris; and I am about to launch my scheme for the financial rehabilitation of Europe.'[56] Keynes recalled in 1942 that the Germans and neutrals were called 'with a view to discussing a general project of international financial reconstruction, which, in the event, never came off. How much subsequent evil might have been avoided if only they had!'[57]

Their presence gave the German delegates a direct means of communicating, not least to Keynes, their anxiety about the economic situation in Germany.[58] It made it far easier for Allied officials to talk with both German representatives and neutral financiers on how to make possible Germany's paying for food imports, especially from the neutral powers. In April, the neutral financiers and German officials discussed with Keynes and other Allied representatives such issues as how Germany, with existing debts to

---

[50] Vol. 10, p. 423.

[51] On Germany's continued desire for a loan, see: Document starting 'At the end of the Conference at Brussels...', folder 2/663, box 203, EMHP. *FRUS, PPC, 1919*, x, p. 66. 'Facts given out...', Brussels, 15 Mar., para. 10, box 43, NDP. Davis was instructed on 14 March to 'make it clear to French that' any credit to Germany for food was 'out of the question and beyond discussion': 'For Davis from Rathbone', 14 Mar., box 43, NDP.

[52] 'Facts given out...', Brussels, 15 Mar., para. 1, box 43, NDP.

[53] Vol. 10, p. 426.

[54] Keynes to FAK, 16 Mar., PP/45/168/9/157–8, KP.

[55] Vol. 10, pp. 426–7; Vol. 16, pp. 415–17. *FRUS, PPC, 1919*, x, pp. 76, 78, 107–8, 145–6, 195–6, 209, 298.

[56] Keynes to JNK, 30 Mar., PP/45/168/13/145–6, KP.

[57] Vol. 16, p. 417.

[58] For example, Melchior to Keynes, 11 Apr., box 59, NDP.

neutrals and with her limited liquid assets not available, could secure further credits in neutral countries to revive her trade.[59] The neutrals and Germany were trying to maintain or increase German buying capacity in the neutral countries in the face of the Allies' restrictions.[60]

On 25 March, a report on 'Conditions in Germany' by a British official who had spent three weeks in Berlin was prepared for the IWC. It spoke of worsening underfeeding, desperate unemployment, the weakness of the government, and the need for credit to restart industry. 'The most impressive fact in Berlin at present is the way in which everyone is reckoning with the probability or inevitability of Bolshevism.... Everybody is convinced that Bolshevism would inevitably spread from Germany to the rest of Europe.' There was a danger of 'the reactionaries' being strengthened. 'Democratic' circles believed the Armistice 'involved a compact to conclude peace on the basis of President Wilson's Fourteen Points'. Cecil wrote on his copy of this report: 'a terrific report—I do not see how Europe can be saved.'[61] Keynes, too, saw this report. But he *did* see how Europe could be saved. On 25 March, the day 'Conditions in Germany' was prepared as a Cabinet paper, Keynes obtained FS approval for food supplies on the left bank of the Rhine which 'in effect involves the handing over of supplies to the Germans in anticipation of payment'.[62] That same day he wrote the introduction to a proposed scheme for reparations that would not leave Germany in an impossible position.[63] Within weeks, he had proposed a 'grand scheme for the rehabilitation of Europe'.[64]

There was urgency in the efforts of the German delegation, neutral representatives, and others to make possible Germany's paying for food imports. For example, on 29 April, Hoover wrote that 'Germany is being fed from hand to mouth', and could not produce funds to cover food more than thirty days ahead of delivery.[65] On 30 April, Keynes told the FS that 'all the liquid

[59] Melchior to Keynes, 7 Apr.; unsigned (Melchior?) to Keynes (Tg. No. 74), 7 Apr.; Melchior to Keynes, 9 Apr.; Melchior to Keynes, 11 Apr., box 59, NDP. Neutral Finance Committee, minutes, 8 Apr., 3–4, box 58, NDP. M. Warburg to Comte de Lasteyrie, for Keynes, 26 Apr., box 61, NDP.

[60] O. Rydbeck to Keynes, 27 Mar.; Melchior to Keynes, 11 Apr., box 59, NDP; see, e.g. minutes, meeting with German Finance Committee, Versailles, 2 May, 3, box 58, NDP. Minutes, 13th meeting, FS, 15 May, 4–5, box 46, NDP.

[61] 'Conditions in Germany', War Cabinet Paper, ref. no. B/425, 25 Mar.; copy marked by Cecil in box 18, RHBP.

[62] Minutes, 6th meeting, FS, 26 Mar., para. 6 and Annex D (memo by Keynes); see also minutes, 8th meeting, FS, n.d., box 59, NDP. There was to be British lending to Germany for supplies, using German gold deposited in Brussels as security: see, e.g. untitled circular by Keynes, 6 May, box 58, NDP.

[63] RT/14/58–61, KP.

[64] Vol. 16, pp. 428–36; see below.

[65] Hoover to E. F. Wise, 29 Apr., box 60, NDP; see also unsigned letter to Sec., Food Section, 26 Apr., box 60, NDP; Keynes to Davis, 24 Mar., box 59, NDP.

resources of Germany would be required for the payment of food', and that, despite Germany's need for raw materials, no resources existed to pay for them.[66] In dealings in the FS and with German officials in April–May, Keynes was seeking to ensure the supply of food and, if possible, raw materials to Germany; but he was impatient with the Germans over their slowness in surrendering assets in payment for supplies made to them.[67]

In a joint meeting of the Food and Finance Sections on 8 May, it was agreed that the Allied commitments of supplies to Germany far exceeded the assets Germany was prepared to put forward.[68]

Mr Keynes said that the position ought once more to be put to the Germans very frankly. They still have substantial assets, such as their South American properties, and it is for them to choose whether they will provide the finance or go without the food. At present they did not propose even to begin the despatch of the next consignment of gold until May 15th.

In a meeting of the FS with the German officials on 12 May, Keynes 'pointed out that food had already been delivered to the full amount of the gold deposited at Brussels. He stated that unless the Germans could provide some further finance, Mr. Hoover would have to stop all shipments of food, and that in consequence there would be no deliveries of food in June.' Keynes foreshadowed a scheme to allow the sale of requisitioned securities in neutral markets.[69] Having had to press the French earlier in the year to allow Germany to use its gold to buy food, Keynes was now pressing the Germans to do so to the necessary extent.[70] It was not until 22 May, when Keynes told the Germans that 'food shipments had stopped, and would only be made as the corresponding amount of gold was deposited to the account of the Allies',[71] that Germany declared itself 'ready to send 18 million pounds sterling to Amsterdam to the credit of the food account'.[72] In April–May, Keynes was also involved in seeking the lifting of all blockade restrictions on the importation of food into enemy countries and the relaxation of financial restrictions on Germany.[73]

[66] Minutes, 11th meeting, FS, 30 Apr., box 58, NDP.

[67] See, e.g. minutes, meeting with German Finance Committee, Versailles, 2 May, box 58, NDP; minutes, 13th meeting, FS, 15 May, 6, box 46, NDP. *FRUS, PPC, 1919*, x, pp. 231, 238.

[68] Minutes, joint meeting, Food and Finance Sections, 8 May, box 18, RHBP; see also *FRUS, PPC, 1919*, v, pp. 523–4.

[69] Minutes, FS meeting with German Financial Commission, Versailles, 12 May, box 58, NDP. See also 'Note', FS meeting with German Delegates, Versailles, 12 May, box 18, RHBP.

[70] 'Note', FS meeting with German Financial Delegates, Versailles, 20 May, para. 1, box 58, NDP.

[71] 'Proposed Minutes', meeting with Germans, 22 May, para. 1, box 61, NDP.

[72] *FRUS, PPC, 1919*, x, p. 305; see also p. 295.

[73] FRUS, PPC, 1919, x, pp. 202, 230–1, 241–2, 294, 304. 'Proposed Minutes', meeting with Germans, 22 May, para. 4, box 61, NDP.

3.1.2 Food for Austria

Among Keynes's criticisms of Hoover's proposed Financial Constitution for
the Relief Council in January was that it made no provision for Austrian
relief.[74] The US appropriation of $100 million for relief excluded financial
assistance to enemy countries.[75] Keynes wanted Britain and other European
allies not to have to pay cash to the USA for US produce shipped to relief
countries.[76] Instead, as Sir William Goode, British Director of Relief, wrote in
1920: 'in order to relieve the bitter distress in Austria, Great Britain, France,
and Italy each borrowed from the United States Treasury 16,000,000 dollars to
be expended in food supplies of American origin for Austrian relief'.[77]
Writing in the wake of controversy surrounding *The Economic Consequences*,
Goode attributed the initiative for this arrangement for averting famine to
Keynes's 'resourceful vision of an England humane, although victorious'.[78]
Keynes worked closely with Hoover in arranging the credits (in two instal-
ments),[79] in the provision of supplies to Austria,[80] and in overcoming diffi-
culties such as Italian obstruction of transporting supplies,[81] and French
insistence on greater security for advances to Austria when Keynes and
Hoover believed this was already amply covered.[82] The need, in the face of
Italian obstruction, to arrange provisioning of rolling stock in the former
Austro-Hungarian Empire 'with entire freedom of movement over all railways
regardless of political boundaries'[83] may have contributed to Keynes's antipathy to the barriers created by successor states.

---

[74] Keynes to Hoover, 29 Jan., box 81, ARAPP.
[75] Davis to Keynes, 30 Jan., box 81, ARAPP.
[76] Vol. 16, p. 391; Keynes to Hoover, 29 Jan., box 81, ARAPP.
[77] *Economic Conditions in Central Europe (1)*, Misc. Series No. 1, Despatch from Sir William
Goode (Parliamentary Paper, 1920), p. 6; Hoover on this: *FRUS, PPC, 1919*, x, p. 321.
[78] On Keynes and Goode, see, e.g. vol. 17, pp. 197–9; vol. 18, p. 176. L/20/26–7, KP. See Ch. 4,
this volume.
[79] *FRUS, PPC, 1919*, x, pp. 33, 179; H. A. Siepmann to Hoover, 17 Apr.; Hoover to Siepmann,
18 Apr.; Keynes to Hoover, 20 Apr., box 81, ARAPP.
[80] Hoover to Keynes, 1 Mar. (two letters); Keynes to Hoover, 2 Mar.; Siepmann to Hoover,
17 Apr.; Keynes to Hoover, 1 May, box 81, ARAPP; Memo by Keynes, 'Annex K. Purchase of
Austrian Property on Italian Account', 26 Mar. (encl. with Keynes to Davis, 24 Mar.), box 59,
NDP.
[81] See, e.g. Lansing to Buck, 4 Mar., box 5, RLP. *FRUS, PPC, 1919*, iv, pp. 255–63, 269–70.
[82] *FRUS, PPC, 1919*, x, pp. 297–8, 321–3; Keynes to Hoover, 1 May, box 81, ARAPP; Minutes,
14th meeting, FS, 22 May, para. 12, box 58, NDP.
[83] *FRUS, PPC, 1919*, iv, p. 263; see also pp. 269–70.

3.2 WAR DEBTS, AND EUROPEAN REHABILITATION[84]

We have seen that in the autumn of 1918, Keynes was involved in discussions resulting in the Zimmern–Percy proposals for debt cancellation and continued inter-Allied economic organization, and that in November 1918, he proposed to Bonar Law that Britain seek complete cancellation of inter-Allied war debt. Keynes recognized that the idea would not appeal to the US Treasury, and would depend on 'the judgment of the President'.[85] On 11 December 1918, W. G. McAdoo (the outgoing Treasury Secretary) wrote to Wilson's aide, Colonel House, opposing frequent suggestions 'in important but unofficial quarters in both London and Paris regarding the possibility of the cancellation of all' inter-Allied war debts. McAdoo made clear that US lending to foreign governments would be greatly decreased, loans for purchases outside the USA would be promptly discontinued, and the Treasury would not consider or discuss suggestions to cancel or diminish in value existing debts owed. That 'would not meet with the approval of Congress or of our people who would thereby be subjected to heavy additional taxation'.[86]

While Klotz was in mid-December again attempting to tie France's debt repayments to the level of reparations it received, McAdoo was opposed to any link between war debts and reparations. He, Wilson, and Glass (the new Treasury Secretary) did not want debt cancellation discussed at the peace conference.[87] Loan questions, they insisted, must be settled in Washington. On 2 February 1919, Davis wrote to Wilson opposing any general financial undertaking by the USA arising from the war, including dismissing, as 'a blank check on the US', a scheme by which the USA would contribute to exchange stabilization.[88] Deeply suspicious of the Allies' intentions, Wilson thanked Davis for his letter 'about the concerted movement which is on foot to obtain an interlocking of the United States with the continental governments in their whole financial situation. I was already aware of the effort and on my guard against it'.[89]

In March, Keynes again proposed cancellation of inter-Allied war debts.[90] This was in a paper for the new Chancellor of the Exchequer, Austen Chamberlain, also to be conveyed to Wilson through House. Keynes had five main reasons for cancellation. First, by alleviating the intolerable financial

---

[84] Cf. Tillman, *Paris Peace Conference*, pp. 267–75.   [85] Vol. 16, p. 419.

[86] *FRUS, PPC, 1919*, ii, p. 539.

[87] *FRUS, PPC, 1919*, ii, pp. 540–8, 555; O. Crosby to Keynes, 7 Jan. 1919, RT/1/21, KP.

[88] Davis to Wilson, 2 Feb., box 10, PMWP.

[89] Wilson to Davis, 5 Feb., box 11, NDP; see N. G. Levin, *Woodrow Wilson and World Politics* (Oxford, 1968), p. 143.

[90] Vol. 16, pp. 419–28; M. Keynes, *Essays*, pp. 169–70; see also vol. 2, pp. 170–9.

situation of debtor countries, it would facilitate more moderate reparations, and perhaps territorial, demands. Second, hostility between debtors and creditors would be generated by the continuing debts. Third, the debts threatened financial stability; repayment imposed a crushing burden. Keynes stressed that large-scale international indebtedness was relatively recent, and was a fragile system. Insistence on war debt repayment threatened capitalism itself. We see here both an anxiety about the durability of capitalism in the circumstances of 1919, and a stage in the development of Keynes's hostility to great international capital movements. Fourth, debt repayments raised the same transfer problem as reparations—a need for all debtor countries to run major trade surpluses. Fifth, repudiation would become an important political issue in European countries, possibly entangling creditor nations in the maintenance of a particular type of government or economic organization in the debtor countries. Insistence on debt repayment by Russia would strengthen the Bolsheviks. Keynes did not believe that war debts would be paid for more than a very few years, because Europe 'will not pinch herself in order that the fruit of her daily labour may go elsewhere'. He concluded that 'expediency and generosity agree together, and the policy which will best promote immediate friendship between nations will not conflict with the permanent interests of the benefactor'. Keynes expected sympathy for his proposal from US representatives, but needed their advice on how to carry 'less-formed' US public opinion. It was believed in some circles, and alleged in US newspapers in 1920, that Wilson and his financial advisers accepted the idea of debt cancellation. Thomas Lamont denied this: Keynes 'used to deplore the fact with us but he accepted our attitude as unequivocal'.[91]

Nonetheless, some American officials were willing to contemplate, as Bernard Baruch hinted to Wilson on 29 March, some 'adjustment of the present terms of our loans to the Allies'. Baruch wrote to Wilson on the problems of restarting the European economies, especially Germany's. He also suggested 'the advancing of a further limited amount of money to France, Italy, Belgium and the new governments ... to start their industries going'.[92] Baruch's letter reflected growing concern with what the SEC on 7 and 9 April described as the 'extreme urgency' of Europe's economic situation. Cecil had submitted a British delegation note on 'the General Economic Position in Europe'.[93] The note, first drafted by Brand,[94] advocated comprehensive

[91] Lamont to F. H. Simonds, 30 Dec. 1920, box 33, NDP.
[92] Baruch to Wilson, 29 Mar. 1919, p. 5, unit VI, BBP.
[93] *FRUS, PPC, 1919*, x, pp. 103, 110–13.
[94] Brand to Keynes, 9 Apr. 1919, RT/1/79–80, KP. The paper has similarities with Brand's 'Financial Situation', 5 Apr., box 18, RHBP, and with Keynes's draft on his bond scheme: vol. 16, p. 431 ff.

policies for each country on such matters as currency and transport; urged the restoration of private enterprise; and ended by saying that Europe's need for capital could not be met by private enterprise alone, perhaps needing a scheme of guarantee and insurance for lending. In response to this paper, House initiated an informal committee, including British, French, and US officials, including Brand, Keynes, and Monnet, to report on Europe's economic position. As we shall see, it proved abortive.

In this context, and with the Americans having again refused cancellation of war debts, Keynes in mid-April proposed 'a grand scheme for the rehabilitation of Europe'.[95] Keynes wrote that the USA was providing generously 'for the urgent food requirements of the non-enemy countries of Europe', but 'may not be able to continue indefinitely her present assistance'. A 'bolder solution for the rehabilitation of the credit and economic life of Europe than is now available' was needed. Keynes stressed the danger to order in Germany and elsewhere, the threat of Bolshevism, and the desperate position of nearly all European countries, in 'need of outside assistance . . . if they are to restore their countries and re-commence the normal activities of peace'. Britain was unable to help others on the scale required: how to repay her own debts to the US Treasury was the chief problem of her external finance. The 'economic mechanism of Europe is jammed', 'production has to a great extent ceased', and 'it is difficult to see how the population can be maintained'. This was 'the greatest financial problem ever set to the modern world'. Removal of obstacles to private enterprise, though necessary, was inadequate.

Keynes's proposal was that the enemy and new states would issue bonds; German bonds would be issued to a present value of £1,000 million. Interest payments would be guaranteed by both the enemy and Allied governments, and some neutrals. Roughly three-quarters of the German bonds would go to the Allied and Associated governments for reparations, and 7.6 per cent to neutrals for discharging existing debts, leaving a fifth for purchasing food and raw materials. The bonds 'could be used to settle war debts, to provide collateral for international loans, or to finance much needed imports from Britain and the United States'.[96] The Keynes plan involved the League of Nations, which could, by economic means, punish guaranteeing governments which failed to meet their guarantees.

Keynes tried to sell his bond scheme—a 'form of world-wide co-operation'—to the USA as an alternative to direct bilateral assistance by the USA. For France, 'the greatest gainer from the scheme', it was 'a way out for her almost overwhelming financial difficulties'. 'The acute problem of the

---

[95] Vol. 16, pp. 428–36; for drafts, see RT/16/1–12, KP.
[96] M. Keynes, *Essays*, p. 157; see vol. 16, pp. 431, 436.

liquidation of inter-ally indebtedness, though not disposed of, is sensibly ameliorated.' In renewing trade, the plan offered mutual advantage to Europe and America. It offered hope, and a protection against Bolshevism. Various authors have described this scheme as a small-scale Marshall Plan[97]—except, of course, that it involved lending rather than grants.

Austen Chamberlain strongly backed Keynes's scheme.[98] Chamberlain mentioned Keynes's proposals in the IWC on 16 and 17 April, and circulated a copy. It was neither endorsed nor rejected;[99] for Keynes, this was 'getting [it] through the Cabinet'.[100] Chamberlain later defended it, against criticism by Brand, as much superior (in giving credit) to cancellation of war debts, and as more likely to be acceptable to the USA.[101] Brand had observed that the scheme did not solve the debt problem, and raised practical difficulties about marketing these bonds.[102] On 23 April, in a meeting of the Big Three, Lloyd George urged the need for Keynes's 'scheme for re-starting Europe', given widespread unemployment and the absence of trade: 'Unless something of the kind was done', Melchior, 'the best of the German Delegates' and one 'who desired peace', 'would not be able to make peace'. Wilson quoted Hoover on Europe's hopelessness and the danger of Bolshevism. Not referring to the Keynes plan, he urged the raising of the blockade, a move Clemenceau opposed. Lloyd George said 'there was the same paralysis in countries that had no blockade':[103] more was needed.

That night, Lloyd George gave Wilson a long letter on Keynes's scheme. Hoover prepared an analysis of it, suggesting that it should have appealed to US magnanimity rather than false self-interest, but that 'With considerable amendment, it is a good plan, and a great advance over any hitherto offered.'[104] Keynes had 'quite satisfactory conversations' with Davis and Hoover[105] (though Lamont was probably not encouraging).[106] When Davis cabled the details to Washington with seemingly favourable commentary,[107] it provoked violent opposition in Washington. Rathbone, Leffingwell, and Strauss all vigorously opposed the plan, sending Davis and Lamont strongly

[97] Harrod, *Life*, p. 288; see also p. 327; Tillman, *Paris Peace Conference*, p. 269.

[98] Vol. 16, pp. 428–9; RT/16/13–16, KP.

[99] Cabinet meetings of 16 and 17 Apr. 1919: CAB/23/10, fols. 13, 15, PRO.

[100] See Keynes to FAK, 17 Apr. 1919, PP/45/168/9/166, KP. Vol. 16, p. 428; Keynes to H. Temperley, 17 May 1932, CO/11/253, KP.

[101] Vol. 16, p. 437.

[102] A copy of Brand's comments, an annexure to a document entitled 'The Economic Situation in Europe. II', is at box 18, RHBP.

[103] *FRUS, PPC, 1919*, v, pp. 151–2.

[104] Hoover, 'Memo on Keynes Plan of League Bonds', 25 Apr., box 81, ARAPP.

[105] Vol. 16, p. 437 ff.

[106] BBD, 25 Apr.

[107] Davis to Rathbone, 24 Mar., box 57, NDP; paraphrase in box 130, CGP.

worded cables, soon endorsed by Glass, who was away.[108] The Keynes plan should not be discussed with Britain.[109] It was 'financially indefensible and politically impossible' in the USA.[110] It would discredit the League 'by making it a debt collecting agency', and jeopardize the Treaty in Congress.[111] It relied on US government lending, not private initiative.[112] It was inflationary,[113] as perhaps Keynes accepted.[114] Glass, like his officials, regarded this as a matter for discussion in Washington and not at Paris.

Keynes reported that 'Unofficial conversations continue in spite of the prohibition of the United States Treasury', including a dinner between Davis, Lamont, J. C. Smuts, and Keynes on 3 May. But otherwise, the Treasury representatives 'crept to heel'.[115] Davis and Lamont told Washington that they always opposed the scheme[116] (though they also quoted Wilson as wishing 'to devise some practical means for affording certain assistance to Europe, especially the newly constituted governments, always provided America retains freedom of action and does not get involved in guarantees').[117] The Keynes plan brought to a head tensions between Bernard Baruch, who wanted the US Treasury to lend for European reconstruction, and the official Treasury view.[118] Evidently fearing that it was a means of pressing for US acceptance of the Keynes plan, Lamont had already insisted that the committee, which House had initiated and to which Baruch had agreed, of American, British, and French officials, to examine European economic conditions, should not function.[119] Baruch argued that US government action was needed; Davis, the Treasury man, after hearing from Washington, stressed that credits should be extended by bankers and commercial channels. Baruch seemingly sympathized with the US and other government guarantees of bonds envisaged in the Keynes plan; Davis vigorously opposed them.

On 1 May, in the Big Three, Lloyd George argued that relaxation of the blockade of Germany, which Wilson also supported, needed to be accompanied by a scheme such as Keynes's to meet Germany's need for credit for food

---

[108] Rathbone to Glass, 29 Apr., box 130, CGP; Glass to Leffingwell, 1 May; to Cooksey, Treasury, 1 May, box 130, CGP; Glass message to Leffingwell was relayed: 'From Leffingwell to Davis', 2 May, box 46, NDP.

[109] 'For Davis from Rathbone', 28 Apr., box 130, CGP.

[110] 'For Davis from Leffingwell and Rathbone', 26 Apr., box 130, CGP.

[111] 'For Davis from Leffingwell', 28 Apr., box 130, CGP.

[112] 'For Davis and Lamont from Strauss', 28 Apr., box 130, CGP.

[113] 'For Davis from Leffingwell', 28 Apr., box 130, CGP.

[114] Vol. 16, p. 437.

[115] Vol. 16, p. 437 ff.

[116] Davis and Lamont to Rathbone, Leffingwell, and Strauss, 1 May, box 46, NDP.

[117] Davis and Lamont to Rathbone and Leffingwell, 29 Apr., box 16A, NDP.

[118] See esp. Davis to Baruch, 1 May, box 46, NDP. BBD, 29 Apr. and 10 May.

[119] BBD, 25 Apr. Baruch to Davis, 30 Apr. and 2 May; Davis to Baruch, 1 May, box 46, NDP.

and raw materials. Wilson denied this.[120] On 2 May, Keynes dissented in a British Empire Committee to a proposal for further British credits to Germany for raw materials: he wanted a general scheme, not just a British one.[121] Davis and Lamont drafted for Wilson a letter of reply to Lloyd George, dismissing the Keynes plan.[122] It asserted the need for international cooperation to solve Europe's confused state, but this 'should not, so far as America is concerned, take the form of a guarantee upon bonds.'[123] Congress would not authorize it; lending should be private wherever possible; Germany needed working capital, but was being stripped of it by reparation demands that the USA had resisted, and the USA could hardly be asked to make that good; the American investing public had 'reached, and perhaps passed, the point of complete saturation in respect of investment'. Keynes partly accepted American criticism of his plan as enabling 'us to extract more reparation', but said that Germany's real problem was 'that she has practically no liquid capital', a problem the Americans ducked. Keynes thought Wilson's letter 'indicates a spirit far too harsh for the human situation facing us'.[124]

On 5 May, the SEC (at which Keynes was present) had resolved to draw the attention of the Council of Heads of States to 'the extreme urgency of supplying raw materials to Europe', without which 'there is no hope for the peace of Europe'.[125] 'As a consequence of this resolution', Keynes believed, the Council of Four met on 9 May, with Keynes present.[126] Cecil said that to get Europe to work again, credits for raw materials purchases were needed, and the blockade should be further relaxed.[127] Wilson said that further expert advice was needed on the financial problem. It was agreed, at Wilson's proposal, to ask a committee of economic advisers for 'a systematic suggestion' on 'the means of assisting the nations which are in immediate need of both food, raw material and credit'.[128] Keynes initially regarded this committee (on which he and Cecil, with Brand, represented Britain) as a distinct step forward.[129] He came to think it ineffective.

---

[120] *FRUS, PPC, 1919*, v, p. 396.

[121] Vol. 16, p. 443.

[122] Wilson to Lloyd George, 5 May, box 16A, NDP. The copy in KP is dated 3 May: RT/16/33–4, KP; see vol. 16, p. 440.

[123] Undated 'Suggestions for letter' from Wilson to Lloyd George, box 16A, NDP.

[124] Vol. 16, pp. 439–42.

[125] *FRUS, PPC, 1919*, x, p. 233.

[126] Vol. 16, p. 444; Minutes at *FRUS, PPC, 1919*, v, pp. 521–5.

[127] NDP, box 16A, contains a 'Summary of Memorandum by Lord Robert Cecil on the Economic Situation of Europe', which, an annotation suggests, 'resulted in the whole study'. It foreshadowed economic breakdown, and urged official US help.

[128] *FRUS, PPC, 1919*, v, p. 524.

[129] Vol. 16, p. 444; see also pp. 441–2.

Keynes believed that this committee arose out of Wilson's rejection of his—the British—plan.[130] This was probably an important factor. But other influences were pointing in the same direction. As we have seen, House had in April initiated a similar committee; but its work was aborted because of Lamont's fears of its being used to promote the Keynes plan. The SEC resolution of 5 May, which prompted creation of the committee, arose from a recommendation to the SEC from the Raw Materials Section on 2 May, that supply of raw materials to the countries most in need of them (Poland, Czechoslovakia) was essential 'for the peace of Europe'.[131] Wilson's letter rejecting the Keynes plan said that he had asked his advisers in Paris about the action needed for European recovery.[132] Davis and Lamont produced papers which argued for credits to new and weaker European states, and for reducing or cancelling interest on US loans to the Allies.[133] But the USA would help the Allies reach a more sensible policy towards Germany by refusing to adopt the Keynes plan.[134] Lamont and Davis proposed non-governmental European and American committees to coordinate a 'general scheme of credits that are to be extended through banking and commercial channels'. They argued that if 'the American people' lent significantly to European countries, 'the close interest that will result will surely prove a great, permanent factor in increasing the harmony and peace of the world'.[135] Given the impact European disorder would have on the USA, recovery was in America's 'almost immediate self-interest'.[136]

On 7 May, Baruch wrote to Wilson urging US, British, and French aid to the weaker European states, including credits from the US government, conditional on 'the establishment of equality of trade conditions and removal of economic barriers'. He also urged, where necessary, US adjustment of the terms of payment of principal and interest on loans to other states. Baruch wrote that America had an obligation to help Europe. 'Economic inequality and barriers were among the causes of the war.' Peace depended on 'the restoration of normal conditions and ... the granting of an equal opportunity to all'.[137]

---

[130] Vol. 16, pp. 445–6.

[131] 'Report by Committee on Supply of Raw Materials and Sales of War Stocks', 2 May, box 18, RHBP. *FRUS, PPC, 1919*, x, p. 233.

[132] See also, e.g. House to F. A. Vanderlip, 5 May, box 16A, NDP.

[133] 'Memorandum Re Financial and Economic Situation in Europe', 3 May, folder 2/630, box 203, EMHP; Memo of same title, 13 May, box 18, RHBP. See also 'Observations Upon the European Situation', undated, folder 2/635, box 203, EMHP (also box 16A, NDP). Reasons for attributing these to Davis and Lamont include Davis–Baruch letters, 1 and 2 May, box 46, NDP; Davis and Lamont to Leffingwell, 27 May, box 16A, NDP; Vol. 16, p. 438.

[134] 'Memorandum', 3 May, 3, folder 2/630, box 203, EMHP.

[135] 'Observations', 4–6, folder 2/635, box 203, EMHP.

[136] Davis and Lamont to Leffingwell, 27 May, box 16A, NDP.

[137] Baruch to Wilson, 7 May, 2, 5, unit VI, BBP.

On 29 April, F. A. Vanderlip, an American banker, wrote to House proposing 'an international loan for the rehabilitation of industry in Europe',[138] so as to avoid revolution. The impetus would come from cooperation between Dutch, American, Scandinavian, and perhaps South American private investors (though some government cooperation was essential in the administration of the loan). Europe would be treated as a whole. Credit would be 'expended in the countries where the credits were given, for food, raw material, tools and machinery, and rolling stock'. To ensure a moderate interest rate, countries receiving credits would give security by pledging specific taxes to their repayment. On 1 May, a memorandum elaborating the Vanderlip plan was prepared.[139] Failure to restart industry 'for all ... may mean a breakdown in European civilization which will involve the whole world'. The risk of revolution meant that all individual commercial loans lacked security. House regarded Vanderlip's plan as important, and encouraged consideration of it.[140]

The view which motivated many such initiatives, and which Keynes was to expound in *The Economic Consequences*, was set out by a subcommittee of the new committee on European finance:[141]

The European problem is in reality a single whole. Central and Eastern Europe cannot be prosperous unless Western Europe is prosperous, i.e. unless the former can export its agricultural and other produce to the latter, and unless the latter has the purchasing power to buy it.... Unless international credit is re-established international trade will not recover: instead of one international market there will be different and separate groups of restricted markets within which business will as far as possible be carried on by something like barter.

As the committee worked, efforts continued to get US help for Europe. On 15 May, Brand and Monnet met with Lamont, trying to get large US credits. Lamont said he was seeking Wilson's agreement.[142] On 16 May, Hoover drafted what he modestly called 'Another Plan for the Financial Rehabilitation of Europe'.[143] It proposed forgiveness of interest on all inter-Allied debts for three years, US government credit to certain states, and a German bonds scheme—a plan in Keynes's spirit. On 18 May, L. P. Sheldon, of the US War Trade Board and Food Administration, signed his 'Rough Memorandum on the Creation of Interest Bearing Certificates to be Used in Paying Unfavorable

---

138 F. A. Vanderlip to House, 29 Apr., box 16A, NDP.
139 'Memorandum in Regard to an International Loan', 1 May, folder 2/835, box 208, EMHP.
140 House to Vanderlip, 5 May, box 16A, NDP.
141 'Memorandum', 12 May, para. 3, box 18, RHBP. This is presumably the memorandum 'A' mentioned at vol. 16, p. 446.
142 'Discussion with Mr Lamont May 15 1919', box 18, RHBP.
143 Box 16A, NDP.

Trade Balances Between the International Group'.[144] It proposed an ingenious and complex scheme, not unlike Keynes's Clearing Union plan before Bretton Woods.

On 22 May, Keynes reported that he and Davis had prepared a draft report which was 'at complete variance with...the reparation chapter of the draft treaty'. But Keynes lamented that the 'Americans do not really intend to do anything; and even apart from that no concrete proposal capable of being put into force can come into existence in the unreal atmosphere of Paris'. Keynes also wrote that Davis had promised to propose to Wilson that interest on inter-Allied debt should be remitted for three years, which would be a real contribution to British and general problems.[145] On 27 May, Keynes reported that Davis definitely stated that Wilson had decided to propose this to Congress, and to recommend relaxation of the conditions governing the use of the $1,000 million at the disposal of the War Finance Corporation for helping American exporters. But Davis had said it was exceedingly unlikely that Congress would 'do anything whatever for the finance of Europe' beyond these measures. Keynes insisted that Britain must 'not allow ourselves to be manoeuvred into taking the place of the United States' in lending.[146]

In a cable to Washington on 27 May, Lamont and Davis sought to persuade the Treasury to support a much more active official US policy, and were clearly fearful that they would not. Lamont and Davis made American aid to Europe conditional on there being 'no preferential tariffs...discriminatory against American nationals, and...no exclusive concessions granted calculated to work to our disadvantage'—the recurrent US concern for an open, non-discriminatory trading order. The cable said that Wilson had seen it, and would want the Treasury's views. It held out the prospect of Wilson embarking on a campaign to persuade Congress and public opinion of the need for US help to Europe, something of which Davis and Lamont had sought to persuade Wilson.[147]

The report of the European finance committee,[148] which appears to be dated 4 June,[149] urged the need for western *government* credits for 'the New States and Eastern Allies' to obtain raw materials, and to guarantee currency reorganization. The latter would involve replacing existing currencies with

---

[144] Box 16A, NDP.

[145] Vol. 16, pp. 447–8.

[146] Vol. 16, pp. 464–5.

[147] In their 'Observations', 6, folder 2/635, box 203, EMHP.

[148] RT/16/26–8, KP. 'Final draft of Committee Report. Directed by 4 Heads of State', box 44, NDP.

[149] The date of printing appears to be 4 June. Some copies were distributed on 5 June: untitled note on memo, dated 5 June, box 44, NDP.

'a new currency based on a definite unit of real value' issued 'under the control of some independent authority satisfactory to the Governments contributing to the Guarantee Fund': a form, it seems, of international currency. Given thinking by American officials along comparable lines,[150] it is not possible to attribute authorship of this scheme principally or solely to Keynes. The report argued that Germany's capacity to pay reparations was far less than the Reparation Commission, and the draft Treaty, envisaged. Indeed, 'if the collapse of Germany is to be avoided', her need for imports and working capital required such action as a loan to Germany from the Allied and Associated Governments, and the reparation chapter permitting Germany to sell bonds ranking in front of all reparation payments. The Committee described the German situation as the key to the whole European financial problem, and urged modification of the draft Treaty. The Report also covered the financial difficulties of France, Italy, and Britain, and the legal limits on US government lending. Keynes insisted on a statement referring to these difficulties along the lines of that which appeared: 'Some members of the Committee were doubtful if private credits and enterprise would be adequate to meet the situation.'[151] That the committee's report should raise the question of whether Britain needed a US loan shows how greatly Anglo-American economic power relations had changed, and the discussions resulting in this sentence showed disagreement over the adequacy of private credits.

On 6 June, Keynes sent a copy of the committee's report to Sir John Bradbury, saying he doubted much would come of it. Keynes reported 'that the Americans intend to make it a condition of remitting interest that we should make a large loan of new money to France for the purchase of wool'. Keynes argued that Britain should itself remit interest, and could not do that *and* lend new money to France.[152] The committee's report was never discussed by the Council of Four.[153] Thus this latest of many attempts to get the leaders to focus on restarting the European economy ended in failure.

In the spring and summer of 1919, schemes for European rehabilitation proliferated away from Paris as well as there. For example, on 14 May *The Manchester Guardian* carried a lucid article by J. A. Hobson proposing an international loan scheme under the League. An American official in Paris described it as 'the Keynes memo in slightly different dress'.[154] Hobson said

---

[150] See, e.g. Lamont's and Davis's 'Observations', 3, folder 2/635, box 203, EMHP. Hoover's 'Another Plan'; Davis and Lamont to Leffingwell, 27 May, box 16A, NDP.

[151] See: BBD, 27 May; Davis to Keynes, 31 May and 3 June; Keynes to Davis, 2 June, box 46, NDP.

[152] Vol. 16, p. 472.

[153] Vol. 16, p. 445; Tillman, *Paris Peace Conference*, p. 271.

[154] Note on letter, W. H. Buckler to Davis, 16 May, box 16A, NDP.

that economic action by the League would help greatly 'to establish confidence in it, not merely as an organ of peace, but as an instrument for the practical co-operation of nations upon the economic plane'. Keynes probably shared this view, but it contrasted with the belief that the League's tackling economic issues would destroy its effectiveness.[155] Hobson also advocated reducing reparation demands 'to a manageable sum', and revising the economic clauses of the draft Treaty 'to secure the largest measure of free trade compatible with national sovereignty'.

Amongst the reasons rehabilitation proposals were not adopted was the persistence of laissez-faire thinking. Baruch recorded on 21 May that Marc Wallenberg, a Swedish banker, 'thought the world would get on its feet better and quicker by having as little governmental assistance as possible, and that the business men and traders of the world would soon get together, if the governments would get out of the way. This view seems to be gaining headway.'[156] As we shall see, this attitude helped defeat further proposals for international action, including the Amsterdam memorial process of 1919–20, in which Wallenberg was involved.

3.3 REPARATIONS[157]

The differences between the Keynes and Hughes approaches to reparations before the peace conference went unresolved, dividing the British delegation at Paris throughout the conference, with Lloyd George alternating between the two approaches. The contentious issues included what Germany owed (not least whether to include pensions and separation allowances, as was decided); whether to fix a sum in the Treaty or, as was decided, leave this to a Reparation Commission; what Germany could pay; the time period over which payments would be made; in what proportions reparations should go to particular countries; what priority, if any, Belgium should get; guarantees to ensure that Germany paid; and provisions for a treaty with Austria.

Although not a member of the Conference's Commission on Reparations, Keynes expressed his opinions to his political masters, in his unofficial dealings with officials from other states (most importantly, the US team), and to some extent even in his official dealings with other states. His words

---

[155] For example, White to Lodge, 14 Apr., 5, box 53, HCLP.
[156] BBD, 21 May.
[157] See also, e.g. RT/14, KP. Tillman, *Paris Peace Conference*, ch. 9.

and deeds were therefore a combination, not always a happy one for him, of his own views and those he was required to advance.

On Germany's obligation to pay, a key divide was between those, such as Hughes and the French, who asserted Germany's obligation to pay the whole cost of the war, and those, such as the American lawyer John Foster Dulles[158] and Britain's James Headlam-Morley,[159] who argued that there had been an Armistice contract with Germany which limited her liability. But there was American apprehension that European states would argue 'that if the United States prevented them from getting what they claimed, the United States should itself assume the financial burden of satisfying their claims'.[160] Britain sought to increase her proportion of reparations by including pensions paid to war widows, and separation allowances paid to the wives of combatants. The USA resisted vigorously, but Wilson finally accepted their inclusion.

There were also keen differences on Germany's capacity to pay. Within the US delegation, the limits on German capacity to pay were widely stressed. For example, on 14 January, Henry White wrote to Henry Cabot Lodge of the impossibility of German reparations through a long series of years being sufficient to prevent an increase of French taxation.[161] On 11 February, Davis told the American peace commissioners that much less could be 'extorted' from Germany than was widely expected, and that British Treasury officials 'felt much as we did in this matter'.[162] On 8 March, Davis wrote that the French were:

seeking for large indemnities combined with crippling trade restrictions on Germany, and while they recognize in private that huge indemnities imply heavy exports from Germany in competition with their exports combined with a diminished market for French products in Germany owing to restricted consumption, their political utterances in the past make them decline to say so in public, or to recognize the dilemma in their acts. British official positions seem somewhat to our surprise to be similarly hampered at least in part.[163]

The point about the impossibility of huge reparations while crippling the German economy was also made by, for example, Rathbone and Baruch (including to Keynes and others).[164] Keynes shared this view.

[158] See, e.g. Dulles, 'Analysis of Debate on Principles Governing Reparation', 24 Feb., folder 2/781, box 207, EMHP; US delegation meeting, 11 Feb.: *FRUS, PPC, 1919*, xi, pp. 28–32.

[159] See, e.g. J. Headlam-Morley, *A Memoir of the Paris Peace Conference 1919*, ed. A. Headlam-Morley, R. Bryant, A. Cienciala (London, 1972) p. 162.

[160] T. H. Bliss diary, 11 Feb., box 244, T. H. Bliss papers, LOC.

[161] White to Lodge, 14 Jan., box 53, HCLP.

[162] *FRUS, PPC, 1919*, xi, p. 31.

[163] Davis to Rathbone, 8 Mar., 7, box 43, NDP.

[164] Rathbone to Davis, 14 Mar., box 43, NDP; Baruch to Wilson, 29 Mar., unit VI, BBP. BBD, 30 Apr.

On 15 March, Davis presented to the Big Three a recommendation from Edwin Montagu, Loucheur, and himself, designed to end the deadlock on Germany's obligation and capacity to pay: that a demand be made upon Germany to pay a capital sum of 30 billion dollars over thirty years, half in foreign and half in German currency. This was, he said, roughly the limit of Germany's capacity to pay, and it met 'the damage done by Germany for which she is liable under the strictest interpretation of the exchange of notes between President Wilson and the German Government, as modified by the Allies on November 4 and accepted by President Wilson'. Figures three or four times this suggested by 'some eminent bankers' were 'utterly impossible'. Davis also recognized that the removal of German shipping and foreign investments eliminated much of the invisible receipts that covered her pre-war trade deficit.[165]

Davis wished to avoid demands that would lead Germany to refuse to sign the Treaty. He recognized, as did others,[166] that this would confront the Allies with the choice between publicly reducing their demands, or a military occupation to force acceptance or to collect themselves the amount demanded.[167] Davis put to Lloyd George the 'strong probability that forcing an unwilling people to work for a generation to discharge a large debt will cause unrest which may again disturb the peace of the world through agitation for repudiation, and it may also in time produce an effect on the public opinion of the world which will react upon the Allies'. Davis recommended that 'In order to provide for future action which may be rendered necessary by unforeseen circumstances, a commission should be created from the Powers interested, with powers to modify, suspend, extend, and possibly even cancel, payments that may accrue over a long period of years'.

Lloyd George appeared to accept Davis's arguments of 15 March; but was soon again 'fortified by Lord Sumner's assurance that the Germans could be milked for £11b'.[168] Keynes became involved in the argument between the Davis and Sumner-Cunliffe approaches[169]—disputing Sumner's figures, serving on a committee to harmonize the opposing view, and drafting with Brand a schedule of annual payments based on the smaller of the opposed estimates. But with Cunliffe and Sumner unwilling to budge, Lloyd George did not

[165] 'Arguments' by Davis, for Montagu and Loucheur, at meeting with Wilson, Lloyd George, and Clemenceau, Paris, 15 Mar., and 'Mr. Norman Davis' Argument' to Lloyd George on reparations, box 44, NDP.

[166] For example, Lansing to Smith, 23 Mar., 5, box 5, RLP.

[167] 'Mr. Norman Davis' Argument', 15 Mar., box 44, NDP.

[168] Skidelsky, *Hopes*, p. 364.

[169] Vol. 16, p. 448; E. Montagu to Keynes, 22 Mar. 1919, L/19/10, KP; Keynes to Kerr, 25 March 1919, RT/1/71–2, KP.

accept it. Lloyd George gyrated between moderation and severity. Whether Britain was represented in meetings by Cunliffe and Sumner, or Keynes and Montagu, depended on Lloyd George's purpose at the time.[170]

In late March, Lloyd George, as Skidelsky put it, 'clutched at Klotz's proposal that they leave out of the Treaty any definite figure of total sums owing or capacity to pay, rejecting Keynes's alternative suggestion that only Germany's capacity to pay be left undetermined. The Reparations Commission was given up to 1921 to work out what Germany owed and what it could pay, subject only to the proviso that it pay £1b on account.'[171] Lloyd George's proposal for a permanent Reparation Commission[172] was debated in a succession of meetings. Issues included whether the Commission would determine what Germany owed, her capacity to pay, or both of these; and whether they would take into account her capacity to pay over a finite period (e.g. thirty years), or seek payment of her full obligation over as long a period as necessary. British and French reluctance to fix a reparations figure in the treaty, and American reluctance to press them too hard, were influenced by British and French fears that their governments would fall if their publics learned that Germany could not pay the amounts they expected. Henry White wrote that Lloyd George 'knows, and his financial experts tell him, that it is quite impossible for his promises to be carried out'.[173] In a meeting of the Big Three on 25 April, Wilson stressed that the Treaty would diminish Germany's economic capacity, but that Germany would need 'a greater foreign commerce than she had had before the war if she was to be able to pay'.[174]

The plan to postpone fixing German payments still left the question of what categories of damage were to be included in its obligation. Though Wilson doubted whether pensions and allowances could be embraced by the wording of the Allied memorandum of 5 November 1918,[175] he recognized their importance for Britain to maximize her share of the total reparation payments.[176] By 28 March, a memorandum by Keynes for Lloyd George showed 'so little, really' between the French and British on the proportions, but a 'combative' French position.[177] In late March and early April, Keynes was actively involved in negotiations with the USA and other powers on categories of claims.[178] Keynes was embarrassed, and Wilson and his advisers

---

[170] See, e.g. VCMcCD, 31 Mar., see also, e.g. MacMillan, *Peacemakers*, p. 198 ff.
[171] Skidelsky, *Hopes*, p. 365; cf. M. Keynes, *Essays*, p. 169.
[172] 'Secret Letters of James A. Logan, Jr', vol. 2, 56, Hoover Institution.
[173] White to Lodge, 3 Apr., p. 3, box 53, HCLP, see also, e.g. VCMcCD, 2 Apr.
[174] *FRUS, PPC, 1919*, v, p. 232.
[175] 'Secret Letters of James A. Logan, Jr', vol. 2, p. 51, Hoover Institution.
[176] VCMcCD, 1 Apr.   [177] Vol. 16, pp. 449–50.
[178] See, e.g. VCMcCD, 3 Apr. and adjacent dates.

were in early April becoming increasingly angry, about the British and French 'playing for advantage in the division of the spoils'.[179]

In early April, Wilson agreed to the inclusion of pensions and separation allowances.[180] What finally persuaded him was a legal opinion by Smuts arguing that they could be regarded as falling within the terms of the Armistice understanding with Germany.[181] Smuts believed that the total claim made against Germany would be scaled down to Germany's capacity to pay within thirty years. Including pensions and separation allowances, while increasing the nominal claim against Germany, would simply increase Britain's share of the actual claim made.[182] The scaling down was not done, and Smuts was soon working with Keynes and others to moderate the demands.[183]

On 5 April, the Big Four discussed the proposal of the British and American financial experts that Germany be required to pay what she could over thirty years.[184] Lloyd George, accompanied only by Sumner, pressed Sumner's view that Germany should pay the full amount of reparations due up to her capacity, not just up to her capacity within thirty years. House and Davis pointed out that 'President Wilson had understood that by including pensions, the total amount was not increased, owing to the thirty years limit, but that their inclusion only formed a more equitable basis for distribution'.[185] Davis insisted that eliminating the time limit would increase the reparations, and give Germany no cause for hope. In the end, House accepted the deletion of any time limit on capacity to pay. 'This concession destroyed the assumption that including pensions would make no difference to the total amount Germany would be called on to pay.'[186] The inclusion of war pensions and separation allowances thus trebled Germany's liability.[187]

Keynes, Lamont, and Loucheur produced the next draft of the reparation clauses.[188] Keynes joined Sumner in attending with Lloyd George when the Big Four met on 7 April, and clearly had some influence on Lloyd George.[189] The meeting of 5 April had added the words 'and the enemy Governments

[179] VCMcCD, 2 and 4 Apr.

[180] 1 Apr. was the famous meeting at Wilson's house: see, e.g. Tillman, *Paris Peace Conference*, p. 245. Wilson's decision was rapidly conveyed to Keynes and others: VCMcCD, 1 Apr. It became clear in the Big Four on 5 Apr.: FRUS, PPC, 1919, v, p. 29 ff; Mantoux, P., *The Deliberations of the Council of Four (Mar. 24–June 28, 1919): Notes of the Official Interpreter*, ed. A. S. Link (2 vols., Princeton, 1992), i, p. 154 ff.

[181] Smuts's opinion is at RT/14/92–3, KP, and, e.g. Zimmern, *Convalescence*, pp. 199–203.

[182] Skidelsky, *Hopes*, pp. 365–6.   [183] See, e.g. RT/14/121–2, KP.

[184] FRUS, PPC, 1919, v, pp. 21–35.   [185] See also VCMcCD, 5 Apr.

[186] Skidelsky, *Hopes*, p. 366.

[187] Thirlwall, *Policy Adviser*, pp. 84, 112; extract of Keynes speech, Zimmern, *Convalescence*, pp. 196–8.

[188] FRUS, PPC, 1919, v, p. 44.   [189] See FRUS, PPC, 1919, iv, pp. 45–7.

accept' to the war guilt clause.[190] Whether intentionally or not, the Lamont-Keynes–Loucheur draft did not include this enemy acceptance of responsibility; it was re-inserted by the Big Four.[191] After the 7 April meeting, Lamont and Keynes worked on a further version of the reparations clauses, and the British draft on categories was examined by officials.[192]

Keynes was involved in negotiations over the Belgian claim (with some US support) for priority in reparation payments as the only country forced into the war through the violation of a Treaty.[193] Although, during a stand-off between Belgium and the Big Three, Belgian financial experts made a direct approach to Keynes,[194] he favoured Belgium's being required to use reparation payments after the first £100 million to repay her debts to the Allies.[195] Keynes was defeated by Hankey and Lloyd George in his attempt to require Belgium to pay for government property in German territory ceded to Belgium.[196]

The German officials sought to influence the reparations debate among the Allies. In early and mid-April, Melchior and Max Warburg put to British and US officials that Germany looked to America for a just peace, that the threat of Bolshevism in Germany was 'hourly growing', and that German opinion meant that no German delegation would dare to sign a treaty with heavy indemnities and other savage provisions. These views were relayed to Wilson and other members of the US delegation.[197] As we have seen, Keynes had formed his own views on reparations long before.

3.3.1 Desperate Efforts to Change the Treaty

On 4 May, Keynes sent Chamberlain and Bradbury some 'general impressions' on reparations and other provisions.[198] Keynes regarded the reparation chapter as showing 'a high degree of unwisdom in almost every direction'. The Reparation Commission could not possibly work. The US delegation had been left with 'the bitterest feelings towards their principal European

---

[190] *FRUS, PPC, 1919*, v, p. 22.   [191] Ibid., p. 44.

[192] Ibid., p. 63; see also, e.g. pp. 302–7.

[193] Ibid., pp. 31 ff, 52–3, 58, 344–51. Cf. vol. 10, pp. 27–32. 'Secret Letters of James A. Logan, Jr', vol. 2, pp. 53–5, Hoover Institution; VCMcCD, 2 May.

[194] *FRUS, PPC, 1919*, v, p. 390. VCMcCD, 30 Apr. (and 1 May). See also 'Secret Letters of James A. Logan, Jr', vol. 2, p. 55, Hoover Institution.

[195] *FRUS, PPC, 1919*, v, pp. 446–8; vol. 10, p. 31; VCMcCD, 3 May.

[196] *FRUS, PPC, 1919*, v, pp. 448–9.

[197] 'Memorandum as to Meeting at Chateau Villette Today (Apr. 16, 1919)' (by T. Lamont), encl. memo. by Max Warburg, folder 2/654, box 203, EMHP; see Melchior to Keynes, 9 Apr., box 59, NDP; Ferguson, *Paper*, pp. 213–15.

[198] Vol. 16, pp. 450–6.

associates' over reparations: 'In fighting week after week preposterous demands on the part of ourselves and the French they have got into a habit of arguing and working in the interests of the enemy which is not likely to disappear in the future'. Keynes regarded many other provisions as humiliating Germany, and undermining her sovereignty. The chapter on the occupation of Germany was open 'to the most terrible abuse', and the Treaty as a whole was unworkable. The German financial representatives, 'nervous and broken-spirited' at Treves in January, were now in good spirits; 'Spartacism is for the moment, at any rate, under control'; the German 'food position is no longer immediately desperate'; and Keynes could not believe that the Germans would sign the Treaty in its present form. Keynes was 'exceedingly pessimistic'. Only a 'simple form of peace' could work.

On 7 May, the draft Treaty was handed to the Germans, and was made public.[199] In a letter to his mother on 14 May (in which he wrote 'well, I suppose I've been an accomplice in all this wickedness and folly'), Keynes said that he was seeking to be relieved of his duties by early June. He wrote that the Germans would not sign the Treaty, that they could not keep its terms if they did, and that 'nothing but general disorder and unrest could result. Certainly if I was in the Germans' place I'd rather die than sign such a peace'. Keynes was persuaded not to press his resignation, and over subsequent weeks was much involved in attempts to ameliorate the terms of the treaty. In early June, believing he had failed, Keynes resigned in protest.[200]

There were many protests, including some resignations, among US officials also.[201] William C. Bullitt, in resigning, in effect accused Wilson of betraying his principles.[202] On 22 May, Lansing described growing opposition as almost a mutiny. Among those telling Lansing of their disgust at the Treaty were Ray Stannard Baker, Norman Davis, and Hoover, and he was hearing 'that the Britishers over here hold similar views'.[203] There was much talk of Germany's not signing, and of Allied delegates such as Smuts not doing so. Churchill told Baruch that 'we were asking too much of Germany', and that 'in the hour of our triumph we should temper our terms with justice'. Churchill gave £2,000 million as Germany's maximum capacity to pay.[204] Hoover 'thought Lloyd George would attempt to take the world leadership away from President

[199] See MacMillan, *Peacemakers*, p. 477.

[200] Vol. 16, pp. 458–74.

[201] See, e.g. copies of letters dated 15 May from A. A. Berle, Jnr, J. V. Fuller, Samuel Eliot Morison, G. B. Noble, all to J. C. Grew, Sec.-Gen., Am. Commission to Negotiate Peace, vol. 43, Lansing papers, LOC; see Boemeke et al., *Treaty of Versailles*, ch. 8.

[202] Bullitt to Wilson; Bullitt to Lansing, 17 May, vol. 43, Lansing papers, LOC.

[203] Lansing to John W. Davis, 22 May, 1, 3, box 5, RLP.

[204] BBD, 22 May. Churchill later described the economic clauses as 'malignant', 'silly', and 'obviously futile': *The Second World War*, i, *The Gathering Storm* (London, 1949) p. 6.

Wilson and . . . denounce the Treaty and stand for a new deal'. McCormick found it 'amusing to hear criticism from Davis, Keynes, and others who, when they have been talking to the Big Four, agree with everything they say and make no strong protest'.[205] But the criticisms from Davis and Keynes were simply the arguments they had been using for many weeks or months.

An exchange of letters ensued between the German delegation, protesting against the draft Treaty, and the Allies defending it.[206] Count Brockdorff-Rantzau claimed it would mean the deaths of millions of Germans.[207] He said Germany laid down her arms on the basis of accepting responsibility for restoration of Belgium and northern France, but not for more than that.[208] Wilson said of one Allied letter that it 'gave a conclusive reply to the German letter but provided no ray of hope'.[209] On 20 May, Loucheur told Baruch, Davis, and Lamont that the reparations clauses were 'a mistake, and that his acquiescence in them was due to the political conditions in France'.[210] Loucheur and these US officials (and perhaps McCormick) sought the agreement of Wilson and Clemenceau that American, British, French, and Italian experts should discuss with the German delegation what 'would give them some hope for the future'.[211] It appears that some officials wanted talks to explain the Treaty provisions to the Germans, and some to negotiate changes in them.

A Big Three meeting on 21 May was overshadowed by fear that Germany would not sign the Treaty. Wilson suggested that experts of both sides discuss the financial and economic conditions, to 'demonstrate to Europe that nothing had been left undone which might have induced the Germans to have signed'.[212] Clemenceau thought this would help Germany; but Lloyd George was willing to make some concession to ensure Germany signed. Wilson said:

[T]he experts who had discussed with the German Financial Experts at Villette found Herr Melchior a very sensible man. Melchior was now one of the German Delegates . . . . The United States Experts had, all along, said that the present scheme of reparation would not yield much. This was Mr. Norman Davis' view, and Mr. Keynes, the British expert, shared it. He himself wanted the Allies to get reparation. He feared they would get very little. If it could be shown to Melchior that the Reparation Commission was allowed to consider the condition of Germany and to adjust the arrangements accordingly from time to time, it might enable him to persuade the German people.

No action was agreed.

[205] Hoover and McCormick in VCMcCD, 22 May.
[206] See, e.g. *FRUS, PPC, 1919*, v, pp. 723–4, 741–3; vi, pp. 32, 38–42.
[207] *FRUS, PPC, 1919*, v, pp. 738–40. Keynes knew 'no adequate answer' to this: vol. 2, p. 146.
[208] *FRUS, PPC, 1919*, vi, pp. 38–42.   [209] Ibid., v, p. 801.
[210] BBD, 20 May.   [211] BBD, 20 (and 21) May. VCMcCD, 21 May.
[212] *FRUS, PPC, 1919*, v, pp. 800–1.

On 26 May, Keynes wrote to Austen Chamberlain urging that, now that the full bearing of the Treaty could be seen, the only way of avoiding disaster was 'to discuss it with the Germans and to be ready to make substantial concessions'.[213] Keynes would stay on if such discussions were agreed upon; but otherwise would resign immediately. He wrote:

The settlement which [Lloyd George] is proposing for Europe disrupts it economically and must depopulate it by millions of persons. The new states we are setting up cannot survive in such surroundings. Nor can the peace be kept or the League of Nations live. How can you expect me to assist at this tragic farce any longer, seeking to lay the foundations, as a Frenchman puts it, 'd'une guerre juste et durable'?

As we shall see, Lloyd George did seek to ameliorate the Treaty, and Keynes stayed on until 7 June.

3.3.2 Provisions for Austria

Meanwhile, provisions for Austria were also deeply contentious. In fighting for moderation, Keynes cited, and may have been strongly influenced by, the frequent messages he received in the second half of May from Sir Francis Oppenheimer in Vienna.[214] Oppenheimer stressed Austria's chaotic state and need for foreign assistance; the willingness of moderate Austrians to work with the Allies if they intended to rebuild Austria; the danger of Bolshevism, perhaps coming from Hungary or Germany, and of unstoppable demands for fusion with Germany, if the Allies did not show such intention; and the need for different treaty provisions from those for Germany.

In the Big Four on 22 May,[215] Wilson sought to set reparations at a low level; Lloyd George, Orlando, and Klotz opposed leniency. Lloyd George had taken Sumner and Cunliffe to the meeting. That same day, Keynes wrote to Hankey protesting the draft terms for Austria.[216] No appreciable indemnity would be got from Austria. The Reparation Commission would become 'one of the most hated instruments of foreign domination ever invented'. It was absurd to provide 'for the surrender of milch cows to Italy, Serbia and Roumania... when the children of Austria are dying in such numbers for want of milk that the allied and associated governments are doing all in their power to rail condensed milk into the country.' Keynes thought that

---

[213] Vol. 16, pp. 459–60.
[214] Telegrams on 18, 21, 23, and 25 May, and 'Memorandum' and 'Report', RT/23/3–40, KP; Vol. 16, pp. 460, 463. No biography of Keynes appears to mention Oppenheimer.
[215] *FRUS, PPC, 1919*, v, p. 830 ff.
[216] Vol. 16, pp. 461–3.

provisions specifically suited to Austria were needed, rather than simply applying the terms of the German treaty to Austria, as was in effect proposed.

The next morning, Clemenceau added the liberalizing influence of Loucheur and Tardieu to join Klotz and Jouasset on the committee on reparations from Austria, Hungary, and Bulgaria. Lloyd George added Smuts and Keynes to join Sumner and Cunliffe.[217] This reflected Lloyd George's inability to decide firmly between the alternative approaches, while searching for ways to produce a more acceptable peace. But Smuts and Keynes, both opposing reparations demands on the successor states, believed that 'the British representation cannot be fundamentally divided against itself, and it is necessary to choose'.[218] Their efforts to force Lloyd George to choose, by initially asking to being excused from serving,[219] may have contributed to the Big Four's agreeing on 26 May that new proposals on reparations and financial clauses for the new states could be considered.[220]

On 29 and 30 May, Keynes attended meetings of the Austrian reparation commission, and 'stirred things up'.[221] McCormick recorded:[222]

Keynes and Lord Sumner... continued fight over Austrian reparation clauses, Keynes trying to modify them considerably, saying Austria broke and ought to be helped financially. Lord Sumner saying that the present clauses fair and flexible. Committee agreed with Lord Sumner, and Keynes stated he would fight it out before Big Four.

Keynes wrote that he had made 'a final protest... against murdering Vienna, and did achieve some improvement', by leaving 'the actual figure of reparation to be exacted from Austria... vague'. On 30 May, Keynes took to his bed with exhaustion, rallying from time to time for particular tasks. Writing to Philip Kerr on 30 May, Keynes asked Lloyd George to have the 'cruel and unwise' clause in the Austrian treaty on delivery of milch cows withdrawn. Lloyd George raised the matter, but let it drop for want of support.[223]

On 30 May, Keynes also suggested that the draft treaty be presented to Austria 'without the reparation chapter, reserving this until the position with Germany is more settled'.[224] The main argument against modifying the Austrian reparation provisions was that this would prejudice negotiations with the Germans; hence a document unsuited to Austrian realities. The Austrian treaty, without financial or reparations details, was handed to the

---

[217] *FRUS, PPC, 1919*, v, p. 864.   [218] Vol. 16, p. 460.
[219] Smuts to Lloyd George, 26 May 1919: copy at RT/23/65, KP; see also vol. 16, pp. 460–1. On their absence from the Commission on the morning of 26 May: *FRUS, PPC, 1919*, vi, pp. 43–4.
[220] *FRUS, PPC, 1919*, vi, p. 43; see also pp. 64–7. BBD, 22 May.
[221] VCMcCD, 29 May; vol. 16, p. 466.   [222] VCMcCD, 30 May.
[223] Vol. 16, pp. 465–70.   [224] Vol. 16, p. 467.

Austrian plenipotentiaries on 2 June.[225] Discussions continued on Austrian reparations. On 4 June, Keynes 'went to a meeting of the Council of Four on Austrian reparation, but had no success. The reparation chapter for Austria is to be the same as for Germany except that no definite figures are mentioned and there is more provision for letting her off later.'[226]

3.3.3 Responding to German Counterproposals

On 29 May, the Allies received counterproposals from Germany, and they became 'the one topic of conversation'.[227] Keynes wrote on 1 June that 'the German reply is of unequal merit but remains an unanswerable exposure of all our wickedness'.[228] The Germans protested, *inter alia*, that the Treaty conflicted with the terms upon which the Armistice was signed.[229]

Some at Paris favoured no extended discussion with, or concessions to, Germany; others (such as Davis and Hoover, and Lloyd George) believed that concessions should be made. As before, there were some who thought Lloyd George might swing to the 'extreme liberals if it looks popular at home'; Wilson thought that 'he would not dare'.[230] Lloyd George was worried by the opposition to the German Treaty developing in Britain, including in the Cabinet.[231] Botha and Smuts were unwilling to sign.[232] Churchill told Baruch that 'if we had thought we could get the kind of peace which the Germans offered us, we would have considered' it 'a great victory and a brilliant peace'.[233] One example of opposition in Britain was a letter from several public figures, including Gilbert Murray, John Masefield, and H. G. Wells, published in *The Manchester Guardian*. It argued 'that the Saar and East Prussian solutions will poison international relations, that the indemnity reduces Germany to economic servitude, that the proposals, taken as a whole, belie the spirit of the Fourteen Points, and thus in substance constitute a breach of faith with a beaten enemy, and that the draft treaty as it stands can have no endurance, and that on such a basis it is impossible to establish any true league of nations.'[234]

---

[225] 'British Delegation Daily Bulletin', 2 June 1919: copy at RT/23/41, KP; Lansing to Polk, 4 June, 2, box 5, RLP.

[226] Vol. 16, p. 472.   [227] VCMcCD, 31 May.   [228] Vol. 16, p. 470.

[229] *FRUS, PPC, 1919*, vi, p. 330.   [230] VCMcCD, 30 May.

[231] For reports reaching American officials, see: Gordon Auchinloss diary, 2 June, group no. 580, box 3, Auchinloss papers, Yale.

[232] On Botha, see Lansing to Polk, 4 June, 3–4, box 5, RLP.

[233] BBD, 31 May–1 June.

[234] Precis quoted from White to Lodge, 29 May, 3, box 53, HCLP.

With American officials pressing for fixing a sum for reparations, Lloyd George told Baruch that the German counterproposal 'was a powerful document, and required answering'.[235] In seeking alternatives for reparations provisions,[236] Lloyd George sought memorandums from Keynes and from Cunliffe and Sumner. On 2 or 3 June, Keynes gave Lloyd George a memorandum on the Prime Minister's proposal that Germany undertake the physical restoration of France and Belgium, other damages being settled in the Treaty.[237] Keynes estimated the aggregate claims against Germany at £6,300 million. Allowing for German loss of territory, this reduced to £5,000 million, a figure the Germans would find hard to refuse. The restoration of Belgium and France could be put at £2,000 million, leaving £3,000 million 'required in cash or its equivalent', spread over not 'too long a period'. Keynes wrote that by fixing such a definite sum, 'a great many of the present powers of the Reparation Commission would be unnecessary and some concessions could, therefore, be made to the German objections against the present dictatorial and far-reaching powers of that body over the internal economy of Germany'. Keynes shared the German anxiety over the powers of the Reparation Commission, and over other detailed foreign control of German economic life, such as waterways.[238] Keynes wrote on 6 June that Lloyd George disliked both his and the Cunliffe-Sumner approaches 'equally and was unable to get anyone to recommend to him the middle course which he wanted. As a result he has himself gone on the small committee which is to consider whether any change is to be made. I anticipate that something will result but nothing that is the least good'.[239]

It was said that Lloyd George threatened on 2 June not to sign the Treaty unless a fixed sum for reparations was included. Clemenceau was firmly resistant to change. Wilson, though agreeing in substance with some of Lloyd George's proposals, was annoyed with his gyrations on the Treaty, seeking to change provisions on which he had earlier insisted. Wilson was not disposed to make changes just to get Germany to sign: heavy demands were just, and would be an historic lesson. Wilson took this stance despite several American officials, including Lansing, urging greater flexibility.[240]

---

[235] BBD, 31 May–2 June. VCMcCD, 31 May.
[236] Vol. 16, p. 467; BBD, 2 June. *FRUS, PPC, 1919*, xi, p. 199 ff.
[237] Vol. 16, pp. 467–9.
[238] Keynes to Davis, 5 May, box 32, NDP.
[239] Vol. 16, p. 472; Mantoux, *Deliberations*, ii, p. 287.
[240] *FRUS, PPC, 1919*, xi, pp. 218–19, 222; Lansing to Polk, 4 June, 3; to Smith, 5 June, box 5, RLP. BBD, 2 June.

On 1 June, Davis had given Wilson 'observations' on the German reply, agreeing with the Germans on the positions 'which we have always taken, namely, that it was a mistake not to fix...a definite amount which Germany shall pay, and that the amount so fixed should be in relation to the amount of damage which she is obligated to repair and such as she may reasonably be expected to pay within one generation'.[241] Davis stressed the centrality of Germany to Europe's economic prosperity, her need for working capital, and the dangers of delay in setting a feasible sum. He also argued that a fixed sum was needed if French and other European credit were to be restored; this was widely believed in the US camp.[242] Davis reiterated his key observations in a large meeting of US officials which Wilson chaired on 3 June to discuss the German counterproposals. Davis, Lamont, and Baruch argued for fixing a definite sum now, not least 'to do away with the functions of the Reparations Commission which most worry the Germans'.[243] On 4 June, Hoover wrote to Wilson that Germany 'will not sign the Treaty without considerable modification', and that 'if she refuses we will have extinguished the possibility of democracy [in Germany] in favor of either Communism or reaction'— a dichotomy Keynes was to use. Hoover urged Wilson to accept British proposals for modification that were in line with Wilson's own original positions.[244]

3.3.4 Keynes's Resignation

In December 1918, Keynes had written that the Treasury authorities accepted that the peace conference 'is the last work I do for them and that when it is over I am a free man'.[245] What was important about his resignation in June 1919 was not that he left the Treasury but that he did so before the conference was over, with little notice, and with strong protests against the Treaty.

On 12 April 1919, Keynes said he intended to leave the Treasury when 'our affairs with Germany have come to a head', perhaps within six weeks; and perhaps sooner, 'as at any moment the best plan may seem to be to chuck.'[246] He stressed Europe's desperation. We have seen that he had decided by

[241] 'Personal and Confidential Observations' of Davis to Wilson, 1 June, 1, box 16A, NDP.

[242] See, e.g. White to Lodge, 6 June, box 53, HCLP.

[243] *FRUS, PPC, 1919*, xi, p. 198.

[244] Hoover to Wilson, 4 June, box 9, H. Hoover papers, Hoover Institution.

[245] Keynes to FAK, 23 Dec. 1918, PP/45/168/9/141, KP; see also Keynes to FAK, 13 Oct. 1918, PP/45/168/9/129–30, KP.

[246] Keynes to FAK, 12 Apr. 1919, PP/45/168/9/164–5, KP; cf. Keynes to JNK, 30 Mar., PP/45/168/13/145–6, KP.

mid-May definitely to resign from the Treasury in protest at the terms of the Treaty, and had written to Chamberlain about his intentions. Urged to stay on by Chamberlain, his mother, Smuts, and perhaps others, Keynes had done so, seeking to effect changes in the Treaty.[247] By the end of May, he was suffering greatly from fatigue,[248] and deeply stressed. On 31 May, H. A. Siepmann, a Treasury official working with Keynes, wrote to him: 'The battle is lost here [and] must be won elsewhere.'[249] On 3 June, Keynes wrote:[250]

The P.M., poor man, would like now at the eleventh hour to alter the damned treaty, for which no one has a word of defence, but it's too late in my belief and for all his wrigglings Fate must now march on to its conclusion. I feel it my duty to stay on here so long as there is any chance of a scheme for a real change being in demand. But I don't expect any such thing. Anyhow it will soon be settled and I bound for home.

On 5 June, Keynes wrote to Lloyd George that 'The battle is lost', and he was 'slipping away from this scene of nightmare' on 7 June.[251] To Davis he wrote: 'You Americans are broken reeds.'[252]

Lloyd George continued to wriggle. Lansing recorded that on 4 June, the US economic advisers 'were shell-shocked by receiving word that Lloyd George had changed his mind and now favored an indefinite amount'. Lloyd George now wanted to give Germany three months in which she could suggest a reparation figure. Lansing wrote: 'A chameleon has nothing on Lloyd George.'[253] The USA pressed for a fixed sum (not least to secure 'what the world instantly requires, a new basis of credit'), and some concessions, including 'the retention by Germany of certain amounts of working capital in the form of ships, gold, and investments abroad'. Lloyd George insisted: 'Any figure that would not frighten [the Germans] would be below the figure with which he and M. Clemenceau could face their peoples in the present state of public opinion.' Nonetheless, the American delegates insisted that the reparation clauses had 'been prepared with scrupulous regard for the correspondence leading up to the Armistice of November 11, 1918'[254]— a proposition many American officials believed was untrue.

---

[247] Vol. 16, pp. 458–60, 469–70. Other letters between Keynes and FAK are in PP/45/168/9, KP. Chamberlain and Bradbury letters at RT/1/100–1, 110–11, KP.

[248] Vol. 16, p. 470; see also, e.g. p. 464.

[249] Siepmann to Keynes, 31 May 1919, RT/1/122, KP.

[250] Vol. 16, p. 471.

[251] Vol. 16, p. 469.

[252] Vol. 16, p. 471; see Davis to Keynes, 6 June, box 11, NDP; for correspondence with others, incl. Hoover, see RT/1/127 ff, KP.

[253] *FRUS, PPC, 1919*, vi, p. 240; Lansing to Smith, 5 June, pp. 4–5, box 5, RLP.

[254] *FRUS, PPC, 1919*, vi, pp. 261–7; see also pp. 337, 480.

Wilson went on to accept, as Lloyd George and Clemenceau wanted, that a figure should not be fixed immediately.[255] But there were to be no changes in the reparation provisions of the Treaty.[256] On 23 June, the German delegation gave way to Allied pressure and agreed to sign the Treaty.[257] Melchior did not.[258]

3.4 CONCLUSION

Before leaving Paris, Keynes referred to the probability of the SEC moving to London.[259] He was probably aware of Cecil's proposals that the SEC provide the means for continued international consultation and cooperation on economic issues until 'the setting up of new machinery for economic consultation under the League of Nations'.[260] On 28 June, the Big Five authorized the SEC to suggest 'methods of consultation'.[261] An SEC subcommittee proposed an international economic council comprising delegates of ministerial rank, with its first meeting in Washington by 15 September—a clear bid for governmental action on Europe's economic crisis, and to ensure US involvement and leadership. Hoover and Dulles immediately cabled Wilson urging his acceptance, and stressing the need for a governmental committee to 'co-ordinate our economic support so as to maintain political stability in Europe without stifling individual initiative'.[262] The League was later to play some modest role in financial and economic issues; but such calls for American leadership met firm refusal.

As we have seen, Keynes's principal ideas on the central economic issues of the PPC—relief, especially feeding Germany and Austria; war debts, and proposals for lending to restart the European economy; and reparations—were widely shared, though largely ineffective, at Paris. His resignation left him free to persuade a wider world of their urgency, and thus, he hoped, to give effect to them. They were already widely shared in liberal circles in Britain. But it was above all to the USA, whose economic power was essential to a satisfactory European settlement, that Keynes had appealed, unavailingly, in Paris, and to which he would appeal again in the coming months.

[255] *FRUS, PPC, 1919*, vi, pp. 264, 273–5, 480–5, 564–5.
[256] See *FRUS, PPC, 1919*, vi, p. 338.
[257] Ibid., p. 644.
[258] Ferguson, *Paper*, pp. 222–3; cf. Mantoux, *Deliberations*, i, p. 478.
[259] Vol. 16, p. 473.
[260] *FRUS, PPC, 1919*, vi, p. 741; see also x, pp. 355–6, 414 ff; Tillman, *Paris Peace Conference*, pp. 272–5.
[261] *FRUS, PPC, 1919*, vi, p. 743; see also x, pp. 430–1.
[262] Hoover and Dulles to Wilson, 10 July, box 8, Hoover papers, Hoover Institution.

4

Appeals Unanswered: From Amsterdam to Lausanne

> It is on America that everything depends, & I see no chance of affecting opinion there.
>
> R. H. Brand to Keynes, 29 October 1919[1]

Within three weeks of leaving the peace conference, Keynes, encouraged by Smuts,[2] had begun to write a book on the Treaty and the economic condition of Europe. He was uncertain whether he would persevere with it.[3] Cecil[4] and others encouraged him to do so, and *The Economic Consequences of the Peace* was published in December 1919. In the months of writing, Keynes was involved in a number of discussions of the needs of post-war reconstruction, including with a group of European and American financiers meeting in Amsterdam in October and November. This chapter sets out his role in the Amsterdam process of private financial diplomacy; the argument of *The Economic Consequences*; criticisms of it; its impact in the USA; Keynes's subsequent role in debate on post-war reconstruction leading up to its sequel, *A Revision of the Treaty*, which appeared in January 1922; and, briefly, debate on reparations and war debts down to 1933.

Keynes was a brilliant and influential expositor of ideas that many others shared. He aimed to shape public opinion, which he and other idealists believed supremely important. While he continued to believe that free trade promoted peace, he also continued to believe that post-war conditions required international action to restart the economic mechanism and thereby create the context in which free trade could promote peace: the laissez-faire doctrine of leaving economic reconstruction to private finance and private enterprise was not enough. The early liberal institutionalism which his views

---

[1] F1/5/108, KP.

[2] See, e.g. extracts from Keynes to Smuts, 8 and 12 June 1919, L/35/141, KP.

[3] Keynes to JNK, 25 June 1919, PP/45/168/13/152–3, KP. On his mixed emotions, see, e.g. MacMillan, *Peacemakers*, pp. 488–9. Boemeke et al., *Treaty of Versailles*, pp. 485–6, 580.

[4] Cecil to Keynes, 31 July 1919, L/19/44–5; 11 Aug., PP/45/63, KP. On the book, see Cecil to Keynes, 31 Dec. 1919, FI/5/211–16, KP.

represented was an important step away from laissez-faire. Keynes joined others in appealing—at Amsterdam and in *The Economic Consequences*—for US leadership in the international action they prescribed. The refusal of the USA to exercise that leadership, not least because its Treasury remained committed to a form of laissez-faire, left Keynes throughout the 1920s to devise means of acting without the USA. When, in the 1930s and especially 1940s, it seemed the USA might provide leadership for international action which he believed necessary, he paid close attention to persuading US opinion-leaders and policymakers of that need.

The years immediately after the First World War were an extraordinary time of transition. Pre-war security had given way to disorder in Europe. The fear of extremism, including Bolshevik revolution, was great in many countries. The war had destroyed an old order, and a new one was yet to be built, or to grow naturally. There had been a decisive shift of economic power from Britain to the USA, though Britain retained significant power. The transfer was not smooth. Many Americans feared that plans, including Keynes's, for US leadership would exploit them, and relieve Britain of responsibilities she should carry. Britain was uneasy about her own loss of power to, and growing dependence on, the USA.[5] Moreover, a paradigm shift was taking place in thought about how to deal with economic problems: laissez-faire, both domestic and international, was being challenged by the growth of ideologies of greater government intervention and inter-governmental action in economic affairs. The Amsterdam memorial stressed the role of business, and sought a liberal trading order; but its emphasis on a comprehensive plan of governmental leadership was alien to the laissez-faire ideas still dominant in Washington.

4.1 A WORLD UNRESTORED: AMSTERDAM AND THE MEMORIAL

After the peace conference, further schemes were proposed in various quarters to provide relief against dire poverty and revolution; for countries to stabilize their finances, reorganize their currencies, and settle the issues of reparations and war debts; and to provide capital to restart the European economy. In July 1919, Keynes agreed, at Norman Angell's request, to join an Economic Subcommittee of the Fight the Famine Fund. Angell, who wrote admiringly of Keynes, wished to use famine relief as a means of getting 'sounder public

---

[5] See, e.g. John W. Davis diary, 11 Feb. 1920, box 103, file 102, 108, Davis papers, Yale.

opinion on broader issues of international policy'.[6] Others on the Subcommittee included J. A. Hobson, Leonard Woolf, G. D. H. Cole, and Sir George Paish.[7] Keynes wrote to Sir John Bradbury on 21 July with a proposal to help Germany finance necessary imports.[8] In the USA, Herbert Hoover,[9] Colonel House,[10] Benjamin Strong (Governor of the Federal Reserve Bank of New York),[11] Fred I. Kent of the Federal Reserve Board,[12] and Edward Stettinius, Snr, of J. P. Morgan & Co.,[13] were among those promoting rehabilitation schemes for Europe; and in Britain, Paish[14] and R. H. Brand.[15]

Keynes was among those financial experts (many of whom had been at Paris) who met, unofficially, in Amsterdam on 13–14 October, and again on 2–3 November 1919.[16] The experts agreed a 'memorial' which, signed by leading figures in many countries, was submitted to governments in mid-January 1920. The meetings were initiated by Dr G. Vissering, Governor of the Bank of the Netherlands, who had helped prepare the Vanderlip scheme (and who was to write the Dutch foreword to *The Economic Consequences*), and Fred I. Kent. The fear of Bolshevism,[17] and more general fear of European calamity,[18] were important motivations.

---

[6] Angell to Keynes, 20 July 1919, L/19/43, KP; see also Keynes to FAK, 6 Aug. 1919, PP/45/168/10/9–10, KP.

[7] See, e.g. CO/1/198 ff, KP.

[8] Keynes to Bradbury, 21 July 1919, T1/12358, PRO.

[9] Hoover, 'Memorandum on the Economic Situation of Europe', 3 July 1919, box 37, Kent papers, Princeton; speech by Hoover, 16 Sept. 1919, box 27, NDP.

[10] House diary, 3 Aug. 1919, binder 17, 13; 19 Sept., binder 17, 43; 22 Sept., binder 16, 47; 21 Oct., binder 16, 55, 57, EMHP.

[11] Ferguson, *Paper*, p. 226 n.

[12] See undated notes on *American Credit Organization*, box 24, Kent papers, Princeton.

[13] See, e.g. E. R. Stettinius, Snr papers, U.Va.: Kent to Leffingwell, 1 Aug. 1919, box WY9; Stettinius to J. P. Morgan & Co., 2 Aug., box WY8; Stettinius to Celier, and to H. P. Davison, 2 Aug., box WY3.

[14] On hostility to Paish, see: House diary, 3 Jan. 1920, binder 17, EMHP. Doc. starting 'In consequence of unfortunate statements by Sir George Paish...', Jan. 1920; doc. starting 'A unique demonstration...', Jan. 1920, box 13, PMWP. Paish called on the US Ambassador, John W. Davis, who regarded his League bonds scheme as 'rather fanciful': diary, 2 Mar. 1920, box 103, file 102, 108, Davis papers, Yale. House also discussed international finance with Paish: House diary, 30 June, 59, EMHP. For Keynes's view of Paish as 'silly' and 'pathetic', see Keynes to Bonar Law, 10 Oct. 1922, L/22/60–2, KP.

[15] Box WY7, E.R. Stettinius, Snr papers, U.Va.

[16] The participants in Oct. were: Vissering, Kent, Keynes, Raphael Georges Lévy (Paris), Paul Warburg (New York), C. E. ter Meulen, J. van Vollenhoven, P. J. C. Testrode, and G. H. M. Delprat, of Amsterdam, with H. M. Moll as secretary. For the conferences, see: FI/5, EC/7/1/9, KP; Paul M. Warburg, 'History of the European Memorandum', box 14, PMWP. Minutes are in: box 46, Kent papers, Princeton (pp. 1–16 only); box 10, PMWP; see vol. 17, p. 128 ff; Ferguson, *Paper*, pp. 225–6.

[17] See, e.g. minutes of Oct. meeting, 5 (Warburg), 8 (Vissering), box 10, PMWP.

[18] Vol. 17, p. 129.

At the first meeting in Amsterdam, Vissering, Kent, Keynes, and others expounded their own remedies for Europe's troubles. Keynes proposed an international currency to facilitate international trade, possibly created under League auspices.[19] He declared that the opportunity to create such a currency was missed in Paris,[20] presumably a reference to the scheme suggested in the 4 June report, drafted by Keynes and Davis, on European finance. But Keynes's international currency proposal again attracted little support, not least for fear of inflation, and because US agreement was unlikely.[21] An important cleavage was between those such as Keynes who favoured using the League as a mechanism for international economic cooperation, and those opposed to doing so. Echoing the remedies he had promoted at Paris, and which would soon appear in *The Economic Consequences*, Keynes also proposed reduction of reparations, with priority to the devastated countries; a fund 'to aid the new countries'; cancellation of inter-Allied debt; capital levies in at least some countries; prevention of inflation through monetary restraint; and an international loan, with customs duties or payments due from Germany as security. Paul Warburg and Kent said that the USA would not join in Keynes's scheme, because most of the sacrifice would be asked from the USA, where taxes were already heavy, and cancellation would enormously affect the general good faith and character of loans in future.[22] Warburg and Kent agreed that 'Congress never would allow the creation of any new bonds to help Europe', but disagreed on how ready private American investors might be to invest in Europe.

A scheme drafted by Keynes and Warburg (with Lévy, concerned about France's interests, joining in) envisaged renewed international lending, public and private, with the borrowing countries free to decide how to use the funds.[23] Keynes's draft proposed too specific a commitment to intergovernmental lending for his colleagues, including Warburg, who foresaw American opposition[24] (the memorial as finally agreed did not specifically propose such *public* lending).[25] The amended draft proposal was remitted to a second Amsterdam meeting planned for 2 November, including prominent figures from Switzerland and Scandinavia and, Keynes hoped, Robert Brand.[26]

[19] Minutes of Oct. meeting, 2, 12–13, box 10, PMWP.

[20] Minutes of Oct. meeting, 9, box 10, PMWP.

[21] Glass said an international currency would need legislation, which Congress at present would refuse: Glass to M. K. C. Adams, 1 Nov. 1919, box 429, CGP.

[22] Minutes of Oct. meeting, 10, 15, box 10, PMWP.

[23] Vol. 17, p. 129; PMWP (box 13) contains drafts, and box 14 part of a draft in Keynes's hand. It starts 'When once the expenditure...', as at vol. 17, p. 139, but differs from the final version. See also 'History', box 14, PMWP.

[24] See Warburg to Hoover, 13 Jan. 1920, box 10, PMWP.

[25] See vol. 17, pp. 140–1.

[26] Minutes of Oct. meeting, 17–19, box 10, PMWP; see below. 'History', 8–9, box 14, PMWP.

Keynes wanted the document completed at the second conference to be submitted to the League.[27] It was also agreed that Dutch participants would prepare a plan for international barter, though Keynes did not welcome such a scheme.[28]

While in Amsterdam, Keynes also saw Melchior, who had come from Hamburg at Keynes's request to see him. Keynes's notes of their discussion refer to 'Pressure of pop[ulation] from the East—Anti-Semitism' and 'Need of Relations with Russia'.[29] Keynes was then writing *The Economic Consequences*, and it may be that his emphasis there both on population and on Germany's need to restore its relations with Russia (and perhaps also references to Polish anti-Semitism) were influenced by Melchior—though his 'grand scheme' in April had already highlighted Europe's difficulty in sustaining its population.[30] In England between the two Amsterdam meetings, Keynes rallied support for the Amsterdam scheme with Cecil, Arthur Salter (to become general secretary of the Reparation Commission), Bradbury, Andrew McFadyean, and Brand.[31]

The amended Warburg–Keynes document was discussed at the meeting in Amsterdam on 2–3 November, at which Keynes was present.[32] The most important outcome was agreement on a final text of this 'memorial', for which further signatures would be sought, before submitting it to the League Council.[33] It stressed the catastrophic dangers urgently threatening, the importance of individual effort and the restoration of normal conditions, and the need for international cooperation, which would in turn 'promote the world spirit for which the League stands'. The memorial urged the League to invite leading governments to convene an urgent meeting of financial representatives to consider the economic crisis and its remedy. It drew attention to the danger of inflation, urging the balancing of budgets, without excessive taxation; and the importance of Germany's not being 'rendered bankrupt', and of reparation demands being within Germany's capacity to pay without engendering 'a spirit of despair and revolt'. It asked: '[S]hould not the United States and England consider how far they can ease the burden of their Entente

----

[27] Vol. 17, p. 129.

[28] Minutes of October meeting, 25, box 10, PMWP.

[29] EC/7/1/10, KP; see vol. 10, pp. 427–9; vol. 17, pp. 130–6.

[30] See, e.g. vol. 2, p. 183 ff; see Keynes to FAK, 2 Oct. 1919, PP/45/168/10/19, KP; vol. 16, p. 433.

[31] Vol. 17, p. 136; vol. 10, p. 130; Salter to Keynes, 21 Oct. 1919, FI/5/15, KP. On Brand, see 'History', 14–15, box 14, PMWP. FI/5/103–8, KP.

[32] Marc Wallenberg was amongst the new participants: vol. 17, p. 141. See Keynes to Warburg, 20 Oct. 1919, box 10, PMWP; Vissering's opening speech: 2 Nov. 1919, at box 24, Kent papers, Princeton; for Keynes on Wallenberg, L/19/25, PP/45/168/13/148–50, KP.

[33] The text is at vol. 17, pp. 136–41.

debtors either by abandoning interest charges or by cancelling a portion of the [debts]?' The memorial also urged the need for working capital to restart the European economy, and a more comprehensive scheme than could be done through normal banking channels. This international cooperation in the granting of credit should involve no government control of trade, should encourage 'the supply of credit and the development of trade through normal channels', and should attract 'the real savings of individuals', to avoid inflation. It required the best obtainable security.

The US Treasury made clear its opposition to the memorial from the moment Kent (to Warburg and Keynes's regret) sought its approval before he signed.[34] Carter Glass wanted European financial difficulties kept separate from the League, which was facing strong opposition in the Senate. He believed that some, at least, of the memorialists were promoting self-interest at American expense. The administration opposed further inter-governmental lending, and believed the crucial task was the revival of European private enterprise, free of governmental control, through private finance.[35]

Warburg saw Davis and House, and sought to have the administration *not* oppose the memorial.[36] Warburg believed some relief of France's debt to the USA could be used to gain France's 'active cooperation in putting Europe on a basis that will insure future peace and economic conditions in which orderly society may be preserved'. Warburg claimed that the memorial did not necessarily mean there would need to be US government, rather than private, lending. Davis was unmoved.[37] As a result of his discussions, Warburg suggested and it was decided, despite Keynes's opposition, to present the memorial to the different governments rather than the League.[38] This was done on (or soon after) 15 January 1920; but not before further complications.

There was a strong body of signatures for the memorial in all countries where they were sought, except France. British signatories included Cecil, Asquith, Reginald McKenna, Lord Bryce, Lord Inchcape, and Brand. Keynes was not among them, for he decided, after consulting Brand and Cecil, that his book made it unhelpful for him to sign, not least because the book's depiction of Wilson could alienate American support.[39]

[34] Vol. 17, pp. 141–2; Warburg to Davis, 17 Nov. 1919, box 10, PMWP; Glass to Rathbone, 13 Nov. 1919, box 101–2, CGP.

[35] 'History', 17, box 14, PMWP; see, e.g. Davis to Warburg, 7 Jan. 1920, box 10, PMWP.

[36] Warburg letters to Davis, 17, 19, 20, and 26 Nov. 1919, box 10, PMWP; House diary, 20 Nov. 1919, binder 16, 65; 3 Jan. 1920, binder 17, 3, EMHP; see also box 114a, EMHP.

[37] Davis to Warburg, 26 Nov. 1919, box 10, PMWP.

[38] Vol. 17, pp. 144–7; 'History', 17–20, box 14, PMWP.

[39] See vol. 17, pp. 148–9; Brand to Keynes, 7 Nov. 1919, FI/5/134; 23 Dec. 1919, FI/5/198, KP; Cecil to Keynes, 31 Dec. 1919, FI/5/211–16; 6 Jan. 1920, FI/5/217–22, KP.

Warburg easily obtained several prominent American supporters for the memorial.[40] These included Hoover, A. W. Mellon (Treasury Secretary, 1921–32), J. P. Morgan, Elihu Root, and Robert L. Brookings. In December, the Secretary of the Interior, Franklin K. Lane, told Warburg:[41]

What you say about Vienna's distress is all too true. I have talked much with Hoover about it. I do not see any possibility of doing anything. Congress is as tight as a clam. We have become entirely nationalistic and selfish. *Poor, poor* people! What a *sad, sad* future is theirs! You cannot be justified in giving them any real word of cheer.

Despite this sympathetic warning, Warburg thought that the Treasury might not oppose the memorial if the objectionable references—to the League and to debts—were changed.[42] By early January, it was clear he had underestimated their objections, which were to the whole memorial.[43] The Treasury's concern arose partly because the European text of the memorial included a paragraph which 'might be construed as an invitation for the cancellation of Inter-Allied debts, such as urged in the recently published book by Mr. J. Maynard Keynes'.[44]

After talks with Davis, Glass, and Leffingwell, Warburg (still hoping to overcome Treasury objections) said that he was proposing the deletion of the memorial's reference to easing the burden of existing debts, and that the memorial be addressed to the Reparation Commision rather than to individual governments.[45] It was too late for the Europeans to change their text; but the US memorial was changed to ask the US Chamber of Commerce (not the government) to designate representatives for the conference, and to eliminate the references to relieving the war debt burden.[46] Hoover, Warburg, and other signatories stressed that the proposed loan was to be on 'a clear-cut business basis that will appeal to the American investor'.[47] Warburg also said that the memorial's proposed loan would be placed in several countries, cooperating together, not solely in the USA.[48]

---

[40] 'History', 15, box 14, PMWP. It appears from box 14, PMWP, that few of those Warburg asked to sign declined.

[41] Lane to Warburg, 15 Dec. 1919, box 10, PMWP.

[42] See 'History', 17–18, 20–1, box 14, PMWP.

[43] Davis to Warburg, 7 Jan. 1920, box 10, PMWP.

[44] Document beginning 'While Secretary Glass' letter …', 30 Jan. 1920, 2, box 14, PMWP; vol. 17, p. 139, para. beginning 'The world's balance …'

[45] Warburg to Davis, 12 Jan. 1920, box 10, PMWP.

[46] See page starting 'In consequence of …', box 13, PMWP; Warburg et al. to Tumulty, 14 Jan. 1920; reply, 17 Jan. box 10, PMWP.

[47] Hoover to Warburg, 10 Jan. 1920; see also Warburg to Hoover, 18? Jan.; Warburg to Davis, 15 Jan., box 10, PMWP; Paper headed 'A unique demonstration …', box 13, PMWP.

[48] Warburg to Davis, 12 Jan. 1920, box 10, PMWP.

Despite signals that the Treasury neither approved nor expressed objection to the memorandum,[49] on 28 January 1920 Glass sent to the US Chamber of Commerce a long letter effectively rejecting the memorandum. Glass's attitude was largely based on the view that European economic recovery would be quickest if private enterprise was left to itself. Glass said that the Treasury agreed with the memorial on the need for increased production, reduced consumption, balanced budgets, currency and credit deflation, and 'prompt and proper determinations by the Reparations Commission which will make possible the resumption of industrial life in Germany and the restoration of trade with Germany'. However, the USA had already given considerable aid to Europe.

The governments of the world must now get out of banking and trade. Loans from government to government not only involve additional taxes or borrowing by the lending government with the inflation attendant thereon, but also a continuance by the borrowing government of control over private activities which only postpones sound solutions of the problems.

Further credits must come through private channels. The great problems were not susceptible of solution by any comprehensive plan, but depended on action by the European governments themselves—to allow gold shipments, to reduce budget deficits (e.g. through disarmament and tax increases), to reduce their claims on Germany to what she could pay, and to encourage the resumption of industrial life. The adoption of such measures should lead to the private investment that Europe needed.[50]

Glass' *Annual Report* for 1919 asserted that Europe's need for financial assistance, though great, had been much exaggerated, because 'we are prone to overlook the vast recuperative power inherent in any country'. The principal factor working to relieve Europe's foreign exchange problems was the inevitable curtailment of her imports and expansion of her exports stimulated by weak exchange rates. That is, there were strong forces of self-equilibration that simply needed time (and political settlement) to work.[51]

An aspect of Glass' letter that gained attention in Europe was the call for 'the movement of goods, of investment securities and, in default of goods or securities, then of gold into this country from Europe', and for the European countries to lift their embargoes on the export of gold. In February 1920, John W. Davis, the US Ambassador in London, listed Glass' statement as a

[49] Note of call, 16 Jan. 1920, box 10, PMWP; Meyer diary, 19 Jan. 1920, box 201, Eugene Meyer papers, LOC.

[50] Glass to H. L. Ferguson, 28 Jan. 1920, box 10, PMWP; see Glass to Warburg, 29 Jan., box 10, PMWP.

[51] Extract, box 10, PMWP.

major reason for unfavourable British sentiment toward America: it was clearly impossible for Europe to send gold to America, and Glass' opposition to 'further governmental loans is exhibited as callousness to Europe's needs'.[52]

Warburg, too, believed that Glass' attitude of 'coolness and aloofness' had 'deplorable' results. He told Leffingwell that Glass did not recognize the difficulties of putting private foreign lending back on an attractive basis, and the need for special security.[53] Warburg nonetheless stressed that the free market views of the memorial coincided with Glass' letter, that the US signatories recognized that cancellation of debt and further US loans were not practical, and that the proposed conference would be unofficial.[54] Warburg believed such a conference could have been 'of the very highest importance at this time when the world is moving without any concerted financial or economic leadership'.

Leffingwell's reply crystallized the issues succinctly.[55] 'It was principally because the memorial made the fatal mistake of reviving the hope of a "comprehensive plan" for having somebody else pay Europe's bills—a hope doomed to certain disappointment—that it was necessary for the Treasury to speak out.' Whereas the memorialists wanted a plan under American leadership, the world must move 'without any concerted financial or economic leadership' because only 'the government of a country can impose its taxes or limit its expenditures'.

The British Government's reply to the memorial was sympathetic, but showed how much Britain now saw itself dependent on the USA for economic leadership. Austen Chamberlain wrote that the British Government agreed that grave economic and social dangers confronted the whole world.[56] Given the importance placed by the memorial on international cooperation, it was obvious that the US government's attitude 'must gravely affect the influence and even the utility' of the proposed conference. While Britain would take part in a 'really representative' conference, it was opposed to further intergovernmental lending, with certain exceptions such as government credits to Austria and Poland to avert famine and restart industrial life.

His Majesty's Government felt compelled publicly to state in November last that, however desperate the need, they could not participate in measures of relief unless they were assured of the co-operation of the Government of the United States of

---

[52] Davis diary, 11 Feb. 1920, box 13, folder 102, 108, John W. Davis papers, Yale.

[53] Warburg to Leffingwell, 4 Feb. 1920, box 10, PMWP.

[54] Document beginning 'While Secretary Glass' letter...', 30 Jan. 1920, box 14, PMWP; see also Leffingwell to Warburg, 2 Feb., box 10, PMWP. On the importance of official support, see Brand to Warburg, 16 Jan., box 10, PMWP.

[55] Leffingwell to Warburg, 11 Feb. 1920, box 10, PMWP.

[56] Chamberlain to Brand, 11 Feb. 1920, copy in box 10, PMWP.

America to an extent which would make it certain that this country would not be called upon to incur additional expenditure in the United States of America. The movements of the foreign exchanges since November last emphasise the difficulty.

Efforts to use Chamberlain's letter to persuade Glass' successor as Treasury Secretary, David Franklin Houston, to give leadership towards European rehabilitation failed.[57] Hoover was 'intensely distressed' that the memorial/ conference question had become so confused, and thought that little could be gained from pursuing it.[58]

By the end of January 1920, if not before, Keynes also had 'no great hopes of any adequate results' from the memorial. Glass' reaction confirmed 'that the Americans are determined to do nothing', and the French situation was 'very unsatisfactory':

All this makes it increasingly probable that things will have to get worse before they can get better. After all the situation is primarily a reflection of the fact that several European countries are living beyond their means. Yet any attempt on the part of governments to reduce the standard of life is politically impossible.[59]

Keynes believed that resolving this impasse required the joint action of the major economies, but especially the USA.

The memorialists recognized the existence of international economic inter-dependence. They believed that the international economy needed management. They saw the USA as a power capable, if it so chose, of creating and sustaining the new order, or, at least, of exercising decisive leadership in that direction. That the USA's decisive role was recognized by the British Government was also clear from Chamberlain's letter. But the USA chose not to play the role of leader. Its refusal was clear in Glass and Leffingwell's letters. That the Democratic administration was constrained by a Republican Senate does not explain its rejection of the memorial. Before his physical collapse in September 1919, Wilson had shown little sign of promoting international economic action. Some of the signatories of the Amsterdam memorial became members of the Harding and Coolidge administrations, and Hoover was President from 1929 to 1933.

The question that remained for the memorialists after the US refusal was whether collective action was possible in America's absence, and whether it could achieve the purpose of the memorialists. In practice, the absence of American leadership was reduced as the USA slowly became more involved in

---

[57] Warburg to Houston, 3 Mar. 1920; Warburg to Leffingwell, 4 Mar., box 10, PMWP.
[58] Hoover to Warburg, 22 Mar. 1920, box 10, PMWP; see Warburg to Hoover, 4 Mar., box 10, PMWP.
[59] Vol. 17, p. 150.

Europe's economic affairs, especially after the Dawes Plan. This increased American role was partly a product of private international economic diplomacy, in which some of the leading figures (such as Kent, Warburg, Dawes, and Young) were Americans. Amsterdam thus proved to be an early exercise in a new private diplomacy within the international elite of financiers and financial experts that was to be important in the 1920s. For example, Kent, Sir William Goode, and others were active in 1920 in unofficial or semi-official capacities in seeking a neutral powers' credit scheme for Austria: Goode described these efforts to Keynes as 'the practical application of your international manifesto'.[60] These talks were part of the process leading to the Austrian reconstruction scheme of 1923.[61] Recollecting 'the stages of progress made from one economic conference to another, culminating in the writing of the Dawes Plan', Paul Warburg later wrote that 'in this progress the first work done by the small group that met in Amsterdam played a useful and historic part—even though history will forget all about it'.[62] Keynes's involvement has received little attention.[63]

4.1.1 Cambridge Meeting, 20–21 December 1919

On 20 and 21 December 1919, a meeting of British civil servants, politicians, and academics was held at King's College, Cambridge, to discuss European rehabilitation. Chaired by Zimmern, participants included Keynes, Blackett (of the Treasury), Angell, Hubert Henderson, and Salter. The conference report[64] suggests that, though some signs of hope for Europe were identified, participants believed that Europe needed external credit. They saw no sign of it from the USA. There was agreement on the need to curb inflation, but dispute on whether it was possible to restore the gold standard. Discussion of an international loan included a proposal that it be combined with 'a new Unit of Account', on which '[i]nternational contracts, import duties, etc., would be based'.[65] The conference report does not attribute views to individuals; but, given the similarity between this proposal and Keynes's at Paris and Amsterdam, it is likely that Keynes was the, or at least an, advocate of this

---

[60] Goode to Keynes, 26 Feb. 1920, L/20/26–7, KP; see also RT/23/77, KP; Kent to Vissering, 28 Jan. 1920, box 28, Kent papers, Princeton.

[61] See vol. 18, pp. 176–7. On this private financial diplomacy, incl. over Austria, see also K. Burk, *Morgan Grenfell, 1938–1988* (Oxford, 1989) pp. 135–45.

[62] 'History', 22, box 14, PMWP.

[63] For example, Harrod, *Life*, pp. 338–9; Skidelsky, *Hopes*, p. 382; cf. Moggridge, *Biography*, pp. 354–6.

[64] FI/4, KP.

[65] FI/4/13–14, KP.

scheme at this meeting. The report says: 'It was agreed that the lending Governments must attach conditions in making the loans to the borrowing Governments as to expenditure, as to reforming their internal currency system and as to making Budgets balance.'[66]

4.2 *THE ECONOMIC CONSEQUENCES OF THE PEACE*

By this time, *The Economic Consequences* had burst upon the world. It argued: First, the Treaty was dishonest in breaking the Allies' pre-Armistice undertaking to Germany to base the peace on the principles enunciated by President Wilson. This undertaking permitted reparations, but not to the extent that they were now demanded. Second, the German economy was being so damaged, and the reparations demands were so great, that there was no way Germany could meet them. To the extent that she tried, her people would be long impoverished, and Britain would be hurt by her export competition. To pay reparations, Germany must earn an export surplus, reducing her imports and increasing her exports (in what goods? to what markets? Keynes asked). Thus, whether Germany tried to pay or not, political relations within Europe would be more and more embittered, and the door would be open for revolution.[67] Given the economic unity of Europe, a stable peace depended on the reconstruction of the European economic system, in which Germany was a central support. To 're-establish life' and 'heal wounds' required 'the magnanimity which the wisdom of antiquity approved in victors',[68] not a Carthaginian peace.

As remedies, *The Economic Consequences* proposed revision of the Treaty to reduce the reparations demands, to moderate provisions on coal and iron, and to create a free trade union; the settlement of inter-Ally indebtedness; an international loan, and currency reorganization; and the revival of German trade with Russia. Keynes predicated the adoption of his remedies on the election of new governments in the major states.[69] Though seemingly unrealistic,[70] McFadyean argued that this judgement was vindicated by subsequent events.[71]

---

[66] FI/4/16, KP.

[67] See, e.g. vol. 2, pp. 158–9; see also vol. 17, pp. 372–3.

[68] Vol. 2, p. 16; see also, e.g. pp. 92, 165, 174.

[69] Vol. 2, pp. 162, 165; see also vol. 18, p. 34.

[70] See *The Spectator*, 20 Dec. 1919.

[71] A. McFadyean, *Reparation Revisited* (London, 1930), p. 2.

Keynes gave colourful—some say unfair[72]—caricatures of the Big Four at Paris.[73] He did 'not reproach Clemenceau for his frank desire to intimidate and humiliate Germany', but blamed the others 'above all, Woodrow Wilson, for agreeing to [that] under the pretence that they were establishing democracy, freedom and economic reconstruction in Europe'.[74] *The Economic Consequences* was later criticized as greatly overestimating how free public opinion left the Big Four to adopt a magnanimous peace.[75] But Keynes believed that public opinion could be changed. *The Economic Consequences* aimed to change it,[76] and did: it is generally agreed that 'Keynes more than any other man helped to create a climate of opinion in Britain and in other countries highly critical of the Treaty of Versailles'.[77]

Let us consider several key aspects of the book: how its ideas about the economic causes of disorder led Keynes back to the classical liberal doctrine that free trade promotes peace; how its remedies were essentially restorative, but required internationally agreed action by states; how it differed from Angell's *The Great Illusion*, but shared much with other post-war writings and with ideas widely argued at Paris; how it reflected Keynes's idealism; and its stress on the need for US help.

4.2.1 Population, Trade, Inflation, Privation, and Peace

The fundamental argument of *The Economic Consequences* is that the economy of Europe operates as a single, interdependent unit, and that it is fragile; that to impoverish Germany, its central support, is to impoverish Europe; and that such impoverishment could well have disastrous political repercussions leading to revolution and war. As Keynes encapsulated it later, given that the claims against Germany were 'impossible of payment', 'the economic solidarity of Europe was so close that the attempt to enforce these claims might ruin everyone'.[78]

The Economic Consequences clearly suggests a link between trade and peace. Keynes argued that obstacles to trade (including currency disorder and

[72] For example, É. Mantoux, *The Carthaginian Peace* (London, 1946), p. 46; see also Thirlwall, *Laissez-Faire*, p. 105; cf. P. Renouvin and J.-B. Duroselle, *Introduction to the History of International Relations* (London, 1968), pp. 282–3.

[73] Vol. 2, ch. 3; vol. 10, chs. 1, 2, and 3.

[74] Thirlwall, *Laissez-Faire*, p. 105; see vol. 2, pp. 32–3.

[75] Thirlwall, *Policy Adviser*, p. 82; see American critics, discussed below.

[76] See vol. 2, pp. 183, 189.

[77] Thirlwall, *Policy Adviser*, p. 80; see also, e.g. Moggridge, *Keynes*, p. 59; A. J. P. Taylor, *The Origins of the Second World War* (London, 1973 [1961]), p. 72.

[78] Vol. 3, pp. 68–9.

inflation) lead to impoverishment, especially because of the need for trade to sustain the population; that privation leads to domestic disorder and extremism (either revolution or reaction); and that these lead to international hostility, perhaps war. Conversely, it seems, free trade promotes prosperity; prosperity promotes domestic order and moderation; and these promote international amity.[79] There is also a vague implication that trade promotes 'the solidarity of man'.[80]

Keynes stressed the need for European countries to trade to feed their populations. As population pressure figured prominently in Keynes's thought over many years, some elaboration is warranted. According to *The Economic Consequences*, 'The great events of history are often due to secular changes in the growth of population and other fundamental economic causes, which, escaping by their gradual character the notice of contemporary observers, are attributed to the follies of statesmen or the fanaticism of atheists.' Thus 'the disruptive powers of excessive national fecundity may have played a greater part' in producing the Russian revolution than Lenin or Czar Nicholas, 'the power of ideas or the errors of autocracy'.[81]

In his 1914 Oxford paper on population, Keynes had adopted an idea which he was to repeat in *The Economic Consequences* and to defend vigorously against Sir William Beveridge in 1922–3: population growth in the New World, especially in the USA, in the late nineteenth and early twentieth centuries, by increasing domestic demand for foodstuffs, raised the cost, and destabilized the certainty of supply, of food to Europe.[82] Keynes asserted that the ratio of exchange between industrial and agricultural products, so favourable to the industrial powers in the late nineteenth century, may have been moving against them since around 1900. Since Europe could not feed itself,[83] these effects threatened to unleash the Malthusian 'devil' which had been 'chained up and out of sight' for half a century.[84] As he had at the PPC, Keynes argued in *The Economic Consequences* that the delicate economic machinery which enabled Europe to feed her growing population before 1914 was shattered by the war.[85] This created one of the great problems for

[79] See, e.g. vol. 2, pp. 62–3, 162. Keynes used the phrase 'peace and prosperity': e.g. vol. 2, p. 169; vol. 3, p. 25; cf. p. 2. On trade and prosperity, see, e.g. vol. 17, pp. 256, 271.

[80] See vol. 2, pp. 170, 181, 187.

[81] Vol. 2, pp. 8–9; cf. vol. 17, p. 436; vol. 19, p. 437.

[82] Vol. 2, pp. 14–15; see also vol. 17, p. 61. See Toye, 'Keynes on population and economic growth', and *Keynes on population*, where Keynes's view is challenged.

[83] For example, vol. 2, pp. 15, 144.

[84] Vol. 2, pp. 5–6. On the ratio of exchange, see vol. 19, pp. 125–37. The ratio of real interchange had moved favourably for the USA: vol. 19, p. 135.

[85] Vol. 2, pp. 7, 15. Keynes stressed pre-war precariousness: see, e.g. vol. 19, pp. 120, 125, 141; vol. 16, p. 433.

a Peace aimed at 're-establish[ing] life'.[86] The populations of Germany and Austria-Hungary had provided the military strength of those countries, and now 'if deprived of the means of life, remain a hardly less danger to European order'.[87] Starvation, already evident in Russia and Austria, posed a grave threat. 'Men will not always die quietly.' Keynes feared that 'in their distress' the starving 'may overturn the remnants of organisation, and submerge civilisation itself in their attempts to satisfy desperately the overwhelming needs of the individual.'[88] Action to sustain Europe's population was urgent.

Keynes wrote: 'If we aim deliberately at the impoverishment of Central Europe, vengeance... will not limp. Nothing can then delay for very long that final civil war between... reaction and... revolution, before which the horrors of the late German war will fade into nothing...'[89] Keynes was careful not to claim that privation, even starvation, necessarily produced revolution. He recognized that men can suffer greatly before 'the limit of human endurance is reached at last', and the sufferer is stirred from lethargy to desperate destructive action.[90] There are thus stages of human reaction to economic privation, though Keynes had not worked out a consistent account of this. Elsewhere, he depicted torpor and action not as sequential stages but as alternatives.[91]

At the time of writing, Keynes did not predict revolution, even in the face of starvation. But the risk was there, either of reaction or of Bolshevism in Germany, possibly heralding 'revolution everywhere'.[92] European civilization itself was in danger. Keynes raised the spectre of 'a new Napoleonic domination' arising from 'a victory of reaction in Germany', and stressed the need to sustain, not humiliate, the 'moderate forces of order' in Germany.[93]

Keynes agreed with the aphorism, attributed to Lenin, that 'the best way to destroy the capitalist system was to debauch the currency'. The arbitrary redistribution of wealth resulting from rampant inflation undermined security and confidence in the equity of the existing distribution, and left contractual relations disordered. Those who gained windfalls were hated, by the impoverished bourgeosie as well as by the proletariat, as 'profiteers'; and inflationist governments encouraged this hatred. But the 'profiteers' were in fact 'the entrepreneur class of capitalists, that is to say, the active and constructive element' in capitalist society. Their loss of self-confidence further undermined the stability of the capitalist system. Ultimately inflation led to reduced production and trade, and to 'the waste and inefficiency of barter'.[94]

---

[86] Vol. 2, p. 16; see also, e.g. Keynes to H. N. Brailsford, 1 Jan. 1921, CO/1/95–6, KP.
[87] Vol. 2, pp. 7–8.   [88] Vol. 2, p. 144.   [89] Vol. 2, p. 170.
[90] Vol. 2, pp. 144, 158–9; see also p. 188.   [91] Vol. 2, p. 144.
[92] Vol. 2, p. 184; see also, e.g. pp. 60, 150.   [93] Vol. 2, p. 184.   [94] Vol. 2, pp. 148–52.

Keynes regarded the dire economic condition of Europe and the inability of Europe, especially Germany and Austria, to sustain existing populations under the terms of the treaties as 'the fundamental problem in front of us, before which questions of territorial adjustment and the balance of European power are insignificant'.[95] Repeatedly, Keynes attacked the Treaty-makers and the Treaty for 'excessive concentration on political objects'.[96] The real issues were financial and economic.[97] Keynes believed that, in an interdependent Europe, the security of one state was not advanced by the destruction of others.[98]

Keynes criticized the Treaty both for the damage it did, and for the opportunity it missed to provide for the economic rehabilitation of Europe: it contained 'nothing to make the defeated Central empires into good neighbours, nothing to stabilise the new states of Europe, nothing to reclaim Russia; nor does it promote in any way a compact of economic solidarity amongst the Allies themselves'.[99] Keynes wished to restore, and perhaps increase, the high degree of freedom of trade that existed before 1914. The barter that was developing he compared unfavourably with 'the former almost perfect simplicity of international trade'.[100] In proposing the renewal of trade with Russia, he said that, regardless of whether communism survived there, 'the revival of trade, of the comforts of life and of ordinary economic motive are not likely to promote the extreme forms of those doctrines of violence and tyranny which are the children of war and of despair'.[101] Keynes proposed that a free trade union be established under League auspices of countries undertaking to impose no protectionist tariffs against other members.[102] Defeated powers and their successor states would be obliged to be members for ten years. 'A free trade union, comprising the whole of Central, Eastern, and south-eastern Europe, Siberia, Turkey, and (I should hope) the United Kingdom, Egypt, and India, might do as much for the peace and prosperity of the world as the League of Nations itself.' The union would retrieve some of the loss of economic efficiency resulting 'from the innumerable new political frontiers now created between greedy, jealous, immature, and economically incomplete, nationalist states.' Keynes wrote:[103]

In a regime of free trade and free economic intercourse it would be of little consequence that iron ore lay on one side of a political frontier, and labour, coal, and blast furnaces on the other. But as it is, men have devised ways to impoverish themselves and one another; and prefer collective animosities to individual happiness.

---

[95] Vol. 2, p. 146.　　[96] Vol. 2, p. xix.　　[97] Vol. 2, pp. 92, 95, 146.
[98] Vol. 2, p. xxi.　　[99] Vol. 2, p. 143.　　[100] Vol. 2, p. 59; see also p. 152.
[101] Vol. 2, p. 187.　　[102] Vol. 2, pp. 168–9.　　[103] Vol. 2, p. 62.

As we saw in Chapter 2, Keynes contrasted his scheme with 'the former German dream of Mittel-Europa': 'an economic system, to which everyone had the opportunity of belonging and which gave special privilege to none, is surely absolutely free from the objections of a privileged and avowedly imperialistic scheme of exclusion and discrimination'.[104]

In advocating a free trade union, and entrusting Germany with prosperity (including by reviving her role 'as a creator and organiser of wealth for her eastern and southern neighbours'),[105] Keynes urged acting on the belief 'that the prosperity and happiness of one country promotes that of others, [and] that the solidarity of man is not a fiction'—'even though the result disappoint us'.[106]

4.2.2 Keynes's Programme for Post-war Reconstruction

We have seen that Keynes and others denied that all the European economy needed was for private enterprise to be left alone to return Europe to work. *The Economic Consequences* repeated the need for international economic action, especially for an international loan, and expressed a further, vaguer hope for development of 'an economic council of Europe' under the League.[107] We may thus view its programme as being an early form of liberal institutionalism.

However, the remedies of *The Economic Consequences* were more modest than Keynes had suggested at Amsterdam (and presumably repeated in Cambridge in December 1919): there is no mention of an international currency, though a guarantee fund for currency reorganization is suggested.[108] Concerned with Europe's urgent needs, and perhaps recognizing that more radical changes would be even less likely of success, the programme of *The Economic Consequences* was fundamentally restorative.

Some of these points emerge crisply from comparing Keynes's drafts with the published book. A draft table of contents listed 'Currency Reform' second in a short list of 'Constructive Proposals':[109] it was far less prominent in the book. A draft declared that 'In a sense this is a reactionary programme since it aims at showing a way by which the present organisation of society can save itself'.[110] A draft preface declared the peace 'disastrous to the established order of Society throughout Europe'.[111] Keynes aimed to suggest 'too late it may be supposed and in vain, some means of amelioration and of safety for a kind of

---

[104] Vol. 2, p. 169.   [105] Vol. 2, p. 186.   [106] Vol. 2, p. 170.
[107] Vol. 2, p. 138; see below.   [108] Vol. 2, pp. 182–3.   [109] EC/7/1/1, KP.
[110] EC/7/1/2, KP.   [111] EC/7/1/5–6, KP; cf. vol. 2, p. xvii; vol. 16, p. 433.

civilisation, which, in spite of its mean imperfections and recent tragical consequences, is still the best next starting point, from which may grow humane improvements and a new social evolution for Western Europe.' That Keynes did not use these sentences may be because they were more critical of existing society, and more radical, than he thought politic. That he wrote them suggests that he was, already in 1919, seeking a 'middle way' between laissez-faire and Marxism: these unused draft sentences presage Keynes's later thought more fully than does the published book. They support Schumpeter's claim that, in its underlying vision, *The Economic Consequences* foreshadowed *The General Theory*.[112]

The book described the European economy before the war as a fragile but effective machine, and aimed to restore it.[113] Keynes's proposals were restorative despite the fragility of the pre-1914 system, and despite the fact that it did not preserve peace. Seeing economic imperialism and exclusionism as significant in causing the First World War, Keynes sought to create a purer free trade system than had existed in 1914, and to reverse the trend to economic and political nationalism. As he was again to do in the 1930s, Keynes asserted that capitalism itself was in danger,[114] and proposed means of saving it. It is true that *The Economic Consequences* asserted that a 'new age' was emerging, and a 'new way' in Britain;[115] but these references were vague, and Keynes made no specific proposals about them.

Keynes's restoration programme was based on classical economics. It included stabilization of exchange rates (whose fluctuations Keynes saw as highly damaging), sound finance (balanced budgets to fight inflation), and free trade.[116] Yet it differed from laissez-faire thinkers in urging a concerted programme of international action.

4.2.3 Keynes's Originality

The Economic Consequences was, in a sense, a post-war exposition of the philosophy underlying Angell's pre-war best-seller, *The Great Illusion*: that the economic interdependence of Europe is such that no state can truly profit from war. In 1919 and after, Angell,[117] Keynes, and other writers such as J. L. Garvin,[118] argued that the German economy was crucial to the European

---

[112] Schumpeter, *Ten Great Economists*, p. 268.   [113] See, e.g. vol. 2, p. 1.
[114] Vol. 2, pp. 148 ff, 179.   [115] Vol. 2, p. 161.
[116] For example, vol. 2, pp. xxiii, 148 ff, 153–4, 178.
[117] N. Angell, *The Peace Treaty and the Economic Chaos of Europe* (London, 1919); *The Fruits of Victory* (London, 1921), much recycled in *Human Nature and the Peace Problem* (London, 1925).
[118] J. L. Garvin, *The Economic Foundations of Peace* (London, 1919).

economy.[119] Others pointed out the striking similarity between *The Economic Consequences* and Angell's *The Peace Treaty and the Economic Chaos of Europe*;[120] and Keynes praised Angell's *The Fruits of Victory*.[121] Angell clearly believed *The Great Illusion* and *The Economic Consequences* came from the same stable.[122]

There were, however, important differences between *The Economic Consequences* and *The Great Illusion*. As D. H. Robertson suggested in 1919, Keynes depicted political control of territory as economically significant, the European economy as extremely fragile, and British and German economic interests as competitive rather than cooperative in a way 'very different from... pre-war optimistic, free-trade, pacific philosophy' such as Angell's.[123] So Keynes did not share Angell's pre-war view, expounded in a chapter on 'The Indemnity Futility', that an indemnity necessarily harmed the recipient. The Ashley–Keynes memorandum had rejected that view; it was the magnitude of the indemnity against which *The Economic Consequences* protested. Angell subsequently claimed that his chapter, while clumsy, was more than vindicated by events; and he referred to Keynes, as others have subsequently, as if he were merely applying the analysis to 'the facts of the case'.[124]

Not sharing *The Great Illusion*'s view of a natural harmony of interests between states, Keynes in 1919 believed that interdependence needed to be managed. This belief was not evident in *The Great Illusion* (which predated the war-time growth of economic controls and damage to the international economy). Keynes did not set out his views on this fully in *The Economic Consequences*, the remedies of which were restorative. But it is clear that Keynes believed that institutional and policy changes were needed to make interdependence work. He was, of course, not alone in this view. We have seen that Hobson and Zimmern had advocated international economic organization, as did others, such as H. N. Brailsford and Garvin.[125] Indeed, Angell

[119] See, e.g. A. Crozier, *Appeasement and Germany's Last Bid for Colonies* (Basingstoke and London, 1988), p. 26.

[120] For example, H. Sanderson Furniss, review of Angell's *Peace Treaty* (London, 1919), *EJ*, 30 (1920), 85.

[121] Angell, *After All*, p. 153. Angell says it was *Fruits* Keynes was praising. Angell to Keynes, 20 Aug. 1920, L/20/56, KP; see also, e.g. Ashworth, *Creating International Studies*, p. 164n.

[122] See, e.g. Angell, *Human Nature*, pp. 40 n., 90, 108 n., 152, and *passim*.

[123] D. H. Robertson, review of *The Economic Consequences*, *EJ*, 30 (1920), 81; see also Robinson, 'Keynes', pp. 22–3.

[124] Norman Angell, *The Great Illusion—Now* (London, 1938 edn.) pp. 86–9, 108–10; see, e.g. Cornelia Navari, 'The great illusion revisited: the international theory of Norman Angell', *Review of International Studies*, 15 (1989), 350.

[125] For example, H. N. Brailsford, *The War of Steel and Gold* (London, 1914), pp. 310–14; Garvin, *Economic Foundations*.

himself after the war somewhat hesitantly advocated 'super-national control' of economic activities.[126]

It is evident from Chapter 3 that the essentials of Keynes's argument were much discussed at Paris, not least by American officials such as Davis, Dulles, Baruch, and Hoover. Keynes proposed in the book the remedies he (and others) had proposed at and after Paris,[127] including referring to various plans which had been advanced for an international loan.[128] Others, not least Angell and Hobson, were criticizing the Treaty on similar grounds to Keynes.[129] For all that its ideas were not original, it is a brilliant work,[130] which scorched its views into the public consciousness of many nations.

4.2.4 Idealism

The Economic Consequences explicitly contrasted Keynes's 'idealistic' approach with the 'realism' of Clemenceau, and acknowledged that Keynes's approach was based on hopes and expectations.[131] Keynes appealed to 'idealism' to avert the misfortunes he predicted.[132]

The realist or Carthaginian approach to peacemaking saw man as 'congenitally ordained to prey upon his fellows'[133] and European history as 'a perpetual prize-fight',[134] making French security dependent on crushing the aggressive Germany. The idealist or Keynesian approach saw 'humanity' and 'European civilisation struggling towards a new order',[135] with economic harmony more important to preserving peace than frontiers or the balance of power were,[136] prosperity likely to diminish power-political conflicts, and the wisest approach to Germany being to reintegrate her into the comity of Europe.[137] There were also two conflicting conceptions of justice. One said that 'reparation for wrongs inflicted is of the essence of justice'.[138] The other urged that that approach can be counterproductive, and that 'nations are not authorised ... to visit on the children of their enemies the misdoings of parents or of rulers'.[139]

[126] For example, N. Angell, *The Economic Functions of the League* (London, 1920) pp. 13–18; cf. Angell, *Peace Treaty*, pp. 98, 108 ff; Angell, *Fruits*, ch. 2.

[127] See vol. 16, p. 445.

[128] Vol. 2, p. 180.

[129] For Hobson, see D. Long, 'J. A. Hobson and Economic Internationalism', in Long and Wilson, *Thinkers*, pp. 164, 171–2.

[130] See Schumpeter, *Ten Great Economists*, pp. 266–7.

[131] For example, vol. 2, pp. 18, 23, 169, 170, 181.

[132] See, e.g. vol. 2, pp. xxii, 144.   [133] Mantoux, *Carthaginian Peace*, p. 180.

[134] Vol. 2, p. 22; see also p. 20.   [135] Vol. 2, p. 23.

[136] See vol. 2, pp. xix, 92, 146.   [137] Vol. 2, pp. 143, 170, 186–7; see vol. 17, pp. 372–3.

[138] Mantoux, *Carthaginian Peace*, p. 158.   [139] Vol. 2, p. 142; see also vol. 18, p. 178.

It was to explain how Clemenceau's realist peace substituted for the idealist peace of Wilson's Fourteen Points that Keynes depicted Wilson as a bamboozled Old Presbyterian.[140] Keynes depicted Clemenceau as a realist committed wholly to the interests of his nation, who saw human nature as unchanging, and the politics of power between France and Germany ('the two rivals for European hegemony') as inescapable. From this view, said Keynes, a demand for a Carthagian peace is inevitable, and a magnanimous peace would merely hasten the revival of the German threat. This was 'the policy of an old man' thinking of the past, not of the future.[141]

Adoption of the realist philosophy of Clemenceau would, in Keynes's view, lead to conflict: it would impoverish Europe, and would need to be enforced by military means. Adoption of the idealist philosophy, and restoring the economic solidarity of Europe and promoting it further through a free trade union, would promote peace. Keynes wanted to engender a 'moral solidarity' of Europe to match its 'economic solidarity'.[142]

Many of the basic beliefs of the inter-war idealists are evident in *The Economic Consequences*. The belief in the possibility of progress is clear in Keynes's references to 'hopes' and 'expectations' for a 'new age', perhaps 'a new world'.[143] There is a strong desire that relations between states be regulated by observance of law,[144] and that undertakings given be honoured. Despite his scepticism about its bias to the status quo, Keynes strongly supported the League.[145] Having regretted the power of the Reparation Commission as arbiter of the economic destiny of Central Europe, including Germany,[146] Keynes asked hopefully:[147]

Transferred to the League of Nations, an organ of justice and no longer of interest, who knows that by a change of heart and object the reparation commission may not yet be transformed from an instrument of oppression and rapine into an economic council of Europe, whose object is the restoration of life and of happiness, even in the enemy countries?

The notion of the League serving justice and not interests was a central idealist assumption which E. H. Carr savaged in *The Twenty Years Crisis*.[148]

There are many references in *The Economic Consequences* to the power of public opinion, another of the recurrent emphases of inter-war idealists.[149] Public opinion is sometimes seen as causing harm,[150] and to be in need of instruction. Providing such instruction was the object of the book.[151]

---

[140] Vol. 2, pp. 23–34.   [141] Vol. 2, pp. 20–3.   [142] See, e.g. vol. 2, p. 187.
[143] Vol. 2, p. 4.   [144] See, e.g. vol. 2, p. 187: 'illegal' blockade of Russia.
[145] Vol. 2, pp. 164–5.   [146] Vol. 2, pp. 133, 135–6.   [147] Vol. 2, p. 138.
[148] Carr, *Twenty Years' Crisis, passim.*   [149] See, e.g. Carr, ibid., p. 31 ff.
[150] For example, vol. 2, pp. 73, 76, 108, 183.   [151] For example, vol. 2, pp. xxii, 189.

4.2.5 Anglo-American Relations

The Economic Consequences contains many references to the dependence of Europe on the USA, both in the economic organization that had developed in the fifty years to 1914,[152] and in the immediate aftermath of the war, when US forgiveness of debts and further US lending were necessary for European reconstruction. In his depiction of Europe before the War, Keynes stressed that the prosperity of Europe depended on cheap food from, and returns on investment in, America, but this equilibrium between the Old World and the New was already under threat before 1914. Keynes asserted that without US financial assistance during the war, both before and after her entry into it, 'the Allies could never have won'. He declared, praising Hoover, that the US relief effort both prevented 'an immense amount of human suffering', and 'averted a widespread breakdown of the European system', in the first half of 1919.[153] This war finance and post-war relief created a European moral debt to the USA.

Keynes spoke of Wilson having real power in Europe because of European dependence on the USA, and—notwithstanding his concern at times about the USA dictating to Britain—regretted that he did not try to use US financial power to secure the Fourteen Points.[154] The Europeans' need for the magnanimity and generosity of America was, Keynes suggested, a strong case for Europeans being magnanimous to each other.[155] Keynes argued that, with France and Italy foolishly basing their budgets on expected reparation receipts, American help was needed to provide an alternative to excessive reparation demands. The USA, 'greatly at fault ... for having no constructive proposals whatever to offer to a suffering and distracted Europe', could, with such proposals, have obviated the reparations dishonesty.[156]

Keynes told readers of the French edition: 'This book was chiefly intended for English (and American) readers.'[157] In writing for American readers, Keynes was making 'an appeal to the generosity of the United States'.[158] In the case of the international loan, Keynes recognized that the USA would not help Europe unless Europe acted, not on the basis of hatred and nationalism, but on 'thoughts and hopes of the happiness and solidarity of the European family'. He wanted the USA to declare conditions on which she would give aid, which would necessarily favour those parties 'in each of the European countries [which] have espoused a policy of reconciliation'. Keynes recognized

---

[152] Vol. 2, p. 13 ff.   [153] Vol. 2, pp. 173–4.   [154] Vol. 2, pp. 24, 31.
[155] Vol. 2, pp. 92–3, 171, 173, 181.
[156] Vol. 2, p. 94. On Wilson's neglecting 'the collective wisdom of his lieutenants', see vol. 2, p. 28.
[157] Vol. 2, p. xix.   [158] Vol. 2, p. 171.

isolationist pressures in the USA, and urged that the USA instead 'interest herself in what may prove decisive issues for the progress and civilisation of all mankind'.[159]

4.3 CRITICISMS OF *THE ECONOMIC CONSEQUENCES*

Although initial reaction to *The Economic Consequences* was far more favourable than Keynes expected,[160] intense attack was soon to come.[161] The most substantial attack came decades later, in 1946, when Étienne Mantoux's passionate and polemical book *The Carthaginian Peace* renewed debate about *The Economic Consequences*.[162] Mantoux had distinguished supporters in R. C. K. Ensor,[163] Hugh Dalton,[164] and Jacob Viner[165]—and his father, Paul Mantoux, who had been interpreter at the PPC.[166] In 1951, Harrod's *Life* robustly defended Keynes.[167] Debate has continued to the present, with much recent scholarship critical of Keynes.[168]

In the writings of Mantoux and other critics of Keynes, three lines of argument stand out. The first is that Germany could have paid the reparations demanded.[169] One argument is that German recovery in the 1920s and rearmament in the 1930s showed what Germany could produce. To this it is replied that German output 'for the enjoyment of a foreign conqueror' would not match German output for German purposes;[170] that in the 1920s Germany received a large inflow of capital rather than losing capital in reparations, so her recovery did not show her capacity to pay reparations;[171]

---

[159] Vol. 2, pp. 181–2.

[160] See, e.g. Keynes to Murray, 26 Dec. 1919, box 44, fol. 143, G. Murray papers, Bodleian Library, Oxford; Keynes to JNK, 31 Dec. 1919, PP/45/168/13/158, KP.

[161] For example, *Parliamentary Debates*, House of Commons, 5th series, vol. 125, 12 Feb. 1920, cols. 290–302.

[162] See, e.g. A. Parker, 'Mantoux v. Keynes', *Lloyds Bank Review*, 3 (Jan. 1947), 1–20; see Parker-Viner correspondence, 1946–7, box 53, JVP.

[163] Mantoux, *Carthaginian Peace*, Intro. by Ensor, pp. v–vii.

[164] Dalton to P. Mantoux, 9 Aug. 1946, box 47, JVP.

[165] J. Viner, review of Mantoux, *Journal of Modern History*, 19 (1947), 69–70; see Viner's correspondence with É. and P. Mantoux, box 47, JVP.

[166] Foreword by P. Mantoux, in Mantoux, *Carthaginian Peace*, pp. ix–xiv.

[167] Harrod, *Life*, p. 323 ff. For adverse reaction, see P. Mantoux to Viner, 29 Apr. 1951; Viner to Mantoux, 9 May, box 47, JVP.

[168] For example, Boemeke et al., *The Treaty of Versailles*; Ferguson, *Pity*; MacMillan, *Peacemakers*.

[169] For example, Mantoux, *Carthaginian Peace*, p. 156.

[170] Vol. 16, p. 377; see M. Keynes, *Essays*, pp. 327–8.

[171] See, e.g., A. Parker to Viner, 9 Aug. 1946, box 53, JVP.

and that the claim that if 'planned appropriately, reparations could have been made out of a *rising* German national income'[172] assumed a Keynesian understanding of aggregate demand which did not exist in 1919. Mantoux also argued that German exactions from occupied territories during the Second World War showed that the problem of currency frontiers was not insoluble.[173] To this, it is replied that the transfer problem—how to remit payments abroad in gold or foreign currency—required Germany 'to pay out, by an excess of exports over imports, the sums demanded by the Allies', which required 'finding foreign buyers for the new goods';[174] that Mantoux did not show how this could be done;[175] and that Hitler's wartime exactions required an army of occupation.[176] Both Keynes and Mantoux realized that only strong measures would make Germany pay.[177] They differed partly on whether to exact reparations by force (as the French and Belgians tried), or whether this was counterproductive (as Keynes believed). The transfer problem, which Keynes debated with Ohlin and Rueff in 1929,[178] has been the subject of continuing debate.[179]

A second, 'realist', critique of *The Economic Consequences* argues that Keynes, in placing his hope for peace in the restoration of Europe's economic solidarity, failed to understand that international politics is inherently a struggle for power, and that prudent statesmanship should generally seek a balance of power; that Keynes failed to see that Germany was inherently expansionist and aggressive, so that a magnanimous peace would merely have hastened the recurrence of military conflict; and that consequently he disregarded, or misunderstood, the needs of French security.[180]

Restoring the economic solidarity of Europe through a magnanimous peace would not have guaranteed peace, as it had not prevented war in 1914. But it could have been combined with political provisions to ensure a balance of power. Preference for a magnanimous peace over a Carthaginian

---

[172] Thirlwall, *Policy Adviser*, p. 119; T. Balogh, *Unequal Partners*, ii (Oxford, 1963), pp. 136–9.

[173] Mantoux, *Carthaginian Peace*; pp. 125–6; Ensor and A. J. P. Taylor agreed with Mantoux: see Mantoux, p. vi; Taylor, *Origins*, p. 70.

[174] Harrod, *Life*, pp. 323–4.

[175] See Mantoux, *Carthaginian Peace*, pp. 117–26.

[176] See Harrod, *Life*, pp. 324–5.

[177] See Mantoux, *Carthaginian Peace*, p. 156.

[178] Vol. 11, pp. 451–80. The debate is at *EJ*, 39 (1929), 1–7, 172–82, 388–408; see also, e.g. L/K/8–16, KP.

[179] For example, Paul Samuelson, 'The Transfer Problem and Transport Costs', *EJ*, 62 (1952), 278–304; H. G. Johnson, 'The Classical Transfer Problem: An Alternative Formulation', *Economica*, 42 (1975), 20–31; D. C. McIntosh, 'Mantoux versus Keynes', *EJ*, 87 (1977), 765–7; Thirlwall, *Policy Adviser*, pp. 119–24; Keylor in Boemeke et al., *Treaty of Versailles*, p. 502; see also Balogh to Viner, 12 Dec. 1929, box 21, JVP.

[180] See, e.g. Thirlwall, *Policy Adviser*, pp. 97, 111.

one requires the counterfactual argument that had such a peace been adopted, economic prosperity and political stability (or something far closer to them than actually ensued) would have followed. The Carthaginian approach was, with some abatements, attempted for the first five years. It proved disastrous. Cranston argues that 'if the policy of economic reconstruction which Keynes recommended had been adopted..., constitutional government would have had as good a chance of success in Weimar Germany as it had after 1945 in the Bundesrepublik',[181] when a magnanimous peace was implemented. Instead, the reparations demands weakened democratic government in Germany, partly by exacerbating Germany's economic difficulties, particularly between 1921 and 1923, and through Brüning's 'subordinating the needs of the economy to the foreign political goal of ending reparations',[182] facilitating Hitler's rise. Ferguson, by contrast, argues that the 'pro-German' Keynes badly advised German governments through these years—for example, encouraging German policies leading to hyperinflation.[183]

Keynes's perception of Germany was that she was not *inherently* aggressive, and that she could be induced to play a peaceful and cooperative role in a European family of nations. Although German ambition had caused the First World War, Keynes regarded the moderate, middle-class government of Weimar Germany as offering international stability.[184] Whether Keynes's view is right, or whether imperialist ambitions were common to German foreign policy at all times from Bismarck to Hitler, and would have been to any possible German government, is beyond the scope of this study.

It is true that Keynes wrote not disapprovingly of German economic ambitions to the east.[185] But he wished these to be pursued peacefully, in an open international economy. *The Economic Consequences* was written before the Anglo-American guarantee to France failed. Though he supported economic magnanimity, Keynes 'never suggested that he would disapprove of military measures to prevent German rearmament',[186] and indeed was in favour of strong measures when Germany did overturn its treaty obligations in the 1930s.[187] *The Economic Consequences* failed to foresee that the war guilt clause would be so much the focus of German unhappiness, and indeed denied it was of real importance.[188] *A Revision* recognized this error.[189]

---

[181] Thirlwall, *Laissez-Faire*, p. 108; see also p. 109.

[182] Thirlwall, *Policy Adviser*, p. 177; see also pp. 89, 114, 118.

[183] Ferguson, 'Keynes and the German Inflation'; Ferguson, *Pity*, ch. 14.

[184] For example, vol. 2, pp. 1, 184.

[185] Vol. 2, pp. 183–7; vol. 3, p. 128; vol. 28, p. 126; see Mantoux, *Carthaginian Peace*, p. 178; Thirlwall, *Policy Adviser*, pp. 97, 105–6.

[186] Harrod, *Life*, p. 317.   [187] See ch. 5, this volume.   [188] Vol. 2, p. 96.

[189] Vol. 3, p. 27.

Keynes was widely criticized as anti-French and pro-German, and he spent much effort rebutting this charge. In 1919, and for years after, the greater threat to European harmony or the balance of power appeared to Keynes and many others[190] to come, not from Germany, but from France. Keynes did not believe that French security was at risk: Germany was weak; and, when she revived, she would look east.[191] But Keynes also argued that a magnanimous peace would better secure French security than a Carthaginian one: it was hopeless to seek security against some future German aggression by pursuing policies that would promote such aggression; Europe's economic rehabilitation (which required Germany's) was France's best guarantee. In the preface to the French edition, he asked: 'Will France be safe because her sentries stand on the Rhine, if her own finances are in a serious disorder, if she is spiritually isolated from her friends, if bloodshed, misery and fanaticism prevail from the Rhine eastward through two continents?'[192]

A further major attack on *The Economic Consequences* concerns its consequences. It is argued that the book contributed significantly to the Treaty's defeat in the USA, and to subsequent US refusal to throw its weight into the European balance of power; and that it generated '*mea culpism*'—guilt over the treatment of Germany at Paris—in Britain and France, which contributed to their failure to resist Germany effectively in the 1930s.[193] The book's impact in the USA is considered below. While it is impossible to know whether European events would have been significantly different without *The Economic Consequences*, there are innumerable testimonies to the great impact of the book on British opinion.[194] But its influence on *mea culpism*, reinforced by Harold Nicolson's *Peacemaking 1919* in 1933,[195] was only one of many background factors generating appeasement.[196] Though Mantoux neglects the fact,[197] Keynes was an early and strong advocate of resistance to the Nazis—as were others who essentially shared Keynes's view in 1919, such as Churchill. Though Keynes received considerable publicity in Germany,[198]

---

[190] For example, Bertrand Russell with Dora Russell, *The Prospects of Industrial Civilization* (London, 1923), p. 90 ff.

[191] See vol. 3, p. 128.

[192] Vol. 2, p. xxi.

[193] Mantoux, *Carthaginian Peace*, p. 17 ff; see also, e.g. D. Thomson (with G. Warner), *England in the Twentieth Century* (London, 1991), pp. 82–3.

[194] For example, Dalton to P. Mantoux, 9 Aug. 1946, box 47, JVP; C. Barnett, *The Collapse of British Power* (New York, 1972), pp. 390–2.

[195] H. Nicolson, *Peacemaking 1919* (London, 1934 [1933]); see, e.g. F. Gannon, *The British Press and Germany, 1936–1939* (Oxford, 1971), pp. 7, 288.

[196] See, e.g. C. Thorne, *The Approach of War, 1938–1939* (London, 1967) p. 11 ff.

[197] See, e.g. Mantoux, *Carthaginian Peace*, pp. 12–13.

[198] See, e.g. vol. 18, p. 18.

it seems unlikely that attitudes to the Treaty there would have been much different had he not written.[199]

4.4 THE IMPACT OF *THE ECONOMIC CONSEQUENCES* IN THE USA

As we have seen, Keynes appealed to US generosity to have his remedies implemented. He has been attacked for encouraging US rejection of the Treaty and retreat into isolationism.[200] If *The Economic Consequences* encouraged the USA into isolationism, it did great harm to its own aim: a form of internationalism in which US action, even leadership, was essential for forgiveness of war debts, and lending to restart the European economy.

There are several reasons for believing that *The Economic Consequences* did not contribute significantly to the Senate's failure to ratify the Treaty of Versailles in 1919–20. The first Senate vote on ratification took place in November 1919, before the book or extracts from it had appeared in Britain, let alone the USA. This vote could not have been affected by an unpublished book of which, probably, no Senator was aware. Both that vote and the second and final vote on ratification, in March 1920, were along lines of cleavage long established. The opposition of the 'irreconcilables' (such as W. E. Borah) to the Treaty,[201] and the nature of the reservations of the more moderate Republicans (led by Henry Cabot Lodge) to the League Covenant,[202] were clear long before the first Senate vote. Moreover, had President Wilson been willing to accept the Treaty with the Senate's reservations, the Senate would almost certainly have ratified it.[203] Wilson's wife and various advisers—most importantly, Colonel House[204]—urged him to accept the Treaty with reservations, but he refused to do so. Finally, the Senate defeat can be convincingly

---

[199] See Balogh, *Unequal Partners*, ii, p. 137 n. 2.

[200] For example, Mantoux, *Carthaginian Peace*, pp. 8–11; Tillman, *Paris Peace Conference*, p. 401; Keylor in Boemeke et al., *Treaty of Versailles*, p. 486.

[201] For example, W. E. Borah to W. F. Brewster, 17 Feb. 1919, box 768; to Frank Kluck, 28 Feb., box 767, Borah papers, LOC; Borah to J. P. Tumulty, 17 Feb., box 50, HCLP.

[202] Lodge to R. L. O'Brien, 28 Oct. 1920, box 59; to Calvin Coolidge, 24 Feb. 1919; to C. I. Barnard, 4 Mar. 1919; to Sen. Frelinghuysen, 24 Mar. 1919, box 50, HCLP; to Corrine Roosevelt Robinson, 5 Nov. 1920, bMS Am 1785 (831), Houghton Library, Harvard; cf. C. R. Robinson, 'My reasons for not believing in the Wilsonian League of Nations', bMS Am 1785.3(49).

[203] See, e.g. Lodge to J. A. Lowell Blake, 3 Dec. 1919, box 50, HCLP; Cravath to Keynes, 20 Oct. 1919, L/19/50, KP; Bailey in R. A. Stone (ed.), *Wilson and the League of Nations* (New York, 1967).

[204] See: House diary, 23 Nov. 1919, p. 67, binder 16; 15 July 1920, p. 65, binder 17; 4 Mar. 1921, binder 17, EMHP; House (unsent) draft letter to Wilson, 8 May 1920, box 121a, EMHP.

explained without reference to Keynes.[205] Though not proof that his book was not decisive, this raises a presumption that it was not.

Nonetheless, *The Economic Consequences* had a considerable impact in the USA even before its publication, especially because of its depiction of President Wilson as being bamboozled. While Keynes was writing, Paul Warburg, though hostile to Wilson, urged Keynes to moderate his draft, and Salter had warned Keynes that his depiction of Wilson would be used against the President and the League.[206] Despite Keynes's naive hope that this not happen,[207] the pre-publication extracts which (at Walter Lippmann's urging)[208] he agreed *The New Republic* should publish had 'an extraordinary impact on public opinion', adverse to the President whom Keynes caricatured.[209] Keynes rapidly regretted allowing the extracts to appear.[210] The book also came to American attention through newspaper[211] and private[212] accounts of it, and its impact, from Britain.

Keynes explained to his American correspondents that his comments on Wilson were written in July 1919, before the President's illness; that if he had been writing after his breakdown, he would 'have spoken more gently of a pitiful and tragic figure...who in spite of everything was the one member of the Four who was *trying* to do right'; that in retrospect, Keynes thought Wilson had substantially maintained his position on reparations until April, and his capitulation may have been significantly due to his impending illness; and that he had written, not to attack Wilson, but to explain how it came about that the Treaty was not 'in accordance with our engagements'.[213] Keynes insisted that his version of Wilson's conduct—of an honourable man duped—was more favourable than the account of the President's friends, which amounted to saying 'that he was insincere when he stated that the peace is in substantial accord with the Fourteen Points'.[214]

[205] H. C. Lodge, *The Senate and the League of Nations* (New York, 1925) has no index reference to Keynes. L. E. Ambrosius, *Woodrow Wilson and the American Diplomatic Tradition: The Treaty Fight in Perspective* (Cambridge, 1987), a detailed account, contains a single, minor reference.

[206] Warburg to Keynes, undated (? Oct. 1919), FI/5/23, KP; vol. 17, pp. 5–6.

[207] Keynes to Frankfurter, 12 and 20 Sept. 1919, box 10, folder 420a, Lippmann papers, Yale.

[208] Hession, *Keynes*, p. 163.

[209] The extracts appeared on 24 Dec. 1919, 14 and 21 Jan. 1920: vol. 30, pp. 54, 64, 84.

[210] Vol. 17, p. 43.

[211] For example, J. M. Tuohy, 'Allied Reparation Policy Arraigned by British Expert', *New York World*, 2 Jan. 1920.

[212] See, e.g. House diary, 30 Dec. 1919, p. 91, binder 16, EMHP.

[213] Vol. 17, pp. 41, 45, 48. Keynes did not use the preface dated Nov. 1919 which referred sympathetically to Wilson's illness: vol. 2, p. xvii.

[214] Vol. 17, p. 48; see also, e.g. pp. 42, 55–6, and Cecil at p. 150.

The book was published in the USA early in 1920, and rapidly became a bestseller. Reviews drew attention to Keynes's depiction of Wilson outdone by Clemenceau and Lloyd George, and this had great impact.[215] A well-balanced review by Joseph P. Cotton used Keynes's attack on the Treaty to show the importance of the League: it was 'now the only instrument at hand (though perhaps a weak one) to do away with the mischief of the treaty'.[216] But many regarded the book as a reason for opposing the League. Though Keynes wished to see the USA enter the League, his book was seized upon by irreconcilables, and gave renewed vigour to their campaign. For example, although Borah's long-standing opposition to the League did not relate to reparations, he was quick to deploy *The Economic Consequences* as further ammunition for his cause: he read, recommended, and quoted the book.[217] He also used E. J. Dillon's *The Inside Story of the Peace Conference*, which had a similar message.[218] Vance McCormick saw the use of Keynes's book by Wilson's enemies—who overlooked its 'pro-German leanings' when they had previously attacked Wilson's 'supposed leniency toward the enemy countries'—as showing that the Senate's attitude was simply anti-Wilson.[219] Keynes gave the irreconcilables a new line of attack.[220]

However, the book was not seized upon by more moderate opponents of Wilson. Lodge, for example, supporting the Treaty's severe treatment of Germany, disagreed with Keynes's argument.[221] His criticisms of Keynes included that he was wrong to see Wilson as a man of conscience; that Keynes described the Big Four but had never been to their meetings; and that his 'remedy'—'that the United States should finance Germany'—was the policy of 'foreign bankers, especially the English'.[222] The latter two allegations were common in attempts to discredit Keynes, and he was at pains to refute them, including arguing that his remedies would not especially advantage Britain.[223]

[215] For testimony to this impact, see, e.g. Scaife to Lansing, 1 Nov. 1920, box 6, RLSP; Lodge to M. Frewen, 26 May 1920, box 58, HCLP.

[216] *New York Evening Post*, 30 Jan. 1920.

[217] Borah to A. J. Beveridge, 9 Feb., box 769; to W. A. James, 9 Feb., box 770; to S. S. Gregory, 10 Feb., box 768; to A. L. Dunn, 24 Feb., box 767, Borah papers, LOC.

[218] For example, Borah to Dunn, 24 Feb. 1920, box 767, Borah papers, LOC; R. Stone, *The Irreconcilables* (New York, 1973), pp. 164–5.

[219] McCormick to Dulles, 16 Mar. 1920, box 3, JFDP.

[220] R. B. Fosdick to Sir E. Drummond, 13 Feb. 1920, box 4, Fosdick papers, Princeton; printed in R. B. Fosdick, *Letters on the League of Nations* (Princeton, 1966), p. 118; Sweetser to Drummond, 4 Feb. 1920, box 5, Fosdick papers.

[221] See, e.g. Lodge to Sir George Trevelyan, 13 May 1919, box 52; to Lord Charnwood, 2 July 1919, box 50; to Henry White, 23 June 1919, box 53, HCLP.

[222] Lodge to Brooks Adams, 4 and 12 Mar. 1920, box 58; to Frewen, 26 May 1920; to J. M. Beck, 30 Sept. 1920, box 58, HCLP.

[223] Vol. 17, pp. 81 ff, 101–9.

Many American supporters of Treaty ratification, and of Wilson, wished to discredit *The Economic Consequences*. Indeed, because the Treaty was more contentious in the USA than in Britain, Keynes found his book aroused more bitter controversy there.[224] Advisers to Wilson such as Baruch, Dulles, Davis, Miller, and McCormick,[225] all of whom Keynes knew, largely responded that the US delegation did try to keep the reparations demands within the Armistice undertakings; that the President's final view on the matter was reasonable, if not necessarily right; that he achieved the best peace public opinion would allow; and that such flaws as there were in the economic and reparations provisions of the Treaty would (or could) be rectified, gradually, through the Reparations Commission and the League, and there was thus no need for wholesale revision of the Treaty. Keynes replied that the alternative to formal revision of the Treaty, gradual modification, meant 'a state of perpetual friction between the Allies themselves and reactions in Central Europe which cannot end otherwise than in the decay and disruption of its life'. Formal revision was also necessary for the resumption of 'that cooperation...between the Old World and the New which is essential for the reconstruction of Europe'.[226]

Dulles and Keynes exchanged respectful letters in *The Times*,[227] and privately.[228] In *The Times*, Keynes seized on Dulles's revelation 'that the President's legal advisers in Paris held the opinion that "pensions and separation allowances are not properly chargeable to Germany"'. Keynes's argument that their inclusion in the reparations demands was a breach of honour received only limited support in the USA (partly because many critics of Wilson were reluctant to give the Fourteen Points and related statements any special status).[229] But Dulles wrote in 1921 that he 'saw in the allied reparations demands a breach of contract as morally unjustifiable as Germany's violation of Belgium'[230]—the parallel Keynes had used in *The Economic Consequences*.[231] Dulles's 1920 letter to *The Times* also revealed that Smuts's memorandum persuaded Wilson to include pensions and

[224] See vol. 16, pp. 39–40, 42, 47, 75–6; vol. 17, pp. 79, 86, 88. On US publications about the Treaty, see Boemeke et al., *Treaty of Versailles*, chs. 8 and 23.

[225] For example, McCormick to Dulles, 16 Mar. 1920, box 3, JFDP.

[226] Vol. 17, pp. 26–30; see also, e.g. vol. 17, pp. 31–2, 39, 77; cf. Lord E. Percy letter, *The Times*, 21 Feb. 1920.

[227] Dulles letter to *The Times*, 16 Feb. 1920; Keynes letter, 19 Feb. at vol. 17, pp. 26–30. A pencilled draft of Dulles's letter was more acerbic: box 3, JFDP.

[228] For example, vol. 17, pp. 31–2; see also, e.g. Dulles, 'The Reparation Problem', *The New Republic*, 30 Mar. 1921; Dulles; 'The Reparation Problem', *The Literary Review*, 6 Aug. 1921.

[229] For example, Lodge to Frewen, 26 May 1920, box 58, HCLP.

[230] Dulles to K. Fullerton, 28 Mar. 1921; Fullerton to Dulles, 9 Apr., box 4, JFDP. Both saw this as an uncommon view. Cf. H. Stephen letter, *The Times*, 27 Feb. 1920.

[231] Vol. 2, p. 91.

separation allowances. Keynes later sought to defend Smuts from the 'substantial injustice' of being saddled with primary responsibility for the reparation demands in their final form: 'he was one of the strongest opponents of the reparation proposals in Paris.'[232]

Davis set out a powerful reply to Keynes in a private paper prepared for Joseph P. Tumulty, Wilson's secretary, who was concerned at the book's impact.[233] Davis argued, *inter alia*, that the war, rather than the Peace, caused the existing troubles; that most of Keynes's remedies relating to reparation, coal and iron, and tariffs were what the American delegation had sought;[234] that the removal of economic barriers was especially important to removing the causes of war; but that 'Mr. Keynes's other two remedies—a cancellation of war indebtedness and a new international loan' were not practical.[235] American opinion opposed the latter two remedies[236] because, as Keynes admitted, Europe could not be relied on to make good use of a loan; because the Allies, including Britain, should first 'forgo their right to strip Germany of her ships and other necessary working capital'; because the money was borrowed and lent in the expectation that it would be repaid; and because America's own condition was not as prosperous as was imagined. Davis urged, not US isolation, but international cooperation, including the USA, not least in 'the removal, so far as possible, of economic barriers and the establishment of an equality of trade conditions'.[237]

In a May 1920 article in New York, Keynes recognized that an international loan and cancellation of war debt had been rendered 'unpracticable', for now at least, by the US attitude and the actual condition of Europe.[238] Keynes did not regret that the Senate had repudiated the Treaty. 'But it will be a disaster for the world if America isolates herself.' He prayed, he said, that 'a new settlement and a new League may even now arise which will command the allegiance of all men'. (This is not to say that Keynes abandoned his belief that the USA should cancel the war debts owed to her: he did not.[239] But he had clear evidence that the USA would not cancel them.)[240]

[232] Vol. 17, p. 99; see also p. 100; and Keynes's extensive correspondence with H. M. V. Temperley, at CO/11/201 ff, KP.

[233] See Fahey to Tumulty, 21 Feb. 1920; Davis to Tumulty, 25 Feb.; G. O. Mayon to Davis, 13 Mar.; untitled, undated (? mid-Mar.) document beginning 'There are many misconceptions...' (hereafter 'Davis draft'), box 32, NDP.

[234] See also draft headed 'III. Remedies', box 32, NDP.

[235] Davis draft, 13, 17, box 32, NDP.

[236] See, e.g. 'Wiping the Slate', *The Saturday Evening Post*, 6 Mar. 1920, 28.

[237] Davis draft, 17, box 32, NDP.

[238] Vol. 17, pp. 76–7.

[239] See, e.g. vol. 17, p. 90.

[240] For example, Oscar Crosby to Keynes, 17 Mar. 1920, L/20/31–2, KP.

Davis wrote to Keynes that they were 'in substantial accord as to what should have been in the Treaty', but Davis believed it was necessary at the time to heed public opinion, 'get the world at peace, and then through the machinery provided in the Treaty, make adjustments'.[241] Davis suggested that Keynes's book increased American 'opposition to our becoming entangled in European affairs', and that a discussion of cancellation of war debts 'only arouses antagonism in the United States'.

In April–May 1920, Davis and Dulles agreed that it was necessary for the Reparation Commission to fix 'a reasonably definite amount' of German reparation, 'setting Germany free to work and pay it off.[242] By January 1921, Dulles, clearly sympathetic to Germany's predicament, was saying that 'the present treaty is not being applied according to its spirit': the spirit, he thought, was reasonable, the application not.[243]

Both Davis and Dulles declined to write fuller, public refutations of Keynes.[244] But in 1920, they and other Americans who had been at the PPC helped Baruch write *The Making of the Reparation and Economic Sections of the Treaty.*[245] For example, Davis urged Baruch to challenge Keynes's interpretation of the reparation chapter, and explain why the USA finally agreed to the inclusion of pensions under the category of 'damage'. He also wanted no passage that could give credence to 'the connection which Keynes attempts to establish between Germany's reparation obligation to the Allies and the Allies' debts to us'. Baruch agreed.[246] In reviewing Baruch's book, Keynes described it as 'the *apologia* of one who...held during the conference broad and enlightened views, and did his best to uphold them (though not to the death)', explaining 'why he finally acquiesced in something so very far from what he himself thought wisdom'.[247] Keynes highlighted that, by exposing documents he (a former civil servant) had not felt at liberty to disclose, Baruch had revealed the stands such Americans as Wilson and Dulles had

---

[241] Davis to Keynes, 19 Mar. 1920, box 32, NDP; Keynes's reply: vol. 17, pp. 38–42; see also Thomas Lamont to Davis, 26 Jan. 1939; Davis to Lamont, 10 Feb., box 33, NDP.

[242] Davis to Wilson, 6 May 1920, box 32, NDP; Dulles to Davis, 1 Apr. 1920, box 3, JFDP.

[243] Memorandum of a conference of the Council on Foreign Relations, 11 Jan. 1921, box 3, JFDP.

[244] On Davis: F. W. Wile to Davis, 15 Apr. 1920, and subsequent documents, box 32, NDP; 'Reply to Keynes' Book by U.S. Government Official', *The Washington Herald*, 17 April 1920. On Dulles: *Révue Economique Internationale*, Brussels, to Dulles, 21 Feb. 1920; Dulles's reply, 26 Mar.; L. B. Stowe to Dulles, 24 Feb.; Dulles's reply, also 24 Feb., box 3, JFDP.

[245] Dulles–Baruch messages, esp. Apr.–July 1920; Dulles to Davis, 11 June; to Lamont, 16 June; Lamont to Dulles, 22 June; Dulles to McCormick, 12 June; to Bainbridge Colby, 16 June, box 3, JFDP; Dulles to Davis, 16 Mar. 1922, box 4, JFDP; P. M. Burnett, 'Report of a Conversation' with Dulles, 23 Mar. 1934, point 12, box 13, JFDP.

[246] Davis to Baruch, 21 June and 10 July 1920; Baruch to Davis, 12 July, box 3, NDP.

[247] Vol. 17, p. 91.

taken against Allied demands.[248] But he rejected Baruch's excuses for their failure. While like 'many others who are secretly ashamed of the treaty, Mr Baruch pins his hopes on the Reparation Commission', Keynes believed that 'it is not by that route...that escape will be found': it was not functioning, and probably never would.[249] Keynes's review illustrates how he came, after the publication of *The Economic Consequences*, to give the dishonour of the Treaty even greater emphasis than he had in the book.[250]

Other episodes in the American debate on *The Economic Consequences* included an acrimonious exchange on the meaning of the Treaty between Keynes and David Hunter Miller;[251] support for Keynes from Paul Cravath;[252] and the preparation by Ray Stannard Baker of *Woodrow Wilson and World Settlement* (1922), which Davis thought too sympathetic to Keynes.[253] Miller, Cravath, and Baker had all been US officials in Paris.

In assessing Keynes's impact, it is important to remember that, not only had the Senate rejected the Treaty before publication of *The Economic Consequences*, but there were other signs of strong isolationism in the USA before the book appeared (to which it alluded).[254] Nonetheless, the judgment that *The Economic Consequences* contributed to America's reversion to isolationism in the 1920s had considerable contemporary[255] and later[256] support, and is hard to dispute. It persuaded many Americans that the Treaty was too punitive, but not that Keynes's remedies, such as debt cancellation, were right. It may be that its greatest effect was to persuade many Americans that the European situation was a vipers' nest from which they had best keep their distance. For example, on 24 February 1920, R. C. Lindsay reported from the British Embassy in Washington that 'it is not easy to exaggerate the importance of the effect on America of Mr. Keynes' book'.[257] Lindsay argued:

[248] See, e.g. vol. 17, pp. 94, 97, 100, 105; Dulles to Baruch, 8 Nov. 1920, box 3, JFDP; Keynes's defence of Dulles is at vol. 17, pp. 99–100.

[249] Vol. 17, p. 96.   [250] See, e.g. vol. 17, pp. 52–8, 91 ff, esp. pp. 97–8.

[251] For Miller, see articles by D. H. Miller in *New York Evening Post*, 6 and 11 Feb., and 27 Mar. 1920; 'The Economic Consequences of the Peace', Address to League of Free Nations Association, 27 Mar. 1920. For Keynes, see vol. 17, pp. 32 ff, 297; see also L/22/23–4, KP; Tillman, *Paris Peace Conference*, pp. 253–4.

[252] See, e.g. vol. 17, pp. 36–7, 43, 45–9; Memorandum of Council on Foreign Relations conference, 11 Jan. 1921; Cravath to Dulles, 8 Mar. 1920, box 3, JFDP.

[253] See, e.g. Baker to Davis, 2 Mar. and 20 Apr. 1922; Davis to Baker 18 Apr. and 26 July, box 3, NDP.

[254] Vol. 2, p. 181. An example is rejection of the Amsterdam memorial when Kent first sought approval for signing it.

[255] For example, A. J. Beveridge letters to Borah and Lodge, 6 Feb. 1920: box 769, Borah papers, LOC; box 58, HCLP; Fosdick to Sir E. Drummond, 20 Feb. 1920, box 4, Fosdick papers, Princeton; Fosdick, *Letters*, 121; Davis to Keynes, 19 Mar. 1920, box 32, NDP; Adams to Lodge, 2 and 9 Mar. 1920, box 58, HCLP.

[256] For example, A. Salter, *Personality in Politics*, p. 141.

[257] R. C. Lindsay to Lord Curzon, 24 Feb. 1920, T1/12516, PRO.

[I]t has decided for some time to come what opinion Americans of moderate education will hold about the Treaty of Versailles. In the first place, it confirms what Americans have always suspected that they are no match for the subtle and unscrupulous diplomatists of old Europe. In the second place and far more important, it shows that Germany, after being led to capitulate on conditions—formulated by an American President—that have been violated, is now being sucked dry. The spectacle of the nations of Europe scrambling for the blood of prostrate Germany offends both the idealism and the business like instincts of the American people.... Herself uninterested in reparations, America's tendency to withdraw from these European complications will be intensified.

Lindsay urged that Anglo-American relations would be served if the British Government would 'somewhat spontaneously dissociate themselves from cooperating in exacting from Germany concessions and reparations which though justified by the Treaty, are really bad business for all concerned'.

The impetus *The Economic Consequences* gave to isolationist tendencies may have contributed to the failure of subsequent attempts to have the Treaty ratified, such as that of April 1921.[258] One of the motives for that attempt was to give the USA moderating power in the Reparation Commission, which Keynes also wanted.

4.5 FROM *THE ECONOMIC CONSEQUENCES* TO *A REVISION OF THE TREATY*

As a result of the Amsterdam memorialists' action,[259] a conference of financial experts, called by the Council of the League, met in Brussels in September–October 1920.[260] Keynes did not attend it. He expected it would not lead Britain and the USA to abandon their 'deflationary policy', which obstructed 'the financial rehabilitation by external loans of all the Continental countries'.[261] The Brussels conference adopted the ter Meulen scheme to furnish impoverished countries with credit for importing raw materials to re-establish their export industries.[262] Keynes believed that such

[258] See, e.g. Herter to Dulles, 14 Apr. 1921; Dulles to Herter, 16 Apr.; Dulles to Hoover, 16 Apr.; Dulles to Allen Dulles, 3 June, box 3, JFDP; Dulles, 'Memorandum on the Importance to the United States of the Economic Provisions of the Treaty of Versailles' (5 Apr.), box 4, JFDP.

[259] Vol. 17, p. 194; 'History', 21, box 14, PMWP; Moggridge, *Biography*, p. 355.

[260] See, e.g. *Survey of International Affairs*, 1925, *Supplement* (chronology, 1920–5) (London, 1928), p. 180; H. A. Siepmann, 'The International Financial Conference at Brussels', *EJ*, 30 (1920), 436 ff.

[261] Vol. 17, pp. 194–5.

[262] Vol. 17, p. 195; see also, e.g. League of Nations, *International Credits: The 'Ter Meulen' Scheme* (London, undated: 1921?).

schemes, 'intended to help small countries like Latvia, are really beside the mark'. A solution was needed to the major problems, including the significant decline in European living standards which he expected.[263] In the autumn of 1920, Keynes was pessimistic about the chances of this.[264] He believed the budgets of such countries as Germany, Austria, Poland, and probably Italy could not be made to balance. He saw signs of moderation in public opinion, but not in France, which he thought increasingly wished to use the Reparation Commission to aid their 'political, military and commercial hegemony of Europe'.[265] Keynes also thought it increasingly clear that the League would not be very useful in its present form.

During 1920, Keynes believed that much of the contemporary discussion of international problems, including at Brussels, was well meaning but useless. Politicians needed to be subjected to 'a real pressure of public opinion'. He increasingly believed (October 1920) that there would be a great deal of suffering before constructive remedial action would be undertaken.[266] But Keynes's own state of demoralized lethargy[267] in late 1920 did not last long. Early in 1921, the renewal of activity on reparations inspired him to renewed journalism.[268] Much of what he wrote in 1921 formed the basis of *A Revision of the Treaty.*

Keynes commented in detail on the sequence of events from the Paris conference on reparations in January 1921, which proposed a scheme of payments he regarded as 'definitely retrograde', with normal period sums four times what he considered justified or possible;[269] through a succession of further meetings, Allied ultimatums to Germany, and German appeals for US mediation; through to Germany's acceptance in May 1921 of the London Schedule of Payments, on threat of occupation of the Ruhr. Keynes was deeply hostile to the ultimatums against Germany, and the sanctions—territorial incursions, and discriminatory tariffs—used. The Treaty was being replaced by 'the intermittent application of force in exaction of fluctuating demands'.[270] This showed 'contempt for the due form and processes of law',[271] and would not raise any money from Germany. When, on 26 April, Briand 'virtually promised the Chamber of Deputies...that the Ruhr would be occupied on 1 May'[272] (which was not done), Keynes developed further his

---

[263] Vol. 17, pp. 196–7.   [264] See, e.g. vol. 17, p. 82.   [265] Vol. 17, pp. 196–202.
[266] Vol. 17, pp. 196–7.   [267] See, e.g. vol. 17, pp. 197–203.
[268] Sources for these events include: vol. 3, chs. 2 and 3, and vol. 17, ch. 11, which contain chronological errors. 'The Reparations Calendar', *Journal of the American Bankers Association*, Mar. 1923, 595–7; Kent, *Spoils*, ch. 3; *Survey*, 1925, *Supplement*, pp. 123–4.
[269] Vol. 17, pp. 207, 209; vol. 3, p. 16. On Lloyd George's 'game', see vol. 17, pp. 210–16; vol. 3, pp. 10, 16.
[270] See also vol. 3, p. 22.   [271] Vol. 17, p. 224; vol. 3, p. 21.
[272] Kent, *Spoils*, p. 133.

twin arguments on the importance of a conscientious observance of inter-national law, and the 'incalculable dangers' of French occupation of the Ruhr.[273] These were to become familiar themes in his response to territorial sanctions, especially the occupation of the Ruhr in 1923. In *A Revision*, Keynes devoted several pages to establishing the illegality, under the Treaty, of occu-pying Germany east of the Rhine.[274] Powerful forces in France were seeking a pretext to 'break the neck of a feared and hated neighbour'. Occupation of the Ruhr was an 'act of war' which would put 'a match to the magazine of Europe'.[275] But Keynes sympathized with Briand in his struggle with Poincaré, who would be even worse.[276] Keynes again urged that, to show goodwill, Britain should relinquish her reparation claims in favour of France.[277]

Keynes applauded the Reparation Commission's determination of Germany's liability on 27 April as being lower even than the estimate in *The Economic Consequences*, for which he 'had suffered widespread calumny'.[278] The Commission's evaluation was 'a signal triumph for the spirit of justice'. The London Schedule, which Germany accepted on 11 May, was a scheme for the payment of this liability. Keynes believed the Reparation Commission evaluation, and the substitution of the London schedule for the Paris pro-posals, represented a return to the Treaty. This was far better than what had been, and was still, threatened—'arbitrary lawlessness based on the mere possession of superior force'. But the Treaty itself remained impossible of fulfilment: though worse had been averted, Keynes believed the sums pro-posed in the London Schedule were still beyond Germany's capacity to pay. This was for the familiar reasons, especially that she could not, and would not be allowed to, develop the necessary export surplus. Keynes urged Germany to accept the London Schedule, 'do her best to obey it', which she should be able to do for some time, and hope and work for the revisions that still remained necessary. By submitting, Germany would 'preserve the peace of Europe', which was 'the paramount interest of everyone'. It would give 'a breathing space . . . during which general opinion can be further crystallised and the cooperation of America secured'. Keynes's encouragement to Germany to accept the terms was widely reported in Germany.[279]

Throughout this period, Keynes continued to stress the importance of the American role. In early March 1921, he predicted that European divisions would mean that no settlement would be reached until America threw 'her arbitral influence into the scales'. She could do so by appointing a

[273] Vol. 17, p. 229.   [274] Vol. 3, pp. 36–40.
[275] Vol. 17, pp. 228–9; see also, e.g. p. 218; vol. 3, p. 25; vol. 18, p. 218.
[276] Vol. 17, pp. 214–18, 229; see vol. 3, p. 15.   [277] Vol. 17, p. 230; see also, e.g. p. 220.
[278] Vol. 3, pp. 24–5.   [279] Vol. 17, pp. 235–40; see also vol. 3, pp. 26–7, 47, 82–3.

representative to the Reparation Commission, without undertaking other responsibilities,[280] and insisting on the impartial determination of reparation proposals, free of any motive other than 'the desire to restore what Germany destroyed': 'America was party to the war and she has no right to divest herself of responsibility now.'[281]

In August–September 1921, Keynes wrote a series of articles for *The Sunday Times*,[282] much of which he recycled in *A Revision of the Treaty*.[283] The articles argued that Germany could not pay the new reparations schedule, except in the first year,[284] and that default and therefore a new reparation settlement were bound to come in 1922. This belief may well have encouraged the French to get in first with the Loucheur–Rathenau agreement on payment in kind of 6 October 1921,[285] which Keynes attacked for unilaterally altering the Allies' shares of reparations, and increasing Germany's obligation.[286] Though Keynes did not think payment in kind was in general superior to payment in cash, he saw political advantages in agreements on payment in kind that reduced the aggregate reparation burden.[287]

The articles also argued that a major German expansion of exports to try to meet the reparations bill would hurt other trading countries,[288] but was not likely to happen. Keynes stressed that he was not arguing that Germany could pay nothing, and that it would be to 'fall into the protectionist fallacy' to think 'that the receipt of an indemnity is necessarily injurious to those that receive it'. But British industry would suffer more than French, while Britain received less in reparations. This divergence of interest between France and Britain, with the greater French interest in exacting reparations, could be redressed by Britain's cancelling France's debt to her, and giving France priority in reparation receipts, in exchange for a moderate reparation settlement.[289] Keynes was to repeat this analysis, with its stress on German exports competing with Britain's, over subsequent years.[290]

Keynes argued that America could only hope for war debt repayment by the expansion of European exports into her own market and the disordering of

[280] Vol. 17, pp. 225, 236.   [281] Vol. 17, p. 231.   [282] Vol. 17, ch. 12.

[283] Compare, e.g. vol. 3, p. 49, and vol. 17, p. 245, re Germany's 'inevitable default' in 1922; see also PP/45/168/10/52–66, KP.

[284] Keynes employed three measures of capacity to pay: see vol. 17, pp. 245–7; vol. 3, p. 50 ff.

[285] Kent, *Spoils*, pp. 148–9; vol. 17, pp. 249, 283–6; vol. 3, pp. 49, 59–64.

[286] Vol. 3, pp. 60–1; see also vol. 17, pp. 283–4; see FI/2/8 ff for Keynes's correspondence with Melchior.

[287] Vol. 3, pp. 62–4, 120.

[288] See vol. 17, p. 256: persistence in the present demands 'may do much injury to the normal equilibrium of international trade, and thus impoverish everyone'.

[289] Vol. 17, pp. 252–3.

[290] For example, vol. 21, p. 261 (1924).

her export industries, and that America would be wise to cancel the debts as part of 'a new world settlement'. Instead, the USA insisted on war debt repayment, and raised her tariffs, making it harder for her debtors to repay her. Further grounds for 'an *all-round* cancellation' were 'connected with the origins of the debts, which are not chiefly economic', and that America's pursuit of debt repayment embittered her relations with Europe.[291]

Just as he had done in *The Economic Consequences*, Keynes described how partnership between the Old World and the New had been disrupted by the war.[292] Europe had moved from creditor to debtor. 'The old equilibrium is destroyed, but a new one is not yet established.' The 'restoration of some equilibrium' was to be central to Keynes's thinking, in different ways, until his death. In discussing American lending to Europe, Keynes wrote of foreign investment along lines that he was to develop over subsequent years. He saw large-scale foreign investment as a recent and unstable phenomenon. There could be mutual advantage, as in the nineteenth century, in an old country's investing in a new country, helping to develop it, and being repaid from the abundant profits of this virgin land. 'But the position cannot be reversed.'[293] Lending from a new country to an old did not have the benefit of a '*real* sinking fund', out of which it could be repaid.

The interest will be furnished out of new loans, so long as these are obtainable, and the financial structure will mount always higher, until it is not worthwhile to maintain any longer the illusion that it has foundations. The unwillingness of American investors to buy European bonds is founded in common sense.

Keynes's mind was turning to '[f]ar-reaching schemes of social improvement'; but 'in the realm of immediate action, the ancient doctrine of Liberalism' still held good, and suggested such projects as a capital levy; general disarmament—'the form of economy least injurious and most worth while'; 'freedom of trade and international intercourse and co-operation', by which 'the limited resources of mankind could be employed to his best advantage'; and a reduction and control of the birth rate, so that 'men might cease to trample one another to the wall'.[294] Keynes also advocated what was to become a recurrent theme:[295] an active countercyclical policy by 'the banking authorities of the world.'[296]

A Revision of the Treaty, published in January 1922, surveyed the major developments on reparations in 1920–1, and elaborated key arguments from *The Economic Consequences*. Keynes defended himself from attacks, such as on

[291] Vol. 17, pp. 277–8; vol. 3, p. 114.   [292] See, e.g. vol. 2, p. 143; vol. 17, p. 272.
[293] Vol. 17, p. 274; vol. 3, p. 111.   [294] Vol. 17, pp. 270–1.
[295] The 'falling off of effective demand': vol. 17, p. 243.   [296] Vol. 17, p. 263.

his alleged hostility to France. *A Revision* reveals a good deal of Keynes's thinking about economic forces making for conflict or harmony; idealism more generally; the needs of post-war reconstruction; and relations between the USA and Europe. Let us consider these issues in turn.

4.5.1 Economic Determinants of Political Conflict or Harmony

There are two major ways in which *A Revision of the Treaty* adds to, or alters, Keynes's view of how economic forces make for political harmony or conflict. It became clearer that he saw those who identify their interests with trade as more likely to pursue peace than those who do not; and he now saw growing profits, rather than privation, as more likely to promote working-class revolution.

In *A Revision*, Keynes again lamented national boundaries cutting across economic units. In criticizing the drawing of the Polish–German border in Upper Silesia after the 1921 plebiscite, Keynes wrote of national self-determination:[297]

The Wilsonian dogma, which exalts and dignifies the divisions of race and nationality above the bonds of trade and culture, and guarantees frontiers but not happiness, is deeply embedded in the conception of the League of Nations as at present constituted. It yields us the paradox that the first experiment in international government should exert its influence in the direction of intensifying nationalism.

This passage contrasts the forces Keynes believed made for amity between states—the bonds of trade and culture—with forces making for conflict—the divisions of race and nationality. Keynes evidently believed that those who recognize that their well-being depends on trade will be much more likely to pursue policies of international 'peace and amity'[298] than those who do not. In explaining why British opinion would accept his remedies, he wrote:[299]

Great Britain lives by commerce, and most Englishmen now need but little persuading that she will gain more in honour, prestige, and wealth by employing a prudent generosity to preserve the equilibrium of commerce and the well-being of Europe, than by attempting to exact a hateful and crushing tribute, whether from her victorious Allies or her defeated enemy.

This brought out clearly what is implicit in *The Economic Consequences*—that if states can be brought to recognize that their well-being is promoted by trade, they will pursue policies of peace which restore and promote the health

---

[297] Vol. 3, p. 8; cf. vol. 2, p. 39.   [298] Vol. 3, p. 130.   [299] Vol. 3, p. 124.

of the international trading system, and not policies of tribute-exaction and violence.

A Revision was much concerned with the enforcement of massive reparation demands through French incursions into Germany east of the Rhine, which breached the peace of Europe. Keynes believed that the French acted on a philosophy of struggle for power and denial of mutual interest in the prosperity of all. Adoption of this philosophy led to conflict. The alternative philosophy asserted that it is in the interests of all to promote the prosperity of all, including of defeated enemies, and that this can be done through making trade possible, and encouraging it. Adoption of this philosophy leads to, or at least promotes, peace. The ideas that the public and those in authority have concerning where their interests lie are decisive. Keynes was actively engaged in promoting one conception of where those interests lay.

Keynes's contrast between French realism and his own idealism, explicit in *The Economic Consequences*, is implicit in *A Revision*. But *A Revision* gives more attention to political provisions for French security than *The Economic Consequences* had. Keynes's contempt for many French politicians[300] and 'corrupt Parisian finance',[301] his hostility to France's policy of territorial sanctions,[302] and his opposition to what he saw as a French policy of European hegemony, were expressed vigorously. But he opposed making British and American concessions to France 'conditional on France's acceptance of a more pacific policy'. He sought to reassure France (as he had earlier)[303] that his proposals would benefit her enormously. In advocating the withdrawal of Allied troops from Germany, in exchange for various guarantees to France, Keynes seems again to have thought that Germany would not be a threat to France unless France provoked her. This was partly because 'Germany's future now lies to the east, and in that direction her hopes and ambitions, when they revive, will certainly turn.'[304]

So in Keynes's thought there were at least two links between trade and peace. The first we identified in *The Economic Consequences*: trade promotes prosperity, which promotes domestic order and moderation, which promotes international amity; the absence of, or obstacles to, trade will lead to impoverishment, which encourages domestic extremism and disorder, which is liable to lead to international conflict. The second (related) link is that those who identify their interests with trade will be more likely to pursue policies of international harmony than those who identify their interests in besting a rival in the struggle for power. This second link is clearer in *A Revision* than earlier; the first was modified in *A Revision*.

---

[300] See, e.g. vol. 3, p. 98.   [301] Vol. 3, p. 74.   [302] For example, vol. 3, p. 25.
[303] For example, vol. 2, pp. xix–xxii, 176–7.   [304] Vol. 3, pp. 121–2, 128–9.

In this sequel, Keynes explained why the worst expectations of 1919 had not come about:[305] the reparations chapter was not being, and would not be, enforced;[306] there had been major US lending to Europe since 1919;[307] the victims of the Treaty had been patient; and 'it is in times of growing profits and not in times of growing distress that the working classes stir themselves and threaten their masters'.[308] Thus Keynes revised his view of the link between privation and disorder. He now wrote:

When times are bad and poverty presses on them they [the working classes] sink back again into a weary acquiescence. Great Britain and all Europe have learnt this in 1921. Was not the French Revolution rather due perhaps to the growing wealth of eighteenth-century France—for at that time France was the richest country in the world— than to the pressure of taxation or the exactions of the old regime? It is the profiteer, not privation, that makes man shake his chains.

Perhaps Keynes too quickly forgot Europe's revolutionary outbreaks since 1917 (to some of which he referred earlier in the book)[309] which were, at least in part, the products of privation. The dichotomy between privation and the profiteer seems misleading: for, in *The Economic Consequences* and later in the *Tract*, it is the contrast between the windfall gains of the profiteer and the impoverished position of the saver and the situation of the worker, which generates discontent. It is not clear why, if it is growing profits that bring revolt, which Keynes had no particular wish to encourage, he looked forward with optimism to the growing health of the European economy, which *A Revision* detected. It is not obvious, here or in *The Economic Consequences*, that Keynes had given the connection between disorder, domestic and international, and economic privation and growth careful examination. He asserted his views *ex cathedra* and elegantly, but with little evidence.

4.5.2 Idealism

Keynes's idealism is evident in *A Revision* in the contrast between the realist and idealist philosophies already referred to, and in the stress on the power, potentially for good, of public opinion, and on the need for law observance in international affairs. Keynes accepted that adoption of his remedies depended on public support, especially in Britain and the USA. He believed that opinion in Britain and some other countries had moved significantly towards him since 1919.[310]

[305] Vol. 3, pp. 115–16; see also Keynes to Kent, 19 Apr. 1921, box 21, Kent papers, Princeton.
[306] On non-enforcement, see also, e.g. vol. 3, pp. 1–2, 5, 45.
[307] Vol. 3, pp. 111–12.   [308] Vol. 3, p. 116.   [309] Vol. 3, pp. 8–9.
[310] See, e.g. vol. 3, pp. xv, 4–5, 69, 115, 125.

Keynes restated the illegality of the territorial sanctions against Germany over reparations,[311] and the inclusion of pensions and separation allowances in the reparation demands.[312] On the latter, Keynes said that 'to their lasting credit, the American delegation [at Paris] had stood firm for the law, and it was the President, and he alone, who capitulated to the lying exigencies of politics.'[313] Keynes wrote that 'the respect shown for legality is now very small'.[314] Nonetheless, he was opposed to the resolution of international issues, such as territorial boundaries, in a legalistic fashion: 'A good decision can only result by impartial, disinterested, very well-informed and authoritative persons taking *everything* into account.'[315] 'International morality, interpreted as a crude legalism, might be very injurious to the world.'[316] There may be, as Keynes appeared to sense, a tension between this scorn of excessive legalism in international affairs and his stress, strongly evident in *A Revision*, on the importance of law observance. He was clearly sceptical of the League's impartiality,[317] and of the capacity of the Reparation Commission as 'a body of interested representatives to give a judicial decision in their own case'.[318]

4.5.3 The Needs of Post-war Reconstruction

Keynes's exposition of remedies in *A Revision* was more modest than in *The Economic Consequences*, and placed considerable stress on sound finance and the natural recuperative powers of economies free of impossible financial obligations. His plan was for Britain and if possible the USA 'to cancel all the debts owing them from the governments of Europe and to waive their claims to any share of German reparation'; 'Germany to pay 1,260 million gold marks (£63 million gold) per annum for 30 years, and to hold available a lump sum of 1,000 million gold marks for assistance to Poland and Austria'; with all the annual payments to go to France and Belgium.[319]

This plan was deliberately simple. It contained no proposal for an international loan,[320] an international currency, a revision of coal and iron provisions, or a free trade union (though support for a high degree of freedom of trade was implicit). Part of the reason for this greater modesty of proposals was that the European economy was in better health, and Keynes was more optimistic about it than he had been in 1919, or even when writing his 1921 *Sunday Times* articles.[321] Furthermore, Keynes's 1919 remedies had, in part

---

[311] Vol. 3, pp. 21–2, 25, 26, 36–40.   [312] Vol. 3, ch. 5.   [313] Vol. 3, p. 104 n.
[314] Vol. 3, p. 37; see also, e.g. p. 40.   [315] Vol. 3, p. 7; see also pp. 71–2.
[316] Vol. 3, p. 94.   [317] See, e.g. vol. 3, p. 21 n.   [318] Vol. 3, p. 82.
[319] Vol. 3, p. 127.   [320] See vol. 3, pp. 111–12.
[321] Cf. e.g. vol. 17, p. 242, and vol. 3, pp. 116–17.

and de facto only, been implemented: the reparations provisions had been abated, there had been major de facto US lending to Europe, and Germany was keeping part of Upper Silesia.

With the changed circumstances came a changed tone, perhaps turn of mind. Keynes wrote that some plans for European reconstruction were too paternal and complicated, and sometimes too pessimistic:

The patients need neither drugs nor surgery, but healthy and natural surroundings in which they can exert their own recuperative powers. Therefore a good plan must be in the main *negative*; it must consist in getting rid of shackles, in simplifying the situation, in cancelling futile but injurious entanglements.

Keynes's proposals aimed 'not to prescribe a solution, but to create a situation in which a solution is possible' to the problems before European finance ministers.[322]

This emphasis on the natural recuperative powers of economies, and on the importance of sound finances, is in the mould of classical economics. In writing of the improving health of the European economy, Keynes identified two remaining obstacles: the unrevised Treaty, and the fact that in most European countries 'there is still no proper balance between the expenditure of the state and its income, so that inflation continues and the international values of their currencies are fluctuating and uncertain'. Keynes's proposals were mainly directed towards these problems.[323] In writing of the collapse of the mark in 1921, Keynes said that Germany was probably headed for either 'social' or 'financial catastrophe'.[324]

4.5.4 Relations Between Europe and the USA

Although *A Revision* emphasized the importance of the USA to a European settlement, it proposed that Britain act unilaterally if the USA would not join in debt cancellation. Keynes argued that US insistence on war debt repayment would require the Allies to reduce their imports from the USA, which ran a balance of trade surplus, and that this would hurt American farmers.[325] It was folly for the USA to restrict imports. America would not insist on war debt repayment because of the damage it would do her own economy.[326] Keynes believed that US public opinion could be changed to support the cancellation of war debts.[327] He seems to have recognized in the Harding administration what he had described in August 1921 as 'a cautious sympathy with

[322] Vol. 3, p. 117. [323] Vol. 3, p. 117. [324] Vol. 3, p. 67.
[325] Vol. 3, pp. 109–10. [326] Vol. 3, p. 113. [327] Vol. 3, pp. 125–7.

Europe'.[328] However, since 'time presses, we cannot rely on American assistance, and we must do without it if necessary. If America does not feel ready to participate in a conference of revision and reconstruction, Great Britain should be prepared to do her part in the cancellation of paper claims, irrespective of similar action by the United States.'[329] This was Keynes's response to the persistent US refusal to undertake the international economic leadership he and others had urged upon her: if America would not act, Britain must act alone. What Skidelsky regards as Keynes's anti-Americanism in the 1920s[330] was really an attempt to find solutions for Europe's problems when the USA had, to Keynes's great regret, refused to participate.

4.6 REPARATIONS AND RECONSTRUCTION, 1922–33

Keynes attended the Genoa Conference of April 1922 as a newspaper correspondent.[331] He wanted the Conference to resolve three issues: reparations and inter-Allied war debts; stabilization of the European exchanges; and reconstruction of Soviet Russia. It was 'the maximum of political unreality' that, when a crisis over German inability to meet reparations demands seemed imminent, this was not to be discussed.[332] Keynes believed that 'the rest of Europe has a strong and urgent interest in Russia's economic restoration' because of 'the hope of markets', 'the danger of plague and famine on our borders', and especially 'the increase of wheat for our consumption'.[333] He proposed government-backed trade and economic assistance to Russia.[334] He lamented that Genoa produced no 'well-considered plan for the economic reconstruction of Europe',[335] though he later referred approvingly to its resolutions as pointing the way to an internationally managed gold standard.[336]

Keynes edited the *Manchester Guardian* supplements on reconstruction in Europe (April 1922–January 1923). The year 1921 having been one of depression, he outlined four 'causes of our misfortunes': war destruction; disorganization due to dismemberment of European empires; hostility due to the war, rivalries between the new states, and 'deep conflict of... principle' with Soviet Russia; and the credit cycle. War destruction was generally

---

[328] Vol. 17, p. 242; see vol. 3, p. 110.   [329] Vol. 3, p. 127.
[330] Skidelsky, *Saviour*, p. 20.   [331] See vol. 17, pp. 354, 379–80.
[332] Vol. 17, pp. 374, 399, 402, 419–20.   [333] Vol. 17, pp. 423–4.
[334] Vol. 17, pp. 419, 424, 434–40.
[335] Vol. 17, p. 422; see also p. 425 on Lloyd George.
[336] Vol. 4, p. 118 n; vol. 6, pp. 302–3, 354; vol. 21, p. 364.

exaggerated and should not take long to rebuild.[337] The supplements outlined Keynes's views on exchange stabilization;[338] the need for population control;[339] the importance of 'the principles of pacifism', namely, disarmament, looseness of imperial control, and free trade;[340] the evils of inflation and of deflation;[341] the need for a settlement of reparations;[342] and the failure of the Genoa Conference.[343]

In August 1922, Keynes proposed a new reparations scheme:[344] a moratorium on payments to enable Germany to stabilize her finances,[345] abolition of most deliveries in kind, dissolution of the Reparations Commission, an end to the occupation of the Rhineland, and a detailed scheme for reducing payments and postponing the obligation to pay until 1930.[346] This is one of a number of such schemes which Keynes proposed in the 1920s.[347] He sought to balance Germany's capacity to pay and the need for reconciliation with her (if only to make her a 'joint defence against... Bolshevist Russia'),[348] with concessions to reconcile France to the disappointment of her larger expectations.[349] Regard to French interests and demands had become a constant theme of Keynes's writings on reparations.[350]

In 1922 and 1923, Keynes had extensive dealings with Melchior, in particular when Keynes visited Hamburg in August 1922 (a trip that left him deeply pessimistic for Germany's prospects),[351] when he served as one of several international experts advising on stabilization of the mark in November 1922,[352] and when Melchior and Keynes sought to influence reparations policy in 1923 (including through approaches to Smuts).[353] In considering whether, as some imply,[354] Keynes's dealings with Melchior are evidence of pro-German bias, it is necessary to consider whether Keynes's view that France constituted the real threat to European order in the 1920s was well founded; and to recognize that Keynes realized that, in his words of 1923, 'savage material' lay 'below the surface in Germany'.[355] He was seeking to help

---

[337] Vol. 17, pp. 426–9.   [338] Vol. 17, pp. 355–69; vol. 18, pp. 70–84.
[339] Vol. 17, pp. 440–6, 449–53; vol. 18, p. 26.   [340] Vol. 17, p. 450.
[341] Vol. 4, pp. 1–53; vol. 18, pp. 75–8.   [342] Vol. 18, pp. 32–44.
[343] Vol. 17, pp. 420–5.   [344] Vol. 18, pp. 18–26, 32–43.
[345] See also vol. 18, p. 89.   [346] Vol. 17, pp. 35–6; vol. 18, p. 24.
[347] See also, e.g. vol. 18, pp. 97–9, 188. On dealing with Bonar Law and Baldwin on reparations late in 1922, see PP/45/168/10/82–3, KP.
[348] Vol. 18, p. 43.   [349] Vol. 18, p. 37.
[350] See, e.g. vol. 17, pp. 253–5, 432; vol. 18, pp. 37, 92; vol. 3, pp. 121–2, 129.
[351] Keynes to FAK, 2 Sept. 1922, PP/45/168/10/77–8, KP.
[352] Vol. 18, p. 61 ff; see also, e.g. vol. 18, pp. 27–8.
[353] For Keynes's 1923 correspondence with Smuts on reparations, see FI/12, KP; note by Melchior, FI/2/73, KP. On their influence, see L/43/45, 50–1, KP.
[354] Ferguson, 'Nerve', 23; Ferguson, 'Keynes and German Inflation'; Ferguson, *Pity*, p. 400ff.
[355] Vol. 18, p. 108.

stabilize the German economy and strengthen the forces of moderation, which he believed Melchior exemplified, to prevent that German savagery re-surfacing.

In December 1922, Keynes urged a British financial policy to prevent a 'disastrous' French occupation of the Ruhr. Britain should 'not be content with a passive protest' if France went ahead.[356] Keynes feared it would injure France's own economy; greatly damage the German economy, enraging her people, and producing 'a reactionary *Putsch*'; and end the prospects of substantial reparations payments.[357] The invasion contravened the Treaty of Versailles.[358] Keynes criticized solutions predicated on an international loan as unattainable.[359] Despite great economic damage to Germany, he was convinced passive resistance could not readily 'be broken down by purely economic causes' (such as unemployment), as France hoped.[360] Soon after the occupation of the Ruhr, Melchior told Keynes that France 'does not want reparation but direct or indirect annexation and we must defend the frontiers until the last day'.[361]

Keynes consistently urged Britain to seek French evacuation of the Ruhr and agreement on fixing the German liability at 50 billion marks, with the time for repayment determined with American guidance.[362] Britain should offer to cancel all inter-Ally debts and to allow the other Allies an absolute priority over British receipts from Germany. If France refused, Britain would withdraw her troops from the Rhineland and abandon France 'to work out her present policy to its bitter conclusion'; Britain would continue to demand repayment of war debts and her share of reparations.

In June 1923, Keynes applauded the 'real opportunity' given to Austria 'of reconstructing her economic life': reparations were suspended, her exchange stabilized, and a considerable loan guaranteed. He condemned French obstruction of a constructive scheme for Hungary.[363] Keynes described the Dawes Report as 'the finest contribution hitherto to this impossible problem'.[364] However, he doubted whether it would work.[365] The moratorium on payments was too brief.[366] Though the loan under the Dawes plan was diplomatically and psychologically crucial, the amount was small compared with Germany's need of working capital.[367] Though 'under cover of it the French may leave the Ruhr',[368] the scheme adopted did not preclude further

---

356 Vol. 18, p. 92.   357 Vol. 18, pp. 105–8, 121, 214.
358 Vol. 18, pp. 133, 206–10; see also vol. 3, pp. 35–40.
359 Vol. 18, pp. 137, 150–6; see also, e.g. p. 16.
360 Vol. 18, pp. 164–5.   361 Melchior to Keynes, 2 Feb. 1923, FI/2/48, KP.
362 Vol. 18, p. 204; see also pp. 214–15.   363 Vol. 18, pp. 176, 178.
364 Vol. 18, p. 241; see pp. 241–6, applauding the McKenna report.
365 Vol. 18, pp. 259, 261, 286.   366 Vol. 18, pp. 237–8.
367 Vol. 18, pp. 255–6.   368 Vol. 18, p. 259.

territorial sanctions, as it should.[369] Establishing foreign control over the banking, transport, and fiscal systems of Germany was incompatible with human nature; patriotic Germans would try to end it.[370]

Keynes continued to advocate cancellation of war debts.[371] In 1925,[372] 1928,[373] and 1932,[374] he endorsed the French argument that the loans were simply one form of contribution to the war effort, which allies contributing in other ways—especially human losses—could not justly be expected to repay. In 1925 he again urged America to forgive, or reduce, war debts so Britain could do likewise. He proposed that a proportion of reparations received by France go to settling her debts.[375]

Keynes wrote in 1926 that 'the United States lends money to Germany, Germany transfers its equivalent to the Allies, the Allies pay it back to the United States government'. He asked: 'How long can the game go on? The answer lies with the American investor.' Debt cancellation would only become an unavoidable burning issue when the circular flow of paper was impeded.[376] This happened in 1929–33.

In January 1928, Keynes favoured Germany's facing an early crisis 'by restricting payments...to what can be made out of current surplus', rather than 'putting off the evil day' by borrowing.[377] Seeing war debt cancellation as interlinked with reparations, as he long had, he urged resettlement of the Dawes scheme.[378] However, Keynes thought the Young Committee was premature because borrowing precluded real insight into Germany's capacity to produce an export surplus and meet the transfer problem. He urged evacuation of the Rhineland, removal of the 'controls at present established in Berlin', and reduction of 'the annuities below their present figure', but without Germany's losing 'transfer protection'.[379] He wanted Britain's proportion of reparations maintained.[380]

Keynes applauded the Young Plan's reduction in the sums demanded—to almost exactly what he had said in 1919 was practicable[381]—and their being 'spread so as to be lighter in the near future and heavier in later years'.[382] He praised the link created between concessions in war debts and reparations,[383] and heralded the Bank for International Settlements (BIS) as 'a nucleus for [a] super-national currency authority'.[384] Nonetheless, 'privately Keynes did not expect the Young Plan to be successful'.[385] He criticized it for placing 'the

---

[369] Vol. 18, pp. 246–8.   [370] Vol. 18, p. 260; cf. p. 241.
[371] See, e.g. vol. 9, ch. 5; vol. 18, p. 335.   [372] Vol. 18, pp. 265–6.
[373] Vol. 9, p. 48; vol. 18, p. 302.   [374] Vol. 18, pp. 383–4.
[375] Vol. 18, p. 268; vol. 9, p. 46.   [376] Vol. 18, pp. 281–2.   [377] Vol. 18, p. 295.
[378] Vol. 9, p. 52.   [379] Vol. 18, pp. 305, 314–15, 329, 342; see also pp. 317–18, 333, 358.
[380] Vol. 18, pp. 326–40.   [381] Vol. 18, p. 343.   [382] Vol. 18, p. 332.
[383] Vol. 18, pp. 335–6; see also pp. 345–6.   [384] Vol. 18, pp. 335, 344; see below.
[385] Vol. 18, p. 346.

liability to transfer the *whole* of each annuity in foreign currencies' on Germany: Young had effectively ignored the transfer problem.[386] Keynes doubted Germany's capacity to raise sufficient foreign capital.[387]

In 1930, Keynes's *Treatise on Money* argued, with Taussig, that 'when foreign investment is increasing, the terms of trade turn against the lending country and in favour of the borrowing, wages falling in the former and rising in the latter'.[388] The adverse changes were sometimes substantial. Keynes had applied his analysis to his debate in 1929 with Ohlin in *The Economic Journal* about the German transfer problem. He depicted reparations as 'a compulsory process of foreign investment' without 'cumulative offsets in subsequent years' or direct stimulus to German exports: '*if* the payment of reparations involves a substantial change in the terms of trade..., then it will probably be necessary to force down the rate of money earnings in Germany by means of a painful (and perhaps impracticable) process of deflation.'[389]

In *A Treatise* and elsewhere,[390] Keynes depicted the contribution of war debts and reparations to the development of the slump during which he was writing. High interest rates were a major cause of the slump; among the factors keeping them above what genuine borrowers could afford were 'the general return to the gold standard, and the settlement of reparations and the war debts'. The market rate of interest must come down, or 'the obstinate maintenance of misguided monetary policies' would 'continue to sap the foundations of capitalist society'.[391]

Visiting America at the time, Keynes welcomed Hoover's June 1931 moratorium of one year on all inter-governmental payments.[392] He was in Germany when Brüning declared in January 1932 that Germany could not resume reparation payments after the moratorium: 'everyone naturally attributes all the miseries of the acute deflation which is occurring to reparations, with the result that there is now a strong moral determination on the part of almost everyone that reparations must come to an end'.[393] Keynes pressed for 'the total cancellation of reparations and war debts...within the present year'.[394] However, in urging the Lausanne Conference of June–July 1932 to present 'a complete plan' to the Americans, he stressed that an end to payments should come through agreement: 'It is of great importance for

[386] Vol. 18, pp. 333–5. [387] See vol. 18, p. 347. [388] Vol. 5, p. 300 n; see below.
[389] Vol. 5, pp. 306–7; see also pp. 310–11.
[390] Vol. 8, p. 132; see also, e.g. vol. 21, p. 214 (1932).
[391] Vol. 6, pp. 338–45.
[392] Vol. 18, pp. 355–7; see also vol. 20, pp. 558–61.
[393] Vol. 18, p. 364; see also p. 366. On Keynes's talk with Brüning, see FI/2/97, 97A; L/32/7, KP.
[394] Vol. 18, pp. 367–8; see also p. 377.

the future of international relations that Treaties should not be broken and that debts should not be repudiated.'[395]

Lausanne's effective end to reparations gave Keynes 'a comfortable feeling' that the mess of Versailles 'at last' was 'cleaned up'. It also removed the 'preliminary impediments' to the world's taking 'strong doses of tonic to recover its economic health', which he urged.[396] Ramsay MacDonald wrote to Keynes: 'You have indeed been vindicated again and again for what you did in 1919.'[397]

When, in December 1932, Congress sought payment of war debts, Keynes developed two new arguments for cancellation: first, 'there . . . never were any profitable assets corresponding to the sums borrowed', making the debt 'pure usury'; and, second, 'the value received at the time was far less than that represented by the principal sums today' because of profiteering wartime prices, and subsequent deflation.[398] He urged Britain to agree to pay what is demanded but declare immediately that, failing a satisfactory settlement, there would be no further payments.[399] Britain paid the instalment due on 15 December. Just before the next instalment (June 1933), Keynes urged suspending payment pending further discussion—neither payment nor default.[400] After a token payment, of which Keynes approved, Britain made no more payments.

4.7 CONCLUSION

In his approach to post-war reconstruction after the First World War, Keynes was concerned, to varying degrees at different times, with seven aspects of post-war reconstruction: loosening the 'paper bonds' of war debts and excessive reparation demands; ensuring adequate relief; producing a flow of capital to restart the European economy; re-integrating the defeated enemy in an interdependent international economy; promoting free trade; creating a new international monetary system; and encouraging appropriate domestic policies, especially the restoration of budgetary balance. We have seen that Keynes placed particular stress on the role of Europe's relations with the USA, especially Anglo-American relations, in achieving these objectives.

The Economic Consequences mentioned all of these factors, but had little to say on the international monetary system. *A Revision of the Treaty* was most

---

[395] Vol. 18, p. 374; see also pp. 372, 375.   [396] Vol. 18, p. 379.
[397] Vol. 18, p. 380.   [398] Vol. 18, pp. 383–4; see also, e.g. vol. 21, pp. 214–15.
[399] Vol. 18, p. 386; see pp. 381–2.   [400] Vol. 18, p. 389.

concerned with debts and reparations. As those two issues settled into a clear, if unsatisfactory, course, and US lending to Europe took place but without official planning, Keynes's attention turned increasingly to the shape the international monetary system should take. This forms an important part of our discussion in Chapter 5.

5

Towards the Middle Way in Theory: The Inter-war Evolution of Keynes's Thought

Keynes's approach to inter-war economic and political problems was as a liberal thinker seeking a middle way between laissez-faire and Marxian socialism, as an economist increasingly dissatisfied with existing theory in the face of massive and enduring unemployment, and as an idealist exponent of a rule of law in international politics. This chapter surveys Keynes's inter-war writings, especially from 1922, on international monetary issues and investment abroad; international trade; population pressure; economic threats to domestic order; 'the middle way'; the mature liberal institutionalism of *The General Theory*; and international political issues, reflecting his idealism. We trace Keynes's thinking especially through such works as *A Tract on Monetary Reform* (1923), his 1920s pamphlets on liberalism and other issues, *A Treatise on Money* (1930), early 1930s writings on the Depression and protection, including his 1933 article on national self-sufficiency, and *The General Theory* (1936).

In these writings, we see reference to several economic factors as influencing the prospects for domestic and international order and peace: trade relations, foreign investment and debts, the exchange rate regime and balance of payments constraint, population pressure, and economic crises (both inflation and deflation). We have seen that Keynes grew up with the classical liberal view of free trade as an agent for peace, and that at the end of the First World War he combined this with a belief in the need for management of international economic interdependence. We have also seen that his hostility to the gold standard developed before the First World War. For several years he advocated a managed currency while still holding to the view that free trade promotes peace. However, as his thinking developed away from international laissez-faire, he came to doubt that free trade under the gold standard and laissez-faire in international lending was conducive to peace. For some time in the early 1930s, he advocated protection and greater national self-sufficiency, including in finance. In 1936, however, *The General Theory* suggested that the principal economic cause of war (the 'competitive struggle for markets') could be eliminated, and 'unimpeded' trade could be to 'mutual advantage', if countries were able to maintain full employment. This was best done by simultaneous pursuit of national policies for full employment within an international monetary system which, unlike the gold standard, did not pit the interests of one country against another.

5.1 INTERNATIONAL MONETARY RELATIONS AND INVESTMENT ABROAD[1]

As we saw in Chapter 2, Keynes presented India's gold exchange standard of 1893–1914[2] as foreshadowing the ideal currency of the future, and he valued internal price stability above exchange rate fixity. We also saw that, as early as 1913, Keynes saw the gold standard as too dependent on chance, and wanted a more rational and stable standard, subject to international control.[3] In 1909, he had planned one day to write a book entitled 'Proposals for an International Currency'.[4] In late 1914, Keynes had expressed the hope that the war would bring international regulation of the gold standard: if 'gold is at last deposed from its despotic control over us and reduced to the position of a constitutional monarch', a historic step toward human self-government would have been taken.[5] During the war, Keynes generally opposed suspending the gold (exchange) standard, because that would diminish British assets and credit, and encourage Germany.[6] But, as we have seen, he was willing to abandon the exchange rate during the July 1917 exchange crisis.

At the end of the war, with the gold standard having been generally abandoned, and with exchange rates floating, there was lively discussion of alternative models to replace it.[7] In January 1919, Keynes advocated regulating the exchanges and gold exports.[8] Perhaps reflecting his 1917 experience, and foreshadowing his opposition to return to gold at the pre-war parity, he

---

[1] For useful surveys, see: D. E. Moggridge, 'Keynes and the International Monetary System, 1909–46', in J. S. Cohen and G. C. Harcourt, *International Monetary Problems and Supply-Side Economics* (Basingstoke and London, 1986); D. E. Moggridge and S. Howson, 'Keynes on Monetary Policy, 1910–1946', *Oxford Economic Papers*, 26 (1974) 226–47; A. H. Meltzer, *Keynes's Monetary Theory* (Cambridge, 1988) ch. 5.

[2] See vol. 1, ch. 2, esp. pp. 21–2; vol. 15, pp. 70–1; vol. 19, p. 521.

[3] See vol. 1, p. 71; vol. 19, pp. 506–8; vol. 20, pp. 157–65.

[4] Moggridge, 'International Monetary System', 56.

[5] Vol. 11, p. 320; see also p. 325.

[6] See esp. vol. 16, pp. 7–15, 143–9, 168, 208–9, 215–22; see Ch. 2, this volume.

[7] *Survey of International Affairs*, 1937, i, p. 123.

[8] Vol. 17, pp. 168–71; T/36, KP.

opposed 'overvaluing sterling': Britain had 'no sufficient incentive to make great sacrifices to maintain [sterling] at an artificial level'. He advocated an international currency at Amsterdam in October 1919, but found little support; he probably did so again at the Cambridge meeting in December. *The Economic Consequences* listed 'a disordered currency system which renders credit operations hazardous or impossible' as one of the 'obstacles to the revival of trade'. In proposing an international loan, Keynes suggested allying this to European currency reorganization; but no detailed scheme was suggested.[9]

However, Keynes devoted considerable attention to international monetary relations in reporting from Genoa in April 1922, and in the *Manchester Guardian* supplements from April 1922 to January 1923, material from which he reused in *A Tract on Monetary Reform*, published in December 1923.[10] The *Tract* developed Keynes's thought in four ways important to this study: the belief that inflation can lead to revolution; a renewed stress on population; the centrality of monetary reform to post-war reconstruction; and the importance of reform by individual states. We consider the third and fourth points now, the others later.

The *Tract* advocated, as Keynes had previously,[11] stabilization of market exchange rates ('devaluation') rather than deflation to restore pre-war values.[12] Keynes stressed the necessity to control budget deficits and so inflation if exchange rates were to be stabilized.[13] He opposed restoring the gold standard, which subjected prices and employment to external and arbitrary determination. The *Tract* proposed building a system of managed currency out of the system of floating exchanges then operating. While the supply of foreign exchange would be regulated to avoid purely temporary fluctuations in exchange rates, these managed rates would be adjustable to preserve internal price stability: that is, long-term flexibility combined with short-term fixity. Keynes's objective of internal price stability (and, with that, stability of trade and employment) would take precedence over exchange rate stability, as in India, whereas the gold standard placed internal price stability at the mercy of exchange rate stability.[14]

The *Tract* portrayed abandoning, or not returning to, the gold standard as one of the manifestations of the new economic order that was replacing the nineteenth-century order. The gold standard worked well then, when it was accompanied by a high degree of internal price stability. 'But the war has

---

[9] Vol. 2, pp. 154, 182–3.
[10] See vol. 17, pp. 355–69, 380–6; vol. 4, pp. xii–xiii, and *passim*; see also vol. 9, pp. 164–87.
[11] For example, vol. 17, pp. 355–69, 409–10.   [12] Vol. 4, pp. 117–25; see also p. xvi.
[13] See vol. 4, pp. 88, 144–5.   [14] See, e.g. vol. 4, pp. 126–7, 141, 149, 153.

effected a great change.'[15] In disregarding the unemployment resulting from the pre-war system, the Cunliffe Report of 1918, which proposed returning to gold at the pre-war parity, belonged to 'an almost forgotten order of ideas'. Everyone was now primarily interested in preserving the stability of business, prices, and employment, and was unlikely to sacrifice these for the pre-war parity.[16] Yet 'the Report remains the authorised declaration of our policy'.[17]

The *Tract* emphasized the action of individual states, rather than international cooperation, in currency reform and exchange stabilization, especially if international cooperation aimed to restore, rather than to replace, the gold standard. Keynes thought international cooperation unlikely.[18] Instead, the Treasury and Bank of England should put domestic price stability before exchange stability. Exchange stability could also be aimed at, as a secondary objective, through cooperation with the Federal Reserve Board in a common policy.[19] But it was not clear whether the Federal Reserve Board would act wisely, or with due regard to British interests. Keynes argued:[20]

With the existing distribution of the world's gold, the reinstatement of the gold standard means, inevitably, that we surrender the regulation of our price level and the handling of the credit cycle to the Federal Reserve Board of the United States. Even if the most intimate and cordial co-operation is established between the Board and the Bank of England, the preponderance of power will still belong to the former.

Keynes thought it rash to surrender Britain's freedom of action to the Federal Reserve Board, whose courage and independence were unproven.[21] He recommended for the USA the parallel policy as for Britain: 'to aim at the stability of the commodity value of the dollar rather than at stability of the gold value of the dollar'.[22] If Britain and the USA were both successful in this policy, 'our secondary desideratum, namely the stability of the dollar-exchange standard, would follow as a consequence'. '[I]ntimate cooperation between the Federal Reserve Board and the Bank of England' should 'develop out of experience and mutual advantage, without either side binding itself to the other.'

We have reached a stage in the evolution of money when a 'managed' currency is inevitable, but we have not yet reached the point when the management can be entrusted to a single authority. The best we can do, therefore, is to have *two* managed currencies, sterling and dollars, with as close a collaboration as possible between the aims and methods of the managements.

[15] Vol. 4, p. 132 ff at p. 134; see also p. 138; vol. 5, p. 149.
[16] Vol. 4, p. 138; see also, e.g. p. 128.   [17] Vol. 4, p. 153.
[18] Vol. 4, pp. 118 n., 128.   [19] Vol. 4, p. 147.
[20] Vol. 4, p. 139. On US financial power, see, e.g. vol. 4, pp. 76, 134, 139–40.
[21] Vol. 4, p. 140.   [22] Vol. 4, pp. 158–9.

Other countries would base their currencies either on sterling or on dollars.

From at least 1924, when he likened investment abroad to a flight of capital, Keynes argued that the extent of such investment damaged Britain's interests.[23] The British system of laissez-faire in investment was 'not very ancient and is practised nowhere else'. Defaults by foreign governments on their borrowings were worldwide and frequent. Trustee Acts gave a powerful artificial stimulus to British investment elsewhere in the Empire.[24] The effect was 'to starve home developments by diverting savings abroad and, consequently, to burden home borrowers with a higher rate of interest than they would need to pay otherwise'. Investment abroad also 'so affects the foreign exchanges that we are *compelled* to export more in order to maintain our solvency', perhaps 'by lowering the price of our products in terms of the products of other nations'. This was especially so when Britain was seeking to 'pay our debt to America'.[25] Keynes proposed legislative change to remove the bias against home investment.[26]

From 1923 to 1925, Keynes campaigned for a managed currency, and, as gold standard restoration became unavoidable, for devaluation rather than sterling's pre-war parity.[27] He responded to the return to gold with *The Economic Consequences of Mr. Churchill* in July 1925.[28] Though again attacking the gold standard as dependent on 'pure chance' and reflecting indifference to economic distress, the pamphlet was really an attack on returning to gold at the pre-war parity, which involved 'the deliberate intensification of unemployment'.[29] It argued that sterling had been revalued by 10 per cent, depressing exports. Restoring competitiveness required a cut in money wages. This would only come through industrial disruption and unemployment—unless, as Keynes proposed, there was agreement on a general cut, compensated by a fall in the cost of living.[30] (In June 1928, Keynes said deflationary finance had produced a million unemployed.[31] By contrast, he praised Poincaré for fixing the franc at about one-fifth of its pre-war gold value, thus avoiding deflation.)[32]

In the 1920s, Keynes consistently stressed the preferability of 'deliberate control of the currency' over the gold standard.[33] He described the BIS in 1929 as 'a nucleus for the super-national currency authority... a rational monetary system' requires.[34] Keynes repeated that unfulfilled[35] hope before

[23] Vol. 19, pp. 202, 275 ff; see also p. 323; vol. 30, p. 8; see also, e.g. vol. 19, p. 93 ff.
[24] Vol. 19, p. 279 ff.   [25] Vol. 19, p. 236.
[26] Vol. 19, pp. 282, 285–8.   [27] See Harrod, *Life*, pp. 420–2; vol. 9, pp. 188–206.
[28] Vol. 9, pp. 207–30; see also, e.g. vol. 19, p. 386.   [29] Vol. 9, pp. 224, 218.
[30] Vol. 9, p. 228; see also vol. 20, pp. 59, 102–6.
[31] Vol. 9, p. 85; see vol. 6, pp. 56–8, 94–5; vol. 18, p. 349.   [32] Vol. 9, p. 82.
[33] Vol. 9, p. 292; see also, e.g. p. 224.   [34] Vol. 18, p. 335; see also pp. 344–5.
[35] See vol. 21, p. 368; vol. 26, p. 221.

the Macmillan Committee on Finance and Industry (1929–1931),[36] on which he served, and in his *Treatise on Money* in 1930.[37] By then, the international economy had slumped.

Keynes saw the slump as partly due to excessive US interest rates dragging gold from most other countries, causing 'a credit contraction everywhere'.[38] This contraction showed how the gold standard transmitted economic fluctuations.[39] The gold standard also represented a great constraint on national policies to combat the slump.[40] Keynes argued that it keeps a country's investment policy and its current rates of interest linked to those in the other gold standard countries, since departure from them would lead to a loss of gold.[41] Keynes wanted the international monetary system to facilitate global expansionism, and enable individual countries to attempt national expansionism.

In his Macmillan Committee evidence in February–March 1930, Keynes nonetheless recognized the 'dangers' of abandoning the gold standard and of depreciation (such as loss of interest earnings in sterling). It was best to stay on gold until all other expedients were tried.[42] Keynes favoured tariffs, bad in the long-run,[43] but desirable to alleviate the slump;[44] measures to increase 'home investment';[45] and 'a concerted policy between the leading central banks of the world ... to raise prices'. All central banks should lower Bank rates together so none lost 'gold to his neighbours'.[46] Keynes also proposed Bank of England measures to overcome the international constraint on domestic policy—for example, greater Bank reserves,[47] and greater regulation of lending abroad.[48] In October 1930, the report of the Economic Advisory Council's Committee of Economists, which Keynes chaired, expressed grave objections to devaluation 'because of its reactions on our international credit', and said that 'none of us are prepared to recommend it at the present time'. But the Committee suggested 'that it may conceivably become necessary in the future for a number of countries to join together in making drastic changes in an international currency system which is serving us so ill'.[49]

Keynes's *Treatise on Money* was written between 1924 and September 1930, and published in October 1930.[50] It has several aspects of importance to this

---

[36] Vol. 20, pp. 152, 198, 218.   [37] Vol. 6, pp. 361–4. The *Treatise* comprises vols. 5 and 6.
[38] Vol. 13, p. 350; see vol. 20, pp. 2, 599–600.
[39] See, e.g. vol. 5, p. 305; vol. 6, pp. 176, 198, 256; vol. 20, p. 136; vol. 25, p. 273.
[40] See, e.g. vol. 6, pp. 231–2, 251, 255–6, 276, 335 ff; vol. 13, pp. 109, 111–12.
[41] Vol. 21, p. 286.   [42] Vol. 20, pp. 91–3.
[43] See vol. 20, pp. 115–16, 120.   [44] Vol. 20, p. 121; cf. p. 125; see below.
[45] Vol. 20, pp. 125–50.   [46] Vol. 20, pp. 151–2.
[47] Vol. 20, pp. 197–8, 213, 239–40, 256; vol. 6, p. 277.
[48] Vol. 20, pp. 231–8; vol. 6, pp. 278–86.   [49] Howson and Winch, *EAC*, pp. 212, 227.
[50] See vol. 13, ch. 2.

study: discussion of the transfer problem, and of excessively high interest rates arising from political debts and the gold standard, already mentioned; the benefits of profit inflations; the deficiencies of the gold standard, and the desirability of supernational management of currency; the role of power in management of the international economy; laissez-faire in lending abroad as a problem for Britain; and the reliance of free trade on wage fluidity, and discussion of commodity valorization.

The *Treatise* had the same aims for an international monetary system as Keynes had already expounded. The first was stability of the price level (that is, he said, 'the maintenance of industrial stability and the optimum output'[51]) rather than of the exchange rate.[52] Keynes was especially concerned about the cost of deflation.[53] Second, it was necessary to give each country 'adequate local autonomy... over its domestic rate of interest and its volume of foreign lending'.[54] It was both because individual central banks were constrained by the gold standard in tackling their own national problems, and because smaller ones were so much at the mercy of those central banks which were powerful enough to set an inappropriate pace, that Keynes sought 'a solution which is reasonably compatible with separate national interests'.[55]

The *Treatise* recognized the importance of power in the international economy. 'Before the war Great Britain and since the war the United States have had a considerable power of influencing the international situation to suit themselves.' France and the USA were able 'to ignore external disequilibrium for long periods at a time in the interests of their own internal equilibrium', while Britain 'has been forced to disregard internal equilibrium in the effort to sustain a self-imposed external equilibrium which was not in harmony with the existing internal situation'.[56] Under the gold standard, international economic power derived significantly from the gold holdings of states, or under the gold-exchange standard from gold-exchange reserves. Keynes identified in 'gold movements under an old-fashioned international gold standard' the virtue of impacting 'both on the country losing gold and on the country receiving gold, so that the two countries *share* the brunt of any necessary change'. Such reciprocity was precarious when central banks kept their 'reserves, not in the form of actual gold, but in the form of liquid resources at a foreign financial centre'.[57] The concentration of over half the world's monetary gold in the USA and France made their conduct enormously important.[58] The USA also found it easier than Britain to maintain

[51] Vol. 6, p. 15; see also vol. 13, pp. 90–1.   [52] Vol. 5, pp. 149, 263.
[53] See, e.g. vol. 5, pp. 245, 264.   [54] Vol. 6, p. 272.
[55] Vol. 6, pp. 255–7; cf. p. 272; see below.
[56] Vol. 5, p. 148; see also, e.g. p. 305; vol. 6, pp. 206, 241, 255, 274.
[57] Vol. 5, p. 315; see also p. 320.   [58] Vol. 6, p. 266.

internal stability because international trade and lending made up a much smaller share of America's economic life.[59]

Keynes worried that the US and French monetary authorities used their power 'to promote national policies which are out of keeping with the requirements of the international position as a whole', bringing 'about very violent disequilibria in the position of other central banks'.[60] He acknowledged that the Bank of England may have done the same at times in the nineteenth century. But he believed, as he put it in May 1932, that 'we alone can be trusted to use' the 'power of international initiative ... once we have regained it, to the general advantage'.[61]

The *Treatise* accepted that 'there can be a real divergence of interest' between states, it was wrong to expect great 'international disinterestedness' of a nation's central bank, and a solution was needed which was 'reasonably compatible with separate national interests'.[62] In bringing about an international agreement, it was open to the powerful states to be obstructive: the conservatism of France and the independence of the USA were serious obstacles.[63] However, Keynes wished not to 'exaggerate the degree of divergence of interest between different countries'.[64] When there was a major disturbance, as in 1930, 'everyone is in the same boat'. 'Broadly speaking, therefore, co-operation, rightly understood, is in everyone's interest.' Keynes continued:

Now it is the action of the lending countries of the world which mainly determines the market rate of interest and the volume of investment everywhere. Thus, if the chief lending countries would co-operate, they might do much to avoid the major investment disequilibria; that is to say, Great Britain, the United States and France. And if France prefers to live in a gilded grotto, Great Britain and the United States acting together could usually dominate the position.

The idea that Britain and the USA could and should jointly take the lead out of the Depression was a recurrent one in Keynes's writings.[65]

As we saw, the *Tract*, before the widespread return to gold, had sought to start building a new international currency system with currency reform by individual countries. The *Treatise* included a section on the historical novelty of gold's existence as the sole standard of purchasing power, and (picking up Keynes's 1914 image of gold as absolute or constitutional monarch) the prospect of its being dethroned.[66] But the *Treatise* accepted the need to start

[59] Vol. 6, p. 336.   [60] Vol. 6, pp. 256–7.   [61] Vol. 21, p. 57.
[62] Vol. 6, p. 257; see also pp. 273–4, 335 ff.   [63] Vol. 6, p. 301.
[64] Vol. 6, pp. 336–7; see also pp. 346–7.
[65] See, e.g. vol. 9, pp. 126–34; see also A/30/239–40, KP.
[66] Vol. 6, pp. 258–61; see also vol. 9, pp. 161–2; vol. 5, pp. xx–xxi.

with the fait accompli of the gold standard, despite its 'disastrous inefficiency'.[67] A 'scientifically managed world system' could have 'a gold camoufl-
age': 'it is only necessary for the supernational authority so to manage gold as
to conform to the ideal standard.'[68] Keynes thought that 'the best practical
objective might be the management of the value of gold by a supernational
authority, with a number of national monetary systems clustering round it,
each with a discretion to vary the value of its local money in terms of gold
within a range of (say) 2 per cent'.[69] This supernational management should
aim at stabilizing the standard of value in terms of a commodity price index,
and 'abolishing the credit cycle'.[70] Keynes identified 'the unwillingness of the
central banks of the world to allow the market rate of interest to fall fast
enough' as an immediate and future 'evil'.[71]

The minimum method of supernational management was a conference of
central banks. But the ideal would be a supernational bank, perhaps evolved
from the BIS, 'to which the central banks of the world would stand in much
the same relation as their own member banks stand to them'.[72] Keynes
envisaged 'supernational bank money'. Despite differences, this ideal resem-
bles Keynes's 1941–3 Clearing Union (CU) plan.[73] An international currency
was explicit in the *Treatise*, and multilateral clearing implicit.[74] The objectives—for example, liquidity provision[75]—were similar. In both cases, Keynes
was concerned with reciprocity of adjustment,[76] and he recognized, as for
'several other immature international institutions', the need for US support.[77]

We saw in Chapter 4 that the *Treatise* argued that changes in the terms of
trade as a result of changes in the rate of investment going abroad increased
the difficulty of maintaining external equilibrium.[78] Incomes at home suffered little from Britain's investing so much abroad in the nineteenth century,
when investment abroad raised exports.[79] But in 1929–30 the relative attract-
iveness of foreign lending was a serious aggravation of Britain's difficulties.[80]
Economists wrongly attributed the success of Britain's nineteenth-century
laissez-faire policy on foreign investment, 'not to the transitory peculiarities

[67] Vol. 6, p. 302; see also pp. 261, 268–9, 296, 348.
[68] Vol. 6, pp. 268–9; cf. a seemingly disingenuous claim: vol. 21, p. 186.
[69] Vol. 6, pp. 302–3. In 1931, Keynes said 'the ideal currency of the future' need not be 'a
world currency': 'fluctuating rates of exchange' within 'a network of national currencies' might
make adjustments easier 'so long as we have separate banking systems and separate wage and
price structures': Keynes to H. G. Wells, 4 Aug. 1931, CO/11/493, KP.
[70] Vol. 6, pp. 351, 354; see p. 360.   [71] Vol. 6, p. 185.
[72] Vol. 6, pp. 354–63.   [73] See ch. 6, this volume.
[74] See also vol. 6, pp. 296, 358.   [75] Vol. 6, p. 277.
[76] Vol. 6, pp. 315, 320; see vol. 5, pp. 318–19.   [77] Vol. 6, p. 363.
[78] Vol. 5, p. 66.   [79] Vol. 5, pp. 301, 311. See also vol. 6, p. 274 ff.
[80] Vol. 5, p. 313 n. See also vol. 6, pp. 165–6.

of her position, but to the sovereign virtues of *laissez-faire* as such'.[81] Keynes believed that establishing differential terms for home investment relatively to foreign investment may be needed.[82] He suggested means of 'regulating the rate of foreign lending day by day in the interests of domestic short-period equilibrium.'[83] The need to control the rate of new foreign lending, to enable 'sufficient autonomy over the domestic rate of interest',[84] became a recurring theme.

In March 1931, Keynes argued that the international slump required an international cure. The best hope lay in Britain's leadership, and the maintenance of full confidence in London required Britain to stay on gold. As we shall see, Keynes urged a substantial revenue tariff to neutralize the dangers of expansionism.[85] By August 1931, Keynes saw British devaluation as unavoidable. He urged an Empire-based currency union, devaluation, and an end to 'economy'. The only alternative was if an international conference led to the USA and France acting less selfishly in accumulating gold, cancellation of war debts and reparations, and a reversal of international deflation through cheap money and public works everywhere.[86] However, by 10 September 1931, Keynes thought that Britain had lost 'the power of international initiative' to deal with the world depression which 'we seemed to be regaining last May'. Keynes urged the National Government to devalue, and to restrict imports drastically.[87]

Keynes welcomed Britain's departure from gold on 21 September 1931, and sterling's depreciation.[88] Writing within days of Britain's going off gold, Keynes said that it gave industry much-needed relief, and Britain 'a free hand' on economic policy.[89] Keynes wrote that the currency question was now more pressing than protection, and the opportunity for British leadership had returned.[90] Devising a sound international currency policy offered 'immense opportunities for leadership by this country'. Britain could probably 'carry the whole of the Empire and more than half of the rest of the world with us' in evolving a new currency system—a 'reformed sterling standard'—'which shall be stable in terms of commodities'. This British leadership of 'a Sterling Club' would rebuild the financial supremacy of London on a firm basis. A universal settlement was obstructed by the 'Gold Club' (the gold standard countries).

---

[81] Vol. 6, p. 274; see also vol. 20, pp. 331–2.   [82] Vol. 6, p. 169.
[83] Vol. 6, p. 280; see also pp. 299–300; vol. 13, pp. 169–70.   [84] Vol. 21, p. 365 (1935).
[85] Vol. 9, pp. 235–6. See vol. 20, pp. 99–100, 295–6.
[86] Vol. 20, pp. 590–611; see also vol. 9, p. 242; vol. 21, p. 57.   [87] Vol. 9, pp. 240–2.
[88] See vol. 20, p. 617; vol. 9, pp. 243–9.   [89] Vol. 9, p. 245; vol. 21, pp. 13, 56, 230, 285–7.
[90] Vol. 9, pp. 243–4, 247–9; vol. 20, p. 617; vol. 21, pp. 14–21, 57–62; Moggridge and Howson, 'Monetary Policy', p. 237.

The Sterling Club would benefit at their expense, principally that of France and the USA:

Their loss of export trade will be an inevitable, a predictable, outcome of their own action. These countries largely for reasons resulting from the war and the war settlements, are owed much money by the rest of the world. They erect tariff barriers which prevent the payment of these sums in goods. They are unwilling to lend it. They have already taken nearly all the available surplus gold in the whole world. There remained, in logic, only one way in which the rest of the world could maintain its solvency and self-respect; namely, to cease purchasing these countries' exports.

The terms of Britain's re-entering a 'drastically reformed gold standard' would be 'strict'.

In October 1931 and April 1932, in prefaces to foreign editions of the *Treatise*, Keynes reiterated that the collapse of the gold standard in most of the world meant freedom 'to rebuild on a new plan'.[91] Keynes still envisaged two currency groupings, one sticking rigidly to gold. A currency union embracing the British Empire, Japan, South America, Central Europe, and Scandinavia could have a common currency unit, the value of which would be kept relatively stable in terms of traded commodities, and in 'a defined, but not invariable, relationship' with gold. There would be consultations within the Union on common monetary policy.

As the Depression continued, Keynes elaborated schemes for redistributing, or generating new, international liquidity as a means of international refla-tion.[92] In late 1932 and early 1933, looking ahead to the World Economic Conference, he repeatedly advocated such a scheme (most elaborately in *The Means to Prosperity* in March 1933).[93] It was inspired by Hubert Henderson.[94] An international body—the BIS, or a new institution—would 'print gold certificates to the amount of (say) $5,000,000,000', to be treated 'as the lawful equivalent of gold for all contractual and monetary purposes'.[95] The gold notes would be available as reserve money to central banks against the gold bonds of their governments, in proportion to normal requirements for gold reserves. This 'more equal distribution of the world's [monetary] reserves'[96] would facilitate exchange stabilization, the 'simultaneous relief of taxation and in-crease of loan-expenditure in many different countries'[97] necessary to restore prosperity, and abolition of 'abnormal impediments on international trade.'[98]

---

[91] Vol. 5, pp. xxi–xxii.   [92] Vol. 21, p. 187.

[93] Vol. 9, pp. 335–66, at p. 356 ff; see vol. 21, p. 233.

[94] Moggridge, *Biography*, pp. 547–8, 564, 572; vol. 21, pp. 203–4, 233; vol. 18, p. 378; R. H. Brand to Keynes, 20 Dec. 1932; Keynes to Brand, 10 Jan. 1933, CO/1/102–3, 114–15, KP. See also, e.g. vol. 21, p. 215; vol. 9, p. 357.

[95] Vol. 21, p. 216.   [96] Vol. 21, pp. 231–2.

[97] Vol. 9, p. 352.   [98] Vol. 21, pp. 215, 232; see vol. 18, p. 378.

In June 1933, during the World Economic Conference, Keynes proposed devaluation and stabilization of currencies of participants, with windfall profits from the increased nominal value of gold stocks being appropriated for tax relief or public works.[99] He described Roosevelt's Conference bombshell as 'magnificently right in forcing a decision' between gold and contractionism, on the one hand, and US-led expansion.[100] But the Conference failed, because it lacked a definite proposal to debate and mistakenly required unanimity.[101]

Over subsequent years, Keynes continued to urge short-term fixity and long-term flexibility of exchange rates.[102] Urging this at a meeting of economists in Antwerp in July 1935, Keynes nonetheless said that there need not be a uniform international monetary system: let the French franc be fixed in terms of gold, though at a devalued level. What was important for trade was that every country 'be relieved of exchange anxiety', so allowing internal expansion, the moderation of tariffs, and abolition of quotas and exchange restrictions.[103] Keynes urged central bank cooperation, through the BIS, for more even distribution of liquidity.[104] *The General Theory*, which Keynes was still completing, implied the necessity for an international monetary system allowing expansion,[105] and the usefulness of fluctuating exchange rates in obtaining 'equilibrium with the rest of the world'.[106] Keynes increasingly favoured controls on capital movements, both to allow sufficient autonomy over the domestic rate of interest and to make possible de facto stability in fluctuating exchange rates.[107] In December 1935, Keynes wrote again of the need to seek alternatives to the gold standard: it might produce inflation in future, as it had deflation in the past.[108] With this concern, Hubert Henderson in 1937 again proposed 'an international note issue which the different countries would treat as they now treat gold', controlled by an international authority. Henderson's concern now was to limit, not to encourage, the growth of 'internationally accepted purchasing power'. Keynes sympathized with Henderson's objective, but not with his specific proposal.[109] But Keynes wrote little more on international monetary relations until 1940–1, when he began developing the plans considered in Chapter 6. We return to foreign investment later.

[99] Vol. 21, pp. 264–8, 272–3.
[100] Vol. 21, pp. 275–6; C. P. Kindleberger, *The World in Depression* (Berkeley, 1973) p. 212 ff.
[101] Vol. 21, pp. 268, 281–3.   [102] Vol. 21, pp. 295–6, 312, 356–69.
[103] Vol. 21, pp. 356–8; see also, e.g. p. 362.
[104] Vol. 21, pp. 363–4; see also, e.g. vol. 11, pp. 488–9.
[105] See vol. 7, pp. 336–8, 348–9, 382; see below.
[106] Vol. 7, p. 270; see, importantly, vol. 11, pp. 498–501.
[107] Vol. 21, p. 365; vol. 11, p. 501.
[108] Keynes to Brand, 10 Dec. 1935, CO/1/116–19, KP.   [109] Vol. 21, pp. 424–6.

5.2 INTERNATIONAL TRADE

Harrod portrays Keynes's views on free trade versus protection in three phases: until 1930, a staunch 'Free Trader'; 1930–45, an advocate of measures of protection and national self-sufficiency; and 1945–6, 'reversion towards Free Trade'.[110] This is simplistic. Keynes began to abandon the arguments for free trade before 1930. His ultimate 'reversion towards Free Trade', which was incomplete and contingent, was more gradual and earlier than Harrod suggests.

5.2.1 Free Trade Evangelism

We have seen that Keynes was, as he put it, 'of free trade origin',[111] and he advocated it repeatedly before the First World War. *The Economic Consequences* proposed a free trade union to retrieve the economic efficiency destroyed by Europe's 'innumerable' new frontiers, and to promote peace.[112] In 1922 Keynes urged Britain to resist the wave of protectionism passing over Europe. Free trade had become an 'essential defence against a crushing poverty',[113] and was 'a principle of international morals'.[114] In 1923 he denied that protection could cure unemployment.[115]

   In *Am I a Liberal?* (1925), Keynes said that free trade was one of 'only two planks of the historic Liberal platform seaworthy'.[116] Of the 'two arguments for free trade', he still accepted that long-term benefits 'flow from each country's employing its resources where it has a comparative advantage'. But he no longer believed in 'the political philosophy' of laissez-faire 'which the doctrine of free trade adorned'.[117] Although a 1927 speech to Liberal candidates described free trade as one of 'the great good old causes',[118] some handwritten notes in his papers, probably written in 1927, suggest that, though still a free trader, he was increasingly sceptical of some of the arguments used for free trade.[119]

---

[110] Harrod, *Life*, pp. 500, 554–5, 721–2.   [111] Vol. 20, p. 120.
[112] Vol. 2, pp. 168–9.   [113] Vol. 19, p. 3.
[114] Vol. 17, p. 451; see vol. 21, p. 233.
[115] Vol. 19, pp. 143–57. See vol. 7, p. 334; vol. 21, pp. 207, 234.   [116] Vol. 9, p. 298.
[117] See also vol. 9, p. 295. Presumably Keynes meant the idea, which he denied in *The End of Laissez-Faire*, 'that individuals possess a prescriptive "natural liberty" in their economic activities': p. 287. J. S. Mill had not thought this: *On Liberty* (London, 1974[1859]), pp. 164–5.
[118] Vol. 19, p. 648.   [119] 'For Children Only', A/27/138–40, KP.

5.2.2 Protection and 'National Self-Sufficiency'

Keynes's renunciation of free trade came, hesitantly[120] and then boldly, in proposals, first, for emergency tariffs, and, secondly, for greater national self-sufficiency and economic isolation. Keynes moved from admitting that the classical connection between free trade and peace was an argument against a tariff, but one outweighed by the economic emergency; through saying that his proposed tariffs could also help international amity; to denying that free trade did in fact promote peace.

In 1929–30, Keynes opposed lifting the McKenna duties, as this would harm employment.[121] Before the Macmillan Committee in February–March 1930, he proposed new 'well-adjusted tariffs' to alleviate unemployment and boost business confidence.[122] There and in the *Treatise*, he said that free trade doctrine implied a fluidity of money wages which no longer existed;[123] protection *could* increase employment.[124] But Keynes opposed protection as a long-term policy.[125]

The *Treatise* argued that, given a laissez-faire policy towards investment, Britain needed 'a fairly large increase in our exports relatively to our imports'. But he doubted whether an expanding trade surplus was possible given 'the tariff walls against us,... the gradual disappearance, in a world of mass-production and of the universal adoption of modern techniques, of the special advantages in manufacture which used to be ours,' and Britain's relatively high real wages. As well as wishing to encourage home investment relatively to foreign investment, he was even coming round to regarding 'differential prices for home and foreign goods' as preferable to suffering 'indefinitely the business losses and unemployment which disequilibrium means'.[126] The *Treatise* foreshadowed his later advocacy of buffer stocks of commodities by defending valorization schemes and organized restrictions on commodity production in certain circumstances.[127]

Before the *Treatise* was published in October, Keynes had gone further. In April 1930, in the Tuesday Club and the Economic Advisory Council (EAC)'s Committee on Economic Outlook, he had questioned the appropriateness of free trade to present 'abnormalities'.[128] At the Tuesday Club, he said that Balfour's concerns three decades before about the 'perils of a Free Trade country in a Protectionist world' gave 'no hint of what most perplexes to-day

---

[120] See, e.g. vol. 20, p. 120.   [121] Vol. 20, pp. 18, 29, 114–15, 121.
[122] Vol. 20, pp. 115, 121–5.   [123] Vol. 20, pp. 115, 124; vol. 6, pp. 164, 167.
[124] Harrod, *Life*, p. 500; see vol 20, p. 386; vol. 21, p. 207; vol. 7, p. 334.
[125] Vol. 20, p. 120.   [126] Vol. 6, p. 169; see also p. 338.
[127] Vol. 6, pp. 126–7; cf. vol. 21, p. 213.
[128] Vol. 20, p. 330; see also pp. 158, 344; Howson and Winch, *EAC*, p. 58n.

a good Free Trader like myself': that the free trade argument assumes wage flexibility, but that wages were now 'out of equilibrium'. Amongst the arguments for free trade which 'remain', Keynes included 'the international [Free Trade] ideal' and the 'anti-pacific character' of alternatives.[129] By June 1930, Keynes favoured a tariff as a new source of government revenue to finance an expansionary capital programme.[130] In reply to a questionnaire from Ramsay MacDonald to members of the EAC, Keynes said in July that he had 'become reluctantly convinced that some protectionist measures should be introduced'. His reservations included that the 'arguments against tariffs on the grounds of political morality, national and international, ... are just as strong as ever they were.' But protection could be useful 'to increase our favourable foreign balance' by restricting imports; for revenue to solve the budget problem; and to protect industries such as cars, steel, and farming, which 'this country is in the long run reasonably adapted for, and ought always to have'.[131]

The EAC's Committee of Economists, created in July 1930, saw fierce debate over tariffs. In a paper dated 21 September for the Committee, Keynes favoured protection as a short-term means of alleviating unemployment *and* as a long-term policy for industry. He wrote of the 'simply enormous' benefit of a tariff 'as compared with the present state of affairs'.[132] The benefits of a tariff for the terms of trade,[133] 'which economists have always admitted as an academic point', might be very much greater than they were for Britain in the nineteenth century because the gains from specialization in manufactures were now far less: 'now that nearly all the manufacturing countries of the world have decided on a certain measure of self-sufficiency, a country which does not follow suit may pay a much greater price in instability than it gains through specialisation.'[134] Moreover, Keynes said there were 'certain fundamental industries which I should wish to preserve', in particular agriculture, despite some relative inefficiency. Keynes recognized the danger of getting 'into bad habits' with tariffs, and thought protection somewhat deleterious to growth.[135] He separately proposed to the Committee a combination of tariffs and bounties.[136]

The Committee's report in October, though accepting the free trade argument in conditions of high employment, gave sympathetic consideration to tariffs in 'the present emergency'. Among the factors the report said needed to be weighed was 'how much injury we may inflict on international ideals and

---

[129] OC/2/162–4, KP.   [130] Vol. 20, pp. 357–66, at p. 364.
[131] Vol. 20, pp. 378–80.   [132] Vol. 13, pp. 190–4, 199; vol. 20, p. 386.
[133] Defined at vol. 5, p. 64; see p. 66, and ch. 21.
[134] Vol. 13, pp. 192–4.   [135] Vol. 13, p. 199.
[136] Vol. 20, pp. 416–19.

the cause of peace and amity throughout the world'.[137] A majority of members, including Keynes, favoured emergency protection for the iron and steel industry, and a revenue tariff. The Committee was equally divided on 'tariffs plus bounties'.[138] Lionel Robbins, not content like Pigou to dissent to specific tariff proposals, refused to sign the report, and prepared his own.[139] Robbins opposed tariffs on economic grounds, and because a 'tariff is an affirmation of separatism, a refusal to co-operate, a declaration of rivalry. That twelve years after a war which devastated civilisation . . ., we should even be discussing such measures, is a sad reminder. . . that some men lose faith in a great ideal [free trade] when it is not realised quickly. . .' Robbins believed the report did not reflect the general opposition of economists to tariffs.[140] In response, he, Sir William Beveridge, and others, mainly from the London School of Economics and Political Science (LSE), began preparing a manifesto against protection.[141]

In February 1931, Keynes publicly endorsed a scheme of duties on imports and bounties on exports.[142] This scheme was also advanced by him and others in May–June 1931 in an addendum to the Macmillan Committee report discussing safeguards to enable the Bank of England to pursue an expansionary monetary policy.[143] Keynes suggested, or discussed, such a scheme at various times through the 1930s.[144]

In March 1931, Keynes provoked strong attacks from free traders by advocating a revenue tariff in the *New Statesman*.[145] He located 'the root-cause of this slump' in 'the reluctance of other creditor countries to lend'. The best hope for an international cure lay in the leadership of Britain: 'But if Great Britain is to resume leadership, she must be strong and believed to be strong. . . . [O]ur exchange position should be ruthlessly defended today, in order, above all, that we may resume the vacant financial leadership of the world, which no one else has the experience or the public spirit to occupy. . .' A revenue tariff would make expansionism possible while staying on gold. It would do this by benefiting the budget and confidence and, by relieving the pressure on the balance of trade, providing 'a much-needed margin to pay for

[137] Committee report at Howson and Winch, *EAC*, pp. 180–243, at 209.
[138] Howson and Winch, *EAC*, pp. 202–231.
[139] For Robbins's report, see Howson and Winch, *EAC*, pp. 227–31; see also pp. 57–8, 63. EA/1/88–95, KP; vol. 20, pp. 462–6; L. Robbins, *Autobiography of an Economist* (London and Basingstoke, 1971) pp. 151–2, 155–6.
[140] Howson and Winch, *EAC*, pp. 229–30.
[141] *The Manchester Guardian*, 9 Dec. 1930; Robbins, *Autobiography*, pp. 156–8; J. Harris, *William Beveridge: A Biography* (Oxford, 1977) pp. 317–19.
[142] See, e.g. vol. 20, p. 488; A/31/27–9, KP (2 Feb. 1931).
[143] Vol. 20, p. 283 ff, esp. pp. 296–301.
[144] Keynes to A. P. O'Shea, 25 June 1936, GTE/2/4/43, KP; Keynes to C. H. Whittington, 13 and 26 Oct. 1938, EA/1/139–42, 148, KP.
[145] See vol. 9, pp. 231–8; vol. 20, pp. 489–515.

the additional imports which a policy of expansion will require and to finance loans by London to necessitous debtor countries.' Thus, 'the buying power which we take away from the rest of the world by restricting certain imports we shall restore to it with the other hand.' In the existing conditions of mass unemployment, a tariff would increase employment. Keynes argued that 'Free traders may, consistently with their faith, regard a revenue tariff as our iron ration, which can be used once only in emergency. The emergency has arrived.' Although an emergency measure, it would be followed 'not by a return to *laisser-faire*, but by... more comprehensive... national planning'.[146]

The extensive controversy in the *New Statesman* over Keynes's revenue tariff proposal involved the interlocking networks of economists and Liberal thinkers, with Keynes under intense assault.[147] Two lines of reaction are important to this study: the reassertion (e.g. by Robbins) of classical liberal free trade pacificism; and the exposition (by Hobson and Kingsley Martin) of a liberal institutionalist position.

5.2.3 The Classical Liberal Response

Replying to Keynes in *New Statesman*, Robbins described free trade as 'the emblem' of 'Liberalism in international relations': 'what a tragedy that he who shattered the moral foundations of the Treaty of Versailles should now turn his magnificent gifts to the services of the mean and petty devices of economic nationalism'.[148] Robbins looked forward

to a world in which the growth of international business and the migration of capital and labour have so overlaid political frontiers that the big questions of Liberalism and Socialism can be fought out on an *international* basis, with a minimum of obstruction from the vested interests of the local government authorities called States. Because I believe that anything which creates such interests is inimical to peace and welfare, I am opposed to policies of the kind that Mr. Keynes favours.[149]

Keynes made what he admitted was 'a poor retort, perhaps':[150]

I can at least say that my practical aims are to avoid a disastrous process of competitive international wage cutting, and the social strife which this would bring; to enable this

---

[146] Vol. 20, p. 495.

[147] For support for Keynes, see *The Observer*, 8 Mar. 1931; Garvin to Keynes, 5 Apr. 1931, A/31/89, KP.

[148] L. Robbins, 'A Reply to Mr. Keynes', *NS*, 14 Mar. 1931, 100.

[149] Letter from Robbins, *NS*, 28 Mar. 1931 179. M. D. L. Dickson argued that tariffs produce antagonisms which produce war: *NS*, 4 Apr. p. 215. Robbins's *The Economic Causes of War* (London, 1939) advocated a United States of Europe.

[150] Vol. 20, p. 497.

country to resume the financial leadership of the world which we alone are capable of using in the general interest; and to prevent a domestic political reaction which might delay progress towards international peace and interrupt our policy in India.

Sir William Beveridge attacked Keynes in both the *New Statesman*[151] and *The Times*,[152] and sent him proofs of part of the free trade manifesto he and others were writing.[153] Its authors included Robbins, J. R. Hicks, and T. E. Gregory.[154] As it appeared later in 1931, the book began by quoting Marshall, and finished by quoting Keynes saying in 1923 that 'We should hold to Free Trade as a principle of international morals, and not merely as a doctrine of economic advantage':[155]

This was one of Mr. Keynes' three 'dogmas of Peace' in 1923, a life-line through the dangers and disorders of the post-war world. Though in later days it has at times lost its appeal for Mr. Keynes himself, it has not done so for many of those to whom his outlook in international affairs was then an inspiration. It is a lifeline today, as it was eight years ago.

The authors elsewhere associated free trade with 'friendly relations and good feeling' between nations, and with 'international goodwill and co-operation'.[156] Arguing against economic nationalism on the grounds that it engendered political conflict and threatened peace was to be a theme of Robbins's writings throughout the 1930s.[157]

5.2.4 Liberal institutionalism

Writing in the *New Statesman*, J. A. Hobson argued that for Britain to impose tariffs 'to shift some of their unemployment on to other countries ... would be a dangerous betrayal of the internationalism which in the long run is essential to her economic and political security'.[158] But he again urged the need for 'international economic government', with British leadership,

---

[151] *NS*, 14 Mar. 1931, 103.   [152] See vol. 20, pp. 508–12.

[153] Beveridge to Keynes, 19 Mar. 1931, CO/1/43; 21 Apr. 1931, EJ/1/3/210–11, KP; see vol. 20, pp. 512–14. Robbins still asked him to lecture at LSE: Robbins to Keynes, 28 May 1931, PS/5/36, KP.

[154] On Gregory's clashes with Keynes, see, e.g. vol. 20, pp. 113–17; *NS*, 14 Mar. 1931, 103–5.

[155] W. H. Beveridge et al., *Tariffs: The Case Examined* (London, 1931), p. 242; Robbins (*NS*, 14 Mar. 1931, 100) had quoted Keynes as a free trader in 1923; see also vol. 7, p. 334; Robbins, *Autobiography*, p. 194.

[156] Beveridge et al., *Tariffs*, pp. 147, 243.

[157] Robbins, *Autobiography*, pp. 159–65. e.g. *Economic Causes*; see also Robbins, *Money, Trade and International Relations* (London, 1971) ch. 11.

[158] J. A. Hobson, 'A World Economy', *NS*, 18 Apr. 1931, 274; see Long and Wilson, *Thinkers*, pp. 172–4, 178 ff.

to control 'economic forces'. A leader by Kingsley Martin[159] referred to
the article by Hobson, 'who remains an internationalist and a Free Trader,
but who realises that Free Trade must be interpreted' positively. Martin
elaborated:[160]

[T]he best way of making a Free Trade policy effective lies in the adoption of a
courageous attitude on the question of international finance. Falling prices mean
higher tariffs; and price stability against monetary fluctuations is the only sure
foundation on which we can begin to work effectively for tariff reduction. If
Mr. Snowden wishes to preserve *laissez-faire* in matters of trade, his best course is to
abandon *laissez-faire* in matters of finance, and to take the lead in an attempt at
handling the problems of gold and currency on international lines.

Keynes then regarded such proposals as excellent in principle but unachiev-
able in practice within a reasonable period of time.[161]

In mid-September 1931, Keynes again pleaded, barring devaluation, for
tariffs and export subsidies.[162] As we have seen, when Britain went off gold
Keynes wrote that high protection ceased to be urgent, while a sound international currency policy was devised.[163] In February 1932, although not
strongly opposed to a protective tariff, Keynes condemned competitive tariffs
and other 'beggar-my-neighbour' policies as counterproductive because of
retaliation.[164]

In April 1932, while again encouraging protection for iron, steel, and
agriculture, Keynes opposed further 'large-scale tariff experiments' as a bad
example; sterling depreciation weakened the justification for tariffs.[165] In a
November 1932 broadcast, Keynes acknowledged that 'nine times out of ten',
the 'free trader' was speaking 'words of... peace and of good will'.[166] But he
claimed that '[n]ational protection has its idealistic side, too—a side which a
well-balanced national economic policy will try to marry with the peace and
truth and international fair-dealing of free trade'. Keynes illustrated the
benefits of 'balance and security in a nation's economic life' by again supporting protection for British cars, iron and steel, and agriculture. Though he
believed that 'a world wide system of tariffs will increase unemployment
rather than diminish it, in the world as a whole', he argued that, when there
was unemployment, protection in one country would probably 'shift on to
other countries some part of our own burden of unemployment'. Though the

---

[159] See vol. 28, pp. 10–13: not G. D. H. Cole, as Freeden says (*Liberalism*, p. 124 n.)
[160] K. Martin, 'Free Trade: Negative and Positive', *NS*, 18 Apr. 1931, 272.
[161] Vol. 28, p. 11.   [162] Vol. 9, pp. 239, 241–2; vol. 20, p. 610.
[163] Vol. 9, pp. 243–4.
[164] Vol. 21, pp. 53–4, 57, 207; vol. 9, p. 352; vol. 20, p. 614; cf. vol. 9, pp. 237–8.
[165] Vol. 21, pp. 103–4; see also vol. 9, p. 246; vol. 21, pp. 208–9.   [166] Vol. 21, pp. 204–10.

Committee of Economists in 1930 had encouraged consideration of 'inter-Imperial preference' if Britain found itself economically isolated,[167] Keynes now expressed disappointment that the Ottawa Conference 'riveted tariffs more firmly... on all concerned'.

Keynes distinguished protection 'in pursuance of permanent national policies' (such as safeguarding vital industries)[168] from measures (e.g. revenue tariffs) to counter temporary payments imbalances or unemployment. Participation in the international note issue of *The Means to Prosperity* depended on removing the latter.[169] Thus, international monetary cooperation enabled trade liberalization: it would replace protective expedients as guarantor of states' autonomy to pursue full employment policies free of tight external constraint.[170] But tariffs and quotas in 'pursuance of permanent national policies' could remain.

Keynes's 1933 writing on 'National Self-Sufficiency'[171] marked the furthest point of his departure from the idea that free trade promotes peace. 'National Self-Sufficiency' was first delivered as a lecture in Dublin on 19 April.[172] It was published in *The Yale Review* for summer 1933, *Studies* in June, and in the *New Statesman* in July.[173] It produced far less reaction, certainly in the *New Statesman*, than Keynes's call for a revenue tariff had two years before.[174]

'National Self-Sufficiency' argued against free international mobility of goods and capital on the grounds that such mobility could endanger peace; that gains from the international division of labour had diminished; and that such mobility placed individual economies 'at the mercy of world forces'. Keynes proposed a gradual move towards greater 'economic isolation' and 'national self-sufficiency' in goods and finance. His motivations included his desire for Britain to fight unemployment with expansionism, which required freedom from 'interference from economic changes elsewhere'; and his new belief that 'economic internationalism' was inimical to peace. He stressed that he was not 'endorsing all those things which are being done in the political world today in the name of economic nationalism'. The experiences of Russia, Italy, and Germany, and of countries with 'straightforward protectionism', showed 'three outstanding dangers': 'the silliness of the doctrinaire', 'haste', and 'the stifling of... criticism'. If experiments in national self-sufficiency

---

[167] Howson and Winch, *EAC*, pp. 207–8.

[168] Vol. 13, p. 193; vol. 19, p. 194; vol. 21, pp. 103–4, 208–9.

[169] Vol. 9, p. 361; see p. 357; vol. 21, pp. 269–70, 360–3.

[170] See vol. 9, pp. 351, 356–7; vol. 21, p. 362.   [171] Vol. 21, pp. 233–46.

[172] See PS/5/215 ff, esp. pp. 243–86; PP/45/168/10/144–5, KP; Keynes to W. L. Cross, 30 Mar., 11 and 25 Apr. 1933, Za Yale Review, Beinecke Library, Yale.

[173] Vol. 21, p. 233.

[174] Letters, *NS*, 15, 22, and 29 July, and 5 Aug. 1933, incl. Kaldor–Robinson debate on specialization.

went wild, Keynes warned, 'I, at any rate, will soon be back again in my old nineteenth-century ideals.'

Keynes proposed no specific measures (a point underlined by his writing to the editor of *The Yale Review* that the article 'has, of course, nothing to do with the [World] Economic Conference'[175]). But he encouraged cautious experimentation towards national self-sufficiency, allowing policies to evolve with circumstances. As he often did, Keynes contrasted the nineteenth century, on the values of which he was brought up, with the new arrangements and ideas that were evolving. Among the beliefs Keynes attributed to the nineteenth-century free traders, as we have seen, was 'that they were the friends and assurers of peace and international concord and economic justice between nations'. This was the view he saw Robbins, amongst others, take in 1931. Keynes now responded:

We are pacifist today with so much strength of conviction that, if the economic internationalist could win this point, he would soon recapture our support. But it does not now seem obvious that a great concentration of national effort on the capture of foreign trade, that the penetration of a country's economic structure by the resources and the influence of foreign capitalists, that a close dependence of our economic life on the fluctuating economic policies of foreign countries, are safeguards and assurances of international peace. It is easier, in the light of experience and foresight, to argue quite the contrary.

Keynes did not set out this argument in a methodical way. But it seems he had four reasons for this view. The first was that the 'protection of a country's existing foreign interests, the capture of new markets, the progress of economic imperialism'—which Keynes evidently regarded as forces working against peace—'are a scarcely avoidable part of a scheme of things which aims at the maximum of international specialisation and at the maximum geographical diffusion of capital wherever its seat of ownership.'[176] Keynes's reference to economic imperialism here, as a by-product of laissez-faire, is in contrast with his reference to it in *The Economic Consequences*, where he contrasted his proposed free trade union with schemes of economic imperialism like Mittel-Europa.[177] In seeing these things as hostile to peace, Keynes may have been influenced by the arguments of radicals and socialists that protecting investments and maximizing markets were major causes of war.[178]

The second point Keynes made on peace was: 'Advisable domestic policies might often be easier to compass, if, for example, the phenomenon known as

[175] Keynes to Cross, 25 Apr. 1933, Za Yale Review, Beinecke Library, Yale. The sole reference to the World Economic Conference was at vol. 21, p. 244.
[176] Vol. 21, p. 236.   [177] Vol. 2, p. 169.
[178] For example, Hobson, *Imperialism* (e.g. pp. 356–7); Brailsford, *Steel and Gold*; see below.

"the flight of capital" could be ruled out.' Presumably Keynes meant that domestic economic crisis could result in international antagonism, but that such crisis could be better dealt with if, by greater national self-sufficiency, the international constraint on domestic policy was relieved.

Third, Keynes asserted that 'experience is accumulating that remotenesss between ownership and operation is an evil in the relations between men, likely or certain in the long run to set up strains and enmities which will bring to nought the financial calculation.'[179] Keynes's notes for his Dublin lecture elaborate this point.[180] Keynes said that 'remoteness between ownership and operation' was 'historically symbolised for you in Ireland by absentee land-lordism'. After the sentence about this bringing 'to nought the financial calculation', he said:

Take as an example the relations between England and Ireland. The fact that the economic interests of the two have been for generations closely intertwined has been no occasion or guarantor of peace. It may be true, I believe it is, that a large part of these economic relations are of such great economic advantage to both countries that it would be most foolish recklessly to disrupt them. But if you owed us no money, if we had never owned your land, if the exchange of goods were on a scale which made the question one of minor importance to the producers of both countries, it would be much easier to be friends.

His notes and published text continued: 'I sympathise, therefore, with those who would minimise, rather than with those who would maximise, economic entanglements between nations.'[181] That Keynes should say 'above all, let finance be primarily national' seems paradoxical for someone who fought so hard in 1919–20 for further US lending to Europe, and was to do so again during and after the Second World War. But the financial obligations (war debts and reparations) created in and after the First World War had, as Keynes predicted, contributed to political animosity. In the Depression, many countries were staggering under other debts which some were tempted to repudiate.[182]

Fourth, Keynes said that 'At any rate the age of economic internationalism was not particularly successful in avoiding war; and if its friends retort that the imperfection of its success never gave it a fair chance, it is reasonable to point out that a greater success is scarcely probable in the coming years.'[183] Keynes himself had previously argued that economic imperialism, which had made such inroads into economic internationalism by 1914, had been a cause of the First World War, and, in his free trade union proposal of 1919, had

[179] Vol. 21, p. 236; see also Keynes to Lord Salisbury, 7 Nov. 1943, L/43/109–10, KP.
[180] PS/5/243–86, at 253–4, KP.   [181] Vol. 21, p. 236.
[182] For example, New South Wales in 1932; see vol. 21, pp. 94–100.   [183] Vol. 21, p. 237.

sought to reverse the inroads of economic and political nationalism. He now saw the impossibility of that counsel of perfection. It may be that one influence on Keynes in concluding that economic internationalism might not promote peace, and on his protectionism generally, was his work in 1932–3 on Malthus for *Essays in Persuasion* (1933). James Bonar, whose work he used,[184] attributed to Malthus the view that 'identity of commercial interests seldom prevents nations from going to war with each other'.[185]

Keynes described himself as 'inclined to the belief that, after the transition is accomplished, a greater measure of national self-sufficiency and economic isolation between countries than existed in 1914 may tend to serve the cause of peace, rather than otherwise.'[186] (In his lecture notes, the words 'than existed in 1914' were inserted above the line, as if as an afterthought.)[187] The fact that Keynes was 'inclined', rather than certain, in this belief, is highlighted by his describing his arguments on peace as 'questions of doubtful judgement, where each of us will remain entitled to his own opinion'.[188]

'National Self-Sufficiency' was the culmination of a trend in Keynes's thought. He had already urged greater national self-sufficiency in commodities, and doubted that benefits of specialization were as great as in the nineteenth century.[189] He had been urging less foreign, and greater home, investment. He had urged that each state should be free to experiment in economic organization, and not 'be at the mercy of world forces'. The *Treatise* had said that a country's ability to escape international influences would be greater, the less important foreign trade and lending were to its economy.[190] On the connection between free trade and peace, Keynes was in effect responding to those who had restated, as a challenge to him, his own old belief that free trade was an element of international morals.

Keynes made no major attempt to promote the article, unlike other major articles,[191] but held off British and Irish publication until it appeared in *The Yale Review* (a less prominent venue for his ideas than he often used).[192] Keynes told the *Review* that he would be 'pleading for a middle position' between 'nineteenth century ideas' and the 'present reaction towards national self-sufficiency'.[193]

---

[184] Vol. 10, pp. xv, 71 n.; Moggridge, *Biography*, pp. 562–3.

[185] Bonar, *Malthus*, p. 225. But at p. 250 Bonar claimed 'that by ignoring political barriers, free trade may really weaken them'.

[186] Vol. 21, p. 237.   [187] PS/5/243–86, at 254, KP.   [188] Vol. 21, p. 237.

[189] Vol. 21, p. 238.   [190] Vol. 6, p. 336.

[191] For example, 'A Positive Peace Programme', 1938; see below.

[192] On holding back publication, see Keynes to Cross, 30 Mar. and 25 Apr. 1933, Za Yale Review, Beinecke Library, Yale; Keynes to G. O'Brien, 5 Apr. 1933, PS/5/235, KP. There is no sign of the World Economic Conference as a reason for delaying publication. Cf. Skidelsky, *Saviour*, p. 476.

[193] Keynes to Cross, 11 Apr. 1933, Za Yale Review, Beinecke Library, Yale.

As we shall see, *The General Theory* reaffirmed Keynes's abandonment of free trade as a doctrine.[194] But it also argued that if domestic policy (under an international monetary system that allowed it) could ensure full employment, then international trade would cease to be a zero-sum struggle to export unemployment, and become again mutually advantageous.[195] That is, Keynesian policies and international cooperation could restore the conditions for free trade. This view was reflected in Keynes's 1938 proposals for a European League, which he envisaged as 'the nucleus of a new system of freedom in trade and intercourse', including investment, 'so that to be a citizen of the European League would be to enjoy again the old personal liberties'.[196]

Having in 1919 opposed international barter,[197] Keynes urged in October 1938 that Britain's payments disequilibrium be rectified by barter agreements, ensuring that those exporting to Britain spend a reasonable proportion of the proceeds on British exports.[198] This might be facilitated through the raw materials storage proposals he had made in August 1938.[199] Commodity supply and price fluctuations were staggering and grossly inefficient: Britain should offer storage to all Empire producers of specified raw materials, either at no or a nominal charge, provided they ship their surplus produce to Britain. These supplies would remain available to the market. The scheme's immediate purpose was war insurance, but its long-term aim was stabilization of international commodity prices and supply and the general trade cycle.

5.2.5 Reversion to Free Trade?

Harrod referred to Keynes's 'reversion towards Free Trade' in 1945–6.[200] Let us discuss this now, and return to it in Chapter 6. Harrod says that Keynes had 'grave doubts until a very late stage of the feasibility of a return to an open non-discriminatory [trading] system'.[201] This was not least because of Britain's weak trade and foreign exchange position. But, once certain of sufficient international (especially American) cooperation, he reverted to stressing its advantages, subject to easing of adjustment strains. Cooperation embraced both monetary and trade matters and commitments to full employment.

Harrod's picture needs clarifying. In fact, Keynes never reverted to the free trade dogmatism of the 1900s to 1920s.[202] What he sought during the Second

---

[194] Vol. 7, pp. 333–4. [195] Vol. 7, pp. 382–3. [196] Vol. 28, p. 102.
[197] Vol. 2, p. 152; see also p. 59. [198] Vol. 21, p. 483.
[199] Vol. 21, pp. 456–70; see also (e.g. on Empire producers) pp. 473–4, 476, 505–8; vol. 14, p. 331.
[200] See Harrod, *Life*, pp. 554–5, 671–2, 720–2, 734–7. [201] Harrod, *Life*, p. 628.
[202] See, e.g. vol. 26, pp. 325–6; vol. 27, p. 445.

World War, and saw promised in the Washington proposals of 1945, was a qualified free trade. He did not make for the beneficence of free trade such strong claims as were common amongst classical liberals of the nineteenth and early twentieth centuries, and which he had long believed himself.

Moreover, it appears that during 1936–46, and perhaps earlier, Keynes's 'shift related, not to any fundamental change in his economic philosophy, but... to what appeared feasible'.[203] *The General Theory* argued that with full employment established, 'the classical theory comes into its own again', and international trade would become 'a willing and unimpeded exchange... in conditions of mutual advantage'.[204] Keynes had said the same during his most protectionist phase. For example, in 1931, he said that, with resources fully employed, 'a tariff means a diversion of output, not a net increase. I have often argued the free trade case on these lines, and would do so again in the appropriate circumstances. But at present the necessary conditions are not fulfilled.'[205] In 1934, he said: 'When we get back to full employment then we get back to our old beliefs'.[206] By the time Keynes's 1946 article on 'The Balance of Payments of the United States'[207] reiterated the importance of letting 'the classical medicine' work, international cooperation to relieve the balance of payments constraint and to stabilize capital flows, national commitments to full employment, and favourable trends in the US balance of payments, had created his preconditions for 'the classical theory [to come] into its own again'. Keynes's 1933 isolationist arguments can be seen to have been met by 1945–6: domestic policy autonomy seemed guaranteed by a system which was, he hoped, expansionist; international conflict was minimized by ensuring joint gains from economic interactions. Furthermore, Keynes believed at the end of the war that the political conditions for a lasting peace were being created.

On this account, Keynes's view, at least from 1930, may be encapsulated thus: There are substantial, if often overstated, gains from trade. But there are four obstacles to free and non-discriminatory trade: Britain's payments problem; the need for domestic control of the national economy, to enable the application of Keynesian policies; the belief that economic interdependence does not necessarily make for peace; and the desire for vital industries. International cooperation can substantially overcome at least the first three obstacles; the appropriate degree of freedom of trade depends on that cooperation. Keynes believed in 1945–6 that an economic system was being

---

[203] A. Hansen, *A Guide to Keynes* (New York, 1953), p. 225; see Thirlwall, *Laissez-Faire*, p. 26.
[204] Vol. 7, pp. 378, 382–3.   [205] Vol. 20, p. 507; see also, e.g. vol. 21, pp. 269–70.
[206] *Keynes's Lecture Notes by Robert B. Bryce* (transcribed by T. K. Rymes), Modern Archive Centre, King's College, Cambridge: lecture for 19 Nov. 1934, p. 42.
[207] Vol. 27, pp. 427–46 at pp. 444–5.

created which did largely overcome those obstacles. He therefore supported a qualified free trade: the elimination of trade discrimination in conjunction with general lowering of trade barriers, while reserving the right to impose non-discriminatory quantitative import restrictions in the case of an adverse balance of payments. On this interpretation, there is greater coherence to Keynes's view from 1930 than Harrod's account suggests, but his 1945–6 view is more complex.

5.3 POPULATION PRESSURE AND 'THE REHABILITATION OF MALTHUS'

Having before the First World War become a Malthusian pessimist, Keynes frequently referred to overpopulation as an economic and political problem, in 1919, throughout the 1920s, and into the 1930s. He was drawn into controversy through references to population in *The Economic Consequences* and in the Reconstruction supplements in 1922–3,[208] and by attacks on his views from Beveridge in 1923–4.[209]

Keynes's interest in Malthus, evident in his 1914 paper, deepened in the inter-war years. In 1922 he wrote the first version of a paper on Malthus which was to appear in *Essays in Biography* in 1933.[210] He gave a paper on Malthus again in April 1924[211] and perhaps other times; helped James Bonar with a second edition of *Malthus and His Work* and with reprinting the first edition of Malthus's *Essay* in the mid-1920s,[212] and in the 1930s encouraged publication of other works by Bonar on Malthus;[213] proposed a toast to Malthus's memory at a Malthusian League dinner in 1927;[214] and worked in 1934–5 to commemorate the centenary of Malthus's death,[215] leading Bonar to write in June 1935 of 'the Rehabilitation of Malthus'.[216] In a section of *The General Theory* written in the summer of 1935, Keynes claimed Malthus as a forerunner of his analysis of effective demand.[217]

[208] Vol. 17, pp. 440–6. Some material was recycled in his preface to Harold Wright's *Population* (1923), vol. 12, pp. 857–9.

[209] See, esp. vol. 19, p. 139; A/24, KP; Harris, *Beveridge*, pp. 341–2.

[210] Vol. 10, pp. 71–108; see vol. 30, pp. 164–5; P. Hill and R. Keynes (eds.), *Lydia and Maynard* (London, 1989), p. 54.

[211] SS/1, KP.   [212] SS/1, KP; vol. 10, p. 71 n 1.

[213] Keynes to D. Macmillan, 1 Jan. 1931, CO/1/93–4; Keynes to Bonar, 27 Sept. 1937, RES/1/2/105; Keynes to A. Robinson, 6 July 1938, EJ/1/5/209, KP.

[214] PS/3/107–21, KP. For the World Population Conference, 1927, see OC/2/185–6, KP.

[215] SS/1, KP; see vol. 10, pp. 104–8.   [216] Bonar to Keynes, 14 June 1935, SS/1/223, KP.

[217] Vol. 7, pp. 362–4, 371. On time of writing, see below.

Frequently, as we have seen, Keynes wrote of population growth as a background factor behind major upheavals, such as the Russian revolution.[218] In 1922, he saw in Bolshevik Russia nature, 'as she has often done before, . . . restoring by her usual weapons'—such as famine—'the equilibrium between man and his surroundings'. Subsequent population growth seemed to Keynes the greatest danger to Russia's economic future.[219] But in Moscow in 1925, Keynes discovered that such talk was taken badly: 'I should have remembered that Marx, criticising Malthus, had held that over-population was purely the product of a capitalist society and could not occur under Socialism'.[220]

Happy to be associated with 'Malthusian pessimism',[221] Keynes's recurrent argument was that the growth of markets and of resources, including of capital,[222] had to keep pace with population growth (as it had in the nineteenth century)[223] if there were not to be problems of overpopulation,[224] such as unemployment,[225] or low and declining living standards,[226] even starvation. *The Economic Consequences* was pessimistic about 'the diminishing response of Nature for any further increase in the population of the world'.[227] In 1920, Keynes thought it 'as certain as anything can be that the standard of life in Europe is bound to decline seriously below its pre-war level, until the influences of emigration, birth-rate and disease have brought about a new equilibrium' in population.[228] In 1923–4, Keynes attacked Beveridge for allowing the impression that 'Malthus's Devil' could be safely ignored: Keynes feared 'the actual or impending over-population of the older countries', including Britain and Germany.[229] He clearly believed that the pressure of population on a country's resources could produce, not only internal disruption,[230] but pressure for national expansion producing international antagonism. Population control would become 'the greatest of all political questions'.[231]

We have seen how Keynes discussed these issues in 1914 and 1919. In 1923, urging the need for deliberate population control, and for free trade as a central tenet of pacifism, Keynes wrote:[232]

[218] See ch. 4, this volume; vol. 2, pp. 8–9; cf. vol. 17, p. 436; vol. 19, p. 437.
[219] Vol. 17, pp. 437, 439; vol. 19, p. 437.   [220] Vol. 10, p. 91 n; see vol. 29, pp. 437, 441.
[221] See, e.g. vol. 19, pp. 136–7; vol. 17, p. 453.
[222] On the need for saving, see e.g. vol. 17, p. 267.
[223] Vol. 17, p. 442. On population growth as a key attribute of the 19th-century economy, see also vol. 7, p. 307.
[224] Vol. 17, p. 443.
[225] In 1923: vol. 19, p. 79; see also pp. 120–4, 154; cf. vol. 20, p. 318 (1930).
[226] Vol. 17, p. 270; vol. 18, p. 26 (Germany, 1922); vol. 19, pp. 124, 134, 141; vol. 9, pp. 324–5 (1928, 1930); see also vol. 30, p. 7.
[227] Vol. 2, p. 161.   [228] Vol. 17, p. 89.
[229] Vol. 19, pp. 135–6.   [230] See, e.g. vol. 17, p. 267 (1921).
[231] Vol. 17, p. 446; see also, e.g. Keynes to Brailsford, 1 Jan. 1921, CO/1/95–6, KP.
[232] Vol. 17, pp. 451–2.

I include in free trade the abandonment of any attempt to secure for ourselves exclusive supplies of food and material—in spite of what is said below about the pressure of population on resources. For if pressure of population is to lead to a regime of armed and powerful nations grabbing resources from weak holders, our last state will be worse than it ever can be under any alternative policy.

Just as in economic management Keynes sought to substitute rational control for blind forces,[233] so he repeatedly urged the necessity for states to achieve 'conscious control'[234] of their population (including, in time, of its quality), rather than leaving it, to their 'undoing, to the blind forces of nature'.[235] Population control was a prerequisite to any 'far-reaching scheme of social improvement',[236] and would help determine the pace of reaching 'our destination of economic bliss'.[237] Although he denied in February 1924 that he had argued in print for birth control,[238] a deeply controversial topic, Keynes had certainly implied support for it; and he was by 1925 explicitly to advocate it as a means of population control (and for 'the liberties of women').[239] This stress on birth control placed Keynes 'at the forefront of social thinking'.[240]

Identifying during the 1923 election campaign that 'Our problem is to find expanding markets and an increased capital equipment for a growing industrial population', Keynes denied that protection, which would reduce the volume of trade, could help. Population increase contributed to unemployment; this could 'be compensated in no other way than by expanding our international markets so as to sell more goods to pay for the needed imports'.[241] The *Tract* argued that inflation may have destroyed the favourable conditions for saving which in the nineteenth century 'provided [the] proportionate growth between capital and population' necessary for maintaining living standards.[242] In 1924, as we have seen, Keynes argued that Britain needed to invest less abroad, and more at home, 'if our national equipment is to grow as fast as our population and our theoretical standards of life'.[243]

In 1927, Keynes told the Malthusian League that the battle for use of birth control as a check on population was practically won, and the population problem would 'merge in the much greater problem of Heredity and Eugenics': 'Mankind . . . has taken into his own hands out of the hands of Nature the task and the duty of moulding his body and his soul to a pattern.'[244] Keynes's

[233] See, e.g. vol 6, p. 256; A/24/150, KP (1924); see also Freeden, *Liberalism*, pp. 141, 159, 352.
[234] Vol. 17, p. 446; see also pp. 451–3; vol. 12, p. 859; vol. 30, p. 7; vol. 18, p. 125; vol. 21, p. 89; vol. 19, p. 437; vol. 9, p. 292.
[235] Vol. 30, p. 7; see also, e.g. vol. 17, p. 453.   [236] Vol. 17, pp. 270–1, 453–4.
[237] Vol. 9, p. 331; see also vol. 21, p. 89.   [238] Vol. 19, p. 139.
[239] Vol. 9, p. 303. For material on birth control, 1922–6, see SS/3, KP.
[240] Freeden, *Liberalism*, p. 160; see also p. 167.   [241] Vol. 19, pp. 152, 154.
[242] Vol. 4, pp. 29–30.   [243] Vol. 19, p. 284.   [244] PS/3/114 (see also 112), KP.

interest in eugenics brought together his concern to check population growth
with his belief in the power of heredity. (In 1944, Keynes resigned as vice-
president of the Malthusian League, of which he had not heard for many years,
and repudiated its call for control of population growth among 'poorer'
sections of society.)[245]

With population growth slowing by the 1930s, Keynes gyrated between
thinking this helped or hindered economic welfare.[246] Toye depicts a recant-
ing of his earlier neo-Malthusian beliefs on population dating from 1928.[247]
In *The General Theory*, Keynes said that passing 'from a period of increasing
population into one of declining population' would lengthen each phase of
the trade cycle.[248] In 1937, Keynes stressed the effect of population changes on
the demand for capital,[249] and argued:

With a stationary population we shall ... be absolutely dependent for the maintenance
of prosperity and civil peace on policies of increasing consumption by a more equal
distribution of incomes and of forcing down the rate of interest ... If we do not, of set
and determined purpose, pursue these policies, then without question we shall be
cheated of the benefits which we stand to gain by the chaining up of one devil
[population], and shall suffer from the perhaps more intolerable depredations of
the other [unemployment].[250]

In that event, 'a chronic tendency towards the underemployment of resources
must in the end sap and destroy [capitalist] society'. Thus the declining trend
of population complicates the task of maintaining capitalism by reforming it,
but it does not render the task impossible. Given that *The General Theory* saw
the maintenance of full employment as necessary to overcome the 'competitive struggle for markets' as a cause of war,[251] and that Keynes saw stationary
population as complicating the task of maintaining full employment, it
follows that he saw stationary population as in this way complicating the
overcoming of one economic cause of war.

On the other hand, *The General Theory* also referred to 'the pressure of
population' as itself an economic cause of war.[252] Attaining 'equilibrium in
the trend of their population' was necessary to avoid the interests of one
country being set against those of its neighbours. This reference sits naturally

[245] L/44/1–5, KP.
[246] Vol. 20, pp. 318, 320–1; vol. 6, p. 168; vol. 9, pp. 324–5, 331; vol. 21, p. 89; vol. 20, p. 517.
On the slower rate of population growth, see also vol. 20, pp. 391, 543, 573; vol. 21, pp. 316, 403.
[247] Toye, 'Keynes on population and economic growth', p. 15 ff.; Toye, *Keynes on Population*,
pp. 8–9, and p. 187 ff.
[248] Vol. 7, p. 318. On the impact of population growth on the interest rate, see also vol. 20,
p. 543.
[249] Vol. 14, pp. 124–33, at p. 131; see also p. 161.   [250] Vol. 14, p. 132.
[251] Vol. 7, pp. 381–2; see below.   [252] Vol. 7, pp. 381–2.

with Keynes's earlier, recurrent discussions of overpopulation as a cause of disruption. *The General Theory's* discussions of the effects of declining population *and* of population pressure reflect twin tendencies in discussion of population in the 1930s. For example, in 1935, during which Keynes wrote the sections of *The General Theory* referring to population, *The Economic Journal,* which he edited, published a review by C. W. Guillebaud of E. F. Penrose's *Population Theories and their Application, with Special Reference to Japan* (which discussed the connection between population and conflict, including in Manchukuo), and a review by A. M. Carr-Saunders of Enid Charles's *The Twilight of Parenthood*[253] (which reflected the 'growing national unease with under-population'[254] in the mid-1930s). Carr-Saunders, whom Keynes knew,[255] was then writing his *World Population,* which also discussed population pressure as a cause of war[256]—a popular topic in the 1930s. In a pamphlet responding to *The General Theory,* A. L. Rowse argued that, since Germany, Italy, and Japan were promoting population growth at the same time as they sought more territory for their populations, Keynes's view on the need for population equilibrium for peace led to a pessimistic view of the prospects for peace.[257]

5.4 ECONOMIC THREATS TO DOMESTIC ORDER

Over time, Keynes identified various ways in which domestic economic disorder produces domestic political disorder (e.g. revolution); and, at times, he suggested that this could produce international political conflict.

We saw in Chapter 4 that *The Economic Consequences* depicted impoverishment as causing domestic and international political disorder. By contrast, *A Revision of the Treaty* claimed that 'it is in times of growing profits and not in times of growing distress' that working class revolt comes.[258] Keynes feared the occupation of the Ruhr in January 1923 might precipitate acute unemployment in Germany:[259]

The combination of economic distress with patriotic rage might at last drive Germany desperate. A movement of violence from reactionary Bavaria, aided perhaps by the

---

[253] *EJ*, 45 (1935), 545–7 and 164–7, respectively.   [254] Freeden, *Liberalism*, p. 344.

[255] See, e.g. EJ/1/5/234, 419; UA/14/2/58–65, KP.

[256] A. M. Carr-Saunders, *World Population* (Oxford, 1936) at, e.g. pp. 321–6.

[257] A. L. Rowse, *Mr. Keynes and the Labour Movement* (London, 1936), p. 56. Keynes thought this pamphlet 'quite well done', and encouraged its publication: Keynes to H. Macmillan; to Rowse, 12 May 1936, GTE/2/4/225–7, KP.

[258] Vol. 3, p. 116.   [259] Vol. 18, p. 108.

Communist left, would face us with a German government ... of more savage material [than hitherto], such material as we know with only too much reason to lie below the surface in Germany.

But in July, as the Ruhr occupation continued, Keynes found that 'half the population is torn and divided against itself by fierce political dissensions, and the other half is apathetic'.[260]

Keynes frequently wondered whether capitalism could survive. In the early years after the First World War, he stressed the danger to capitalism from inflation; but as deflationary forces in Britain persisted through the 1920s, and with the Depression, his focus turned to deflation as the danger.

5.4.1 Inflation

The Economic Consequences in 1919 asserted that inflation, combined with popular hatred of entrepreneurs as profiteers, could threaten domestic stability.[261] *A Revision* (1922) stressed the role of the profiteer, not privation, in producing revolt.[262] The *Tract* (1923) reiterated these beliefs. The order of society would decay unless means were found to stabilize the standard of value.[263] It depicted inflation turning businessmen into profiteers as part of the process by which inflation affects different classes unequally.[264] Where the profiteer was seen to gain from 'lucky gambling' rather than in some rough proportion to his contribution to society, 'the psychological equilibrium which permits the perpetuance of unequal rewards', one of the essential props of capitalism, was destroyed.[265] Moreover, inflation, which enriched many entrepreneurs, impoverished savers:[266] the continued drawing of voluntary savings into investments depended on price stability.[267]

Keynes saw inflation as impoverishing the middle class throughout Europe.[268] He valued highly the beneficent and stabilizing role the middle class played. For example, *The Economic Consequences* appears to have seen the German middle class as the bastion of moderation and order in Germany and, through that, of peace.[269] In *A Short View of Russia*, in 1925, Keynes asked: 'How can I adopt a creed which ... exalts the boorish proletariat above the bourgeois and the intelligentsia who, with whatever faults, are the quality in life and surely carry the seeds of all human advancement?'[270]

The *Tract*'s account of inflation was based on the quantity theory of money. Government budget deficits were the principal cause of inflation. Sound

---

[260] Vol. 18, p. 185.   [261] Vol. 2, pp. 149–50; vol. 9, pp. 57–8.

[262] Vol. 3, p. 116.   [263] Vol. 4, p. xiv; see also p. 36.   [264] Vol. 4, p. 1.

[265] Vol. 4, p. 24.   [266] Vol. 4, p. 55.   [267] Vol. 4, pp. 4–17.

[268] Vol. 4, p. 29.   [269] Vol. 2, p. 184.   [270] Vol. 9, p. 258; see also p. 297.

public finance was part of Keynes's prescription.[271] However, Keynes believed that conservative notions on currency were self-defeating: it was innovation that would preserve society.[272] Those 'absolutists of contract' who, for example, prefer 'inequitable and disastrous' inflation to a capital levy, 'are the real parents of revolution'.[273]

Keynes, happy himself to profit from speculation, did not attribute moral blame to profiteers. They were active entrepreneurs whose windfalls were consequence, not cause, of inflation.[274] But whereas profiteers were depicted in those early post-war writings as becoming an unintentional threat to capitalism, the *Treatise* (1930) applauded their role in progress. Keynes wrote that 'the wealth of nations is enriched, not during income inflations but during profit inflations', that is, 'when prices are running away from costs'.[275] Keynes wrote of the great progress during 'the rise of European prices during the sixteenth and seventeenth centuries as a result of the flow of precious metals from America':

[T]he greater part of the fruits of the economic progress and capital accumulation of the Elizabethan and Jacobean age accrued to the profiteer rather than to the wage earner. Never in the annals of the modern world has there existed so prolonged and so rich an opportunity for the business man, the speculator and the profiteer. In these golden years modern capitalism was born.

Citing the example of Shakespeare, who died rich, writing during this great profit inflation, Keynes wrote, only partly in jest: 'I offer it as a thesis for examination by those who like rash generalisations, that by far the larger proportion of the world's greatest writers and artists have flourished in the atmosphere of buoyancy, exhilaration and the freedom from economic cares felt by the governing class, which is engendered by profit inflations.'[276]

Keynes was keen to have historians give greater recognition to the effects of economic, especially monetary, factors in history.[277] In particular, he stressed 'the extraordinary correspondence between the periods of profit inflation and of profit deflation respectively with those of national rise and decline.' This was true of the post-war period also: 'France has been rebuilt since the war and her foreign investments greatly augmented, neither by exceptional

---

[271] See, e.g. vol. 4, p. 8.

[272] Vol. 4, p. xiv; see also, e.g. vol. 7, p. 380; vol. 9, pp. 296–7, 299. *The End of Laissez-faire* argued that 'devotees of capitalism are often unduly conservative, and reject reforms in its technique, which might really strengthen and preserve it, for fear that they may prove to be first steps away from capitalism itself': vol. 9, p. 294.

[273] Vol. 4, pp. 55–7.   [274] Vol. 2, pp. 149–50.   [275] Vol. 6, pp. 135–7.

[276] Vol. 6, p. 137 n. See J. Robinson, *Economic Philosophy* (London, 1964), p. 74. Robbins, *Money*, p. 13; Strachey, *Coming Struggle*, pp. 203–4; cf. vol. 6, pp. 139–40.

[277] See, e.g. vol. 6, pp. 134–5, 138 n., 139 n.

efficiency nor by exceptional thrift, but by a steep profit inflation which has already lasted for a full decade'.[278]

Whereas the *Tract* had depicted inflation as hostile to capital accumulation, the *Treatise* saw a profit inflation as being accompanied by an abnormal growth of capital wealth (though also by greater inequality of wealth). Keynes believed that 'today a tendency towards a modest profit inflation would accelerate our rate of progress, as compared with the results of a modest profit deflation'. But he expressed 'a preference for a policy today which, whilst avoiding deflation at all costs, aims at the stability of purchasing power as its ideal objective'. Prefiguring the argument of *The General Theory*, he wrote: 'Perhaps the ultimate solution lies in the rate of capital development becoming more largely an affair of state, determined by collective wisdom and long views.'[279]

5.4.2 Deflation

The threat to capitalism which the *Treatise* explicitly identified was deflation, not inflation. Keynes wrote of misguided monetary policies during the slump of 1930 as sapping the foundations of capitalist society.[280] As the Depression deepened, he referred to the danger of mass unemployment doing untold damage to social stability;[281] and said in September 1931 that if 'economy' were carried far, greatly intensifying unemployment, it might 'produce social effects so shocking as to shake the whole system of our national life'.[282]

In December 1930, writing on 'The Great Slump of 1930', Keynes insisted that the possibilities of economic progress remained great, but that 'we have involved ourselves in a colossal muddle, having blundered in the control of a delicate machine, the working of which we do not understand.'[283] The 'immense burden of bonded debt, both national and international' contracted since 1914 was increased by 'every fall of prices'; and a fall to the pre-war level of prices would represent a great threat to social stability: 'it must be doubtful whether the necessary adjustments could be made in time to prevent a series of bankruptcies, defaults, and repudiations which would shake the capitalist order to its foundations. Here would be fertile soil for agitation, seditions, and revolution. It is so already in many quarters of the world.'

In December 1933, again foreshadowing *The General Theory*, Keynes raised the possibility that 'the inability of the rate of interest to fall ... brought down

---

[278] Vol. 6, pp. 143, 144.   [279] Vol. 6, pp. 142, 144, 145.
[280] Vol. 6, pp. 344–6.   [281] Vol. 9, pp. 126–34; see also A/30/239–40, KP.
[282] Vol. 9, p. 238; see also Keynes to H. Belshaw, 24 May 1932, L/32/113, KP.
[283] Vol. 9, pp. 126–34; see also A/30/239–40, KP.

civilisations' in the past, since unemployment caused in a rich society by too high a rate of interest 'causes more discontent than natural poverty'.[284] *The General Theory* saw this as a potential threat to present-day capitalism. Keynes referred to the nineteenth century as having an 'average level of employment [which] was... substantially below full employment, but not so intolerably below it as to provoke revolutionary changes'. But the contemporary problem was that a lower interest rate was needed to produce tolerable average employment than seemed likely to be established by manipulating the money supply.[285] In advocating international economic collaboration during the Second World War, Keynes attributed to economic suffering much blame for 'preparing the soiled atmosphere in which the Nazis could thrive'.[286]

5.5 BETWEEN LAISSEZ-FAIRE AND MARXISM

In both the 1920s and 1930s, therefore, Keynes saw capitalism as vulnerable. Laissez-faire provided no answer. But Keynes was hostile also to Marxian socialism. Like other liberals,[287] he sought to find a middle way between the two that, by reforming capitalism, would save it, and make it more worth saving. This project was evident in Keynes's 1920s pamphlets, and in unpublished drafts. Like other Liberals at a time of Liberal decline and seemingly increased need for economic interventionism, Keynes also struggled with the relationship between his liberalism and Labourite socialism.[288] We will see this reflected in, for example, his approach to socialist arguments on the causes of war, and on foreign policy, in the 1930s.

Keynes believed that, with a shift away from nineteenth-century economic conditions,[289] new economic ideas were needed. The 'most violent interferences with stability and with justice' in the nineteenth century came from changes in the price level, but the consequences of such changes were no longer tolerable, especially with fluctuations more violent than before.[290] In *The End of Laissez-Faire* (on which Keynes lectured in 1924, and published in

---

[284] T. K. Rymes, *Keynes's Lectures, 1932–35: Notes of a Representative Student* (Basingstoke and London, 1989), p. 127; see also p. 128.

[285] Vol. 7, p. 308.   [286] Vol. 25, pp. 279–80; vol. 26, p. 14.

[287] For example, H. Macmillan, *Reconstruction* (London, 1933), ch. 9; id., *The Middle Way* (London, 1938). Keynes saw liberals in all parties: vol. 9, p. 310; vol. 21, pp. 491–500.

[288] For example, vol. 9, pp. 307–11; vol. 19, pp. 472–3, 638–48; vol. 21, pp. 372–3, 500–4; vol. 28, pp. 107, 123. O'Donnell, *Philosophy* pp. 323–4, 381–2.

[289] Vol. 9, pp. 303–6. A (1926?) draft table of contents for 'Essays on the Economic Future of the World' started: '1. Transitional character of 19th century', A/2//9, KP.

[290] For the greater violence of fluctuations, see, e.g. vol. 20, p. 317 (1930).

1926), he said that laissez-faire was fixed in the popular mind in the nineteenth century 'as the practical conclusion of orthodox political economy',
and had 'its most fervent expression in free trade'.[291] Keynes cited Mrs
Marcet's *Conversations on Political Economy* (1817) as teaching that 'the
interests of nations, as well as those of individuals, so far from being opposed
to each other, are in the most perfect unison'. That private and social interest
were in harmony remained in the popular mind despite the attempts of
economists from John Stuart Mill onwards to dislodge it.[292] The continued
predominance of laissez-faire was helped by the intellectual weakness of the
alternatives—protectionism, and Marxian socialism.[293] Keynes sought 'improvements in the technique of modern capitalism by the agency of collective
action'. Capitalism, 'wisely managed', could 'probably be made more efficient
for attaining economic ends than any alternative system yet in sight', but 'in
itself it is in many ways extremely objectionable'.[294] Keynes sought a path
between individualistic capitalism and socialism, combining 'economic
efficiency, social justice, and individual liberty'.[295]

Am I a Liberal? (August 1925)[296] depicted the 'middle course' as being
between Fascism and Bolshevism, and between laissez-faire and socialism.
Neither of the latter pair offered a middle course between the former ex-
tremes.

The transition from economic anarchy to a regime which deliberately aims at con-
trolling and directing economic forces in the interests of social justice and social
stability, will present enormous difficulties both technical and political. I suggest,
nevertheless, that the true destiny of New Liberalism is to seek their solution.[297]

The 'coming political struggle' was *not* 'best described as capitalism *versus*
socialism'.[298]

A Short View of Russia (1925) was sympathetic to the possibility 'that
beneath the cruelty and stupidity of New Russia some speck of the ideal
may lie hid'.[299] But Keynes was 'not ready for a creed...which uses deliberately the weapons of persecution, destruction, and international strife'. Its
policy found 'a characteristic expression in spending millions...to stir up
trouble abroad' (although it was perhaps no worse than other 'greedy, warlike,
and imperialist' governments).[300] Marxism-Leninism was not a solution to

---

[291] Vol. 9, pp. 278–80; see p. 272 ff.   [292] Vol. 9, pp. 280–2.
[293] Vol. 9, p. 285.   [294] Vol. 9, pp. 292–4.
[295] See also, e.g. vol. 9, pp. 309–311. 'Thoughts on reading Hobson's Free Thought', 2 Apr.
1926, A/2/48, KP. For some of the intellectual background, see Freeden, *Liberalism*, e.g. pp. 137,
149, 161–4, and *passim*.
[296] Vol. 9, pp. 295–306; see also vol. 29, pp. 434–42.
[297] Vol. 9, p. 305; see also vol. 29, pp. 438–9.   [298] Vol. 9, p. 310.
[299] Vol. 9, p. 271.   [300] Vol. 9, p. 258.

the problem of war, then, in part because it was itself a cause of conflict. Keynes wrote that 'we have everything to lose by the methods of violent change. In Western industrial conditions the tactics of Red revolution would throw the whole population into a pit of poverty and death'. Keynes believed that for modern capitalism, which was 'absolutely irreligious', 'ultimately to defeat religious Communism', it had to be many times as efficient: but, having been greatly successful in the nineteenth century, was now only moderately successful.[301] Keynes said that 'Russia will never matter seriously to the rest of us, unless it be as a moral force'.[302] As in the earlier years of the Bolshevik period,[303] he wanted to help and not to hinder Russia.

In the mid-1920s, Keynes drafted outlines of proposed books to be entitled 'An Examination of Capitalism',[304] and 'Essays on the Economic Future of the World'.[305] A draft for the former suggests that he was considering a link between capitalism and war, though he regarded capitalism as 'essentially internationalistic'. He wrote: 'Our object [is] to preserve as much of the capitalistic machine as is compatible with sound morals'. His minimum programme covered 'population' and 'eugenics'.[306] Keynes saw the alternative to capitalism as being economic collapse.[307]

Keynes's quest for a viable middle way was made more urgent by the Depression, which increased the appeal of extreme alternatives to the existing order. In 'Economic Possibilities for Our Grandchildren' (1930), Keynes depicted the present economic suffering as arising 'not from the rheumatics of old age, but... from the painfulness of readjustment between one economic period and another.'[308] He rejected 'two opposed errors of pessimism': 'the pessimism of the revolutionaries who think that things are so bad that nothing can save us but violent change, and the pessimism of the reactionaries who consider the balance of our economic and social life so precarious that we must risk no experiments.'

In writing *The General Theory*, Keynes believed himself to be providing the economic theory to underpin the policy prescriptions he had made over several years for a managed capitalism.[309] He looked to President Roosevelt to show in practice that it could be achieved. His open letter to Roosevelt in December 1933 began:[310]

---

[301] Vol. 9, pp. 267–8.   [302] Vol. 9, p. 270.

[303] Vol. 2, pp. 183–7.

[304] A/2/1, 2; see also A/2/6, KP. See Keynes to President of Cornell, 1 June 1926, PS/3/90–2, and 18 Aug., L/26/66, KP. He was to have lectured on 'An Examination of Capitalism'.

[305] A/2/9, KP.

[306] A/2/1, KP; see also, e.g. Keynes to Brailsford, 3 Dec. 1925, CO/1/98, KP.

[307] A/2/6, KP.   [308] Vol. 9, pp. 321–2.

[309] See, e.g. vol. 21, p. 355.

[310] Vol. 21, p. 289. For origins and promotion of this letter, see A/34/1 ff, KP.

You have made yourself the trustee of those in every country who seek to mend the evils of our condition by reasoned experiment within the framework of the existing social system. If you fail, rational change will be gravely prejudiced throughout the world, leaving orthodoxy and revolution to fight it out.

Keynes wrote from Washington in 1934: 'Here, not Moscow, is the economic laboratory of the world.'[311] After the publication of *The General Theory*, Keynes took particular interest in spreading 'the leaven' of his ideas in the USA, where classical economics was especially strong.[312]

In a radio talk in 1934 in which he denied that the economy was self-adjusting, Keynes declared that '[we are] at one of those uncommon junctures of human affairs where we can be saved by the solution of an intellectual problem, and in no other way. If we know the truth already, we shall not succeed indefinitely in avoiding a clash of human passions seeking an escape from the intolerable. But I have a better hope.'[313] He was then writing the book, *The General Theory*, which he believed would solve that intellectual problem.

It is frequently overlooked that *The General Theory* arose from Keynes's deep anti-Marxism as well as from his opposition to laissez-faire economics.[314] In the 1920s and 1930s, Keynes contrasted his belief that the great problem was the intellectual one of developing 'a coherent scheme of progress' with that of Marxists, who believed they had such a scheme, which simply needed to be implemented.[315] Keynes also suggested that his alternative to Marxism (and to laissez-faire) would prevail because the Marxist idea that interests ruled the world was wrong.[316]

Keynes believed Marxism was hostile to political liberty, wrong in its diagnosis of the unreformability of capitalism, substituted a less (an even less) efficient system,[317] and did so at great cost in the transition. In 1934, describing himself as 'a defender of liberty *on principle*', Keynes said that Marxism was ready 'to sacrifice the political liberties of individuals in order to change the existing economic order': 'My own aim is economic reform by the methods of political liberalism.'[318] Keynes had little use for

---

[311] Quoted from Skidelsky, *Saviour*, p. 506; see also, e.g. vol. 21, p. 278.

[312] Keynes to A. P. Lerner, 3 Apr. 1938, EJ/1/5/81–2, KP; vol. 29, p. 270.

[313] Vol. 13, p. 492; see also Keynes to A. Le Jeune, 22 Nov. 1934, A/34/208–9, KP.

[314] There is no reference to Marx in the index to Peter Clarke's excellent *The Keynesian Revolution in the Making, 1924–1936* (Oxford, 1988). Moggridge, *Biography*, pp. 469–70, merely has Keynes 'tone deaf' to Marx; Skidelsky, *Saviour*, deals well with Keynes's anti-Marxism: p. 514 ff, and *passim*.

[315] Vol. 10, p. 67. See also, e.g. vol. 28, pp. 31, 34, 36 and *passim*; vol. 21, pp. 35, 38.

[316] Vol. 7, pp. 383–4; see also vol. 28, pp. 34–6, 42; cf. vol. 9, p. 286, for laissez-faire and business support.

[317] See, e.g. vol. 17, p. 269.   [318] Vol. 28, pp. 24–30.

class analysis,[319] nor for class politics.[320] As we have seen, he saw greater value in the middle than in the working class.[321] He said in 1943 that, despite many efforts, he would never know 'what dialectic materialism is'.[322]

Though Keynes respected Beatrice Webb, he had little sympathy in the 1930s for her admiration, or that of others, for the Soviet model: for him, the dominant Soviet realities then were wasteful incompetence and terror.[323] Keynes was deeply hostile to the influence of Marxism, especially among Cambridge undergraduates.[324] In March 1938, he said that 'Communism has a lot to feel responsible for in its effect on mind and morals.'[325] In 'My Early Beliefs' (September 1938), he depicted 'the unsurpassable individualism of our philosophy' as immunizing his generation, unlike its successors, against the 'virus' of Marxism. Here he connected Marxism with Benthamism and materialist ethics generally, as a worm 'gnawing at the insides of modern civilization'.[326] In January 1939, he took a more mellow view of the young Communists, some of whom (probably including John Strachey) he admired.[327]

In 1934, Keynes wrote for the *New Statesman* on G. B. Shaw's commentary on H. G. Wells's interview with Stalin.[328] Keynes saw Marx's picture of the capitalist world as having become outdated by the 'dizzy pace' of change since the nineteenth century. Restating his long-standing view,[329] Keynes described 'the contemporary *economic* value' of *Das Kapital* as essentially '*nil*'. Its appeal he found inexplicable.[330] Keynes saw Marxism as an offshoot of classical economics whose intellectual foundations he could destroy by destroying classical economics. Ricardo and Say had 'foisted on economics the idea that supply creates its own demand'.[331] Marx was amongst those who took this to mean that nothing can be gained from interference in a capitalist economy.[332] Marxism was thus 'a highly plausible inference from

---

[319] For example, vol. 28, pp. 56–7.

[320] Vol. 19, p. 441; see Fitzgibbons, *Vision*, pp. 173, 176–7.

[321] See, e.g. vol. 9, pp. 258, 297.

[322] Keynes to L. Woolf, 24 May 1943, L/43/69, KP; see also L/43/74; UA/14/2/46; L/42/102, KP. On Soviet philosophy as 'lunatic rubbish', see L/43/77, 81, KP.

[323] See, e.g. vol. 21, pp. 243–4; vol. 28, pp. 17–19, 57–9, 72. Keynes to B. Webb, 23 Dec. 1937, L/37/91–2; see also L/37/2, KP. Webb was probably right to see vol. 7, p. 374, as anti-Soviet: Webb to Keynes, 4 Feb. 1936, L/36/29, KP; cf. Keynes's misjudgement at vol. 30, pp. 19–20.

[324] Skidelsky, *Saviour*, p. 514 ff; see, e.g. vol. 10, p. 442; vol. 28, pp. 27, 35. On what Keynes found 'detestable' in the Soviet Union in 1925, see vol. 9, p. 258.

[325] Keynes to A. Robinson, 25 Mar. 1938, EJ/1/5/102, KP.

[326] Vol. 10, pp. 445–6; see Fitzgibbons, *Vision*, pp. 64, 94–5.

[327] Vol. 21, pp. 494–6 (Jan. 1939). On Strachey, see below.

[328] Vol. 28, p. 30 ff.   [329] For example, vol. 9, pp. 258 (1925), 285–6 (1924–6).

[330] Vol. 28, p. 38; original emphasis; see also, e.g. vol. 28, p. 42.

[331] *Keynes's Lecture Notes*, 23 Nov. 1933, p. 15. See Rymes, *Representative Student*, p. 83.

[332] *Keynes's Lecture Notes*, 29 Oct. 1934, p. 10. See Rymes, *Representative Student*, p. 135.

the Ricardian economics': 'So much so, that, if Ricardian economics were to fall, an essential prop to the intellectual foundations of Marxism would fall with it.'[333] Keynes set out to attack both Marxism and laissez-faire, twin 'forces of nineteenth-century orthodoxy' born of Say and Ricardo, in their 'citadel': classical economics.[334] He said in his 1934 commentary on Shaw-Stalin-Wells that there was a 'third alternative which will allow us to escape'.[335] Indeed, his letter to Shaw in 1935 foreshadowing *The General Theory* as a book 'which will largely revolutionise...the way the world thinks about economic problems', said that '*in particular,* the Ricardian foundations of Marxism will be knocked away'.[336] *The General Theory* itself stated that the answer to Marxism is to be found along the lines of Silvio Gesell's 'reaction against *laissez-faire* built on theoretical foundations totally unlike those of Marx in being based on a repudiation instead of on an acceptance of the classical hypotheses'.[337]

In January 1939, Keynes, while urging an 'amalgam of private capitalism and state socialism', stressed 'a profound connection between personal and political liberty and the rights of private property and private enterprise'.[338] The 'middle way'[339]—moving from 'nineteenth-century *laissez-faire*' to 'liberal socialism'[340]—was crucial 'in our struggle with the totalitarian states and in making ourselves safe from them'. Keynes thought diehards for laissez-faire, especially out-of-date ministers and 'Treasury school' civil servants, were becoming a heavy handicap in that struggle.[341]

5.6 CAPITALISM AND WAR: *THE GENERAL THEORY* AND MATURE LIBERAL INSTITUTIONALISM

The General Theory's discussion of causes of war needs to be seen in the context of the vigorous debate on this in the mid-1930s, in particular the debate amongst liberals and socialists on whether capitalism caused war. This debate was especially active in 1935, during the summer (and perhaps autumn) of

---

[333] Vol. 13, p. 488; cf. Marx as a successor to Malthus, rather than Ricardo, on effective demand: vol. 7, p. 32; see also vol. 10, p. 91 n.

[334] Vol. 13, p. 488. On the term 'classical economics': e.g. vol. 7, p. 3 n; vol. 29, pp. 270–1.

[335] Vol. 28, p. 32, see also *Keynes's Lecture Notes,* 29 Oct. 1934, p. 10.

[336] Vol. 13, pp. 492–3; vol. 28, p. 42. Emphasis added. For Shaw-Keynes exchange: vol. 28, pp. 30–42.

[337] Vol. 7, pp. 353–5.   [338] Vol. 21, pp. 492–3.

[339] Martin attributed this phrase to Keynes: vol. 21, p. 494.   [340] Vol. 21, p. 500.

[341] Vol. 21, p. 497.

which Keynes wrote the chapters of *The General Theory* touching on this issue.[342] Let us consider five instalments of this debate.

1. In January 1935, an article by J. A. Hobson in the *New Statesman*, encapsulating ideas he had expressed over many years,[343] argued that underconsumption produced an international competition for markets and for profitable investments which endangered 'world-peace'. The solution to this 'vital conflict of interests between nations' was to establish 'fair and equal access of members of all nations to the resources of the common world, including credit', and simultaneous pursuit internationally of policies for increasing consumption (e.g. by wage-raising and social services) to overcome underconsumption.[344]

2. *The Nature of Capitalist Crisis* by John Strachey (1901–63) was published in March. In 1925, as a non-Marxian socialist, Strachey's *Revolution by Reason* had argued, like Hobson, that underconsumption 'led to the race for markets, economic Imperialism, [and] war'.[345] It proposed policies to create effective demand and coordinate production to overcome underconsumption.[346] Strachey became a Marxist in 1931. In *The Coming Struggle for Power* (1932), he contrasted his argument that capitalism was unreformable with the views on managed capitalism of 'the most optimistic of all capitalist theorists, Mr. J.M. Keynes'.[347]

There is, in fact, a complete contradiction between our diagnosis of the present situation and that of Mr. Keynes. And this contradiction arises precisely from a basic difference of opinion as to whether there is a causal chain between the historical development of capitalism and the recurrence of crisis and war, or whether their coincidence is, as Mr. Keynes says, 'nothing but a frightful muddle.'[348]

Strachey (an admirer of Mosley's before becoming a Marxist) wondered whether Keynes, who was seeking to save capitalism by some measure of socialization and combining this in the early 1930s with a form of economic

[342] On 9 July, Keynes wrote to his mother: 'I began the *last* chapter of my book [ch. 24] this morning.' On 26 December, he wrote: 'I finished my book on Tuesday'. PP/45/168/10/154–5, 158–9, KP. The preface (p. xxiii) was dated 13 Dec. That Keynes was working on chs. 23 and 24 mainly in the summer is deduced from his correspondence with Hobson (July–Aug. 1935, CO/3/275–8, KP) and with Eli Heckscher (Keynes to Heckscher, 15 May 1935, RES/1/2/70–1, KP), and when chapters went to Harrod and Joan Robinson: vol. 13, pp. 526, 542, 634, 650, 653.
[343] See J. A. Hobson, *Confessions of an Economic Heretic* (London, 1938) p. 109 ff; Long and Wilson, *Thinkers*, p. 176 ff.
[344] J. A. Hobson, 'The High Road to Peace and Prosperity', *NS*, 19 Jan. 1935, 67–8.
[345] J. Strachey, *Revolution by Reason* (London, 1925), pp. 73, 87.
[346] Strachey, *Revolution*, pp. 128–9.
[347] Strachey, *Coming Struggle*, p. 94. See P. Clarke, *Liberals and Social Democrats* (Cambridge, 1978), p. 260.
[348] Strachey, *Coming Struggle*, p. 202.

nationalism, would end up, like Mosley, a Fascist.[349] In 1933, Keynes's 'National Self-Sufficiency' appeared in two parts in the *New Statesman*. In the issue in which the greater part appeared, a leading article juxtaposed Keynes's views on the benefits of managed capitalism combined with economic nationalism and Strachey's views (in *The Menace of Fascism*) on the danger of Fascism arising from British capitalism, including from attempts to save it.[350] When Mosley congratulated Keynes on his articles, Keynes replied that he wrote as he did 'not to embrace you, but to save the country from you'.[351]

In 1935, Strachey's *The Nature of Capitalist Crisis* reiterated the impossibility of a middle way between unstable capitalism and communism,[352] and expounded 'the Marxist explanation of why recurrent war is inevitable to capitalism'.[353] The world faced a choice between 'communism or barbarism'.[354] In 1937, Strachey attacked Keynes's claim that the future of Spain would not be decided by the civil war; Keynes 'refused to face the plain fact that either the Fascists will conquer Spain or they will not'.[355] Gradually, in the later 1930s, Keynes in theory, and Roosevelt in practice, influenced Strachey away from communism and towards Keynesian reformism.[356]

3. From February to April 1935, an exchange ran in the *New Statesman* on whether capitalism caused war.[357] It was reprinted as a book.[358] H. N. Brailsford, Harold Laski, and Frank Hardie argued, against Sir Norman Angell, that capitalism caused war, either through the need for capitalists to sell or invest abroad, with efforts to fence off markets or protect investments producing political conflicts.[359] Leonard Woolf argued that 'the existing protectionist, imperialist structure of capitalist society must almost inevitably sooner or later produce war'.

[349] Strachey, *Coming Struggle*, p. 205. Keynes had praised Mosley's 'manifesto' of 1930, before he became a Fascist: vol. 20, pp. 473–6.

[350] 'The Meaning of Fascism', *NS*, 15 July 1933. See J. Strachey, *The Menace of Fascism* (London, 1933), pp. 41, 234–5.

[351] Quoted from Skidelsky, *Saviour*, p. 478.

[352] J. Strachey, *The Nature of Capitalist Crisis* (London, 1935) at, e.g. p. 354.

[353] Ibid., pp. 359–64.   [354] Ibid., p. 379.

[355] J. Strachey, letter, *NS*, 24 July 1937, 143.

[356] H. Thomas, *John Strachey* (London, 1973), pp. 175, 182–4, 273; Clarke, *Liberals*, p. 274; see also A. Robinson to Keynes, 28 Mar. 1938, EJ/1/5/94, KP; J. Strachey, *A Programme for Progress* (London, 1940); see below.

[357] See *NS*, 2 Feb. 1935, 134 (critic, citing Angell's *Preface to Peace*); 9 Feb., pp. 169–70 (Brailsford); 16 Feb., pp. 210–11 (Woolf); 23 Feb., pp. 241–3 (Angell); 2 Mar., p. 278 (Brailsford, Laski); 9 Mar., pp. 311–2 (M. Munro, 'A Socialist'); 23 Mar., pp. 416–7 (J. P. M. Millar); 30 Mar., pp. 451–2 (Hardie); 6 Apr., pp. 483–4 (Angell).

[358] H. Brinton (ed.), *Does Capitalism Cause War?* (London, 1935).

[359] See also, e.g. H. N. Brailsford, *Property or Peace?* (London, 1934); *Why Capitalism Means War* (London, 1938). For Hardie-Angell correspondence, see MS. Eng. Lett. c 458, fols. 102, 103, 107; MS. Eng. Lett. c 459, fol. 197, Bodleian; see also MS. Eng. Lett. d 448, fol. 172.

4. In April and May, a further exchange arose from an article by Lord Lothian (previously Philip Kerr), a Liberal, who distinguished between the socialist view that capitalism was the main cause of war, with universal nationalization the only remedy, and the Liberal view that the root cause of war lay in the absence of world government. The 'political international anarchy, with its tariffs, embargoes, quotas and so forth' was 'preventing the international division of labour' and causing 'the apparent breakdown of capitalism'.[360] Clement Attlee replied that Lothian was wrong to deny that capitalism is the main cause of war.[361]

5. In late May, Julian Bell reviewed T. H. Wintringham's *The Coming World War* as 'a general statement of the Marx-Leninist view of the nature and causes of war, and of the contemporary international situation'.[362]

Given Keynes's intimate links with the *New Statesman*,[363] he was undoubtedly aware of the debate on whether capitalism caused war, and the debate arising from Lothian's article. In 1936, after *The General Theory* was published, his contributions to the *New Statesman* showed contempt for the idea of organized worker resistance to rearmament, which Brailsford had advocated during and after the 1935 exchange. When Abba Lerner and Paul Sweezy urged Keynes to recognize British foreign policy as driven by capitalist class interests, he replied that capitalists and communists were a tiny proportion of public opinion, and that the dominating fact of British foreign policy was 'the blind determination of the average man to keep out of war'. He described as 'brilliant' an article by Norman Angell[364] which argued that it was capitalists who were refusing to risk war, when those on the left would fight to uphold collective security.[365]

There is no direct evidence that Keynes read Julian Bell's review. Bell (1908–37) was the son of Clive and Vanessa Bell, long-standing friends of Keynes's. Having known Julian Bell 'from his earliest days',[366] Keynes established 'warm relations' with him when he went up to King's in 1927. Skidelsky writes that Bell's 'conversion to Marxism affected Keynes personally': Keynes told Bell and others that Marxism was founded on a 'silly mistake' of Ricardo's.[367] It is

---

[360] Lord Lothian, 'Liberalism and Labour', *NS*, 27 Apr. 1935, pp. 582–3.

[361] Letter from C. R. Attlee, *NS*, 4 May 1935, pp. 616–17.

[362] J. Bell, 'War and Revolution', *NS*, 25 May 1935, p. 756.

[363] Letters concerning *NS* affairs in Jan.-Mar. 1935 are at: *NS*/1/4/43–67, KP; vol. 28, pp. 43–5.

[364] N. Angell, 'The New John Bull', *Political Quarterly*, 7 (1936) 311–29.

[365] Vol. 28, pp. 46–57. For Keynes's hostility to Brailsford, see pp. 59–60, 68, 147–8, 183, 185–6, 199–202.

[366] Keynes testimonial for Bell, 8 Mar. 1934, PP/45/26/11, KP; see Bell, *Old Friends*, p. 43.

[367] Skidelsky, *Saviour*, pp. 686, 515–7; see also 293–4, 296, 339, 496. On Bell, see also Clarke, *Liberals*, pp. 259, 261.

clear from their correspondence and a glowing testimonial,[368] and from Keynes's memoir after Bell's death in the Spanish civil war,[369] that Keynes followed his career closely.

There is more direct evidence of Keynes's interest in Strachey's *The Nature of Capitalist Crisis*. It was reviewed mildly favourably by G. D. H. Cole in the *New Statesman* in March 1935,[370] and quite favourably by Keynes's Cambridge colleague, Maurice Dobb, in the July-September number of *Political Quarterly* (which Keynes had helped to found).[371] In September 1935, while working on *The General Theory*, Keynes urged Joan Robinson to write her overdue review of Strachey for *The Economic Journal*.[372] Keynes's note to Robinson referred to the link between Marx and Ricardo. That note, and especially Robinson's review,[373] suggest a connection between Strachey's book and *The General Theory*; namely, that in the face of the inability of orthodox economics to conquer the 1930s crisis of capitalism, Strachey concluded that capitalism was doomed, whereas Keynes wanted to replace orthodox economics with an economics that would reform capitalism. Strachey addressed the Marshall Society in Cambridge in late 1935 or early 1936, possibly before Keynes completed *The General Theory* in December 1935.[374]

5.6.1 *The General Theory*

When, in the summer of 1935, Keynes wrote the concluding chapters (23 and 24) of *The General Theory*, he in effect entered the debate on whether capitalism caused war. Though much has been written on the writing of *The General Theory*,[375] little has been said about the writing, or importance, of these references to war and peace.[376] Keynes rejected both the classical

[368] PP/45/26, KP.

[369] Vol. 10, pp. 358–60; see also vol. 28, pp. 73, 77; Skidelsky, *Saviour*, p. 635; Moggridge, *Biography*, pp. 612–13.

[370] G. D. H. Cole, 'Marxism trenchantly restated', *NS*, 16 Mar. 1935, pp. 384–9.

[371] M. Dobb, review, *Political Quarterly*, 6 (1935), 441–3. On Keynes and *Political Quarterly*, see, e.g. vol. 28, pp. 2, 57.

[372] Vol. 13, p. 651.

[373] *EJ*, 46 (1936), 298–302. Strachey's reply (*Programme*, pp. 303–5) implies that his view is closer than hers to Keynes's.

[374] D. Patinkin and J. C. Leith (eds), *Keynes, Cambridge and 'The General Theory'* (London and Basingstoke, 1977), pp. 51–2. On Marshall Soc.: A. Cairncross, *Austin Robinson* (Basingstoke and London, 1993), pp. 39, 78–9.

[375] For example, vol. 7, pp. xv–xvii, xxii–xxiii; L. R. Klein, *The Keynesian Revolution* (2nd edn., London and Basingstoke, 1968); Kahn, *Making*; Clarke, *Revolution*.

[376] For example, D. Patinkin, *Anticipations of the General Theory?* (Oxford, 1982), p. 14. H. P. Minsky, *John Maynard Keynes* (New York, 1975), p. 159.

liberal position that international laissez-faire promoted peace, and the socialist claim that capitalism necessarily caused war. There was a competitive struggle for markets, as Brailsford and others said, and that was the most important economic cause of war; but the pursuit of Keynesian economic policies would create sufficient demand and investment opportunities at home that this struggle would be abated. The problem was not inherent in capitalism, but could be remedied by policies which, Keynes insisted, would not destroy capitalism but make it work.[377] This middle position—that successfully managing capitalism would eliminate the economic causes of war—was directly analogous to Keynes's view that the classical economists were wrong to see economies as self-equilibrating, socialists were wrong to think that capitalism was necessarily destructively unstable, and it was by managing capitalism that it could be stabilized at high levels of employment.

The crucial passages are in chapter 23, in which Keynes discussed mercantilism and other precursors of his thinking, and in chapter 24, which considers the society which may evolve from the application of his theory.[378] Chapter 24 argued that such a society would involve 'a somewhat comprehensive socialisation of investment' to ensure full employment, but otherwise retain 'the traditional advantages' of capitalism: efficiency and freedom.[379] Against the advocates of laissez-faire, Keynes defended 'the enlargement of the functions of government' which he proposed 'as the only practicable means of avoiding the destruction of existing economic forms in their entirety', and perhaps of avoiding authoritarianism. The 'world will not much longer tolerate the unemployment' associated 'with present-day capitalistic individualism'. Against socialist critics, Keynes argued that only that degree of socialization was necessary as would achieve full employment, and that market forces could otherwise determine the allocation of resources.

Keynes then proceeded to capitalism's alleged tendency to cause war:[380]

War has several causes. Dictators and others such, to whom war offers, in expectation at least, a pleasurable excitement, find it easy to work on the natural bellicosity of their peoples. But, over and above this, facilitating their task of fanning the popular flame, are the economic causes of war, namely, the pressure of population and the competitive struggle for markets. It is the second factor, which probably played a predominant part in the nineteenth century, and might again, that is germane to this discussion.

---

[377] Vol. 7, pp. 380, 381–3; see Robbins, *Economic Causes*, pp. 31–2.

[378] Vol. 7, pp. 348–9, 381–3.

[379] Vol. 7, pp. 378–81. This discussion was influenced by Keynes's role in Liberal debates over many years. On these, see, e.g. Freeden, *Liberalism*, p. 137; see also, e.g. vol. 14, pp. 132–3.

[380] Vol. 7, pp. 381–3.

The reason was 'that, under the system of domestic *laissez-faire* and an international gold standard such as was orthodox in the latter half of the nineteenth century, there was no means open to a government whereby to mitigate the economic distress at home except through the competitive struggle for markets'. This had been discussed by Keynes in chapter 23. The solution rested in Keynes's new economic analysis:

[I]f nations can learn to provide themselves with full employment by their domestic policy (and, we must add, if they can also attain equilibrium in the trend of their population), there need be no important economic forces calculated to set the interest of one country against that of its neighbours.... International trade would cease to be what it is, namely, a desperate expedient to maintain employment at home by forcing sales on foreign markets and restricting purchases, which, if successful, will merely shift the problem of unemployment to the neighbour which is worsted in the struggle, but a willing and unimpeded exchange of goods and services in conditions of mutual advantage.

In short, Keynes's argument was both that laissez-faire did not have the tendency to peace claimed for it, and that a reformed capitalism along the lines he advocated would much improve the prospects for peace. Keynes said that 'the new system might be more favourable to peace than the old has been'. It is not clear whether by this Keynes meant simply that past causes of war would be absent, or that with these gone *and* with freer trade, some of the mechanisms classical liberals claimed were the means by which free trade actively promoted peace would work again. Such mechanisms included the creation by trade of vested interests in peace, and the promotion of moral solidarity between nations trading with each other.[381]

In chapter 23, 'Notes on Mercantilism...', Keynes had contrasted mercantilism with free trade doctrine, using Heckscher's 'masterpiece', *Mercantilism*, which had been published in English in 1935.[382] Keynes wrote:[383]

The mercantilists were under no illusions as to the nationalistic character of their policies and their tendency to promote war. It was *national* advantage and *relative* strength at which they were admittedly aiming. We may criticise them for the apparent indifference with which they accepted this inevitable consequence of an international monetary system. But intellectually their realism is much preferable to the confused thinking of contemporary advocates of an international fixed gold standard and *laissez-faire* in international lending, who believe that it is precisely these policies which will best promote peace.

[381] On these mechanisms, see above and, e.g. D. Baldwin, *Economic Statecraft* (Princeton, 1985), p. 78.

[382] See Keynes to Heckscher, 15 May 1935, RES/1/2/70–1, KP; see also RES/1/2/22, 23, 69, 72, KP. For early basis for 'Notes', see Rymes, *Representative Student*, pp. 83, 93, 129.

[383] Vol. 7, pp. 348–9.

Keynes continued:

Never in history was there a method devised of such efficacy for setting each country's advantage at variance with its neighbours' as the international gold (or, formerly, silver) standard. For it made domestic prosperity directly dependent on a competitive pursuit of markets and a competitive appetite for the precious metals.

This was because, under the gold standard, 'where the quantity of the domestic circulation and the domestic rate of interest are primarily determined by the balance of payments, as they were in Great Britain before the war, there is no orthodox means open to the authorities for countering unemployment at home except by struggling for an export surplus and an import of the monetary metal at the expense of their neighbours'. Keynes suggested that the fierceness of the struggle was abated when new supplies of gold and silver were abundant; but more recently 'it has tended to become increasingly internecine'. This would explain why Keynes thought that the competitive struggle for markets might again play a predominant part in causing wars.[384]

The gold standard was thus not the appropriate international monetary system. Instead, Keynes argued:[385]

It is the policy of an autonomous rate of interest, unimpeded by international preoccupations, and of a national investment programme directed to an optimum level of domestic employment which is twice blessed in the sense that it helps ourselves and our neighbours at the same time. And it is the simultaneous pursuit of these policies by all countries together which is capable of restoring economic health and strength internationally, whether we measure it by the level of domestic employment or by the volume of international trade.

It must be to these passages that Keynes was referring when he said in the subsequent (and final) chapter that he had 'mentioned in passing that the new system might be more favourable to peace than the old has been', and that he wished to 'repeat and emphasise that aspect'.[386]

In suggesting that laissez-faire in international lending may not be conducive to peace, Keynes probably was not agreeing with the socialist argument that investments abroad created interests which the state, obedient to capitalist interests, would protect. Rather, he seems to have been concerned that investment going abroad meant a higher interest rate at home than otherwise,[387] thus making it harder to reduce unemployment, and so contributing to the competitive pursuit of markets which bred animosities. The constraint

---

[384] Vol. 7, pp. 381–2.
[385] Vol. 7, p. 349. On multiplier effects under foreign trade: vol. 7, pp. 120–2.
[386] Vol. 7, p. 381.   [387] Vol. 7, p. 337.

that flight of capital imposed upon advisable domestic policies was an argument he had used in 'National Self-Sufficiency'.

Keynes's prescription for peace, therefore, was an international monetary system that, unlike the gold standard, allowed an autonomous rate of interest, and domestic policies to ensure full employment (and, preferably, the simultaneous international pursuit of these policies). 'There would still be room for the international division of labour and for international lending in appropriate conditions.' But trade would be marked by mutual advantage, not internecine struggle.[388]

Keynes criticized the classical economists (including himself as late as 1923) for their denial that protection might increase domestic employment.[389] He accepted the mercantilist argument that, in a society with 'a monetary system which rigidly links the quantity of money to the stock of the precious metals, it will be essential for the maintenance of prosperity that the authorities should pay close attention to the state of the balance of trade.'[390] But it did 'not follow from this that the maximum degree of restriction of imports will promote the maximum favourable balance of trade':

It is, indeed, arguable that in the special circumstances of mid-nineteenth-century Great Britain an almost complete freedom of trade was the policy most conducive to the development of a favourable balance. Contemporary experience of trade restrictions in post-war Europe offers manifold examples of ill-conceived impediments on freedom which, designed to improve the favourable balance, had in fact a contrary tendency.

That Keynes should write this is not surprising in the light of his previous references to the special circumstances of Britain in the nineteenth century, and to the follies of various protectionist experiments.[391] He went on to stress: 'There are strong presumptions of a general character *against* trade restrictions unless they can be justified on special grounds.' Whereas in 'National Self-Sufficiency' and elsewhere he had sought to play down the gains from international specialization, he now wrote that 'The advantages of the international division of labour are real and substantial, even though the classical school greatly overstressed them.' He urged moderation in the pursuit of 'the precious metals', not least because 'an immoderate policy may lead to a senseless international competition for a favourable balance which injures all alike.'[392]

Keynes wrote that 'if our central controls succeed in establishing an aggregate volume of output corresponding to full employment as nearly as is practicable, the classical theory comes into its own again from this point onwards.'[393] This comment was made in specific reference to leaving the

---

[388] Vol. 7, pp. 382–3. [389] Vol. 7, p. 334.
[390] Vol. 7, pp. 337–8. [391] For example, vol. 21, p. 243 ff.
[392] Vol. 7, pp. 338–9. [393] Vol. 7, p. 378.

domestic allocation of resources to market forces. But it appears that Keynes also envisaged the international corollary, namely, that there could be a high degree of freedom of trade under such circumstances. Early in the book, Keynes referred to the classical doctrine of 'the unqualified advantages of *laissez-faire* in respect of foreign trade' as amongst the propositions 'which we shall have to question.'[394] But, with full employment achieved, the objections to free trade disappear. By creating the right international monetary system, and by pursuing full employment at home, the conditions could be created for a return to unimpeded trade.

5.6.2 Keynes, Strachey, Hobson, and Meade

In urging this, *The General Theory* set out a liberal institutionalism that echoed the approaches of John Strachey in 1925, and of Hobson, and was to be echoed in the writing of James Meade. In *Revolution by Reason*, Strachey advocated domestic policies for full employment through combating under-consumption,[395] within an international monetary system that allowed it,[396] combined with free trade.[397] It was implicit that this would remove under-consumption as a cause of war. In 1925, Strachey had set out, or implied, the elements of Hobson's view, which Hobson repeated in January 1935, and which Keynes, *mutatis mutandis*, expounded in *The General Theory*. By contrast with the underconsumptionist approaches of Strachey and Hobson, *The General Theory* pointed to increasing investment to combat unemploy-ment. But, as Keynes pointed out, both approaches were concerned with effective demand;[398] and Keynes advocated state control of the propensity to consume as well as of investment.[399] Making allowance for Keynes's analysis not being underconsumptionist, the views of Hobson and Strachey in 1925 are fundamentally similar to *The General Theory*'s discussions of war and peace. They all appear to have wanted the simultaneous pursuit by states of full employment policies, within an international monetary system that did not pit the interests of states against each other (and in Hobson's case gave equal access to credit); and these could combine with free trade as an economic policy promoting peace.

As the socialist A. L. Rowse put it, *The General Theory* 'omits to notice the competitive struggle for profit' as leading, at least as much as the forces

---

[394] Vol. 7, p. 21.   [395] Strachey, *Revolution*, pp. 128–9.

[396] See Strachey, *Revolution*, esp. pp. x, 47, 52–3, 97. Other references to Keynes are at pp. 35 n, 90, 224–8.

[397] Strachey, *Revolution*, pp. 195, 204.   [398] Vol. 7, p. 364 ff; vol. 29, p. 211.

[399] See, e.g. vol. 7, pp. 219, 378; see also, e.g. vol. 14, pp. 16–17, 132; vol. 21, pp. 36–7.

Keynes did mention, 'to the rivalries of modern imperialism and to war'. That is, Keynes 'sheers off this most fundamental of questions' by disregarding the need to increase and protect investments abroad as a major cause of war, when some writers, such as Laski, thought it the most important.[400]

There is no evidence as to whether Keynes wrote as he did on the implications of his theory for war and peace because he was influenced by reading Strachey or Hobson, or other particular writers on the economic causes of war. But something can be said of Keynes's generally underrecognized relations with Strachey and Hobson. In 1926, Keynes had written sympathetically to Strachey about *Revolution by Reason*.[401] He followed some, at least, of Strachey's Marxist writings. But despite Strachey's stress in 1925 on 'effective demand',[402] Keynes did not acknowledge him as a precursor in *The General Theory*. In January 1940, Strachey sent Keynes a copy of a book, presumably *A Programme for Progress*, 'about which we spoke eighteen months ago at your house at Tilton': 'you will see at a glance how greatly I have been affected by "the general theory", partly directly and partly by reaction'.[403]

Seven pages of *The General Theory* are devoted to Hobson and Mummery's theory of underconsumption as a precursor of Keynes's own economic theory.[404] This discussion of Hobson is sometimes presented as Keynes's 'making amends'[405] for a deeply hostile review of Hobson's *Gold, Prices, and Wages* in 1913.[406] Skidelsky says Keynes 'refused to review any more of his books'.[407] They met in Liberal circles in the 1920s, but Hobson's writings frequently attacked Keynes.[408] In 1926, Keynes wrote three pages of critical but sympathetic 'Thoughts on reading Hobson's *Free Thought*'.[409] Later that year, referring to *The Living Wage* by Brailsford, Hobson, and others, Keynes told Brailsford that, although he didn't 'quite subscribe to Hobson's doctrine of under-consumption', he held a notion 'perhaps kindred' to Hobson's, that stimulating demand would have cumulative effects.[410] In April 1930, while working on the *Treatise*, Keynes told Hobson that 'the essential truth has been

[400] Rowse, *Labour Movement*, p. 55.

[401] See Keynes to Strachey, 5 Jan. 1926; Strachey to Keynes, 19 Nov. 1925 and 6 Jan. 1926, CO/11/190–4, KP; Thomas, *Strachey*, pp. 51–2.

[402] Strachey, *Revolution by Reason* at, e.g. p. 94; Skidelsky, *Saviour*, pp. 246–7, 702 (attributing *Revolution by Reason* to Mosley).

[403] Strachey to Keynes, 21 Jan. 1940, L/40/7, KP.

[404] Vol. 7, pp. 364–71; see also vol. 29, p. 211; *Keynes's Lecture Notes*, 23 Nov. 1933, p. 16.

[405] See, e.g. Skidelsky, *Saviour*, p. 535; see also vol. 13, p. 634; Clarke, *Liberals*, p. 273.

[406] Vol. 11, pp. 388–94.   [407] Skidelsky, *Hopes*, p. 218.

[408] See Clarke, *Liberals*, p. 227; see also pp. 226–42, 268–74.

[409] A/2/48–50, KP; J. A. Hobson, *Free Thought in the Social Sciences* (London, 1926). It attacked Keynes at p. 81.

[410] Keynes to Brailsford, 27 Nov. 1926, CO/1/100–1, KP; H. N. Brailsford, J. A. Hobson, A. Creech Jones, and E. F. Wise, *The Living Wage* (London, 1926).

in you', and how very near their views were.[411] The *Treatise* noted affinity between Keynes's analysis and Hobson's underconsumption theory, but stressed the differences between them.[412] In 1931, after its appearance and Hobson's article 'A World Economy', they entered into correspondence which ended (1 November 1931) with Keynes, stressing the failure of the interest rate to fall sufficiently, looking ahead to *The General Theory*.[413] In December 1931, writing of 'the great tribe of Hobsons', Keynes lauded Hobson's 'absolute honesty and independence of mind'.[414] In a 1934 broadcast, Keynes aligned himself with Hobson and other 'heretics' who disputed the orthodoxy that capitalist economies were self-adjusting.[415] In July–August 1935, as Keynes was writing the last chapters of *The General Theory*, Keynes and Hobson corresponded about Hobson's early history as a heretic, and the similarities and dissimilarities between their ideas.[416] Hobson applauded *The General Theory*, especially commending 'Concluding Notes' as 'exceedingly impressive indicators of a social economic policy'.[417] In 1938, commending Hobson's autobiography, *Confessions of an Economic Heretic*,[418] Keynes wrote of his 'fine record' as a 'heretic'.[419] (It is a striking omission that, having objected to the chapter of *The General Theory* in which Hobson appeared as, in Keynes's words, 'a tendentious attempt to glorify imbeciles',[420] Harrod did not mention Hobson in his *Life* of Keynes.)

Writing soon after publication of *The General Theory*, the young Oxford economist James Meade, a Keynesian and a free trader who was to play important roles during the Second World War, set out a programme of international economic cooperation—on employment, reducing exchange rate fluctuations, and barriers to international trade, capital flows and migration—which he argued would reduce the economic causes of war.[421] His argument that the 'wild scramble for external markets' to cure unemployment caused war echoed Keynes, as did his remedy:

[A]bove all it is necessary that countries should meet the problem of unemployment not by developing a favourable Balance of Trade at the expense of others, but by internal expansion, carried out if possible simultaneously in all countries; for the former method, if universally adopted, must lead to general impoverishment and

---

[411] Keynes to Hobson, 23 Apr. 1930, EJ/1/3/212, KP.   [412] Vol. 5, pp. 160–1.
[413] Vol. 13, pp. 330–6.   [414] Keynes to Macmillan & Co., 4 Dec. 1931, CO/3/284, KP.
[415] Vol. 13, pp. 487–8.
[416] Hobson to Keynes, 19 July and 2 Aug. 1935; Keynes to Hobson, 31 July, CO/3/275–8, KP. See vol. 7, p. 365 n.
[417] Vol. 29, p. 209.   [418] (London, 1938). See p. 194 for Keynes.
[419] Keynes to Hobson, 30 Mar. 1938, CO/3/279–80, KP.
[420] Vol. 13, p. 650; see pp. 555, 651.
[421] J. E. Meade, *An Introduction to Economic Analysis and Policy* (Oxford, 1936), p. 371 ff.

eventually to war, whereas by the latter method the way is opened to prosperity and peace.[422]

The General Theory's exposition of a way to remove the economic causes of war was a strong statement of a liberal institutionalist view. Chapter 6 suggests that Keynes and others achieved much in implementing this vision in their planning during the Second World War for the post-war world. If these propositions are true, then Keynes's thinking on this issue should be seen as an exception to Freeden's view of the 1930s as 'a decade of dormancy' in which 'the dominant currents of political thinking in England ... retreated even further into weariness and complacency'.[423] A significant step was taken in liberal thought and the intellectual basis was laid for important action in the 1940s.

5.7 KEYNES AS AN INTER-WAR IDEALIST

Idealist thinking in various forms dominated British thought about inter-national relations for most of the inter-war years.[424] Inter-war idealists were much more likely than pre-1914 idealists to see progress coming through the growth of international organizations. Their central transformative project was to create a rule of law or collective security through the League of Nations, and to sustain it through educating the awakened democracy about inter-national relations.[425] Another important strand, which Hobson embodied, combined economic internationalism with a belief, greatly heightened by the First World War, in the need for, and practical possibility of, international economic organizations or policies that would promote economic welfare and so international harmony. As laissez-faire liberalism had given way to greater state interventionism in the domestic economy, so demands had grown also for international cooperation in economic affairs to maximize welfare.

Keynes, both as a classical liberal who believed that free trade promoted peace, and then as a liberal institutionalist who believed in the need to manage international economic interdependence, belonged (like Hobson, and Angell) to the strand of idealism that stressed economic paths to greater international

---

[422] Meade, *Economic Analysis and Policy*, pp. 386, 388.

[423] Freeden, *Liberalism*, p. 329. But see pp. 351–2.

[424] See, e.g. Bull in Porter, *Aberystwyth Papers*, pp. 33–6; Long and Wilson, *Thinkers*. Carr, *Twenty Years' Crisis*.

[425] See, e.g. Sir F. Pollock, 'The League of Nations and the Coming Rule of Law', in Lord Grey et al., *The League of Nations* (Oxford, 1919); A. Zimmern, *The League of Nations and the Rule of Law, 1918–1935* (London, 1936).

harmony. Keynes's belief that economic policies could promote political harmony was central to his belief in the possibility of progress in international affairs. In the inter-war years, with international organizations developing as a means of international cooperation, including in economic affairs, Keynes was a great advocate and planner of such organizations: for example, his plan to develop the BIS into a super-national monetary authority.

Keynes's views on the high politics of the 1920s and 1930s also mark him clearly as one of the inter-war idealists. His idealism may be seen in his attitude to nine issues: the possibility—indeed, the probability—of progress; pacificism; the rule of law; the League; the need to resist the 'brigand powers' and uphold collective security; the importance of public opinion; disarmament; the process of international cooperation; and the utility of economic weapons, especially as an alternative to war. Keynes's beliefs were fundamentally similar to those of other idealists of his time, such as Zimmern,[426] Murray,[427] and Angell.[428] Keynes had friendly dealings with these, and with many other of the prominent inter-war idealist writers, such as David Davies,[429] Arnold Toynbee,[430] Philip Noel-Baker,[431] Leonard Woolf,[432] Lord Lothian,[433] and the American James T. Shotwell.[434]

5.7.1 The Possibility of Progress

Keynes's belief in the possibility of progress from the 'power politics' of the past to a new order governed by international law and a sense of international solidarity is clear in *The Economic Consequences of the Peace*. We have seen that Keynes explicitly contrasted Clemenceau's realism with his own idealism, Clemenceau seeing any scheme to promote the solidarity of man, through a League or economic means, as sentimental delusion.[435]

---

[426] See, e.g. D. J. Markwell, 'Sir Alfred Zimmern revisited: fifty years on', *Review of International Studies*, 12 (1986), 279–92.

[427] See, e.g. Wilson, *Murray*; West, *Murray*; D. J. Markwell, 'British Social Science and Humanities', in T. B. Millar (ed.), *The Australian Contribution to Britain* (London, 1988), pp. 88, 93–6. For Keynes's regard for Murray, see, e.g. vol. 17, p. 5.

[428] See, e.g. J. D. B. Miller, *Norman Angell and the Futility of War* (London, 1986).

[429] See NS/1/2/214–15, 246–8; NS/1/3/10, 20, 55, KP; see also, e.g. Ceadel, *Semi-Detached Idealists*, p. 283.

[430] See L/32/132–5, KP.

[431] For example, Keynes to Noel-Baker, 23 Mar. 1938, NS/1/4/157, KP: 'My dear Phil...', vol. 28, pp. 109–10.

[432] The complexities of Keynes's relations with Leonard and Virginia Woolf are depicted in the Keynes biographies. See also P. Wilson, *The International Theory of Leonard Woolf: A Study in Twentieth Century Idealism* (New York and Basingstoke, 2003).

[433] See ch. 2, this volume.   [434] See CE/1, KP, for dealings with Shotwell in 1920–1.

[435] Vol. 2, pp. 18–23.

As we have seen, as a young man Keynes believed in the rationality of man. Influenced by events, and perhaps by belated awareness of developments in psychology (e.g. discussion of the group mind),[436] he came over time to develop a darker view of human nature that recognized springs of wickedness within it.[437] *The General Theory* spoke of the natural bellicosity of peoples.[438] By 1938, in the face of totalitarianism and events 'worse than which have not been seen . . . since man became himself',[439] Keynes believed that 'civilisation was a thin and precarious crust' on the vulgar passions and irrationality of human nature.[440] Believing it was 'only maintained by rules and conventions skilfully put across and guilefully preserved', he came to 'honour more than formerly the achievements of our predecessors and the Christian civilisation and fundamental laws of conduct which they established in a savage world'.[441]

Yet Keynes did not lose the liberal and idealistic faith that 'with clear and careful thought and appropriate action the world could be made a better place',[442] and that the key to progress was 'getting our ideas right'.[443] This belief was evident in the closing pages of *The General Theory*, where, as we have seen, Keynes suggested that the adoption of Keynesian economics could eliminate the economic causes of war, and then argued that the fulfilment of his ideas was practical because it is ideas, and not vested interests, that rule the world. Keynes was to work during the Second World War to bring major reform, international and domestic, for the post-war world along these lines. In July 1940, he urged American reformers to remember that civilization is 'a miraculous construction made by our fathers of which they knew the vulnerability better than we do, hard to come by and easily lost'; but he also urged a grand experiment to seek the optimum employment of American resources, with the 'old guard of the Right' recognizing the need for major reform.[444]

5.7.2 Pacificism

Like most idealists, Keynes consistently detested war as irrational and inhumane, but believed it could be necessary and just. We have seen that, in his debating speeches of 1903–5, Keynes expressed a strong preference for peace,

---

[436] For example W. McDougall, *The Group Mind* (1920). See Freeden, *Liberalism Divided*, p. 230; Keynes on being 'pre-Freudian': vol. 10, p. 448.

[437] See, e.g. 'My Early Beliefs': vol. 10, pp. 433–50, esp. pp. 447–50.

[438] Vol. 7, p. 381.   [439] Vol. 28, p. 104.   [440] Vol. 10, pp. 447–50.

[441] Vol. 28, p. 104; see also H. Macmillan to Keynes, 27 March 1938, *NS*/1/4/184–5; vol. 10, p. 314; cf. L. Woolf, *Barbarians at the Gate* (London, 1939).

[442] Thirlwall, *Policy Adviser*, p. 123; see also Robinson, 'Keynes', p. 25.

[443] See, e.g. vol. 9, pp. 294, 325 ff, 335–6; vol. 10, p. 67; vol. 13, p. 344; vol. 25, p. 280.

[444] Vol. 22, p. 155.

though a willingness to go to war, and a belief in the possibility of everlasting peace. His hostility to war was greatly reinforced by the slaughter of the First World War, and throughout the 1920s and 1930s he placed strong emphasis on the desirability of peace. In the 1920s, Keynes contrasted his own abhorrence of war with the delight some others took in it.[445] He came to accept the likelihood of war with 'the brigand powers' of the 1930s, and the necessity to fight; but there is no sign that he abandoned the pacificist credo of its irrationality. (Keynes used the term 'brigand powers' from at least as early as July 1936 to describe Germany, Italy, and Japan.)[446]

Keynes's abhorrence of war appears based on moral and humanitarian grounds, and his beliefs that it could achieve no constructive purpose, and was liable to worsen the general welfare (e.g. by being the catalyst for revolution).[447] His 1926 review of Trotsky's *Where is Britain Going?* stressed the uselessness of force when the problem was not promoting, but finding, a coherent scheme of progress. 'The next move is with the head, and fists must wait'.[448] In 1937 he denied that the struggle between competing ideologies, then bloodying Spain, 'can or will be settled by force of arms.'[449]

Keynes's 'pacifism', as he called it, was always qualified.[450] Though he nowhere specified full criteria, Keynes saw some wars as legitimate: the Allied effort in the Second World War was a just war.[451] He had written in 1937 that 'the first duty of foreign policy is to avoid war', but it could not always be avoided, so the second duty of foreign policy 'is to ensure that, if [war] occurs, circumstances shall be the most favourable possible for our cause'.[452] Keynes believed Britain should only enter a war when 'the vast majority of right-thinking men' are united in support of it.[453] Even then, the majority was not entitled to force an individual to fight.[454]

5.7.3 The Rule of Law

Like other inter-war idealists, Keynes placed much emphasis on establishing the rule of law in international politics, and on promoting observance of moral principles. *The Economic Consequences* condemned the size of the reparations demands as 'a breach of engagements and of international morality comparable with [the German] offence in the invasion of

---

[445] Vol. 10, pp. 52, 57.
[446] Vol. 21, pp. 381–2; vol. 28, pp. 47, 64; Keynes to JNK, 15 July 1936, PP/45/168/10/170–2, KP.
[447] Thirlwall, *Policy Adviser*, p. 102; see vol. 2, pp. 186–7.   [448] Vol. 10, p. 67.
[449] Vol. 28, p. 61.   [450] Vol. 17, pp. 450–1; vol. 28, pp. 57, 99.
[451] Vol. 9, p. 396; see also vol. 22, p. 37; vol. 28, p. 371.   [452] Vol. 28, p. 63.
[453] Vol. 28, pp. 77, 93–4.   [454] See ch. 2, this volume; vol. 28, pp. 51–2, 77.

Belgium'.[455] In denouncing the Ruhr occupation as illegal, Keynes argued that disarmament and peace can never be established without vindication of international law.[456] Law enforcement was essential to 'a League of Nations regime, in which the nations of Europe are to allow their security... mainly to depend upon written engagements instead of their own armed strength'.[457]

In 1927, Keynes drew attention to the lack of 'one essential ingredient of a regime of justice between nations':[458]

The rule of law has two sides—a willingness, spontaneous or induced by sanctions, to abide by the law, and a machinery for altering the law when it is no longer in conformity with opinion. Is it prudent or reasonable for us to engage ourselves to enforce in perpetuity what—at present—there is no adequate machinery to alter? Can the future of the world be handed over to courts of law, except in so far as we are developing *pari passu* a means of international law-making[?]

Keynes wished there to be a rule of law in international politics, but he was deeply critical of the centrepiece of the existing body of law, the Treaty of Versailles. He had believed since 1919 that the means of its revision were inadequate, and he still wished them to be changed.

In the 1930s, as we shall see, Keynes argued repeatedly for action to uphold international law. In August 1936, after the start of German rearmament, Abyssinia, remilitarization of the Rhineland, and the outbreak of Spain's civil war, Keynes wrote that 'brigandage has now gone so far that it is impossible for the time being to depend on rules of law or promises relating to hypothetical cases'.[459] Keynes distinguished 'pacific powers' from 'brigand powers', just as Zimmern distinguished 'welfare states' from 'power states'.[460] Both Keynes and Zimmern identified one group with the breaking of international law, and the other with the goals of upholding law and preserving peace. Though 'pacificists', Keynes and Zimmern believed that war had to be risked to uphold the rule of law. Thus, despite his criticisms of the Versailles Treaty's economic provisions, Keynes sought the judicious enforcement of its political provisions, and revision of its economic provisions through agreement, not unilateral breaking of undertakings.

Keynes's consistent concern to promote the observance and enforcement of international law arose both from its importance in keeping peace, and from its being part of international morality. He strongly believed that morality was not to be interpreted as a crude legalism.[461] Rather, it included a strong sense of honour, which meant that the powerful did not exploit ambiguities in their

---

455 Vol. 2, p. 40; see also p. 91.   456 Vol. 18, p. 209.
457 Vol. 18, p. 133.   458 Vol. 30, p. 9.
459 Vol. 28, p. 55.   460 Vol. 28, pp. 47–8 (e.g.); Markwell, 'Zimmern', p. 286.
461 Vol. 3, p. 94.

undertakings to their own advantage;[462] and it embraced a sense of justice that, as we have seen, precluded visiting on the children of one's enemies the misdoings of parents or of rulers.[463]

5.7.4 The League of Nations

There is little evidence regarding the degree of interest Keynes took during the First World War in proposals for a League of Nations.[464] He attended a meeting in October 1914 with Dickinson, Hobson, Russell, and others to discuss Dickinson's ideas for a 'League of the nations of Europe'.[465] His work at Paris touched the League only tangentially. In 1919, he wanted to make the world's economic rehabilitation, including an international loan, the League's first task.[466] In May 1919, he believed the peace treaties, by undermining peace and prosperity, doomed the League.[467] *The Economic Consequences* was less pessimistic.[468] Contrary to those who believed that the League provided the means for Treaty revision, Keynes argued that its unanimity requirement, the entrusting of revision to an unwieldy Assembly, and the recognition of the territorial integrity and existing political independence of all members gave the League 'an almost fatal bias towards the *status quo*'. Nonetheless, Keynes supported the League, which he said might become a powerful instrument of peace. He believed Articles 11–17, which provided safeguards against the outbreak of war, made 'substantially less probable war between organised great powers such as that of 1914'. Yet two years later, he showed that these provisions were being flouted by French army incursions into Germany east of the Rhine, and, in 1923, by the occupation of the Ruhr.[469] In *A Revision of the Treaty*, Keynes doubted the wisdom of the League's deciding detailed frontier questions.[470] Its exalting 'the divisions of...nationality above the bonds of trade and culture' meant that 'the first experiment in international government' intensified nationalism.

In November 1920, Keynes wanted the League (the value of which he then doubted) to concentrate on the prevention of war.[471] But in 1923 he thought that, for the present, its best scope was in fields 'not the subject of acute controversy between the major powers, but where, [without] the League, the

---

[462] Vol. 2, pp. 37–8; vol. 3, p. 38.   [463] Vol. 2, p. 142.
[464] Harrod, *Life*, p. 252, seems speculative.   [465] Ceadel, *Semi-Detached Idealists*, p. 204.
[466] See chs. 4 and 5; see also, e.g. vol. 16, p. 428; vol. 17, pp. 128–50 and *passim*.
[467] Vol. 16, p. 460; see also vol. 17, pp. 77, 202–3.
[468] Vol. 2, pp. 164–5; see Harrod, *Life*, pp. 312–13.
[469] Vol. 3, pp. 36–40; vol. 18, pp. 206–9.   [470] Vol. 3, pp. 6–8.
[471] Vol. 17, pp. 202–3.

necessary organisation' would be lacking. He welcomed the League's restoration of Austria.[472] In 1930, he wrote on the League's enforcing its will, applauding its Draft Convention for Financial Assistance to the victims of actual or threatened aggression as 'an extraordinarily effective way of giving greater reality to the decisions of the League'.[473]

Over many years, Keynes believed the involvement of the USA in, or at least alongside, the League was important to its success, and its absence from the League a major handicap.[474] In October 1928, Keynes condemned the Anglo-French arms agreement, which the USA regarded as seeking to import through the back door what they had rejected at the 1927 Geneva naval conference.[475] British negotiations with France exhibited 'minds back in the framework of the old pre-war diplomacy'. In so far as particular friendships were still necessary, it was 'intimate conversations and arrangements with the U.S. and with *no-one* else' that Britain should have. They were the two countries in the world truly pacific, and, with overwhelming combined naval power, could provide guarantees of the future peace of the world. This must be, Keynes said, in the context of passionate British support for the growing structure of the League, and willingness to make sacrifices for disarmament and to accept arbitration on all matters whatsoever. 'We, America and the League of Nations can keep the peace', he declared.

In 1930, seeking money for *The Nation* from David Davies, advocate of an international police force,[476] Keynes wrote of 'the support we have been able to give to questions of the League and international appeasement'.[477] Keynes was an active supporter of the Peace Ballot in 1935, intended to arouse and demonstrate public support for the League and disarmament.[478] However, in the 1930s, he attacked the League's unanimity requirement, saying that progress can be made without universal agreement,[479] and that the League was 'based on the false assumption that all nations alike are equally desirous of peace and justice'. As the realization became ever clearer that this assumption was false, and that some states 'ensue war', in late 1935 he welcomed the 'evolution of the League ... to embrace only the genuine peace-lovers'.[480] This evolution would strengthen it. Despite hesitancy in 1936 about commitments to help resist all aggression,[481] in a 'Positive Peace Programme' in March 1938

---

[472] Vol. 18, pp. 176–7.   [473] Vol. 20, pp. 332–42 at p. 337.

[474] Vol. 17, pp. 77, 152, 278; vol. 20, p. 337; vol. 21, p. 374.

[475] Keynes speech, 16 Oct. 1928, OC/5/212 ff, KP. For the 'Anglo-French compromise', see *Survey of International Affairs*, 1928, p. 61 ff.

[476] D. Davies, *The Problem of the Twentieth Century* (London, 1930).

[477] Keynes to Davies, 6 Jan. 1930, NS/1/2/214–15, KP; see also NS/1/2/216, 246–8.

[478] L/35/60, 68 ff, KP.   [479] Vol. 21, p. 282; see also p. 371; vol. 17, p. 374.

[480] Vol. 21, p. 374; see vol. 20, pp. 335, 342; vol. 21, p. 282.   [481] Vol. 28, p. 53.

Keynes proposed constructing, within the League, new regional Leagues—especially a European pact—with 'definite undertakings to one another'.[482] This pact would be a new, long-term attempt at collective security, with sanctions, arbitration, defence collaboration, free trade, and help for Jewish refugees. Keynes was thus thinking along the same lines as many other idealists: that a system of collective security—the League or something else—depended on its members making genuine and strong commitments against aggression. Keynes's 1938 plan, like those of some other idealists, arose from the belief that the League had failed to uphold the collective system, most importantly over Abyssinia, making war more likely; he wrote in August 1936 that 'no one now puts much trust in it'.[483] Britain was partly to blame. Her inadequate responses to world crises—and hence the League's—were partly due to 'the pacifism of the average League supporter today'.[484]

Thus, while Keynes believed that a league of states that would prevent war could be created, and though he was sometimes optimistic for the League itself, he identified several major flaws in it. These included bias towards the status quo; inadequate attention to enforcing its will; popular pacifism that weakened the will of many states to uphold the collective system; the unanimity requirement; and the absence of the USA.

5.7.5 The Need to Resist the 'Brigand Powers'

Although Keynes favoured revision of some Treaty provisions[485] and of some European frontiers,[486] he never believed that this justified Hitler's demands and methods. Keynes was hostile to Germany's Nazi regime from the outset. He objected to its political illiberality,[487] its autarkic economic policies,[488] but above all its international 'brigandage'. He was involved in helping German Jews and other refugees from 1933 on.[489]

When Germany withdrew from the Disarmament Conference and the League in October 1933, Keynes saw a hideous dilemma between allowing them to rearm as they chose, 'or the horror of a preventive war'.[490] This dilemma—between the need to resist the brigand powers and the desire for peace—recurred over subsequent years.[491] The need for a strategy of resistance

---

[482] Vol. 28, pp. 99–104.   [483] Vol. 28, p. 51; see also pp. 64–6.

[484] Vol. 28, pp. 56–7.   [485] See vols. 2 and 3.

[486] See vol. 28, pp. 101, 118–19.   [487] See, e.g. vol. 28, pp. 21–2, 25.

[488] Vol. 21, pp. 243–4.

[489] See, e.g. D. H. Robertson to Keynes, 4 May 1933, GTE/1/15, KP; UA/14/2/107, KP; MS SPSL 238/8, fols. 361–2; 238/9, fols 414–8; 237/8, fols. 290–359 (various); 55/5, fol. 45; 23/3, fol. 228 ff, Bodleian.

[490] Vol. 28, pp. 20–1.   [491] See, e.g. vol. 28, pp. 48–9.

to brigandage was clear to Keynes, but he was not always certain on tactics—over which issues to acquiesce (e.g. Spain), and over which to act (e.g. aggression in China). Keynes's stress, especially during the Spanish civil war, on the need for peace, his opposition to risking war over Spain, and his contempt for suggestions that the British Government was pro-Fascist, contributed to the perception of him among some on the left, such as Kingsley Martin, editor of the *New Statesman*, as an 'appeaser'.[492] Some others, thinking Keynes pro-German after the First World War, and believing *The Economic Consequences* to have helped create the climate for appeasement, have also been inclined to see him as an appeaser.[493]

These views are, at best, simplistic.[494] There was no trace of pro-German sentiment in Keynes's approach in the 1930s: the attempt to establish Germany as a stable and pacific democracy in the European comity having failed, and the savage element in Germany (which Keynes had identified before and after the First World War) having triumphed, Keynes had no illusions about Hitler's Germany. He insisted in 1938 that the Treaty of Versailles, French policy in the 1920s, and 'our own weakness and betrayals since then' had caused 'our troubles';[495] but the effects of *The Economic Consequences* were irrelevant to Keynes's own views of how to deal with Hitler. Parker has defined the British policy now associated with the word 'appeasement' as 'offering concessions to Germany in an attempt to make the United Kingdom more secure from the threat of German attack'.[496] Keynes did not support such a policy. Where Chamberlain opposed working with Moscow, Keynes urged it. Keynes opposed giving concessions to Hitler in Europe to save British colonies. As we shall see, he did not support Munich.

In 1936 Keynes explicitly denied that seeking 'an understanding with the brigand powers ... is more likely than any other [policy] to keep this country out of war'.[497] At the end of 1935 he had written: 'World peace requires two conditions. Those nations which have a real and abiding will to peace must combine to preserve it; their joint action must be sufficiently imposing to make the risk of war too great to be undertaken except by a gambler or a madman.'[498] These themes dominate Keynes's extensive writings, especially in

[492] K. Martin, *Editor* (London, 1968) ch. 12, esp. pp. 241–2. See C. H. Rolph, *Kingsley* (London, 1973), pp. 211, 227–8, for Martin's focus on Spain; see vol. 28, p. 45 ff.

[493] Cf. Mantoux, *Carthaginian Peace*, p. 13.

[494] Cf. Skidelsky, *Fighting*, p. 26 ff.

[495] Vol. 28, p. 99. On evils flowing from Versailles, see Keynes to H. Butler, 6 Apr. 1939, CO/1/138, KP.

[496] R. A. C. Parker, 'Economics, Rearmament and Foreign Policy: The United Kingdom before 1939—A Preliminary Survey', *Journal of Contemporary History*, 10 (1975), 640. See also R. A. C. Parker, *Chamberlain and Appeasement* (Basingstoke and London, 1993).

[497] Vol. 28, p. 47.   [498] Vol. 21, p. 374.

the *New Statesman*, on international issues in the mid- to late 1930s.[499] In 1925, he had declared: 'I am against pacts'.[500] But in 1936, he stressed the need for a close accord with France, an understanding with Russia, and 'the habit of intimate conversation' with Washington.[501] He had, in late 1935, written of a gradual evolution towards a new League of peace-loving nations.[502] The new European pact he proposed in 1938 would contain definite undertakings on resistance to aggression, majority rule with voting weighted towards major powers, but no specific guarantees of the status quo. There would be new 'Leagues' for other regions of the world.[503]

In this political project of resistance to the brigand powers, as in his economic projects of international reform, Keynes emphasized the leadership of the major powers, especially Britain and the USA. Britain should give leadership on sanctions against Italy[504] and Japan,[505] in effective cooperation between pacific nations,[506] and, with France and Russia, in the formation and leadership of a new European League.[507] The USA would head an American League.[508] Keynes continued[509] to see US cooperation in world affairs as crucial: to give a new League of peace-loving nations power;[510] to make the threat of sanctions against Japan in 1937 effective;[511] and later to provide wartime finance. In March 1938, Keynes sent a copy of his 'Positive Peace Programme' to President Roosevelt, saying:

The tragedy is that the right-minded show no indication of supporting one another. You will be reluctant to support us; we are reluctant to support France; France is reluctant to support Spain. At long last we shall get together. But how much harm will have been done by then?[512]

At least until the outbreak of the Second World War,[513] Keynes did not see resistance to the brigand powers in ideological terms. He denied that ideological issues could be settled by force.[514] He saw the world divided into 'liberal' and 'totalitarian' states,[515] but he was prepared, even keen, to ally with one totalitarian power (the Soviet Union) to defeat more dangerous ones.[516] Particularly after the purges of 1937, however, he did not trust Stalin: he saw

[499] See vols. 21 and 28.
[500] Vol. 9, p. 301.
[501] Vol. 28, p. 47; see also pp. 46, 55.
[502] Vol. 21, p. 374.
[503] Vol. 28, pp. 100, 102.
[504] Vol. 28, p. 66.
[505] Vol. 28, pp. 185–6.
[506] Vol. 28, p. 47.
[507] Vol. 28, pp. 100–1, 104.
[508] Vol. 28, p. 102.
[509] See vol. 17, p. 30.
[510] Vol. 21, p. 374.
[511] Vol. 28, pp. 83, 86.
[512] Keynes to FDR, 25 Mar. 1938, box 53, PSF, FDR papers, FDR Library, Hyde Park, NY.
[513] See vol. 22, p. 24.
[514] Vol. 28, pp. 61–2.
[515] Vol. 28, pp. 73, 126; cf. p. 61.
[516] See, e.g. vol. 28, pp. 117, 122–6.

the foreign policy of all dictators as almost invariably opportunist, and he anticipated the Nazi–Soviet Pact.[517]

Keynes highlighted four problems in the formation of British policy in the 1930s: Britain's reluctance to make commitments to 'minor people who may be attacked', when Britain's immediate interests did not seem threatened by an eastward-looking Germany;[518] the public's blind pacifism;[519] the difficulty of knowing how to act under great uncertainty;[520] and the obsession of some with the Empire.

Let us trace Keynes's comments on specific issues. First, Abyssinia: in September 1935, Keynes wanted, in the event of Italian aggression against Abyssinia, economic sanctions against Italy, but not a blockade, and financial assistance to Abyssinia.[521] He believed that these measures would make military sanctions unnecessary, though if Italy treated these sanctions as if they were an act of war and took warlike action against the League powers, it would be necessary to contemplate further measures. Keynes insisted in July 1937 that firm action early in the crisis would have stopped Italy and 'saved the League of Nations'.[522]

Second, the Spanish civil war: though he saw the republican government as 'suffering aggression', Keynes did not wish Britain to make 'final commitments' too soon.[523] He supported attempts to secure a general ban on intervention.[524] In July 1937, Keynes argued that Spain's greatest interest lay with peace on any terms; the civil war would not settle Spain's future. Delay and caution were essential in British policy towards Spain—for the sake of peace, to give time for the pacific powers to prepare for any war, and for Germany and Italy to 'persuade the rest of the world that they are the enemies of the human race'.[525] Britain should not enter a war, such as that in Spain, for which there was not overwhelming public support.[526] Keynes's approach put him in opposition to many associates on the left. Keynes's first article in the *New Statesman* urging the avoidance of war over Spain was a response to calls for action over Spain, and the abandonment of non-intervention.[527] Immediately prompting Keynes to write was a leader by H. N. Brailsford, urging naval and aerial controls on Spain that would hurt General Franco, and British encouragement for the despatch of aeroplanes and volunteers for the Republican side.[528] Keynes's article was immediately preceded by a leader by

---

[517] Vol. 28, p. 72.   [518] Vol. 21, p. 381; see also vol. 28, p. 75.
[519] Vol. 28, p. 57; see also pp. 53, 55, 64.   [520] See, e.g. vol. 28, pp. 49, 54, 117, 120, 131.
[521] Vol. 21, pp. 370–2.   [522] Vol. 28, pp. 65–6; see also p. 55.
[523] Vol. 28, pp. 48–50.   [524] Vol. 28, p. 55.
[525] Vol. 28, pp. 62–4; see also pp. 80–1.   [526] Vol. 28, p. 77.
[527] Vol. 28, pp. 58–60.
[528] [H. N. Brailsford,] 'The Last Chance in Spain', *NS*, 3 July 1937, pp. 4–5.

Kingsley Martin, arguing that British policy, in helping Franco, had not made war with Italy and Germany less likely: a strong stand would have deterred them, and Keynes was wrong to think that 'the policy of delay' was a peace policy.[529] It is not obvious that Keynes was mistaken about Spain in 1936–7. But in March 1938, Keynes urged that, unless there was a negotiated peace with Catalan and Basque independence, France should be given a free hand, with full British support, 'to end the Spanish war'.[530]

Third, Japanese aggression in China: in September 1937, Keynes wanted economic sanctions by the League powers and the USA against Japan, initiated by Britain.[531] In October, he said that the difference between Japan and Spain was that with Japan, 'there is something specific which would be effective if done and might command sufficient general assent to be practical politics', whereas this had not been clear for Spain.[532] By November, Keynes concluded that, without such sanctions, China should conclude a peace, even with loss of territory; Britain should use all her influence to get China the best possible terms.[533]

Fourth, *Anschluss*: Keynes responded to the forced union of Austria with Germany in March 1938 with 'A Positive Peace Programme', a powerful article in the *New Statesman*,[534] already cited for advocating a new European pact under British, French, and Soviet leadership. Explicitly siding with Churchill against Chamberlain, it stressed the need to appear formidable to preserve peace. Keynes went to great trouble to get national and international press coverage for this article, and sent it to many British and other political leaders, describing it to some as a proposal 'to revive collective security'.[535] To Churchill, he wrote: 'I have shared the general admiration of your magnificent speeches in the House of Commons.'[536]

Fifth, Czechoslovakia: Keynes's attitude to Munich is sometimes used to suggest that he was an appeaser. In his Positive Peace Programme, Keynes had urged that, to help establish a new European pact, Czechoslovakia should try to negotiate with Germany over the Sudeten Germans, even if this meant frontier changes. 'Racial frontiers are safer and better to-day than geophysical frontiers'.[537] He believed, perhaps wrongly, that frontier changes would leave Czechoslovakia defensible. He wrote in August that 'Germany is *equally* vulnerable to air-raids'; and the Czechs 'unaided can give a pretty

529 [K. Martin,] 'The Policy of Delay', *NS*, 10 July 1937, pp. 60–1 (Keynes at 61–2); see vol. 28, pp. 59–60.
530 Vol. 28, p. 101.   531 Vol. 28, pp. 82, 86.
532 Vol. 28, p. 88; see also p. 83.
533 Vol. 28, p. 93. See also Keynes to M. Fry, 25 Aug. 1940, L/40/102, KP.
534 Vol. 28, pp. 99–104.   535 See *NS*/1/4/141 ff at, e.g. 156, KP.
536 Keynes to Churchill, 23 Mar. 1938, *NS*/1/4/153; reply at 186, KP.   537 Vol. 28, p. 101.

good account of themselves'. But Soviet assistance was the key: 'She will have to be the first to lend material assistance. (Will she?).' Keynes was clear that Czechoslovakia's 'integrity apart from frontier revisions' had to be safeguarded. Though he expected that there would be frontier revision and that this was the best remedy in the long run, he urged that, with Hitler knowing he would be beaten in a world war, Britain 'should bluff to the hilt; and if the bluff is called, back out'.[538] Keynes later wrote that the Soviet Union was 'greatly to blame' for Munich.[539] An 'honourable settlement could have been secured without any risk to peace, if an unambiguous stand had been taken [jointly] by this country, France *and Russia*'. But Chamberlain was 'bought off by Germany's agreeing to forgo a fleet and soft-pedalling on the Colonies'.[540]

So, although for some months before Munich Keynes had advocated frontier revisions, and he foresaw the Munich settlement a month ahead,[541] he neither advocated nor welcomed that settlement. Kingsley Martin has suggested that he wrote to Keynes for advice on what to publish over the Czech crisis, and Keynes's advice carried great weight with him in deciding to write the infamous *New Statesman* leader of 27 August 1938 urging frontier revision and the avoidance of world war.[542] The letters between Martin and Keynes do not fit well the description of asking and giving advice on what to write.[543] Martin wrote the leader himself, of his own volition.[544] Keynes criticized him for it,[545] as did many others.[546] To make a *public* statement of this kind would defeat Keynes's policy of 'bluff to the hilt'; Keynes had written to Martin that 'I prefer, meanwhile, meiosis[547] and bogus optimism in public'.[548] Keynes was contemptuous of a comparable leader in *The Times* on 7 September.[549] He had written on 29 August, 'I should [have] thought that Mrs Chamberlain could have told [her husband] that kindness and concessions are the worst way to handle an hysteric'.[550] Although Keynes declared during the Czech crisis his belief in evading '*immediate* evils', and though he saw some potential benefits in the Munich settlement, it is misleading simply to label as an appeaser someone who regarded Munich at the time as 'one of the worst pieces of trickery in history', and urged 'a union of forces against Chamberlain'.[551]

---

[538] Vol. 28, pp. 117–19.   [539] Vol. 28, p. 122; see also pp. 125–6.
[540] Vol. 28, pp. 125–6; original italics.   [541] Vol. 28, p. 118.
[542] K. Martin, *Editor* (London, 1968) pp. 254–7; cf. Barnett, *Collapse*, p. 537; see also Gannon, *Press*, p. 178; Skidelsky, *Fighting*, pp. 35–6.
[543] Vol. 28, pp. 115–18.
[544] See Rolph, *Kingsley*, p. 245; E. Hyams, *The New Statesman* (London, 1963), pp. 210–12.
[545] See Martin to Keynes, 9 Sept. 1938, and Keynes to Martin, 11 Sept.: vol. 28, pp. 118–19.
[546] Rolph, *Kingsley*, pp. 245–6.
[547] That is, understatement, esp. ironic understatement.   [548] Vol. 28, p. 117.
[549] Vol. 28, pp. 120, 122.   [550] Keynes to FAK, 29 Aug. 1938, PP/45/168/10/223–4, KP.
[551] Vol. 28, pp. 120, 122 (1 Oct. 1938), 123; see Thirlwall, *Policy Adviser*, p. 101.

Sixth, the Second World War: although not expecting war over Danzig,[552] Keynes defended the war when it came as being for 'the defence of freedom and of civilisation'.[553] In October 1939, he believed it unwise to be precise on acceptable peace terms, 'for a compromise peace must depend on circumstances which we cannot anticipate'.[554] He was hostile to any advocacy of a peace with Hitler.[555] In December 1939, he denied that it was 'reactionary' to wish 'for the ideals of the Western powers to triumph over Germany and the Soviet Union'.[556] In the summer of 1942, Keynes believed it was too early for a Second Front in Europe, and opposed encouragement to communist revolutions against the fascists.[557] He probably believed the war should be fought in a way that prevented the Soviet Union having 'it all her own way in Europe'.[558] During and immediately after the war, though he was keen to have Soviet cooperation in the post-war order, Keynes did not really expect it, and he was unhappy about the spread and misuse of Soviet power: for example, he supported Western resistance to Soviet arrests of anti-communist Poles in May 1945.[559]

5.7.6 The Power of Public Opinion

Keynes's view, like that of many other idealists, was that public opinion was powerful, though not necessarily well directed, but could be changed: thus, a better world could be moulded by shaping public opinion. He came to recognize that public opinion reflected 'vulgar passions', and was often ignorant and myopic.[560] But his belief that it could be changed, and that this was the only way of influencing 'the hidden currents, flowing continuously beneath the surface of political history',[561] explains his prolific output of 'essays in persuasion'[562] in the inter-war years, and later his 'missionary' role for the Bretton Woods proposals.[563]

---

[552] Vol. 28, p. 131; M. Keynes, *Essays*, p. 179; Bell, *Old Friends*, p. 46; Keynes to FAK, 22 Aug. 1939, PP/45/168/10/233–4, KP; Skidelsky, *Fighting*, p. 44.

[553] Vol. 22, p. 37; see also p. 150; vol. 28, p. 371.

[554] Vol. 22, p. 37; see also, e.g. Keynes to F. Hardie, 18 Nov. 1939, MS Eng. Lett. c459, fol. 70, Bodleian.

[555] See, e.g. Hyams, *NS*, pp. 219–21.

[556] Keynes to L. Elmhirst, 10 Dec. 1939, W/2/137–8, KP.

[557] Vol. 28, pp. 169–70; see also vol. 25, p. 10; Hyams, *NS*, 230–1.

[558] Vol. 28, p. 194.

[559] Vol. 28, pp. 207–15; 'Sanity in Poland', *NS*, 12 May 1945, 297–8; see also, e.g. vol. 28, pp. 169–70, 193–4.

[560] See, e.g. vol. 2, pp. 85–99; vol. 9, p. 225; vol. 17, p. 453.   [561] Vol. 2, p. 188.

[562] See vol. 22, p. 38; vol. 9.   [563] Vol. 26, pp. 102–3.

5.7.7 Armaments

In the 1920s, Keynes, like most idealists, was a strong advocate of multilateral disarmament, and unilateral disarmament if necessary.[564] Pre-Keynesian economics favoured economy and disarmament.[565] Thus, in 1921, Keynes asserted that 'general disarmament is the form of economy least injurious and most worth while'.[566] Keynes did not believe economies—including 'reduction of the Army even to a point incompatible with our exerting agreed influence in Europe'—would leave Britain unprepared. A 'happy and prosperous people at home' was 'the best form of preparedness', and, though 'incompatible with the other forms of preparedness', should be followed.[567]

Keynes also believed that disarmament would set an example to other countries, would reduce the likelihood of attack, and would help promote collective security. In 1921, agreeing to serve on a League of Nations Union committee on disarmament, Keynes wrote that the League would 'stand or fall with its success on the Disarmament question'.[568] Britain should set 'a very good example, even at the risk of being weak, in the direction of arbitration and of disarmament'.[569] His optimistic view of 'civilised man' led him to write in 1923: 'The world is not so savage that it is usual to attack those who are harmless. It is the bold and armed nation which provokes enemies.'[570] Deeply concerned at the danger of French hegemony in Europe, Keynes denied that it was in the general interest to disarm Germany, yet to leave France unprecedentedly armed,[571] and he attacked French incursions into Germany.

By July 1933, in the midst of the Disarmament Conference, Keynes realized that on disarmament 'the agreement of all is necessary before anyone dare move'.[572] In a deteriorating international climate, and with a new macroeconomics, Keynes came to advocate rearmament. *The General Theory* showed that expenditure on arms could add to employment.[573] But Keynes's basic reason for advocating rearmament was his perception of the international political environment. In 1936, he declared that the brigand powers 'know no argument but force', that 'inadequate armament on our part can only encourage' them, and that 'the collective possession of preponderant

---

[564] See, e.g. vol. 9, p. 301; vol. 17, pp. 241, 271, 319, 451–2.
[565] See H. Bull, *Strategic Arms Limitation: The Precedent of the Washington and London Naval Treaties* (Chicago, 1971), p. 32.
[566] Vol. 17, p. 271; see also vol. 19, pp. 2–4; vol. 18, p. 271.   [567] Vol. 19, pp. 2–3.
[568] Vol. 17, p. 241; see Cecil's letter of thanks to Keynes, 25 July 1921, L/21/85, KP.
[569] Vol. 9, p. 301.   [570] Vol. 17, p. 451.
[571] Vol. 18, p. 130.   [572] Vol. 21, p. 277.
[573] Vol. 7, p. 129; see also vol. 9, pp. 286, 354–5; vol. 21, p. 60.

force by the leading pacific powers is, in the conditions of to-day, the best assurance of peace'.[574]

In the 1930s, Keynes advocated rearmament for foreign policy, not economic, reasons (though in 1939 he applauded those benefits). He mainly proposed increases in loan expenditure without reference to rearmament, 'of all forms of expenditure the most unproductive'.[575] He argued for rearmament even when, in early 1937, he saw inflation as a greater danger than unemployment. He and the Treasury then agreed that £400 million could be borrowed over five years for rearmament without inflation, if the expenditure were carefully planned; but he also proposed raising taxes to pay for the main part of the cost of armaments.[576]

Keynes was a member of the Committee on Economic Information which in 1938 drew attention to the dangers from rearmament to Britain's exchange position.[577] Yet Keynes in 1937 had viewed with greater equanimity than the Treasury the prospective worsening of Britain's trade balance;[578] and some of his 1938 suggestions for how Britain could sustain trade deficits (e.g. borrowing in Canada) met with Bank of England opposition.[579] (The US downturn which started in 1937 was evident by 1938.) Keynes repeatedly urged tighter control on British nationals sending capital funds overseas: as he wrote in April 1939, 'the whole of our liquid capital resources must be concentrated henceforward to meet the adverse balance of trade and to provide for political loans'.[580] In January 1939, although appearing sceptical about the prospect of war, Keynes condemned the lack of preparation for it—for example, in plans for wartime controls—as potentially disastrous. Failure to use unemployed resources—for example, 'unemployed miners and others to dig underground shelters'—seemed 'insanity'. However unfairly, Keynes said that what he thought would '*employ* our resources', the Chancellor and Treasury thought would '*exhaust* them'.[581] In May 1939, Keynes regarded rearmament as a 'grand experiment' in achieving full employment, and he clearly saw himself as helping to reassure trade unionists and their leaders over rearmament.[582] It may be that Keynes underestimated the difficulties arising from shortages of suitably skilled labour.[583]

---

[574] Vol. 28, p. 48; see also pp. 49, 53, 55–6, 76.   [575] Vol. 21, p. 528; see also pp. 463, 532.
[576] Vol. 21, pp. 390, 404–9; see also G. C. Peden, *British Rearmament and the Treasury, 1932–1939* (Edinburgh, 1979), pp. 71–2, 79, 81, 179.
[577] Parker, 'Economics', pp. 642–3.   [578] Vol. 21, p. 391; see Peden, *Rearmament*, p. 91.
[579] Peden, *Rearmament*, p. 98–9; Howson and Winch, *EAC*, p. 149.
[580] Vol. 21, p. 512; see R. A. C. Parker, 'British rearmament 1936–9: Treasury, trade unions and skilled labour', *English Historical Review*, 96 (1981), 316.
[581] Vol. 21, pp. 498–9; original emphasis; see Howson and Winch, *EAC*, p. 145; see also T. W. Hutchison, *Keynes versus the 'Keynesians'. . . ?* (London, 1977), pp. 49–50.
[582] Vol. 21, pp. 528–32; see Parker, 'British rearmament', p. 343.
[583] See Parker, 'British rearmament', esp. p. 318 ff; cf. vol. 21, p. 530.

5.7.8 The Process of International Cooperation

Like other idealists, Keynes consistently stressed the importance of inter-national cooperation. Indeed, he was a leading advocate of it in economic matters, and in security and other fields. But his aspirations came to be joined with sceptical pragmatism about the *process*. He believed that attempts at international cooperation did not often achieve their goals. In 1946, he declared: 'There is scarcely any enduringly successful experience yet of an international body which has fulfilled the hopes of its progenitors.'[584] Inter-national conferences are prone to several flaws:[585] aiming at an unattainable and unnecessary unanimity;[586] attacking symptoms, not the disease;[587] be-coming 'unwieldy polygot debating societ[ies]' in which the forces of the status quo have the advantage;[588] and inadequate prior preparation of specific proposals.[589]

As we have seen before, Keynes believed that international cooperation in economic[590] and political[591] matters requires the leadership of major powers. Ambitious goals could only be achieved under exceptional circum-stances. One CU draft 'doubted whether a comprehensive scheme will ever...be worked out, unless...through a single act of creation made possible by the unity of purpose and energy of hope' springing from military victory.[592] Cooperation required that national interest was subsumed into that of the world as a whole.[593] This is a function both of the proposals, which must be mutually advantageous,[594] and of the participating states, which must identify their national interest with the global interest. Much depended on the personal qualities of the participants in international endeavours. This was the point of Keynes's description of the Big Four in *The Economic Consequences*.[595] He highlighted the inhibiting effect of the language barrier.[596] He stressed the value of friendly informal relations:[597] virtue is more often found in individuals in their private than in their public capacities.[598]

---

[584] Vol. 26, pp. 215–16.   [585] See vol. 26, p. 101.
[586] See vol. 21, pp. 277, 282–3, 359; vol. 17, p. 371.
[587] Vol. 9, p. 357; see also vol. 21, p. 268.
[588] Vol. 2, p. 164.   [589] Vol. 21, pp. 268, 281.
[590] For example, vol. 20, p. 497; vol. 9, p. 235; vol. 21, pp. 57, 59, 62.
[591] For example, vol. 28, pp. 99–104.
[592] Vol. 25, p. 170; see vol. 26, p. 189; R. Gardner, *Sterling-Dollar Diplomacy in Current Perspective* (New York, 1980), p. 81.
[593] Vol. 7, p. 335.   [594] See vol. 2, p. 179; vol. 6, p. 274; vol. 9, p. 249.
[595] See vol. 2, p. 17; vol. 17, p. 8.   [596] Vol. 2, p. 19 n; vol. 10, pp. 412–13; vol. 26, p. 101.
[597] Vol. 18, p. 291.   [598] Vol. 2, p. 40.

5.7.9 The Utility of Economic Weapons

At various times, Keynes considered five different forms of economic weapons in international politics: financial assistance to victims of aggression; 'sanctions' (i.e. prohibition of commercial and financial transactions between one's own and an enemy state); blockades, which seek to stop all the enemy's commercial and financial transactions with all other countries; reparations demands; and control of an occupied country's resources. Our immediate interest in these is Keynes's belief that economic weapons could be powerful in enforcing the rule of law, and as alternatives to the use of military force, but Keynes's consideration of some of them arose in other contexts.[599]

In 1930, Keynes wrote supporting the League's Draft Convention for Financial Assistance to the victims of threatened or actual aggression.[600] The League would borrow in world money markets, and, in the event of war or threat of war, lend to the victim. Keynes argued that such financial aid could make the difference between war and peace, especially where a lesser power could be helped to deter attack from a major power. He believed the availability of foreign finances was crucial to any war effort. Keynes repeated his belief in the value of financial assistance in 1935 and 1938.[601]

When, in September 1935, Italy appeared likely to invade Abyssinia, Keynes urged the League powers to prohibit commercial and financial transactions with Italy on the part of their own nations, but not to blockade Italy, and forthwith to ratify the draft Protocol of Financial Assistance, because lending Abyssinia (say) £10,000,000 coupled with removing embargoes on the export of arms could turn Italy's 'unwise risk . . . into an insane one'. Keynes wondered whether closing the Suez Canal to Italy would be legal, but said nothing could be more decisive than this.[602] As we have seen, he later believed that firm action at the time of the invasion would have saved the League.[603] In September 1937, Keynes believed it highly likely that a threat to Japan from the British Empire, the other League powers, and the USA to 'sever all trade relations with her unless she mends her ways . . . would be effective'. It was one of the clear opportunities for decisive action. American cooperation was crucial. Keynes believed sanctions against Japan would have united public support, which was essential. He insisted that the world immensely underestimated the effect of economic sanctions strictly applied in appropriate circumstances.[604] Thus, Keynes thought economic sanctions could be

---

[599] See, e.g. vol. 26, pp. 340–1. [600] Vol. 20, pp. 332–42.
[601] Vol. 21, p. 371; vol. 28, p. 101. [602] Vol. 21, pp. 370–2.
[603] Vol. 28, pp. 65–6; see also pp. 55, 83, 88. [604] Vol. 28, pp. 82–8.

effective where there is a clear-cut case for them, something specific which could be done, sufficient countries participating, united public support, and they are applied strictly and wholeheartedly. However, the case Keynes cited to show that sanctions could work—Germany during and immediately after World War I[605]—is an instance, not of sanctions, but of blockade, which, as Keynes pointed out in 1930, 'could scarcely be enforced by purely peaceful means'.[606] (He believed that starvation had defeated Germany in the First World War.)[607]

In October 1939, stressing the importance of financial exhaustion of the enemy and considering Germany's capacity then to trade through neutral neighbours, Keynes wanted blockades concentrating on preventing the flow of essential goods, forcing import prices as high as possible, and undermining her export trade, thus curtailing her purchasing power.[608]

In 1942, Keynes proposed a post-war technique 'by which Germany [could] be required to pay over annually a large sum to those financially responsible for maintaining the peace of the world'. Gross receipts from German exports would be paid into an international institution by all countries purchasing German exports. A certain proportion would go to the international peace-keeping body, the balance being transferred to Germany to pay for her imports and other general purposes. The machinery would exist to impose a complete financial blockade by increasing the proportion of her export proceeds to be withheld if Germany breached any undertakings.[609] This proposal was endorsed by the Malkin committee.[610]

As we have seen, in 1919 Keynes saw the reparation demands, given their magnitude and the destruction of the German economy, as continuing the war by economic means, and he opposed this.[611] In 1943, Keynes proposed post-war economic measures such as control of German stocks of sensitive raw materials, and prohibition of arms or aircraft manufacture, to inhibit Germany's recreating her war economy.[612]

5.8 CONCLUSION

In 1923, Keynes saw the task for Liberalism as 'finding a *via media* to peace abroad and contentment at home'.[613] We have seen how he struggled to find

---

[605] Vol. 28, p. 88.   [606] Vol. 20, p. 333; see also vol. 21, p. 370; vol. 28, p. 74.
[607] Vol. 10, p. 396.   [608] Vol. 22, pp. 16–20; see also vol. 16, pp. 218–19.
[609] Vol. 26, pp. 337–41.   [610] See ch. 6, this volume.
[611] See esp. vol. 2, p. 173; see also vol. 25, p. 9.   [612] Vol. 26, pp. 370–3.
[613] Vol. 19, p. 146.

that *via media*. By 1936, he had devised an economic theory which he believed, if implemented internationally, offered real prospects of peace and prosperity. The Second World War was to provide an opportunity to construct, for the post-war world, an international economic order based in part on these ideas.

6

Anglo-American Cooperation for Internationalism: Keynes's Second World War Vision for a Post-war World

From July 1940 until his death in April 1946, Keynes returned to the Treasury to work on wartime and post-war issues, including several visits to the USA between 1941 and 1946 (listed in the chronology at the start of this book). Keynes contributed to the plans made for the post-war international order in three principal ways. First, he played a leading role in the creation of the Bretton Woods institutions: the International Monetary Fund (IMF) to maintain stable but adjustable exchange rates and facilitate balance of payments adjustment, and the International Bank for Reconstruction and Development (IBRD, or World Bank). Second, he negotiated the settlement of Britain's Lend-Lease obligation to the USA, and a US loan to help Britain through its immediate post-war balance of payments difficulties. Third, he played a role in Anglo-American discussions resulting in publication of US proposals on trade and employment at the same time as the loan in December 1945.

Arising from negotiations that were often difficult and distressing, and in which this patriot fought hard for his country,[1] these measures embodied, albeit imperfectly, Keynes's liberal vision for the post-war international economy, especially his desire to lay an economic basis for a durable peace through 'international government in economic affairs'[2] based on Anglo-American cooperation. This international government, combined with domestic Keynesianism, would give effect to the ideal of *The General Theory*: simultaneous pursuit of full employment policies within an international system which allowed, and perhaps assisted, such policies; all this allowing a form of unimpeded trade.[3] Although the elements of Keynes's vision were evident early in the war (1939–41), it was not clear to him for some years that post-war circumstances (such as Britain's balance of payments, and US domestic

---

[1] See Skidelsky's magnificent 3rd vol., *John Maynard Keynes: Fighting for Britain, 1937–1946*. Many, but not all, of the issues and events covered in this chapter are discussed at greater length there.

[2] Vol. 25, p. 280.   [3] Vol. 7, pp. 348–9, 382–3.

and international economic policy) would make possible its realization. Especially before 1941 and at times later, he believed that Britain might have no choice but to rely post-war on bilateral trade and currency arrangements—in essence, an Empire-based economic bloc. After July 1941, Keynes made a leap of faith that cooperation with the USA was sufficiently likely to make a sustainable multilateral system possible to warrant working zealously to design and institute such a system.[4] The influences that led Keynes to that view and sustained his zeal in the face of serious obstacles and anxieties, and which thereby contributed to the post-war order being based on open trade rather than a return to economic blocs, are not often discussed in any detail.[5] The influence of others—such as Lionel Robbins, and James Meade—who had taken part in inter-war discussions of economic causes of war and peace, and who now served in government roles, was at times important.

These various influences can be seen by examining a range of issues in which Keynes was involved. These include American reaction to his ideas on internal war finance, and his role in external war and post-war finance (above all, the 'consideration' for Lend-Lease, and the 1945 US loan negotiations with their parallel commercial, or trade, talks), international monetary relations, commercial policy, and treatment of Germany. It is not possible here to give other than passing reference to other issues—such as relief,[6] or commodities,[7] or Keynes's concern over the abuse of Soviet power in Eastern Europe in 1945–6.[8]

6.1 BACKGROUND

From early in the war, discussions of war aims often considered post-war economic arrangements. In 1939 it was natural that there was, as Keynes identified, a 'tendency to think of peace aims in terms of avoiding last time's mistakes'.[9] Before the fall of France, Anglo-French cooperation, reflected in

---

[4] On 'the policy of faith': vol. 23, p. 207.

[5] Cf. Skidelsky, *Fighting, passim*. For the argument that Keynes created international macroeconomics, see D. Vines, 'John Maynard Keynes, 1937–1946: The Creation of International Macroeconomics', *EJ*, 113 (2003), 338–61.

[6] For his initiation of proposals for a fund, battles against extravagance, and criticisms of the United Nations Relief and Rehabilitation Administration (UNRRA), see vol. 22, pp. 23–9; vol. 27, chs. 2, 3; see also, e.g. D. Acheson, *Present at the Creation* (New York, 1970), pp. 101–11, 115–21.

[7] See vol. 27, ch. 3 and Appendix, and references below to buffer stocks.

[8] See, e.g. vol. 28, p. 207 ff. For anxiety over freedom in Czechoslovakia, see Keynes to N. Milnes, 27 June 1945, CO/9/163–4, KP.

[9] Vol. 22, p. 24.

the economic and financial agreements of November and December 1939,[10] inspired various schemes of wartime or post-war federalism or union with France and other free European states.[11] In January 1940, F. A. Hayek wrote to Jacob Viner:[12]

Since the statistical black-out makes it almost impossible to do any work on war problems we are mostly working on utopian post-war schemes (economics of federation and the like) which makes one at least dream of a better future world. On what are the *probable* economic effects of the war we had better try not to think.

In November 1939, Keynes had written of a possible Communist revolution in Germany at war's end: 'What will happen then to the plans of us liberals and federalists?'[13] Winston Churchill was famously to propose the union of Britain and France in June 1940,[14] and later to advocate a form of United States of Europe.[15]

As the war proceeded and it became clear there would not be a compromise peace, more detailed post-war planning became both possible and necessary. US and British officials increasingly discussed specific possibilities—some of them seeming at first quite utopian. In Britain, however, there came to be unlikely allies on the left and right favouring trade and currency arrangements based on the Commonwealth and Empire over a multilateral approach founded on Anglo-American cooperation.

As early as September 1939, the US Secretary of State, Cordell Hull, appointed Leo Pasvolsky his special assistant for peace problems.[16] Pasvolsky shared Hull's strong faith in non-discrimination and free trade.[17] He recorded a discussion in March 1940 with Paul Van Zeeland, former Prime Minister of Belgium.[18] In the 1930s, Van Zeeland had welcomed the 'hegemony' of a great power (such as Britain before the First World War) which promoted free trade.[19] In 1940,

---

[10] See *AR*, 1939, pp. 118, 124–5, 188; W. K. Hancock and M. M. Gowing, *British War Economy* (London, 1949) ch. 7; cf. R. A. C. Parker, 'The Pound Sterling, the American Treasury and British Preparations for War, 1938–1939', *English Historical Review*, 98 (1983), 276.

[11] See, e.g. Harris, *Beveridge*, pp. 367–8. In 1942–43, French and Dutch monetary proposals spoke of generalizing the Anglo-French agreement of Dec. 1939: item 24g, box 9, HDWP.

[12] Hayek to Viner, 20 Jan. 1940, box 39, JVP.   [13] Vol. 22, p. 28.

[14] See *AR*, 1940, pp. 48–9.

[15] For example, Memorandum of meeting between Churchill, Henry Wallace, Stimson, et al., 22 May 1943, box 7, Leo Pasvolsky papers, LOC.

[16] C. Hull, *Memoirs* (London, 1948), pp. 1626–7; R. C. Hilderbrand, *Dumbarton Oaks* (Chapel Hill and London, 1990), pp. 6–7; R. A. Divine, *Second Chance* (New York, 1971), pp. 40–1.

[17] See, e.g. vol. 26, pp. 239–43; Pasvolsky notes, p. 2, box 23, Herbert Feis papers, LOC.

[18] 'Paul Van Zeeland's Ideas on Post-war Economic Reconstruction', 12 Mar. 1940, box 1, Pasvolsky papers, LOC.

[19] See, e.g. P. Van Zeeland, *A View of Europe, 1932: An Interpretative Essay on Some Workings of Economic Nationalism* (Baltimore, 1933), p. 90.

Van Zeeland reported a strong desire in Allied and neutral countries for US leadership post-war in creating a new world order, and real possibilities in the present Anglo-French policies of economic cooperation for a future, broader economic union (presumably of the Allies and the economically advanced neutrals) with fairly free trade and stable exchange rates under an international monetary authority. Pasvolsky also received, for example, Australian proposals of October 1940 on laying the economic foundations of peace through a World Economic Authority to coordinate anti-depression policies.[20]

Keynes himself was thinking about post-war arrangements almost from the outbreak of war. From September 1939, he believed that the USA would help the Allies in their fight for 'civilisation'.[21] Encouraged by Sir George Schuster and Leonard Elmhirst,[22] he wrote 'Notes on the War for the President', dated 2 November 1939.[23] The Notes suggested that US wartime financial assistance to the Anglo-French cause (which help, he believed, would become necessary) should be repaid, in exports, into a post-war Reconstruction Fund as part of America's contribution to that fund. To prevent the Communist revolution in Germany which Keynes feared 'if this war is fought to a finish' (just as he and others had feared Bolshevism in 1919), Keynes wanted Roosevelt to 'offer peace terms of unprecedented generosity (in which the Reconstruction Fund would play a prominent part)' as soon as 'the Hitler gang seems ripe for disappearance'. He listed Germany and Austria among the beneficiaries of reconstruction payments: 'This time it must be clear from the beginning that the indemnity is paid by the victor to the vanquished.'

Because Keynes soon thought an approach to the USA premature, these Notes were not sent to Roosevelt.[24] But on 1 October 1940, Elmhirst wrote to Roosevelt's secretary that 'Mr. Keynes asked me to convey direct to the President' certain ideas. These ideas echoed the Notes. War loans should be non-commercial. Repayments should contribute to post-war reconstruction by the setting up, perhaps immediately, of an International Loan Corporation under US or joint Anglo-US administration. 'Repayment by Great Britain could thus be in the form of goods and services for a general reconstruction program which, if post-war slump and unemployment is to be avoided, will have to be on a world-wide scale.'[25]

When, in November 1940, Keynes was asked by Harold Nicolson at the Ministry of Information for suggestions on how to respond to the German

---

[20] 'Notes on the Re-Statement of Our Aims', 22 Oct. 1940, box 7, Pasvolsky papers, LOC.

[21] See, e.g. vol. 12, p. 74; vol. 22, p. 23. On civilization, see esp. vol. 22, pp. 150, 154–5.

[22] W/2/111–72, KP. On Elmhirst, see vol. 12, pp. 73–4; vol. 22, p. 22; vol. 28, p. 426; Skidelsky, *Saviour*, pp. 522, 693–4.

[23] Vol. 22, pp. 22–9. [24] See W/2/131 ff, 168 ff, KP.

[25] Elmhirst to M. LeHand, 1 Oct. 1940, PPF 4320, FDR papers. There is no sign in L/40, KP, of Keynes authorizing this approach.

'New Order' in Europe, he proposed a plan for the post-war international economy that would have a positive appeal to counter that of the German plan.[26] He feared that Britain would appear to offer only a return to inter-war problems. Keynes proposed that Britain acquire sufficient surplus stocks to help meet Europe's, including Germany's, most urgent post-war require-ments,[27] to be financed through a European Reconstruction Fund: 'a system of international exchange which will open all our markets to every country, great or small, alike, and will give equal access for each to every source of raw material which we can control or influence, on the basis of exchanging goods for goods'; allowing Germany 'under new auspices' to resume her natural measure of economic leadership in Central Europe; measures to prevent wild fluctuations of employment, markets and prices, while promoting extensive international trade; and domestic emphasis on social security and employ-ment policy. Keynes stressed the need not to repeat 'last time's' mistaken neglect of 'the economic reconstruction of Europe'.[28] He wrote that an 'optimistic assumption as to the ultimate outcome of our financial arrange-ments with U.S.A. is implicit throughout'. That is, war debts would not, as last time, long burden economic and political relations.

Keynes's draft, circulated in government departments on 1 December, was modified in the light of comments from various officials, discussed by Keynes with Harry Hopkins in London in January 1941, and sent to Churchill on 30 January.[29] On 23 May 1941, when Keynes was in Washington on Lend-Lease matters, Lord Halifax sent Hull 'two copies of a paper drawn up by a Mr. J. M. Keynes concerning some aspects of post war policy... Mr. Eden is contemplating embodying much of the contents of Mr. Keynes' paper in a speech which he is to make in London on May 29th.' Eden sought the views of Hull and Roosevelt.[30] Roosevelt saw Keynes and Halifax over lunch on 28 May.[31] Keynes reported that Roosevelt had read his paper carefully,[32] and Halifax telegraphed Roosevelt's comments to London that day. Roosevelt recorded: 'I told [Keynes] I did not like the proposed speech of Eden's because while we could all agree on objectives, we could all fight about the machinery to attain them. He got Eden to eliminate the methods—and we should follow that idea over here.'[33]

---

[26] Vol. 25, pp. 7–16.   [27] See also vol. 28, p. 148.

[28] See also, e.g. vol. 27, p. 102.

[29] Vol. 25, pp. 7, 16. On Eden's interest, see Keynes to FAK, 11 Jan. 1941, PP/45/168/11/35–6, KP.

[30] Halifax to Hull, 23 May 1941, OF48, box 2, FDR papers.

[31] See 'Presidential Memorandum for General Watson', 26 May 1941, PPF 5235, FDR papers; vol. 23, pp. 108–12; vol. 25, p. 19; Moggridge, *Biography*, pp. 654, 658; Skidelsky, *Fighting*, p. 116.

[32] Vol. 23, p. 109.

[33] FDR to A. Berle, 26 June 1941, PSF 90, FDR papers; cf. A. Eden, *Memoirs, The Reckoning* (London, 1965), pp. 258–9; Harrod, *Life*, pp. 602–3; vol. 23, pp. 109–10.

In the event, Eden's speech still drew heavily and verbatim from Keynes's draft, making a post-war commitment to 'social security' at home and abroad, with economic health in every country a key to peace. But it was somewhat more general than Keynes had suggested.[34] When Pasvolsky reported Eden's speech to Hull on 7 June, including Keynes's clarification that 'social security' should be taken in a broad and general sense, Pasvolsky complained that while citing Hull on financial arrangements to promote trade, Eden did not cite other points in Hull's post-war programme.[35] 'The vagueness of some of Mr. Eden's statements and the [socialist] character of the Labor Party's ideas certainly argue strongly for joint exploration of post-war problems by representatives of the two governments and for vigorous effort to work out a more or less precise post-war program.'

It was Pasvolsky's desire to clarify post-war plans with the British, rather than Roosevelt's aim to keep matters vague, which was to prevail (though over the years to 1945 there were to be lengthy lacunae in some Anglo-American discussions).[36] Detailed thinking gained impetus from the need to identify the consideration Britain would give for US financial help to run the war. Before discussing this, we consider internal war finance.

6.2 INTERNAL WAR FINANCE: AMERICAN REACTIONS TO KEYNES'S IDEAS

Focusing on how to muster war resources without inflation, Keynes expounded a plan for 'compulsory savings' (or 'deferred pay') in articles in *The Times* in November 1939,[37] elaborating them in a pamphlet, *How to Pay for the War*, in February 1940.[38] Much has been written on the impact in Britain of these proposals, and especially of Keynes's approach to demand management in an inflationary boom.[39] The 'Keynes plan' also received much

---

[34] *The Times*, 30 May 1941.

[35] Pasvolsky to Hull, 7 June 1941, box 7, Pasvolsky papers, LOC. For Hull's programme, see *The Washington Post*, 19 May 1941.

[36] See, e.g. E. F. Penrose, *Economic Planning for the Peace* (Princeton, 1953), pp. 33–4, 50, 119–20.

[37] Vol. 22, pp. 41–51, 74–84.

[38] Vol. 9, pp. 367–439; see also, e.g. Keynes to Hamilton Fish Armstrong, 29 Dec. 1939, box 33, Armstrong papers, Princeton; Thirlwall, *Policy Adviser*, p. 65 ns. 2 and 3.

[39] Skidelsky, *Fighting*, chs. 2–3; A. Cairncross and N. Watts, *The Economic Section, 1939–1961* (London and New York, 1989), pp. 35–6, 232; R. S. Sayers, *Financial Policy, 1939–45* (London, 1956), pp. 80–5; Hancock and Gowing, *War Economy*, pp. 222, 328; cf. pp. 165, 171; Keynes to Irving Fisher, 17 May 1941, box 22, Fisher papers, Yale; Thirlwall, *Policy Adviser*, p. 41; A. S. Milward,

attention in the USA. When Keynes's first articles appeared in November 1939, Ambassador Joseph Kennedy reported the plan in some detail to Washington, including coverage of adverse British press reaction to it.[40] On 1 July 1940, an exposition of *How to Pay for the War*, prepared within the US Treasury, was sent to the Treasury Secretary, Henry Morgenthau.[41] In June 1940, Keynes expounded his scheme for *The New Republic*.[42] He urged that the USA should, by undertaking major war preparations, test (as the New Deal had not) what level of output was necessary for full employment in a modern industrial economy. Compulsory saving would be worth examination when consumption needed curbing and it was necessary to prevent the war boom being 'like the last'—'an orgy of profits, gambling, soaring and disproportionate wages and prices'.

In May 1941, the US Ambassador in London, J. G. Winant, told Morgenthau that he thought Keynes, then in Washington, might be of some help on the programme for saving on which, Winant believed, Morgenthau was having work done.[43] During that visit, Keynes talked with many economists, especially about the American mobilization of resources and the danger of inflation.[44] Keynes's concept of an inflationary gap quickly became, according to E. A. Goldenweiser of the Federal Reserve Board, one of the principal topics of discussion in financial circles in Washington.[45] Goldenweiser believed that 'some form of compulsory saving, as there now is in England and in Canada', might become necessary. When, in July 1941, J. M. Clark of the Office of Price Administration and Civilian Supply in Washington apologized to Keynes for unintended similarity between his own writings and *How to Pay for the War*, Keynes replied: 'There is a quantity of stuff in my "How to Pay for the War" which is now common ground amongst many economists, and I certainly cannot claim it for myself alone.'[46]

War, Economy and Society, 1939–1945 (London, 1977), p. 90; Roll, *Economic Thought*, pp. 517–19; Moggridge, *Biography*, pp. 631–4, 642–8; vol. 22, ch. 4; L. Amery, *The Empire at Bay: The Leo Amery Diaries, 1929–1945*, ed. J. Barnes and D. Nicholson (London, 1988), pp. 561–2, 580.

[40] Kennedy to Secretary of State (for Treasury), 15 and 16 Nov. 1939, HMD, vol. 222, esp. pp. 339–44.

[41] Review by H. C. Murphy, sent to Morgenthau by Haas, 1 July 1940, HMD, vol. 278, pp. 67–76; see J. M. Blum, *From the Morgenthau Diaries: Years of Urgency, 1938–1941* (Boston, 1965), pp. 297, 300.

[42] Vol. 22, pp. 144–55; see Hession, *Keynes*, pp. 315–16. Hession's stress on this article seems well placed.

[43] Winant to Morgenthau, 19 May 1941, HMD, vol. 399, p. 410.

[44] See vol. 23, ch. 5; Hansen, *Guide*, p. 225.

[45] 'Central Banking and the War' by E. A. Goldenweiser, 4 Nov. 1942, box 2, Goldenweiser papers, LOC.

[46] Vol. 23, pp. 191–3.

Keynes's talks with US economists are important partly because his belief that Keynesian economics was taking root in the USA helped to set the context in which he was, in the late summer and autumn of 1941, to devise a scheme for international monetary cooperation that would involve Britain surrendering bilateral protections of her payments position.[47] Keynesian economics, while powerful, had not made a complete conquest.[48] Conversely, Keynes came to think some economists more 'Keynesian' than himself.[49] It is said that he 'chaffed a group of experts assembled to meet him' along these lines during this 1941 visit.[50] This almost certainly refers to discussions with Price Administration officials, whom he believed underestimated the risk of inflation.[51] Keynes wrote in July 1941:[52]

There is too wide a gap here in Washington between the intellectual outlook of the older people and that of the younger. But I have been greatly struck during my visit by the quality of the younger economists and civil servants in the Administration. I am sure that the best hope for good government of America is to be found there. The war will be a great sifter and will bring the right people to the top.

The contrast between the Keynesianism of the younger economists and others, and the laissez-faire approach (especially on international trade)[53] of 'the older people', particularly in the State Department, was to be a recurring phenomenon. Much of the wartime economic diplomacy aimed to reconcile the two approaches.

Amongst the most influential of administration economists was Harry Dexter White, a senior Treasury official whose pro-Soviet sympathies were not then widely known.[54] His Keynesian credentials were reflected in his attitude to wartime inflation and compulsory saving.[55] In October 1941, White told Vice-President Wallace that a proposed plan of compulsory savings excise could be made a satisfactory instrument for the prevention of wartime inflation and post-war depression.[56] This scheme of excises on consumer purchases of commodities, which would be repaid post-war, was inspired by Keynesian analysis of the need to cut consumer spending to prevent inflation. After the USA entered the war (if not before), a scheme of

[47] Harrod, *Life*, pp. 621–2; Hansen, *Guide*, pp. 225–6; see below.

[48] For example, in January 1945, Paul Samuelson wrote that most American economics journals were 'somewhat anti-Keynesian in tone': 'a good deal of the economics profession, especially among the older members, are still unreconstructed'. Samuelson to D. McC. Wright, 20 Jan. 1945, box 6, Wright papers, U.Va.

[49] Hutchison, *Keynes versus the 'Keynesians'...?*, pp. 23, 58.   [50] Harrod, *Life*, pp. 621–2.

[51] Vol. 23, ch. 5, *passim*: e.g. pp. 183–5, 192.   [52] Vol. 23, p. 193.

[53] Vol. 23, pp. 145, 176–8; see below.

[54] See vol. 25, p. 356; Skidelsky, *Fighting*, p. 241 ff.   [55] Harrod, *Life*, p. 637.

[56] White to Wallace, 10 Oct. 1941, encl. memo, item 20d, box 6, HDWP.

forced or compulsory saving more directly along the lines of Keynes's deferred pay was actively considered by Treasury officials and others. During 1942, White sent Morgenthau several memoranda either urging it, or giving it as an option.[57] Amongst White's objectives was funding the war effort so as to facilitate reasonable expansion of consumers' purchasing power in the post-war period.[58] In December 1943, David McCord Wright wrote to Alvin Hansen urging that 'we economists who believe in the use of deficit financing' should preserve their credibility by urging an anti-inflationary package including 'the Keynes plan'.[59]

Keynes's writings over some years were influential, both in Britain and in America, in having the war financed at low interest rates.[60] Through the 1930s, he had been a strong advocate of a continuously low interest rate.[61] In April 1939, Keynes urged the Chancellor of the Exchequer to announce that in no circumstances would he offer loans carrying a rate of interest in excess of 2.5 per cent.[62] He reiterated this, and the general desirability of low interest rates, over subsequent months.[63] Keynes wanted a 'cheap money war' to limit the burden put on the future tax payer. Moreover, he believed that any post-war boom would be short, and as the real post-war problem would be inadequate effective demand, ending the war with a low rate of interest would facilitate the transition to peacetime capital expenditure.[64] He argued that the sacrifices asked from others make it appropriate that loan rates be low; and that high interest rates would threaten, and low rates enhance, the security and stability of financial institutions.[65] Such concerns were also evident in the US Treasury.[66]

---

[57] White to Morgenthau, 31 Mar. 1942; draft memo, White to Morgenthau, 8 Apr.; White to Morgenthau, 20 July, urging 'A New Program for Inflation Control and Government Borrowing'; White et al. to Morgenthau, 28 July; 'Progressive Compulsory Saving and the Control of Inflation', 29 July; all at: item 20d, box 6, HDWP. White to Morgenthau, 7 Aug., item 20e, box 6, HDWP. Draft memos from White to Morgenthau, 13 Apr. and 5 May, urging financing the war by forced savings; White to Morgenthau, 22 Sept., item 20f, box 6. None of these documents cites Keynes. White came to prefer rationing to compulsory lending.

[58] White to Morgenthau, 20 July 1942, item 20d, box 6, HDWP.

[59] Wright to Hansen, 10 Dec. 1943, box 6, Wright papers, U.Va.

[60] Skidelsky, *Fighting*, pp. 22–6, 43, 85–6, 375–7; Harrod, *Life*, p. 582; M. Keynes, *Essays*, p. 183; Blum, *Urgency*, p. 299.

[61] For example, vol. 7, pp. 375–7; vol. 21, p. 389.

[62] Vol. 21, pp. 517, 523; Peden, *Rearmament*, p. 94; Howson and Winch, *EAC*, pp. 148–51.

[63] For example, vol. 21, p. 524 ff; vol. 22, p. 30; Parker, 'British rearmament', pp. 315–16; Moggridge and Howson, 'Monetary Policy', pp. 241–2.

[64] Vol. 22, pp. 35–6; see also p. 30; vol. 21, p. 517.

[65] Vol. 21, p. 523; see also p. 517.

[66] For example, White to Morgenthau, 20 July 1942, 3, item 20d, box 6, HDWP.

6.3 EXTERNAL FINANCE: LEND-LEASE, 'CONSIDERATION', AND THE US LOAN

During the war, Britain faced large current account deficits, as exports dropped but her need for imports remained large. She sold overseas investments to help pay for the war, and incurred substantial debts to the USA and Canada and in 'blocked balances' in the sterling area. In 1944 Keynes argued that in 'waging the war without counting the ultimate cost we—and we alone of the United Nations—have burdened ourselves with the weight of deferred indebtedness to other countries beneath which we shall stagger'.[67] He expected Britain to have severe balance of payments difficulties after the war.

As in the First World War, Keynes's work was crucial in ensuring finance for the British war effort. With Britain's gold and dollar reserves at very low levels, Britain faced the problem of how to pay for supplies that must be paid for in dollars. US Lend-Lease and Canadian assistance were indispensable for this. It was also necessary to prevent those who had sterling from seeking to convert it into gold, dollars, or other currencies which Britain did not have. This produced blocked balances, and left the difficult question of how soon after the war, and on what terms, the balances would be unblocked and sterling convertibility restored.

Keynes advised on exchange controls before rejoining the Treasury in July 1940.[68] We have seen that, in April 1939, he urged a tighter embargo on sending capital funds overseas by British nationals—'national service for saving'—because Britain's liquid capital must be concentrated to meet the adverse balance of trade arising from increased imports due to rearmament, and to provide for political loans.[69] In September 1939 he proposed that the Treasury require British exporters to hand over the foreign currency they earn, and that it acquire the cash equivalent of as much as possible of Britain's invisible exports, while allowing a free exchange on a modest basis.[70] During the war he proposed various tightenings and modifications of exchange controls.[71]

Encouraged by reports that 'practically everyone in Washington and New York is perfectly certain that America would come in in some shape or form if we got into any difficulties or if there was any bombing of London and Paris', Keynes wrote on 20 September 1939 that 'what would be easy, if we handled

---

[67] Vol. 26, p. 11; see also p. 86.   [68] See, e.g. vol. 22, pp. 9–15.

[69] Vol. 21, pp. 512, 515; see Parker, 'Pound Sterling', for background.

[70] Vol. 22, pp. 13–15.

[71] Vol. 22, ch. 3, *passim*; ch. 23, pp. 1–6; Moggridge, *Biography*, pp. 627–8, 634.

ourselves properly, would be to get a complete economic front with America, whilst not asking them to send troops'.[72] By January 1940, disillusioned, Keynes complained to Walter Lippmann that 'no one expects, or even desires' the USA to enter the war, but that he found 'extremely distasteful' 'the idea that there is some sort of moral beauty about neutrality'. He rejected the notion that financial assistance would compromise American neutrality, and said that 'some day I should like to make suggestions, not for an alliance, but for some kind of active benevolence'.[73] Keynes was to be central in negotiating that active benevolence when it came. The story—of great assistance given, but of greater expectations dashed—can only be told briefly here.[74]

On 1 November 1940, Keynes wrote to Edward Stettinius, Jnr, who was already working in the Advisory Commission of the Council of National Defense, forerunner to the Lend-Lease Administration (which he was to head from 1941 to 1943):[75]

We are now very much occupied, as you may suppose, with the future financial arrangements between your Administration and our Government when the pest of the [US] election is out of the way. It is highly important that discussions of such significance both financially and from the standpoint of getting the right and proper relations between the two peoples should not be left too much to the last moment and then hastily improvised.

Keynes believed from his experience in and after the First World War that the way in which Britain received US aid would determine whether there would be subsequent friction and estrangement.[76] It was essential, not least to avoid unnecessary friction, that Britain retain enough assets to leave her capable of independent action.[77]

The announcement of Lend-Lease in January 1941, approved by Congress in March, gave great encouragement.[78] But there was much to be worked out. In the early months of 1941, American pressure increased for the sale of remaining British overseas assets, which could often only be sold at low prices, and whose sale would deplete Britain's assets.[79] The 'show sale' was to be of the British-owned American Viscose Company. Keynes had in 1940 proposed that American subsidiaries of British companies (such as Viscose) borrow dollars on their own credit, these dollars to be made available for British

---

[72] Vol. 12, p. 74; see Parker, 'Pound Sterling', pp. 277–8.

[73] Keynes to Lippmann, 6 Jan. 1940, box 82, folder 1217, Lippmann papers, LOC; W/1, KP.

[74] For fuller treatment, see vols. 23 and 24; Skidelsky, *Fighting, passim*; Moggridge, *Biography*, ch. 25.

[75] Keynes to Stettinius, 1 Nov. 1940, box 646, E. R. Stettinius, Jnr papers, U.Va.

[76] Vol. 23, pp. 22–6 at p. 25; see also L/40/136–8, KP.   [77] Vol. 23, pp. 46–8 at p. 48.

[78] Keynes to Wright, 4 Mar. 1941, box 6, Wright papers, U.Va.

[79] See, e.g. vol. 23, p. 45 ff (esp. pp. 66–71).

dollar purchases.[80] In March 1941, he proposed a scheme to avoid selling British assets in the USA by using them instead as security for loans to Britain from the US Reconstruction Finance Corporation.[81] The need for such action was heightened when, in mid-March, the Budget Director, Harold Smith, promised Congress that commitments pre-dating Lend-Lease would not be covered, as Britain had expected.[82] Encouraged by Winant and his adviser Ben Cohen,[83] Keynes went in May to the USA to explain Britain's financial difficulties, to discuss such issues as the rules of Lend-Lease (including what it would cover), financing commitments pre-dating Lend-Lease, and 'consideration' for Lend-Lease.[84] Much of Keynes's work was with the US Treasury under Henry Morgenthau, and Lend-Lease officials such as Harry Hopkins and Oscar Cox.[85]

Despite Harrod's tentative account[86] of something he once intended not to mention,[87] and Morgenthau's denial to Harrod,[88] it is clear that Keynes had an extremely bad start with Morgenthau.[89] Morgenthau believed that Keynes had come to upset the Viscose sale.[90] Though not strictly true, it is understandable that Morgenthau, who had heard of Keynes's discussions with Cohen about avoiding asset sales, should have suspected this.[91] Reassurances from Halifax and Sir Frederick Phillips took time to calm Morgenthau. Keynes saw Morgenthau privately on 23 May and, as he believed, the air was cleared.[92] Keynes had already formed the view that Morgenthau 'really wants to do his best for us', and that 'we owe him a big debt of gratitude' for his help on the Lend-Lease legislation.[93] On 25 May, Keynes wrote that 'Mr Morgenthau himself is passionately with us, believes that he has at every stage fought our battle and is sensitive to criticism which he thinks misunderstands the excellence of his intentions and the magnitude of his success in fulfilling them,—and, in spite of everything, there is great truth in this'.[94]

---

[80] Vol. 23, pp. 10–11.

[81] Vol. 23, pp. 53–9. This resulted in the 'Jesse Jones loan': vol. 23, pp. 114, 121–2, 134, 151–2, 160–1, 166, 278; Sayers, *Financial Policy*, p. 392 ff. T/247/43, PRO.

[82] See, e.g. vol. 23, p. 53 ff; Winant to Morgenthau, 19 May 1941, HMD, vol. 399, p. 409.

[83] Harrod, *Life*, pp. 596–7; Winant to Morgenthau, 19 May 1941, HMD, vol. 399, pp. 409–11.

[84] See, esp. vol. 23, chs. 2–6.   [85] On Cox, see vol. 23, p. 306.

[86] Harrod, *Life*, pp. 600–1.

[87] Harrod to Viner, 15 and 17 Apr. 1949; Viner to Harrod, 18 Apr. 1949, box 38, JVP.

[88] Harrod to Viner, 15 Apr. 1949, ibid.

[89] Vol. 23, pp. 87–91, 97–100; Blum, *Urgency*, pp. 239, 244–6; Skidelsky, *Fighting*, pp. 103–4.

[90] See, e.g. vol. 23, p. 83; M. Keynes, *Essays*, p. 185. On this episode, see Morgenthau telegram to Winant, 18 May 1941; Winant to Morgenthau, 19 May, HMD, vol. 399, pp. 407, 409–11. 'Memorandum for the Secretary's Diary', 21 May; Cochran to Morgenthau, 21 May; Halifax to Morgenthau, 21 May, HMD, vol. 400, pp. 220–3, 228–9, 230.

[91] See vol. 23, pp. 98–9; Blum, *Urgency*, pp. 239–40.   [92] Vol. 23, pp. 98–9.

[93] Vol. 23, p. 88.   [94] Vol. 23, p. 95.

Subsequent weeks of talks, including in a committee formed by Morgenthau for Anglo-American discussion of Lend-Lease, showed both his sensitivity to criticism,[95] and his willingness to help Britain[96] and the Dominions.[97] Morgenthau declared: 'I would like to feel that I make a contribution toward licking Mr. Hitler'.[98] His assistance included advice on how to get the best deal from Congress[99] and from the State Department over consideration.[100] Morgenthau's advice on dealing with Congress tended to be very cautious;[101] Keynes came to think the administration far too timid in its dealings with Congress.[102] During the talks, Keynes and other British officials needed to respond to press criticism that Britain was trying to expand its trade under cover of Lend-Lease to the detriment of American exporters,[103] and did so with help from the State Department, Morgenthau's office, and perhaps the White House.[104] British exports were to be the subject of the Export White Paper of September 1941, declaring 'that Britain would use for export neither Lend-Lease supplies nor their substitutes nor, so far as possible, scarce materials of any kind'.[105] There is much evidence that, despite annoyances,[106] over these weeks and subsequent years mutual admiration and even affection developed between Keynes and Morgenthau.[107] Yet when Keynes told Morgenthau on 30 June 'that his mission with the U.S. Treasury ... had been completely successful' (though more meetings were to follow in

[95] For example, Transcripts 'Re Aid to Britain', 10 July 1941, HMD, vol. 419, p. 388; 18 July, vol. 422, pp. 154–6.

[96] For example, Transcripts 'Re Aid to Britain', 23 June 1941, HMD, vol. 412, p. 259; 1 July, vol. 416, pp. 180–1; 10 July, vol. 419, p. 392.

[97] For example, transcript of meeting 'Re Aid to Britain', 20 June 1941, HMD, vol. 411, pp. 108, 117, 118, 124, and *passim*; 23 June, vol. 412, pp. 218, 223, 231, 240, 243–9, and *passim*; see also *CW*, vol. 23, pp. 128–34.

[98] Transcript 'Re Aid to Britain', 1 July, HMD, vol. 416, p. 169; see Acheson, *Present*, p. 47.

[99] Transcripts 'Re Aid to Britain', 10 July, HMD, vol. 419, pp. 383, 397–8; 18 July, vol. 422, pp. 148–9, 152–3.

[100] See Keynes to Morgenthau, 18 June 1941, HMD, vol. 412, p. 200; vol. 23, p. 178.

[101] See also, e.g. Acheson, *Present*, p. 54.

[102] For example, vol. 23, pp. 135, 142; vol. 25, p. 369.

[103] Keynes to Lippmann, 24 July 1941, and enclosed British press release on 'British Export Policy', 14 July 1941, box 82, folder 1217, Lippmann papers, LOC.

[104] See Keynes to S. Early, 12 July 1941, PPF 5235, FDR papers; 'Highlights', 10 July 1941, HMD, vol. 410, p. 383; vol. 23, p. 167.

[105] L. S. Pressnell, *External Economic Policy Since the War*, i, *The Post-War Financial Settlement* (London, 1986) p. 10; vol. 23, pp. 197–201.

[106] See, e.g. Cochran to Morgenthau, 20 June 1941, HMD, vol. 411, pp. 89–90.

[107] See, e.g. Harrod to Viner, 15 Apr. 1949; Viner to Harrod, 18 Apr., box 38, JVP; cf. untitled note, 3 June 1941, reporting Morgenthau–Frankfurter conversation, HMD, vol. 404, p. 174A; Robinson, 'Keynes', p. 58, and Moggridge, *Biography*, p. 743, say that intimacy grew at Bretton Woods: see Skidelsky, *Fighting*, p. 354.

July), Morgenthau asked White to get Keynes to confirm that statement in writing.[108] Keynes did so handsomely.[109]

The State Department had responsibility for the consideration for Lend-Lease. From May to July, Keynes discussed this with Hopkins, State Department officials led by Dean Acheson, and Roosevelt. But until 28 July, the day before Keynes left the USA, he had not seen an official American draft, as the US position was itself evolving.[110] Keynes knew by 25 May that consideration was likely to include declaration of common post-war economic policy on the lines of Hull's 'well-known opinions covering non-discrimination, in the presence of free trade bias'. But he thought State Department officials understood Britain's 'probable unavoidable dependence on exchange control and import licensing after the war, and will endeavour to agree to declaration in a form which would not involve us in any lack of candour'.[111]

Earlier in 1941, Keynes had written that the outstanding international economic problem of the post-war world would be how the USA was to redress her unbalanced creditor position. This could be by US lending, or her importing more, or exporting less. 'There is nothing we can do about it, except to try and safeguard ourselves against being ruined by entering into commitments we cannot meet before the period when the solution can be found.'[112] Keynes's fears were further aroused in an exchange with Dr Harry Hawkins, Chief of the State Department's Trade Agreements Division, on 25 June. Hawkins was shocked at Keynes's suggesting that, 'unless some other comprehensive solution was found', Britain might be driven by post-war balance of payments difficulties to bilateralism in trade policy.[113] Keynes was disturbed that Hawkins rejected 'the idea that our choice of where we buy should be influenced by whether we possess means of payment in that place'. In any case, Britain could not make commitments when it did not know what exchange and import controls it would face from other countries.[114]

Keynes's unwillingness to rule out bilateralism caused such alarm in the State Department that Hull mentioned it in mid-August to Roosevelt, and sent him Hawkins's detailed account of his talks with British officials, especially Keynes.[115] Keynes's statements strengthened the State Department's

---

[108] Memo. by White, 30 June 1941, HMD, vol. 415, p. 316.

[109] Vol. 23, pp. 178–80; see Morgenthau to Keynes, 8 Aug. 1941, HMD, vol. 430, p. 133; see also Keynes to Winant, 14 Aug. 1941, box 204, Winant papers, FDR Library.

[110] Vol. 23, pp. 86, 92–7, 101–2, 121, 125–70.   [111] Vol. 23, p. 102.

[112] Vol. 27, p. 19; see also, e.g. Acheson, *Present*, p. 57.   [113] Vol. 23, p. 208; see below.

[114] Vol. 23, pp. 207–8, 145–6; see, e.g. Harrod, *Life*, pp. 606, 610–11.

[115] Hull to FDR, 18 Aug. 1941, encl. memo by Hawkins dated 4 Aug. 1941, PSF 90, FDR Library.

resolve to insist on non-discrimination, the traditional US doctrine to which Hull was deeply wedded. Their resolve strengthened further after a commitment to non-discrimination was not included in the Atlantic Charter.[116] Some British officials believed Keynes had been foolish to be so frank with Hawkins,[117] and Keynes was to regret that the image of him as a bilateralist was to persist in Washington when he was promoting the Clearing Union (CU) as a means to multilateralism.[118]

In the absence of American or British official drafts for consideration, Keynes floated his own thoughts with American officials, and suggested a more detailed draft to London. His suggestions aimed to reconcile what he understood to be American wishes with his views of British interests and practicalities. He wondered whether Britain should offer to take, as part of consideration, a major responsibility for equipping and arming a post-war international police force.[119] To the Americans he suggested a draft committing Britain 'to make such contribution as lies in their power' towards the US purpose of avoiding 'encumbrances which might interfere with the free and healthy flow of normal economic intercourse between nations after the war'.[120] The draft he suggested to London elaborated this with several economic proposals. Anglo-American cooperation to establish 'a post-war economic order which shall promote the freedom of trade, of travel and of intercourse' between all countries would include 'the abatement, as circumstances allow, of all special privileges and discriminations in trade navigation and commerce and the reduction of trade barriers' and 'the maintenance through an appropriate exchange and currency organisation and in other ways of a due equilibrium in the balance of payments between national systems'. An Anglo-American Commission would prepare plans for Anglo-American and broader international economic cooperation.[121] But London allowed Keynes to pass officially to the Americans a draft committing Britain to no more than discussing with the USA 'in due course further measures of cooperation'.[122] Acheson, who (with Roosevelt) had promoted the Anglo-American Commission which London discouraged,[123] regarded such absence of commitment as 'wholly impossible'.[124] Keynes thought the British draft

---

[116] On this episode: W. L. Langer and S. E. Gleason, *The Undeclared War, 1940–1941* (Gloucester, Mass, 1968), pp. 678–92. Generally: R. Gardner, *Sterling–Dollar Diplomacy in Current Perspective* (New York, 1980), pp. 16–20; Hull, *Memoirs*, pp. 975–6, 1151–3.

[117] For example, vol. 23, p. 144; Pressnell, *External Economic Policy*, i, pp. 23–4.

[118] Vol. 26, pp. 245–7.   [119] Vol. 23, pp. 135–6, 137, 141.

[120] Vol. 23, p. 128.   [121] Vol. 23, pp. 139–40.   [122] Vol. 23, p. 165.

[123] Vol. 23, p. 195; FDR's advocacy: vol. 25, p. 202; see CAB 117/52, PRO.

[124] Acheson, *Present*, p. 55; vol. 23, p. 176.

'jejune',[125] and later argued that offering the Americans so little had led them to demand too much.[126]

On 28 July, Dean Acheson handed Keynes the American draft consideration agreement.[127] Keynes 'exploded'[128] at Article 7, which said that both countries would 'provide against discrimination' in either country 'against the importation of any produce originating in the other country'. Keynes believed that this 'saddled on the future' the State Department's 'ironclad formula from the nineteenth century' ruling out imperial preference and other trade and exchange controls which Keynes believed would probably be needed to safeguard Britain's post-war position. Keynes insisted that Article 7 was impossible when Britain would have a large trade deficit and the USA a large surplus. Acheson insisted that it had a more general purpose, only requiring Britain to work out, in cooperation with America, measures to obviate discriminatory and nationalistic practices. The next day, Keynes wrote to Acheson acknowledging the 'excellence and magnanimity of the first part' of Article 7. This was a commitment not to burden commerce between the two countries, which Keynes took to mean 'that there will be no war debts'.[129] 'My so strong reaction against the word "discrimination"', he told Acheson, 'is the result of my feeling so passionately that our hands must be free to make something new and better of the post-war world'. Keynes did not wish a return to economic nationalism, but safeguards for each country's welfare. '[My] vehemence...has deep causes in my hopes for the future.' Keynes took the draft back to London for discussion.[130]

During this 1941 visit, Keynes had received valuable lessons in interagency and interpersonal rivalries and uncoordination within the US executive, and in the impact of oscillations in public and Congressional opinion on dealings with the Administration.[131] It is not possible here to trace through subsequent negotiations in great detail: but Keynes repeatedly encountered the same phenomena.[132] Especially after his 1941 visit, he was conscious that the atmospherics of American politics, and therefore of Anglo-American possibilities, could be adequately sensed only in Washington. He sought in reports to London to convey 'the atmosphere here'.[133] Back in London, he solicited, and circulated to ministers and other officials, letters giving the feel of

---

[125] Vol. 23, p. 162.   [126] Vol. 23, pp. 202, 206.
[127] Vol. 23, pp. 171–8.   [128] Moggridge, *Biography*, p. 661.
[129] Vol. 23, pp. 177, 194; vol. 25, p. 435.
[130] See vol. 23, pp. 171–8; Acheson, *Present*, pp. 55–7.
[131] See, e.g. vol. 23, pp. 106, 113.
[132] For example, vol. 24, pp. 192 ff (e.g. pp. 208–9), 605 ff; vol. 28, p. 218.
[133] Vol. 23, p. 96.

subsequent American developments.[134] Over subsequent years, Keynes was repeatedly fearful of Congress limiting US wartime help to Britain, or rejecting the post-war plans, as in 1919–20. He sought to cultivate public and Congressional, as well as Administration, opinion.[135] Although at times, as in 1941, Keynes's superior and sometimes abrasive style caused difficulties with US officials,[136] he went to considerable lengths to cultivate individuals he believed would be helpful (including Winant and his economic advisers, Cohen and E. F. Penrose).[137]

During August and September 1941, immediately after Keynes's return to London, several elements of the Lend-Lease arrangements he had negotiated were overturned by Congress, or faced other difficulties.[138] Keynes wrote 'that one can take nothing whatever for settled in U.S.A.' as 'every bargain can, and very likely will, be overthrown by Congress'.[139] Yet in early October 1941, Lippmann could write that Roosevelt 'now has the backing of at least three-fourths of the people' and 'can have anything he wants, at a price', and that the internationalist wing of the Republican party was in the ascendant.[140] Keynes replied that, during the 'very bad spell' on Lend-Lease in August–September, the 'Administration did not seem prepared to risk the faintest criticism, however misconceived... Now it is evident that matters are much better and that the Administration was, as usual, unnecessarily timid. But we are very remote from Washington here'.[141]

Keynes continued that 'We are working here on post-war problems, and I am hopeful that the time will come when we shall have something constructive to produce, which you in America will be able to pass on as being conceived in the general interest.' This was a reference to his plan for a CU, which was a means to avoid the trade and monetary bilateralism which the State Department regarded as selfish.[142] Keynes's first draft of this was

[134] For example, Keynes to O. Cox, 22 July 1942, box 17, Cox papers, FDR Library, and (copy) box 150, Stettinius papers, U.Va.; vol. 23, p. 219.

[135] See, e.g. D. Acheson, *Sketches from Life* (London, 1961), pp. 132–4; vol. 24, pp. 541–2, 614; vol. 25, pp. 203–4, 243–4, 249, 376; cf. pp. 256–7.

[136] For example, R. Clarke, *Anglo-American Economic Collaboration in War and Peace, 1942–1949*, ed. A. Cairncross (Oxford, 1982), p. 63; Blum, *Urgency*, pp. 245–6; S. Howson and D. Moggridge (eds), *The Wartime Diaries of Lionel Robbins and James Meade, 1943–45* (Basingstoke and London, 1990), pp. 94–5.

[137] See Penrose, *Economic Planning*, p. 16; see Keynes–Winant letters, box 204, Winant papers, FDR Library; cf. Skidelsky, *Fighting*, p. 105.

[138] See vol. 23, pp. 194–218. Harrod, *Life*, pp. 608–9.

[139] Vol. 23, pp. 210–11.

[140] Lippmann to Keynes, 7 Oct. 1941, box 82, folder 1217, Lippmann papers, LOC; cf. vol. 23, p. 210 n.

[141] Keynes to Lippmann, 4 Nov. 1941, box 82, folder 1217, Lippmann papers, LOC.

[142] See, e.g. vol. 23, p. 177 (per Acheson).

prepared in early September.[143] On 19 September, commenting on his controversial Hawkins conversation, Keynes wrote:

So far from its being my opinion that the bilateral arrangements to which the Americans object are the ideal solution, I have been spending some time since I came back in elaborating a truly international plan which would avoid these difficulties.... Let us start constructively, offering [the Americans] something which would give them all they ask, provided they are really prepared to be truly international minded.... I do not myself see how there can be any alternative except either a variant of my international scheme or a variant of my bilateral scheme, as [incompletely set out by Hawkins].

The State Department did not understand that, while the USA ran massive trade surpluses, no multilateral solution was possible; but economists advising the Administration, such as Alvin Hansen and Jacob Viner, were 'fully alive' to this.[144]

Keynes had told Acheson in July of 'considerable differences of opinion in London about future courses': 'There were some who believed that Great Britain should return to a free trade policy; there was a middle group, among whom he classified himself, who believed in the use of control mechanisms; and there was a third group who leant toward imperial policies'.[145] The immediate effect of the State Department draft on consideration was to ally many of the middle group with the latter, but Keynes was soon to be developing a de facto alliance with the first.

As well as devising his CU plan to obviate the need for bilateralism, Keynes set out in consideration discussions to find 'a formula which should make the commitment to abandon "discrimination" conditional upon the joint Anglo-American effort having created a sufficiently prosperous world to make such discrimination no longer necessary'.[146] Where some, such as Leo Amery, wished to insist on respecting Britain's established economic policies, or make some other proposal to the Americans which Keynes thought derisory, Keynes in late August urged seizing the opportunity, 'which may not recur', for Anglo-American economic cooperation. This would enable Lend-Lease to be settled without Britain being left with a massive war debt to the USA. Moreover, Keynes believed that the State Department, which always regarded the Ottawa imperial preference agreement of 1932 as 'our riposte to the Hawley Smoot tariff' of 1930, was willing to halve that US tariff in exchange for 'modification of Ottawa'. Keynes and others in the Treasury proposed that Britain offer, in its counterproposal to Article 7, 'agreed action by the U.S.

[143] Vol. 25, pp. 21–40.   [144] Vol. 23, pp. 207–10; see below.
[145] Vol. 23, p. 177.
[146] Harrod, *Life*, p. 610; vol. 23, pp. 194–6, 201–10, 224–8.

and U.K., each working within the limits of their governing economic conditions, directed to the progressive attainment of a balanced international economy which would render unnecessary policies of special discrimination'. Britain submitted a modified (perhaps less satisfactory) version of this draft.[147]

The USA rejected the British proposal as inadequate, and on 2 December proposed its own revised draft of Article 7.[148] To the July draft was added reference to 'agreed action' by the two countries, open to like-minded countries, 'directed to the expansion, by appropriate international and domestic measures, of production, employment, and exchange and consumption of goods'. Dean Acheson wrote that by this, 'We were embracing the Keynesian ideas of an expanding economy. If it needed to be managed, let us do it together and not separately.'[149] Thus, in a way, the two strands of American opinion Keynes had encountered earlier in 1941—the free trade enthusiasts in the State Department and among older economists,[150] and the Keynesian outlook of the younger economists and civil servants in the Administration[151]—were coming together. Nonetheless, Keynes regarded Foreign Office promptings to accept the new draft as characteristic appeasement. But he preferred to sign the agreement than to face a public breakdown of the negotiations, which could result in financial arrangements destroying British financial independence after the war.[152] After further US pressure, and reassurance from Roosevelt to Churchill that Article 7 was a commitment to constructive, unfettered discussion and not to pre-specified action, Britain signed the Mutual Aid Agreement, including Article 7, on 23 February 1942.[153] It was under Article 7 that Anglo-American talks were ultimately held on many topics, especially international monetary arrangements, commercial (i.e. trade) policy, commodities and cartels policy, and international investment.[154]

From late 1941, Keynes grew increasingly anxious that Britain's large expenses in the Middle East and India were creating sterling balances which constituted a form of post-war debt. He sought ways to limit this growing

[147] Vol. 23, pp. 202–7. On Ottawa/Hawley-Smoot, see p. 96. For discussion of 'consideration', see T/247/44, PRO.

[148] Vol. 23, p. 224; Acheson, *Present*, pp. 58–9.

[149] Acheson, *Present*, p. 59; see Penrose, *Economic Planning*, pp. 18–19.

[150] Vol. 25, p. 20. Some senior US economists thought Keynes neo-mercantilist: e.g. F. W. Taussig to Viner, 15 May 1936, box 61; F. H. Knight to Viner, 6 Aug. 1940, box 44, JVP.

[151] Vol. 23, p. 193.

[152] Vol. 23, pp. 224–8; Moggridge, *Biography*, pp. 666–7; Keynes to Opie, 2 Mar. 1942, L/O/6–8, KP.

[153] See also Acheson, *Present*, pp. 60–1; Gardner, *Sterling-Dollar*, pp. 58–62; Amery, *Empire at Bay*, p. 707 ff.

[154] See, e.g. memorandum on USA-Britain 'Exploratory Discussions at Washington' on 'Article VII of the Mutual Aid Agreement', 30 Sept. 1943, RG19, vol. 3989, file T-2-9-2, PAC.

debt (including by fighting inflation in countries where Britain was incurring liabilities).[155] Keynes believed that even top US officials did not realize the burden Britain carried through 'our sole financial responsibility for the miscellaneous cost of the war in all areas of hostilities'.[156] He wrote to Lippmann in May 1942 that 'it is indeed the liabilities thus incurred [in India and the Middle East] which are now the main aggravation of our accumulating post-war financial problem.'[157] Was it reasonable, he asked, now with the USA in the war, or even possible, that Britain should continue such sole responsibility? He lamented 'the failure to revise Anglo-American relations, political, financial and economic—in fact, in any field outside the military and supply fields' since US entry. He believed that such a reorientation would have profound effects on the long-term underlying trends of public opinion. He did, however, believe that the reciprocal Lend-Lease arrangement then being worked out was of high political importance, and could involve Britain 'in a pretty considerable liability'. Keynes also believed that Britain's position needed to be understood by American public opinion, and told Lippmann that he could 'do more to help the evolution of opinion in the right direction than any of us'. He therefore fed Lippmann 'fully and frankly' with his thoughts. 'You would be astonished', Keynes wrote, 'if you knew how much of our actual time and energy we [in Whitehall] are now giving to the wider post-war questions with particular regard to Anglo-American relations. But none of this can or should be a matter for public consumption at present.'

Similarly, Keynes continued cultivating Stettinius, now the Lend-Lease Administrator, who was in London in July–August 1942.[158] Keynes believed Stettinius's visit, including discussion of Britain's financial impoverishment through sterling liabilities in India and the Middle East,[159] put him 'in a very much stronger position for giving evidence to Congress on lend-lease matters on first-hand knowledge'.[160] Keynes was much concerned, then as later, with encouraging American understanding that Britain had 'borne the brunt of the

[155] See vol. 23, pp. 216, 222–3, chs. 7 (e.g. pp. 265–76) and 8; M. Keynes, *Essays*, pp. 186–7; Amery, *Empire at Bay*, pp. 899, 1025.

[156] Vol. 23, p. 236.

[157] Keynes to Lippmann, 13 May 1942, box 82, folder 1217, Lippmann papers, LOC; PP/45/187/31–3, KP; see also vol. 23, pp. 233–6.

[158] See vol. 23, pp. 236–43, 247; see also, e.g. p. 314. Stettinius was clearly an admirer of Keynes's; see, e.g. Keynes to Stettinius, 24 July 1942; Stettinius to Keynes, 27 July 1942, box 150, Stettinius papers, U.Va. For Keynes to Stettinius, 15 Sept. 1940, re Keynes's dealings in the First World War with E. R. Stettinius, Snr: box 646, Stettinius papers.

[159] Vol. 23, pp. 237, 263.

[160] See, e.g. Keynes to Cox, 22 July 1942, in Cox papers, box 17, FDR library, and box 150, Stettinius papers, U.Va.

financial sacrifice of the war and *literally alone* amongst the Allies will have suffered a serious reversal of our overseas financial position'.[161] His hopes for a new financial deal with the USA (e.g. to share burdens in the Middle East equally with them)[162] gave way to thinking about how to handle those 'war debts' post-war, and how they might be taken over by the CU.[163]

Soon after returning to England after Bretton Woods and financial talks in Canada, Keynes returned in September 1944 to spend over two months in Washington to negotiate Stage II of Lend-Lease (to cover the period while Britain was fighting Japan only) and the details of war supplies.[164] Among the key issues was negotiation to relax the principles of the Export White Paper to allow Britain 'to use her available foreign resources to maximise her export potential while using American aid to meet other needs'.[165]

In looking ahead to 'Stage III', the period after Victory over Japan day, Keynes gave close attention to Britain's need for American aid, the terms on which it could be accepted, and how to negotiate them. He also emphasized repeatedly the need to expand exports and to exercise stricter economy in overseas expenditure.[166] In a paper written in mid-March 1945, and circulated after revisions to the War Cabinet in May, Keynes proposed terms which would enable Britain to accept whole-heartedly the 'American ideal' of a 'free international economy' (which was far preferable for Britain, if it were practicable, to bilateralism and isolation). Keynes depicted a 'policy of economic isolationism and of economic rupture' with the USA and Canada as 'frantic and suicidal', though he wished Britain to 'feel and appear sufficiently independent' that she could threaten this if the USA insisted on unacceptable terms. Keynes's terms would involve a redistribution of the financial burden of the war, which had fallen unjustly and uniquely heavily on Britain; without the USA and sterling area countries assuming a greater share, Britain would be 'left with a heavier overseas financial burden than Germany, a burden which we shall owe to our *Allies*'. This paper was majestic, but unrealistic as to what the USA would agree when the war was over.[167]

On 13 August 1945, in a paper sent to various Ministers, Keynes wrote of three essential conditions for escaping 'a financial Dunkirk': an intense concentration on the expansion of exports, drastic and immediate economies in overseas expenditure, and substantial aid from the USA on terms which Britain could accept.[168] This paper, which warned that difficult and awkward

---

[161] Vol. 23, p. 247; see, e.g. pp. 276–85, 288–9.   [162] Vol. 23, p. 235.
[163] For example, vol. 23, pp. 259–60, 262.   [164] See vol. 24, chs. 1 & 2. W/6/3/1–58, KP.
[165] M. Keynes, *Essays*, p. 186; vol. 24, p. 215 ff.
[166] For example, vol. 24, pp. 263 ff, 613; see L/B/2, KP, for general background.
[167] Vol. 24, pp. 256–95; see A. Cairncross, *Years of Recovery* (London, 1985), p. 90 ff.
[168] Vol. 24, p. 410.

problems of terms and conditions for US aid remained, shows that, contrary to some claims, Keynes warned before the negotiations of likely difficulties.[169]

With the Japanese surrender in August 1945, Stage II finished sooner than expected, Truman abruptly terminated Lend-Lease,[170] and Britain had much less time for the transition to peace than had been expected. Keynes was sent to Washington to negotiate, with Halifax and Brand, the American aid he had long said would be needed.[171] Keynes sought a sizeable gift or interest-free loan. But US public and Congressional opinion were not disposed to such generosity now the war was won (and, in contrast with the Marshall Plan, the cold war had not conspicuously begun).[172] The argument from equality of sacrifice was rejected as invidious and backward-looking.[173] Keynes secured a loan of $3.75 billion with interest and, as he had expected, with strings attached; but, advantageously, Britain's Lend-Lease obligation was fully settled (by writing off supplies consumed in wartime, and valuing those available for post-war use at $650 million, with this sum to be repaid on the same terms as the US loan).[174] The principal condition of the loan was that Britain restore sterling to convertibility (for sterling area and others alike) within a year of the loan agreement coming into effect. Keynes favoured convertibility, but he resisted as dangerously premature the American insistence on its early introduction, which could threaten the transition to peacetime arrangements, on which he had placed much emphasis. He ultimately secured a clause providing for 'agreed postponement of convertibility after consultation'.[175] The loan agreement also contained a commitment, required by the Americans, that Britain would seek settlement of the sterling balances to scale down her total liability.[176] Though Keynes believed Britain should negotiate with countries with sterling balances to seek in effect a greater contribution to war costs, he opposed making an explicit commitment to sterling area negotiations in an Anglo-American agreement.

The loan negotiations involved great tension between Keynes and London, as well as between the British and Americans; and Keynes had much difficulty

---

[169] H. Dalton, *High Tide and After* (London, 1962), pp. 73–4; Cairncross, *Recovery*, pp. 100–2; Robbins, *Autobiography*, pp. 206–9.

[170] See, e.g. Harrod, *Life*, pp. 704–5.

[171] On the negotiations: Skidelsky, *Fighting*, ch. 12; Cairncross, *Recovery*, ch. 5; Clarke, *Collaboration*, pp. 61–5, 71; vol. 24, ch. 4; Pressnell, *External Economic Policy*, i, ch. 10; Dalton, *High Tide*, ch. 8; Harrod, *Life*, ch. 14; Moggridge, *Biography*, ch. 30.

[172] See, e.g. Harrod, *Life*, pp. 707–8, 727.

[173] See, e.g. vol. 24, pp. 609–10; R. A. C. Parker, *Struggle for Survival: The History of the Second World War* (Oxford, 1990), p. 247.

[174] The loan and Lend-Lease agreements are Cmd. 6708 (1945). For defence of the terms, vol. 28, pp. 218–20; vol. 24, p. 605 ff.

[175] Harrod, *Life*, p. 717.   [176] Cmd. 6708, p. 5.

in persuading official and unofficial British opinion to accept the deal.[177] Robinson regarded Keynes as having won for Britain 'a chance of economic recovery at an absolutely critical moment'. This was Keynes's 'greatest achievement', and his House of Lords speech in December 1945, which clinched the Lords' approval of the loan and Bretton Woods legislation, was 'the greatest debating triumph of his life'.[178] Harrod depicted Keynes as a 'great negotiator', especially of the loan.[179] Others have wondered whether Keynes was the best leader for the loan negotiators, because of his manner, misjudgements of post-war conditions, and 'unreal optimism about US intentions'.[180] Skidelsky gives a graphic account of his tumultuous style.[181] Robbins, who worked closely with Keynes during the war, said that he was 'not always a good *negotiator*', but 'as an *envoy* he was supreme'.[182]

Keynes has been rightly criticized for taking so little notice, before the loan negotiations, of the American desire for commercial policy discussions.[183] After he had arrived in Washington, a team of commercial policy experts, including Sir Percivale Liesching and Robbins, was rushed there to conduct talks simultaneous with the loan negotiations. These talks went well.[184] Keynes played little part,[185] though Harrod asserted that while listening to the talks Keynes was persuaded that it was now safe to agree to greater freedom of trade without fear of mass unemployment and international depression.[186] As a result of the talks, US Proposals for Consideration by an International Conference on Trade and Employment together with a joint Anglo-American statement in which Britain expressed her full agreement on all important points, were published simultaneously with the loan agreement on 6 December 1945.[187] Agreement to these proposals meant that Britain was in effect satisfying the obligations of Article 7 of the Mutual Aid Agreement, and

[177] Robinson, 'Keynes', pp. 62–4; Cairncross, *Recovery*, p. 110; Skidelsky, *Fighting*, p. 419 ff.; Harrod, *Life*, pp. 715, 722–6, and *passim*; Moggridge, *Biography*, ch. 30, *passim*; see, e.g. vol. 24, pp. 598–9.

[178] Robinson, 'Keynes', p. 64; see, e.g. Dalton, *High Tide*, p. 88; Robbins, *Autobiography*, pp. 210–11; Penrose, *Economic Planning*, pp. 315–17.

[179] Harrod to Viner, 15 Apr. 1949, box 38, JVP; see Harrod, *Life*, p. 601.

[180] Clarke, *Collaboration*, pp. 63, 71; cf. p. xix; Cairncross, *Recovery*, pp. 98, 113–14.

[181] Skidelsky, *Fighting*, e.g. pp. 431–35.

[182] Robbins, 'John Maynard Keynes', *The Times*, date unknown (1951 or 1952), copy in folder 1949–51 ca 60, box 6, Wright papers, U.Va; Robbins, *Autobiography*, pp. 208–9.

[183] For example, Cairncross, *Recovery*, p. 102; Pressnell, *External Economic Policy*, i, pp. 274–6; see pp. 276–9, 326–9 on the commercial talks; Robbins, *Autobiography*, p. 204 ff; Moggridge, *Biography*, p. 801 ff; see vol. 24, p. 452; vol. 26, pp. 326–7.

[184] Vol. 24, pp. 538–9; Moggridge, *Biography*, p. 804; see also, e.g. Gardner, *Sterling–Dollar*, ch. 8.

[185] See, e.g. vol. 26, p. 327.

[186] Harrod, *Life*, p. 721; Robbins, *Autobiography*, pp. 209–10; cf. Hansen, *Guide*, pp. 225–6; Robbins to Wright, 2 Oct. 1952, box 6, Wright papers, U.Va.

[187] Published as Cmd. 6709 (1945); see vol. 28, p. 219.

so made possible the final settlement of Lend-Lease.[188] These measures, described as necessary to 'an economic environment conducive to the maintenance of peaceful international relations', included 'an undertaking on the part of nations to seek full employment'.[189] The centrepiece was an International Trade Organization (ITO) to facilitate trade liberalization and the curbing of cartels, and to oversee intergovernmental commodity agreements. As Keynes wanted, non-discriminatory quantitative import restrictions would be allowed as an aid to the restoration of equilibrium in an adverse balance of payments.[190] Tariff preferences would be eliminated 'in conjunction with adequate measures for the substantial reduction of barriers to world trade'.[191] The ITO's Commodity Commission would investigate 'the problem of an international buffer stocks organization'.[192] Keynes had long been advocating, in the face of scepticism on the part of some American officials, buffer stocks to moderate commodity price fluctuations and mitigate the business cycle.[193] He expressed disappointment at 'the lack of enthusiasm which the primary producers seem to feel for plans to keep their prices more stable'.[194]

The effort by members of the Administration in early 1946 to win public and Congressional support for the loan was 'tireless'.[195] A principal argument, which Keynes and others had used, was that the loan was needed to enable Britain to take part in the planned multilateral economic arrangements.[196] American officials, including White, argued that these were necessary to peace.[197]

6.4 INTERNATIONAL MONETARY RELATIONS: THE CLEARING UNION, BRETTON WOODS, SAVANNAH

Accounts of the origins of the IMF begin at various points. Chapter 5 suggested that Keynes's CU plans of 1941–3 were similar to the 'ideal' plan

---

[188] Cmd. 6708, p. 6.   [189] Cmd. 6709, p. 2.

[190] Cmd. 6709, pp. 6–7; Cairncross, *Recovery*, pp. 101–2. The loan agreement also allowed them: Cmd. 6708, pp. 4–5. On their need, see vol. 27, pp. 373–4; vol. 25, pp. 198–9.

[191] Cmd. 6709, p. 5; see Robbins, *Autobiography*, p. 201 ff. On the conjunction: Robinson, 'Keynes', p. 64.

[192] Cmd. 6709, p. 16.

[193] For example, 'Informal Economic Discussions—Subcommittee on Commodity Policy', 22 Sept. 14 and 16 Oct. 1943, box 123, Stettinius papers, U.Va; cf. vol. 25, p. 165.

[194] Vol. 25, p. 414.

[195] Harrod, *Life*, p. 708; see, e.g. papers in box 42, Eugene Meyer papers, LOC.

[196] See, e.g. vol. 24, pp. 257, 290–1, 409, 608, 635; Parker, *Struggle*, p. 247; Moggridge, *Biography*, p. 783.

[197] Speeches and radio talk by White on 4, 9, and 10 April 1946, items 26a-c, box 11, HDWP; see also, e.g. *The Washington Post*, 10 Feb. 1946 (W. L. Clayton).

of the *Treatise*, itself comparable to some of his other inter-war proposals.[198] Some writers attribute the origins of the IMF to Keynes's 1940 Proposals to Counter the German 'New Order'.[199] Some see it as the product of an economic diplomacy in which Britain responded to the challenge of American demands for multilateralism.[200] Others see the origins of the IMF more in Harry Dexter White's proposals for a Stabilization Fund.[201] Each view contains an important element of the history.

The 1943 White Paper setting out the CU plan made no claim to originality in its proposals. They were 'an attempt to reduce to practical shape certain general ideas belonging to the contemporary climate of economic opinion, which have been given publicity in recent months by writers of several different nationalities'. These general ideas were 'born of the spirit of the age'.[202] There were in 1942–3 a variety of monetary schemes—including French, Norwegian, and Chinese[203]—competing with the American and British schemes, with Canada trying to forge a compromise between the latter two. Other alternatives included John Williams's 'key currency' approach.[204] At Bretton Woods, Louis Rasminsky said of the IMF that, as 'so often in the history of ideas a brilliant concept was developed simultaneously and independently in different parts of the world'.[205]

Though others contributed to the 'Keynes Plan' for a CU,[206] there is no doubt that the vision was Keynes's.[207] Having already referred to his inter-war and 1940 thinking, let us take up the evolution of his thought in the summer of 1941. We have seen that Keynes returned from the USA in early August 1941 encouraged by his talk with Roosevelt, and impressed with the quality of the younger American economists, who were overwhelmingly Keynesian. But he was convinced that currency and trade bilateralism, perhaps based on the Commonwealth, would be necessary unless some multilateral plan

---

[198] See D. Worswick and J. Trevithick (eds.), *Keynes and the Modern World* (Cambridge, 1983), pp. 109–12; Meltzer, *Monetary Theory*, ch. 5; Moggridge, 'International monetary system'.

[199] L. P. Mansfield, 'The Origins of the International Monetary Fund', Ph.D. thesis (University of North Carolina, 1960) p. 224; A. Van Dormael, *Bretton Woods* (London and Basingstoke, 1979) ch. 1.

[200] Gardner, *Sterling–Dollar*, chs. 1 and 2, and p. 58.

[201] For example, Morgenthau at Cmd. 6597 (1945), p. 6.

[202] Vol. 25, p. 170. (Cmd. 6437, p. 5.) Amongst those suggested by various writers as precursors of the Keynes plan were Marshall, Irving Fisher, Edgard Milhaud, and Wicksell. For Marshall on an 'international currency', see, e.g. Marshall to Keynes, 19 Dec. 1923. L/M/66.

[203] Papers on these are at, e.g. box 9, HDWP.

[204] J. H. Williams, *Postwar Monetary Plans* (3rd edn., New York, 1947).

[205] Cmd. 6597, p. 10. For the Sept. 1941 plan of E. F. Schumacher, sent to Keynes by Brand, see L/B/35 ff, KP.

[206] See, e.g. Robinson, 'Keynes', p. 54n; vol. 25, p. 269.

[207] See, e.g. Robbins, *Autobiography*, pp. 196, 200.

safeguarded Britain's post-war payments position: and a response was needed to the US draft Article 7. R. J. Shackle of the Board of Trade was advocating what Keynes regarded as an impossible return to laissez-faire.[208] But on 19 August, Kahn, who was working in the Board of Trade, wrote suggesting that the differences between Keynes and the Board of Trade view were probably exaggerated, and that colleagues hoped Kahn could act as a kind of bridge: 'the only fundamental issue is what degree of American co-operation would be necessary in order to justify a return to what might be called a liberal economic system and whether there is sufficient hope of persuading the Americans (either by threats or by blandishments) to make the necessary concessions to justify our approaching them on that line of action'.[209] Kahn quoted Sir Arnold Overton, permanent secretary at the Board, as thinking bilateral measures might be necessary, but hoping there was a chance of avoiding them.[210] Discussions with Robbins and James Meade, academic economists now in the Economic Section of the War Cabinet Office with strong hopes for free trade and for international economic organization,[211] encouraged Keynes to seek a basis for cooperation with the USA.[212] His own long-standing bias was, as earlier chapters have shown, for such cooperation; and he had advocated between the wars a succession of monetary plans, including the ideal scheme of the *Treatise*, that might be dusted down as a basis for this.

Keynes was very conscious of the debate, very evident in and after August 1941, between Dennis Robertson at the Treasury and Hubert Henderson at the Bank of England on the desirability of exchange and trade controls post-war. Interestingly, Robertson, a staunch free trader, wished to encourage all American policy to conform with 'Hull-ism'; for example, he saw US immigration policy, keeping out labour, as adversely affecting world prosperity and peace. Henderson, an advocate of controls, argued that economic nationalism was not the cause of war.[213]

Keynes had by mid-August decided to try to devise post-war currency arrangements that would enable clearer thinking, and perhaps Anglo-American cooperation, on post-war trade.[214] In discussions of consideration in late August, he said that he 'should prefer the policy of faith to a refusal to meet

---

[208] Vol. 25, p. 20; Cairncross and Watts, *Economic Section*, p. 96.

[209] Kahn to Keynes, 'personal', 19 Aug. 1941, L/K/135, KP.

[210] Kahn to Keynes, '*very* personal', 19 Aug. 1941, L/K/136, KP.

[211] J. Meade, *The Economic Basis of a Durable Peace* (London, 1940); Meade, *Economic Analysis and Policy*, pp. 371 ff, 382–8. On Meade, see also, e.g. Vines, 'John Maynard Keynes', *passim*; Robbins, *Economic Causes*.

[212] Interview with J. Meade, 6 Nov. 1985. Worswick and Trevithick, *Modern World*, p. 129; Meltzer, *Monetary theory*, p. 235 n; Robbins, *Autobiography*, p. 196; Penrose, *Economic Planning*, p. 18; Cairncross and Watts, *Economic Section*, pp. 96–7; see vol. 23, pp. 206–7; vol 25, pp. 40–1.

[213] T241/121, PRO.

[214] Keynes to Kahn, 24 Aug. 1941, L/K/142–3, KP; see vol. 25, p. 20, for 21 Aug.

the Americans at all'.[215] Despite difficulties with Lend-Lease and regarding the economic principles of the Atlantic Charter as extremely vague,[216] in late August and early September Keynes devised his 'Utopian plan' for an International Currency Union.[217] It was a scheme of monetary multilateralism that would make trade bilateralism unnecessary, and so enable Britain to do what the draft Article 7 asked. The alternative to such a scheme was 'improvement of the Schachtian device'.[218] It was for this reason that, whereas most US thinking gave priority to commercial policy, Britain put monetary policy first in Article 7 talks.[219] Keynes found 'Whitehall in all its quarters ... surprisingly enthusiastic' about his proposals;[220] they were especially welcomed by those who saw them as making possible 'a liberal economic system'.[221] Hubert Henderson at the Bank of England, preferring to start from bilateral devices, was the conspicuous opponent.

Successive drafts from November 1941 to January 1942 spoke of giving various degrees of 'satisfaction to Mr Cordell Hull' as 'we should be accepting a non-discriminatory international system as the normal and desirable regime'.[222] As we have seen, Keynes's plan was to offer the Americans (to whom Britain owed so much) 'something which would give them all they ask, provided they are really prepared to be truly internationally minded'.[223]

But were they? Alvin Hansen believed then and later that his visit with Luther Gulick to London in September 1941 helped to persuade Keynes that the chances were good.[224] Hansen and Gulick were advisers to the Administration, and Hansen had been described to Keynes as having exercised 'a good deal of influence in Washington'.[225] Hansen was a Keynesian free trader at Harvard who, in the late 1930s, had greatly encouraged the conversion to

[215] Vol. 23, p. 207. On Keynes's stress on Anglo-American cooperation in Art. 7: memo of 1 Sept. 1941, T/247/44, PRO. Keynes saw Winant on 25 Aug.: Keynes to Winant, 14 Aug. 1941, and later notes, box 204, Winant papers, FDR Library.

[216] Vol. 23, p. 202; cf. vol. 27, pp. 135, 168; vol. 26, pp. 348–9.

[217] Vol. 25, p. 33; Keynes to FAK, 6 Sept. 1941, PP/45/168/11/53–4, KP.

[218] Vol. 25, p. 24; see Pressnell, *External Economic Policy*, i, pp. 18–19, 22–4, 69–71.

[219] See, e.g. 'Report of the Canadian Representatives at the "Post-War Economic Talks" ', London, Oct.–Nov. 1942, CU section, p. 15, RG19, vol. 3989, file T-2-9-2, PAC. Keynes to Fisher, 10 Aug. 1942, box 22, Fisher papers, Yale; see vol. 25, p. 189.

[220] Keynes to Kahn, 12 Jan. 1942, L/K/163–7, and ff, KP; see also Keynes to FAK, 21 Dec. 1941, PP/45/168/11/58–9, KP.

[221] See vol. 25, pp. 66–8.

[222] Vol. 25, pp. 51, 81, 122. The wording changed slightly, with satisfaction offered Hull *diminishing* from 'complete' to 'some ... over a wide field'.

[223] Vol. 23, p. 209; for the plan, see vol. 25, pp. 21–40.

[224] Hansen to Viner, 20 Oct. 1941, encl. 'Tentative Draft of Joint Declaration' by USA and Britain, box 38, JVP; Hansen, *Guide*, pp. 225–6; see also 215 n; vol. 25, pp. 41–2; Harrod, *Life*, p. 624; Moggridge, *Biography*, p. 678; cf. Pressnell, *External Economic Policy*, i, pp. 74, 76, 111 n. Skidelsky, *Fighting*, p. 218 pays surprisingly little attention to Hansen and Gulick.

[225] S. E. Harris to Keynes, 20 Feb. 1941, L/41/4, KP.

Keynesian economics of younger American economists, including many who were now working in Washington.[226] He was later involved in discussions in Washington which resulted in Harry Dexter White's proposals for a Stabilization Fund and International Bank.[227] Gulick was an economic official expert on, amongst other things, the Tennessee Valley Authority (TVA).[228] In October 1941, Hansen wrote to Viner concerning post-war Anglo-American economic collaboration, which he had discussed with British officials and ministers, and with Hull and Vice-President Henry Wallace, and was to discuss with Henry Morgenthau.[229] As well as immediate post-war relief measures and an International Finance Corporation to lend for development projects, Hansen proposed coordinated internal economic policies designed to promote active employment and to secure economic stability, and the promotion of world trade through international collaboration:

[T]hese proposals proved [in London] to be a way of bridging to a large extent the gap between those who, like Keynes and Henderson, have been favoring continuation of exchange control and bi-lateral payments agreements for England after the war, and those on the other hand, led by Lionel Robbins, who favor the multi-lateral trade approach.... Keynes and Henderson saw, through this type of approach, the possibility of working on to the Hull type of multi-lateral trade and agreed that, if a broad attack of this sort [e.g. through co-ordinated internal policies] could be made on the whole problem of active employment and trade, everyone would prefer the broadest possible trade relations rather than the narrow bi-lateral arrangements.

We have seen that *The General Theory* envisaged that, if full employment were achieved, trade could again be 'a willing and unimpeded exchange of goods and services in conditions of mutual advantage'.[230] It was never clear whether the Hansen–Gulick proposals had any official standing,[231] and Keynes thought it unsafe to rely on the views of 'New Dealers' when they might be out of office after the war.[232] However, although his hopes were not fully realised,[233] it is clear from British Treasury and Cabinet Office files that Keynes regarded their visit as very important, and was excited and greatly encouraged by it.[234] In particular, their visit encouraged him to believe that

[226] See Galbraith at M. Keynes, *Essays*, pp. 136–7; Klein, *Keynesian Revolution*, pp. 48, 102–3; R. Lekachman, *The Age of Keynes* (New York, 1968), p. 126 ff; Hession, *Keynes*, pp. 297–8.

[227] Harrod, *Life*, p. 638.   [228] Harrod, *Life*, p. 624.

[229] Hansen to Viner, 20 Oct. 1941, box 38, JVP.   [230] Vol. 7, p. 383.

[231] See unsigned and undated memo, 'Conversations on Article VII' starting 'Redvers Opie tells me...', mid-1942, T/160/1377/F18003, PRO; Minutes of ASD (44) (Employment) meeting, 29 Feb. 1944, T/247/25, PRO; Harrod, *Life*, p. 624.

[232] Keynes to Harrod, 14 Nov. 1941, L/41/60–61, KP.

[233] See ASD (44) (Employment), 29 Feb. 1944, T247/25, PRO.

[234] See various letters and references in T247/70, T247/116, T247/121, T247/122, and CAB/87/2, PRO.

the US 'could be sufficiently relied upon to play a positive role' in international economic affairs, especially in the maintenance of high employment,
'to justify risking a program of Anglo-American collaboration designed to
promote a multilateral trading world'.[235] Winant's adviser, E. F. Penrose, who
talked with Hansen and Gulick, and frequently with Keynes, thought that
(though Keynes remained pessimistic about Britain's balance of payments)
Hansen and Gulick 'rendered valuable service by showing Keynes that there
were Americans who were equally concerned with him about the necessity of
placing full employment as high as free trade among the prerequisites for the
postwar economic order'.[236] This may be seen in the change of tone in
Keynes's references to the USA between his early September and November
drafts;[237] his references or allusions to Hansen in each of his November,
December, and January drafts;[238] discussion of the Hansen–Gulick proposals
between Treasury and Bank officials in November, after Keynes had received a
revised statement of them;[239] the inclusion, with Keynes's CU plan and other
papers, of 'a discussion of the International Economic Board and Development Corporation proposed by Professors Hansen and Gulick' in a Treasury
memorandum submitted to a War Cabinet committee early in 1942, including some discussion (especially encouraged by Harrod) of the connection of
the Hansen-Gulick proposals with the CU;[240] and Keynes's interest in March
1942 in Hansen's pamphlet, *After the War—Full Employment*.[241] Keynes's
November and December 1941 drafts saw 'great force in Prof. Hansen's
contention that the problem of surpluses and unwanted exports will largely
disappear if active employment and ample purchasing power can be sustained
in the main centres of world trade'.[242] Keynes was further encouraged in early
November by reports from Washington of discussions between other British
and American officials, including Viner, which showed 'an atmosphere in
which we could discuss the issues rationally and realistically'.[243] Where the
September draft referred to the possibility of the US maintaining high
employment by domestic 'New Deal expedients'[244], by December there was

---

[235] Hansen, *Guide*, pp. 225–6. On timing of the visit, compare Pressnell, *External Economic
Policy*, i, p. 74, and Penrose, *Economic Planning*, p. 15. The visit was *after* Penrose's trip to
Washington, and probably in early/mid-Sept.

[236] Penrose, *Economic Planning*, p. 16.

[237] Cf. vol. 25, pp. 31–2 with pp. 42–4.

[238] Vol. 25, pp. 48 and pp. 59–60, 77 and pp. 91–2, 116 and p. 133.

[239] 'Second Meeting with the Bank', 25 Nov. 1941, T/247/122, PRO.

[240] Vol. 25, p. 108. The full text, unfortunately not reproduced in the *CW*, is in typescript at
T247/70 and in printed form at CAB/87/2, PRO.

[241] Keynes to Opie, 2 Mar. 1942, L/O/6–8, KP.

[242] Vol. 25, pp. 48, 77; see also p. 116.

[243] Keynes to Harrod, 14 Nov. 1941, L/41/60–61, KP.   [244] Vol. 25, pp. 31–2.

reference to the possibility of 'international T.V.A.'.[245] This was before, under the influence of Henry Wallace, that phrase passed into more common usage. Some advisers to Wallace were already advocating such international public works;[246] it may be that Keynes learned of this through Hansen and Gulick, or perhaps from Penrose.

Cordell Hull's deputy, Sumner Welles, re-stated their opposition to tariffs (including US tariffs) and to preferences in a speech on 7 October 1941; unlike some of his colleagues, Keynes found this undisturbing.[247] If Hull stood for trade liberalization as the centrepiece of post-war plans, Wallace was increasingly to stand for policies of full employment and economic development.[248] A long-standing Keynesian, Wallace had been considering, and speaking somewhat generally on, post-war issues in 1940–1.[249] It appears that in the autumn of 1941, Wallace was taking a growing interest in Keynesian ideas, and Anglo-American leadership in post-war reconstruction. It is likely that Hansen and Gulick, fresh from London, helped to crystallize Wallace's emerging ideas.[250] In October 1941, Wallace received White's analysis of compulsory savings excise, in which Wallace had expressed interest.[251] Wallace sent White a paper urging Anglo-American collaboration in an international reconstruction programme, including a redistribution of the world's gold (something Keynes said in his November CU draft the US might 'wish to effect'[252]). On 1 December, White sent Wallace favourable comments on this paper; he also suggested that countries other than Britain be included in the collaboration discussions from the outset.[253] Wallace's interest thus preceded Pearl Harbor,[254] and Morgenthau's request to White on 14 December to prepare a plan for an Inter-Allied Stabilization Fund.[255] In speeches during 1942, Wallace advocated what was likened to a 'New Deal for the world',[256] including 'an international Tennessee Valley

[245] Vol. 25, p. 94; see also p. 139; vol. 27, pp. 122, 156.

[246] N. D. Markowitz, *The Rise and Fall of the People's Century* (New York, 1973), pp. 41, 75 n 10.

[247] See T160/1377/18003/1, T247/121, CAB 117/51, and CAB 117/52, PRO.

[248] H. G. Nicholas (ed.), *Washington Despatches, 1941–1945* (London, 1981), pp. 38, 43–4, 62–3, 95, 132–3.

[249] Markowitz, *People's Century*, p. 45 ff. Wallace had encouraged FDR to read Keynes's views: e.g. Wallace to FDR, 22 Oct. 1937, box 3 (see also box 2), OF1, FDR Library.

[250] See Markowitz, *People's Century*, pp. 59–60, 141; and Hansen's reference to Wallace above. Halifax to Keynes, 1 Nov. 1941, T247/70, PRO.

[251] See above. [252] Vol. 25, pp. 58–9.

[253] White to Wallace, 1 Dec. 1941, item 20g, box 6, HDWP.

[254] Cf. J. S. Walker, *Henry A. Wallace and American Foreign Policy* (Westport, Connecticut, 1976), p. 84.

[255] Van Dormael, *Bretton Woods*, p. 40.

[256] Hilderbrand, *Dumbarton Oaks*, p. 16; Divine, *Second Chance*, pp. 64–6, 78–81. For Wallace's speeches: L. W. Holborn, (ed.), *War and Peace Aims of the United Nations, September 1, 1939–December 31, 1942* (Boston, 1943), pp. 79–85, 132–5, 147–54.

Authority'.[257] In advocating buffer stocks, Keynes drew on Wallace's 1930s talk of an 'ever-normal granary'.[258] In October 1942, Keynes deflected a proposal from a close friend of Wallace's that he write a book on post-war economic proposals to which Wallace would write the introduction.[259] In January 1943, Keynes referred to 'the wonderful blue print for the new world which Mr Wallace is producing, whilst everyone else is doing nothing, or obstructing him'.[260] In September 1942, however, Keynes had been pleased that 'the officials we are mainly dealing with in discussing post-war arrangements are out-and-out New Dealers'.[261]

As we have seen, Keynes's first detailed plan for a CU came in September 1941.[262] His proposals were refined through successive drafts over subsequent months.[263] On 8 and 9 July 1942, written details of White's plan were passed to British officials in Washington, and Keynes had received them by 22 July.[264] On 17 July 1942, when Sir Frederick Phillips called on Pasvolsky and Acheson at the State Department to discuss (again) beginning the discussions referred to in Article 7, he outlined Keynes's CU plan to US officials for the first time, and promised a memorandum.[265] Phillips also saw Morgenthau. Keynes's proposals were refined further until on 28 August a copy went to White.[266] After consultations with the Dominions, European Allies, and others, the Keynes and White Plans were published in April 1943.[267] Negotiations, with Keynes leading for Britain, resulted in a Joint Statement by Experts on the Establishment of an International Monetary Fund in April 1944.[268] These proposals more closely resemble White's than Keynes's plan. International negotiations at Atlantic City in June 1944 and at Bretton Woods in July created the IMF and IBRD.[269]

Keynes said in 1942 that the chief purpose of the CU plan 'was to achieve balance in international payments and so facilitate full employment'.[270] His proposal was for an International CU, based on international bank money.

[257] Holborn, *Peace Aims*, p. 134 (Nov. 1942); Gardner, *Sterling-Dollar*, p. 15; Markowitz, *People's Century*, pp. 48 ff, 58, 70, 79 n 67; see also, e.g. J. McG. Burns, *Roosevelt: The Soldier of Freedom, 1940–1945* (London, 1971), p. 301.

[258] Vol. 27, pp. 22, 112–15, 138–41; vol. 21, pp. 462, 476.

[259] Keynes to Opie, 1 Dec. 1942, L/O/37–8; see also 28–30, KP.

[260] Vol. 28, p. 186; see speech on 28 Dec. 1942 stressing full employment: Holborn, *Peace Aims*, pp. 147–54.

[261] Vol. 28, p. 175.   [262] Vol. 25, pp. 33–40.

[263] Vol. 25, pp. 42–139.   [264] Vol. 25, p. 157. L/P/52–4, KP.

[265] 'Memorandum of Conversation' by Acheson, 17 July 1942, box 1, Pasvolsky papers, LOC.

[266] Vol. 25, pp. 168–95, 449–52. Item 24e, unboxed, HDWP.

[267] See vol. 25, pp. 233–5, 459–68. The CU plan is Cmd. 6437 (1943).

[268] See vol. 25, pp. 437–42, 469–77.

[269] On the process, see, e.g. Van Dormael, *Bretton Woods*; Howson and Moggridge, *Robbins and Meade*; Skidelsky, *Fighting*, chs. 9, 10.

[270] Report on 'Post-War Economic Talks', CU section, p. 2, RG19, vol. 3989, file T-2-9-2, PAC.

This international currency, called 'bancor', would be 'fixed (but not unalterably) in terms of gold and accepted as the equivalent of gold' for settling international balances. The central banks 'would keep accounts with the International Clearing Union through which they' could 'settle their exchange balances with one another at their par value as defined in terms of bancor'.[271] Keynes's scheme thus embraced multilateral clearing between members. The Union was for 'settlement of the ultimate outstanding balances between central banks'.[272] Money earned by exporting goods to one country could be spent on imports from any other.[273] Blocked balances and bilateral clearings would be unnecessary.

Keynes's plan permitted, and in some circumstances required, exchange rate depreciations for deficit countries, and appreciations for surplus countries, within certain limits.[274] In short, it embodied short-term fixity and long-term flexibility of exchange rates. Competitive currency depreciations would be avoided, but states had some autonomy to adjust their exchange rates to safeguard their economies.

The plan aimed at expansionist pressure on world trade by allowing to each member state overdraft facilities, designated its quota, proportionate to the importance of its foreign trade.[275] This would alleviate the cumulative contractionist pressures which arose because debtor countries, trying to preserve their own equilibrium, sought to force exports and cut all imports which are not strictly necessary. The overdraft facility would give resources and time for the necessary adjustments to be made.[276] Keynes proposed rules to provide that equilibrium is restored.[277] These would place some responsibility for adjustment on creditor countries—through charges on credit as well as debit balances with the Clearing Bank, requiring creditor as well as debtor countries to discuss with the Bank how they would restore equilibrium, and in some cases requiring exchange rate appreciation.[278] This onus on creditors, which would promote the expansion of trade markets, was a major innovation.[279] Creditor responsibility was ultimately accepted by the USA in their proposal of a 'scarce currency' clause, allowing other countries to discriminate against the currency and goods of a country whose currency was declared scarce.[280]

---

[271] Vol. 25, pp. 111–12.   [272] Vol. 25, p. 125.
[273] Vol. 25 at, e.g. pp. 168, 270. See p. 399.
[274] Vol. 25, pp. 34–6, 49, 62–4, 79–80, 105–7, 119–20, 174–5, 454, 461–3.
[275] Vol. 25, pp. 112, 118.
[276] Vol. 25, pp. 46–8, 75–7, 112–14, 155, 176, 208–9, 273–4.
[277] Vol. 25, p. 116.
[278] Vol. 25, pp. 27–30, 48–50, 76–80, 96, 117–18, 211, 235.
[279] See, e.g. vol. 25, p. 273; Moggridge, 'International Monetary System', pp. 71–2.
[280] Vol. 25, pp. 386, 440–1, 474.

Though Keynes was for some time uncertain how significant that clause would prove to be,[281] he came to believe it an extremely valuable safeguard.[282]

Keynes wanted provisions to give countries 'an entirely free hand' during the difficult post-war transition period before the institution settled into its normal peacetime role.[283] He proposed controls on capital movements which would allow genuine new investment and movements from surplus to deficit countries, but prevent speculative movements or flights of capital from deficit countries or between surplus countries. Capital control was necessary for countries to have the interest rate appropriate to their domestic economy 'without reference to the rates prevailing elsewhere in the world'.[284] (Keynes had favoured controls of capital movements since at least 1933.)[285] Keynes's early drafts proposed capital controls as an element, though not an essential one, of the multilateral plan; later versions left them to decision by each member state (though requiring controls under some conditions).[286] Keynes argued that the CU would facilitate trade liberalization while allowing 'special expedients' (such as import controls) to help a country regain equilibrium in its balance of payments.[287] It would be especially important in making possible the resumption of trade with Europe during the relief and reconstruction period.[288] It would not unduly diminish national sovereignty; by each state surrendering the right to 'bad-neighbourliness', there would be general gain.[289]

Keynes envisaged the CU using the otherwise idle credit balances with it to finance international bodies concerned with relief and reconstruction, buffer stocks for commodities, and international investment.[290] The CU might also 'set up an account in favour of the super-national policing body charged with the duty of preserving the peace and maintaining international order', and the CU account of a delinquent country could be blocked to enforce a financial blockade.[291] Because the financing of such international economic and political bodies would not depend on national appropriations, but be anonymous and impersonal, the CU would provide 'a genuine organ of truly international government'.[292] Yet Keynes also envisaged that, while the CU

---

[281] Cf. vol. 25, pp. 226 ff, 267 (per Harrod), with p. 230; see pp. 238–9, 268, 281, 309, 322.
[282] Vol. 25, pp. 358–9, 401–2; vol. 26, p. 14; Harrod, *Life*, pp. 643–9, 669, 676–8.
[283] Vol. 25, p. 394; see pp. 118, 135–7, 406–7, 441.
[284] Vol. 25, pp. 52–4, 86–7, 129–30, 149, 186–7, 212–3, 389, 439–40, 465–6; see also pp. 16–17; cf. pp. 275–6.
[285] Moggridge, 'International Monetary System', pp. 58–9.
[286] Cf. vol. 25, pp. 130, 186.   [287] Vol. 25, pp. 121–2, 138; see also pp. 8, 12.
[288] Vol. 25, p. 178; cf. pp. 76, 115.   [289] Vol. 25, pp. 57–8, 89, 131.
[290] Vol. 25, p. 38–40, 58–60, 90–2, 131–3, 189–93.
[291] Vol. 25, p. 59, 90–1, 132, 190; cf. p. 38–9.
[292] Vol. 25, p. 193; see also pp. 276–7.

would be worldwide,[293] the USA and Britain, as founders, would have a special position.[294]

White's plan was different.[295] Keynes stressed the right to exchange rate adjustments; White, stability of rates.[296] White proposed both a Stabilization Fund and an ambitious Bank for Reconstruction and Development. Unlike the CU, which gave each member an immediate addition to its reserves (i.e. the right to an overdraft), the White Plan was contributory, operating in national currencies, not bancor. White's formula for contributions used a broader measure of economic strength than Keynes's quota formula.[297] This had the effect of reducing Britain's share in voting power. White emphasized Anglo-American leadership less,[298] and provided for neither a transition period, nor controls on capital movements.[299]

Keynes initially argued that, despite similar objects, White's plan was unworkable.[300] Above all, Keynes wanted far greater, and less conditional, liquidity provision than White.[301] Keynes distinguished bilateral from multi-lateral clearing, stressing that White's scheme neither disciplined creditors, nor was expansionist.[302] Keynes thought the exchange rate rigidity under White's scheme very excessive.[303] He conceded that either plan could achieve the other's purposes,[304] but thought the differences were important for future use of the CU for various international purposes.[305]

After the publication of both plans in April 1943, negotiations and redrafts ensued, leading to the Joint Statement by Experts in April 1944.[306] In September–October 1943 Keynes finally accepted White's framework, as he had long realized would be unavoidable:[307] there would be a contributory fund. Important issues included American adoption of an international currency (Unitas), Keynes's attempts to monetize it, and its abandonment;[308] compromise on the Fund's size, the British seeking a larger Fund (as they saw it, more adequate quotas) than the Americans would agree to; the British push for disciplines on creditors, resulting in the scarce currency clause; less

---

[293] Vol. 25, p. 123.   [294] Vol. 25, p. 113; see pp. 134–5.

[295] See, e.g. Gardner, *Sterling–Dollar*, pp. 72–6.   [296] See vol. 25, pp. 220, 275.

[297] See vol. 25, p. 162.

[298] See J. K. Horsefield, *The International Monetary Fund, 1945–1965*, i (Washington, 1969) pp. 24, 29; vol. 25, pp. 223–4.

[299] Horsefield, *IMF*, i, pp. 28–9; vol. 25, pp. 225, 275.

[300] Vol. 25, pp. 160–7 at p. 161; see also pp. 158–9.

[301] Vol. 25, p. 216. For detailed comparison: pp. 215–26.

[302] Vol. 25, pp. 160, 215–26, 235, 273.   [303] Vol. 25, p. 220.

[304] Vol. 25, p. 226; see also pp. 278–9, 308–14, 405, 437.   [305] Vol. 25, p. 281.

[306] Vol. 25, ch. 3, pp. 469–77; Horsefield, *IMF*, i, pp. 57–75; Skidelsky, *Fighting*, p. 253 ff.

[307] Compare Moggridge, *Biography*, pp. 692–3, 721–3, with Harrod, *Life*, p. 664; vol. 25, pp. 268, 278–9, 283, 285, 297, 308, 317.

[308] See vol. 25, pp. 342–50, 359, 389, 393, 405, 428–9, 442.

exchange rate flexibility than had been sought by Keynes, who was concerned to allow exchange rate changes if needed for full employment;[309] the adoption, at Keynes's urging, of transitional arrangements;[310] the British push— defeated, as they saw it, finally at Savannah—for 'objective' management by international civil servants rather than national representatives; and the British emphasis on automaticity of drawing rights, as against the greater US stress on conditionality, an issue left unresolved for some time.[311] Keynes famously opposed 'an untried institution' being 'too grandmotherly'.[312]

Keynes claimed that the CU's major purposes were achieved in the proposed IMF.[313] He commended the new plan to the House of Lords in May 1944, emphasizing benefits to an indebted Britain from the transition period; convertibility of currencies; increased world monetary reserves, promoting trade; the disciplining of creditors; and the existence of a permanent institution. The plan, allowing controls on capital movements, ensured 'our power to control the domestic rate of interest... to secure cheap money'. He rejected parallels with the gold standard. The proposals did not prevent bilateral trade agreements.[314]

At Atlantic City in June 1944, Keynes sought greater national freedom to adjust exchange rates, an indefinite transition, larger quotas, and technical, non-political management of the new institutions.[315] In Lionel Robbins's word, Keynes 'dominated' the Bretton Woods Conference of 1–22 July.[316] Its Final Act embodied the Articles of Agreement of both the IMF and IBRD. The USA insisted that both be sited in the USA; Keynes opposed this, and Britain entered its only reservations on this point.[317]

In May 1944, two months before Bretton Woods, the British Government had published its White Paper on Employment Policy, in preparation of which Keynes was only somewhat involved.[318] Keynes welcomed its commitment to maintaining a high and stable level of employment after the war. Though he criticized aspects,[319] it represented 'if one casts one's mind back ten years or so,... a revolution in official opinion'.[320] Also in May, Keynes said

---

[309] See vol. 25, pp. 309, 317–19, 323–4, 383–4, 389, 392, 402–4, 413–14, 473. Memo on Art. 7 talks, 30 Sept. 1943, p. 2, RG19, vol. 3989, file T-2-9-2, PAC; cf. Moggridge, 'International Monetary System', pp. 68–9.

[310] Vol. 25, pp. 476–7. Gardner, *Sterling–Dollar*, p. 121; see also pp. 119–20, 139.

[311] See, e.g. vol. 25, pp. 359, 393, 404–5.   [312] Vol. 25, p. 333; see also p. 404.

[313] See vol. 25, pp. 437–42.   [314] Vol. 26, pp. 9–21; see Gardner, *Sterling–Dollar*, p. 128.

[315] Horsefield, *IMF*, i, pp. 82–7; vol. 26, pp. 68–70, 78–9.

[316] Howson and Moggridge, *Robbins and Meade*, p. 193; see also Robinson, 'Keynes', p. 58; see vol. 26, pp. 112–13, 193; vol. 28, p. 205.

[317] See vol. 26, pp. 84, 87–92; cf. vol. 25, p. 134. For British reservations on siting: Cmd. 6597, p. 24.

[318] Vol. 27, ch. 5; Cairncross and Watts, *Economic Section*, pp. 71–87.

[319] Vol. 27, pp. 375–9.

[320] Vol. 27, p. 364; see Robinson, 'Keynes', p. 57; Moggridge, *Biography*, pp. 709, 714.

that the policy of full employment 'would be immensely easier in practice if we could have a concerted policy with other countries'.[321] He recommended the proposals to be discussed at Bretton Woods as 'providing an international framework' for 'the new techniques associated with the policy of full employment'.[322] Keynes had proposed a provision that the Fund 'shall bear it constantly in mind that the maintenance of employment and output at satisfactory levels throughout the world is their first and overriding duty'.[323] At Atlantic City, he helped the Australians strengthen the emphasis on high employment in the draft purposes of both institutions.[324] Though the Bretton Woods conference encouraged governments to cooperate on the harmonization of national policies aimed at high employment and rising living standards, it rejected an Australian proposal that countries joining the IMF enter into a formal undertaking to maintain high levels of employment.[325] Though Britain supported Australia's proposal, Keynes regarded it as promising to be 'not only good but clever'.[326]

Though saying that Bretton Woods was compatible with trade restrictions,[327] Keynes acknowledged that currency multilateralism pointed the way to trade multilateralism.[328] He stressed the safeguards—from exchange rigidity, competitive devaluations, and US trade surpluses—the Fund secured for Britain.[329] Throughout the negotiations leading to the creation of the IMF, Keynes had envisaged Britain's possible need for IMF assistance.[330]

Appointed a Governor of the IMF and IBRD, Keynes attended their inaugural meeting at Savannah in March 1946. He stressed the need for an 'objective', international and non-political approach.[331] He opposed, in vain, the US plan for highly paid, full-time Directors; US Treasury Secretary Vinson's 'rail-roading' of Washington as the head office site (Keynes wanted New York); and White's stress on conditionality of drawing rights.[332] Keynes argued that the politicization, as he saw it, of the Bretton Woods institutions left them still 'important and useful': despite US dominance, Britain should

---

[321] Vol. 26, p. 5.   [322] Vol. 26, p. 19.   [323] Vol. 25, p. 314.

[324] L. G. Melville to Ministers, 30 June 1944, C-3.9.1.77, RBAA; see material on Australia, box 9, HDWP.

[325] Cmd. 6597, pp. 20–1.

[326] Vol. 27, pp. 383–4; Report by Melville on Bretton Woods, 26 Aug. 1944, pp. 15–16, C-3.9.1.77, RBAA; Markwell, *Keynes and Australia*, pp. 47–9.

[327] Vol. 26, pp. 128–9.   [328] Vol. 26, pp. 190–2.

[329] Vol. 26, p. 189.

[330] Vol. 25, pp. 104–5, 137–8; vol. 23, pp. 284–5; vol. 26, p. 13; Horsefield, *IMF*, i, p. 20; Robinson, 'Keynes', p. 52.

[331] Vol. 26, pp. 215–17; Horsefield, *IMF*, i, pp. 747–9; Robinson, 'Keynes', p. 65; Moggridge, 'International Monetary System', pp. 79–80.

[332] Vol. 26, pp. 208, 217–25; Gardner, *Sterling–Dollar*, pp. 261–4.

participate fully.[333] Keynes set out to 'do our best in the way of staffing' the new institutions.[334] Some suggest that distress over Savannah contributed to Keynes's fatal heart attack on 21 April 1946, though others emphasize the strain of the loan negotiations. Skidelsky argues strongly that earlier writers exaggerated Keynes's unhappiness about Savannah.[335]

As we have seen, Keynes's early CU drafts favoured the Hansen–Gulick proposal for a Board for International Investment.[336] Keynes wanted a 'development organisation (or international T.V.A.)'—complemented by buffer stocks—'to offset a deficiency of effective demand which seems to be endemic'.[337] It would be financed through the CU. Keynes is thus credited with initiating the concept of a link between international liquidity creation and aid.[338]

The idea of an international investment bank was far more novel than a body to deal with exchange problems.[339] The British decided not to propose such a bank in any detail, as they would not be in a position to lend after the war; such a scheme was better coming from the principal creditor.[340] The initiative was in fact taken by White.[341] Where Keynes proposed reconstruction functions for bodies allied to the CU, White separated them from his Stabilization Fund, and proposed an International Bank.[342] It evolved into the IBRD. Though Keynes believed 'that loans from creditor countries to debtor countries in the early post-war period are essential to avoid widespread economic chaos', he thought White's initial plan highly defective. It was necessary to make clear that loans would be made for post-war reconstruction as well as development.[343] Though giving the Bank less attention than the Fund until immediately before Bretton Woods, Keynes became an enthusiastic supporter.[344] He chaired the commission on the Bank at Bretton Woods. The version of it which he and others drafted *en route* to America in June 1944

---

[333] Vol. 26, pp. 220–38. Cf. Moggridge, *Biography*, p. 834; G. Bolton, 'Where critics are as wrong as Keynes was', *The Banker*, 122 (1972), 1387; A. P. Thirlwall (ed.), *Keynes and International Monetary Relations* (London and Basingstoke, 1976), pp. 26–31.

[334] Keynes to Brand, 3 Apr. 1946, L/B/2/309–11; see also 317–22, KP.

[335] Skidelsky, *Fighting*, p. 468. R. F. Harrod, *Reforming the World's Money* (London, 1965), p. 121; Robbins, *Autobiography*, pp. 208–11; Robinson, 'Keynes', pp. 63, 65–6; Penrose, *Economic Planning*, p. 317; Moggridge, *Biography*, p. 834; G. Bolton, 'Where critics are as wrong', p. 1387; A. P. Thirlwall (ed.), *Keynes and International Monetary Relations* (London and Basingstoke, 1976), pp. 26–31.

[336] For example, vol. 25, pp. 59, 91.

[337] Vol. 27, p. 122.

[338] G. Bird, *The International Monetary System and the Less Developed Countries* (London and Basingstoke, 1982), pp. 256–7.   [339] For example, see Georges Theunis at Cmd. 6597, p. 15.

[340] Vol. 25, pp. 195–6, 200, 206.   [341] See box 10, HDWP.

[342] See, e.g. vol. 25, p. 161.   [343] Vol. 25, pp. 419–27, at pp. 425, 427.

[344] For example, Harrod, *Life*, pp. 682, 686; see vol. 25, pp. 373–4, 419–27.

was largely accepted by the USA, despite disagreements over location and management.[345]

Depending on their national interest, some countries (especially Europeans) stressed the Bank's reconstruction role, while others (such as the Latin Americans) wanted at least equal weight given to its developmental role.[346] Keynes's focus was more on reconstruction, which was of the utmost urgency and importance, than on development.[347] At Bretton Woods and in subsequent salesmanship, he lauded the vast benefits which may flow from the Bank: 'There has never been such a far-reaching proposal on so great a scale to provide employment in the present and increase productivity in the future.'[348]

6.5 POST-WAR COMMERCIAL POLICY

As we have seen, Keynes in 1941 outlined differences of opinion in London that remained for many years. Some advocated return to free trade. Some, including Keynes, supported control mechanisms. Some favoured imperial policies.[349] Control mechanisms, such as quantitative import restrictions, could be discriminatory (e.g. under barter or other bilateral agreements), but need not be. What Keynes favoured evolved as post-war prospects changed.

As we have seen in his attitude to Article 7, Keynes initially resisted free trade notions most forcefully as nineteenth-century dogmas inappropriate under such uncertainty about post-war conditions.[350] In the early years of the war, he believed that Britain's payments position could make continued discrimination unavoidable.[351] At least until December 1941, Keynes favoured barter trade,[352] but saw that multilateral clearing would render it redundant.[353] He repeatedly stressed that Britain's payment difficulties would compel quantitative import restrictions.[354]

We have already seen that Alvin Hansen, as early as autumn 1941, believed that Keynes would favour multilateral trade liberalization if it were accompanied

[345] Vol. 26, pp. 67, 84.
[346] Melville to Ministers, 14 July 1944, C-3.9.1.77, RBAA. [J. B. Brigden,] 'The Bretton Woods Conference', p. 4, RBAA.
[347] Vol. 26, p. 72; see also, e.g. pp. 100, 188.   [348] Vol. 26, p. 105.
[349] Vol. 23, p. 177.   [350] Vol. 26, p. 253; see pp. 239–40, 288; vol. 23, p. 208.
[351] Vol. 26, p. 247.   [352] Vol. 25, p. 8; vol. 26, p. 240.
[353] See vol. 21, p. 12; vol. 25, p. 23; vol. 26, p. 241.
[354] See vol. 23, pp. 102, 143, 176; vol. 26, p. 254 ff.

by policies to ensure 'active employment'.[355] It was partly to enable the elimination of discrimination (though not necessarily other restrictions) that Keynes devised his CU plan, which would obviate 'dodges to protect an unbalanced position'.[356] Keynes saw general reduction of trade barriers as dependent on multilateral trade arrangements and multilateral clearing, or a similar monetary system, promoting payments equilibrium and an expansive world economy.[357] An alliance developed between him and those, such as Meade and Robbins, promoting multilateralism in commercial policy, against the empire-centred bilateralism of the Bank of England,[358] though Meade thought that in general Keynes was 'not opposing' their push for trade liberalization rather than working for it.[359] Until at least early 1944, Keynes was sceptical that a multilateral trade agreement could be reached.[360] In June 1944 he advocated a multilateral plan 'directed to the freedom and expansion of international trade, and to the elimination of discriminatory practices, which is fully compatible with the programming of overseas trade', including quantitative import restrictions and bulk purchasing by the state.[361] This was his conception of future British policy. At least until late in the war, Keynes approved infant industry protection, and urged British self-sufficiency in some goods, which required import restrictions.[362]

As post-war plans developed, Keynes increasingly opposed the imperialist-isolationists who resisted them. As early as October–November 1942, he was cited by Canadian experts as saying that bilateralism should be avoided at all costs.[363] Keynes insisted that the Bretton Woods proposals permitted trade restrictions, but came to argue that they pointed the way to 'commercial multilateralism'.[364] By early 1944, if not before, he had become a passionate opponent of trade and currency bilateralism.[365] This would entail a rupture with the USA and much of the world, with Britain in the weakest position ever to sustain economic isolation.[366] He opposed Britain's concentrating trade policy on the Empire.[367]

---

[355] Hansen to Viner, 20 Oct. 1941, box 38, JVP.
[356] Vol. 25, pp. 80, 120, 187; see p. 169.
[357] Vol. 23, pp. 139–40, 209; vol. 26, p. 256.
[358] Cairncross and Watts, *Economic Section*, ch. 7, esp. p. 110.
[359] Worswick and Trevithick, *Modern World*, p. 130; cf. vol. 26, pp. 241–2, 247.
[360] Vol. 26, pp. 273, 284.
[361] Vol. 26, pp. 310, 325–6.
[362] Vol. 26, pp. 252, 261–3, 267–8, 285.
[363] Report on 'Post-War Economic Talks', CU section, p. 1, RG19, vol. 3989, file T-2-9-2, PAC.
[364] Vol. 26, pp. 128–9, 190; cf. p. 25.
[365] Vol. 25, pp. 410–13; vol. 26, pp. 190–2, 314–16; vol. 27, pp. 380–1.
[366] Vol. 26, p. 192.
[367] Vol. 26, pp. 11–12, 191; M. Keynes, *Essays*, p. 207.

Keynes's reaction in December 1944 to Beveridge's *Full Employment in a Free Society* is a measure of how far Keynes had moved from countenancing bilateralism, as he had in 1941. Beveridge emphasized that open, non-discriminatory trade depended on maintenance of full employment.[368] Keynes thought the 'weak spot in the volume' was 'the chapter on international implications': 'I looked in vain for even a shadow of an explanation of how the mysterious system known to me only by its name, namely bilateralism, is supposed to help or prevent' the difficulties of maintaining employment in Britain if there were an American slump.[369]

In his March 1945 paper on terms for a US loan, Keynes argued powerfully against a policy of depending 'on our own self-sufficiency', bilateral trade deals, and the present sterling area arrangements (except as a last resort if American help were unforthcoming and internationalism failed). It would mean a rupture with North America, where it would be seen 'as recklessly disrupting the common Anglo-American front which is the best hope of the world'. Britain's likely current account deficit made it no 'well-chosen moment for a declaration of our financial independence of North America'. Moreover, freedom of trade—not an isolationist or etatist scheme of trade—was, 'on its merits, to our great advantage if it can be made to work'. British trade was not well suited to bilateral arrangements: 'what suits our exporters is to have the whole world as their playground'. Bilateralism would require Soviet-style state planning, at a low standard of life, and a virtual abandonment of all overseas activities involving any considerable expenditure. Only with sterling convertibility could London's position as the financial centre of the greater part of the British Commonwealth and of several other countries be preserved.[370] In advocating the CU and then the IMF, Keynes had depicted multilateral clearing or convertibility as essential to London's position.[371]

We have seen that in December 1945 Britain expressed full support for US proposals for an ITO to oversee the elimination of discrimination in conjunction with reduction of trade barriers, with states reserving the right to non-discriminatory quantitative import restrictions to help restore balance of payments equilibrium. In his December 1945 defence of the policy package comprising Bretton Woods, the US loan, and trade and employment proposals, Keynes insisted that trade planning to preserve external equilibrium was not prejudiced by these proposals. They 'combine the advantages of freedom of commerce with safeguards against the disastrous consequences

---

[368] W. H. Beveridge, *Full Employment in a Free Society* (London, 1944), pp. 210, 239, and part 6, *passim.*

[369] Vol. 27, pp. 380–1.

[370] Vol. 24, pp. 256–95; see also, e.g. vol. 28, pp. 221–2; vol. 25, p. 156.

[371] For example vol. 25, pp. 82, 84, 94, 99–100, 416; vol. 26, p. 12; vol. 24, p. 620.

of a laissez-faire system which pays no direct regard to the preservation of equilibrium and merely relies on the eventual working out of blind forces'. 'Here is an attempt to use what we have learnt from modern experience and modern analysis, not to defeat, but to implement the wisdom of Adam Smith.'[372] Keynes elaborated his remarks on 'the wisdom of Adam Smith' in 'The Balance of Payments of the United States', published soon after his death.[373] In both the Lords speech and the article, he was optimistic that US payments would tend towards equilibrium, not least because the USA was becoming a 'high-living, high-cost country'. Thus Keynes endorsed 'the classical teaching' that 'there are . . . natural forces, . . . the invisible hand, operating towards equilibrium'. He praised the Washington proposals, which aimed at creating a system which allows 'the classical medicine' to work, something inter-war American protectionism had prevented. He was encouraged that, with 'all the most responsible people' in the USA having abandoned protectionism, '[f]or the first time in modern history the United States is going to exert its full, powerful influence in the direction of reduction of tariffs, not only of itself but by all others'. He reiterated the need to supplement the classical medicine with quicker and less painful aids, especially exchange variation and import controls. Keynes's reference to 'modernist stuff, gone wrong and turned sour and silly'[374] appears to refer, at least in part, to those 'Keynesian' isolationists who misinterpreted *The General Theory* 'as an argument for closing national economic systems'.[375]

6.6 THE POST-WAR TREATMENT OF GERMANY

Reflecting his view of 1919, Keynes wrote in his Proposals to Counter the German 'New Order' in 1940 that her neighbours could not develop 'a prosperous, or a secure life with a crushed and ruined Germany in their midst'.[376] In July 1941, Anthony Eden, who (as we have seen) had used those Notes for a speech in May, used very similar words to Keynes's to foreshadow Britain's post-war attitude.[377] Keynes said that the alternative to Germany's being 'allowed to

[372] Vol. 24, p. 621.

[373] Vol. 27, pp. 427–46. The quotations below are from pp. 444–6 and vol. 24, pp. 621–3. See Moggridge, *Biography*, pp. 822–4.

[374] Vol. 27, p. 445.

[375] Robinson, 'Keynes', p. 46; B. Ward, *The Ideal Worlds of Economics* (London and Basingstoke, 1979), pp. 387–9.

[376] Vol. 25, p. 15.

[377] *The Times*, 30 July 1941; cf. Eden's trial run, *The Times*, 30 May 1941; see V. Rothwell, *Britain and the Cold War, 1941–1947* (London, 1982), p. 26.

resume that measure of *economic* leadership in Central Europe which flows naturally from her qualifications and geographical position' was letting the Soviet Union fill the vacuum, which he clearly opposed.[378] He argued that post-war policy towards Germany should favour her economic reconstruction and concentrate preventive measures in the political and military settlement.[379] While he stressed political aspects more than in 1919, his theme— economic reconstruction, necessarily to include Germany—remained the same.

During the Second World War, Keynes—fairly consistently[380]—sought restitution, reparation according to capacity to pay within five years, and the ultimate reconstruction and return to the international economy of a demilitarized but prosperous German buffer state between east and west. In September 1941, Keynes recommended the setting up of a British government committee on reparations and restitution.[381] After discussions in an informal group of officials, the Malkin Inter-Departmental Committee on Reparation and Economic Security was established in late 1942, with Keynes as a member.[382] His December 1942 paper for it on 'Germany's Contribution to the Cost of Keeping the Peace of the World' argued that Germany and Japan, whose conduct created the need, could justly be required to contribute, as the Allies would, to the cost of an international body concerned with maintaining peace.[383] Keynes also proposed restitution of stolen property, and that Germany deliver such goods and services as she could during the occupation towards making good the loss and damage. Germany's capacity would be interpreted by a Reparations Commission within reasonable guidelines.[384]

In September 1943, Keynes outlined to US State Department officials the Malkin recommendations, which largely followed his ideas.[385] The Malkin Committee assumed no dismemberment of Germany. It urged that most action, especially deliveries in kind, should be of a once-and-for-all character within, say, five years after the war. Reparations would depend on Germany's capacity to pay, with the Allied governments agreeing on 'round figures' for their shares 'as part of a broad-bottomed bargain', rather than elaborating 'a detailed inventory of claims'. The Committee recommended confining reparation to the loss of non-military property directly caused by enemy military operations. But reparations obligations must be 'adjusted to the facts of the future as they disclose themselves'. The Committee saw that disarming Germany while the Allies assumed a peace-keeping role would benefit

---

[378] Vol. 25, p. 9; M. Keynes, *Essays*, p. 193.   [379] Vol. 25, p. 10.
[380] Cf. vol. 26, p. 382.   [381] Vol. 26, p. 330; see p. 359.
[382] M. Keynes, *Essays*, pp. 193–5; Moggridge, *Biography*, p. 768 ff; Skidelsky, *Fighting*, pp. 362–3.
[383] Vol. 26, pp. 337–41 at pp. 339, 341.   [384] Vol. 26, pp. 341–6.
[385] Vol. 26, pp. 347–73

Germany's economy but burden the Allies. It therefore supported Keynes's idea of tapping Germany's export trade for a contribution to peace-keeping costs. Germany would pay over time for post-war relief given her. She would admit her guilt.[386] However, the British government did not adopt the Malkin principles, leaving policy for future decision.[387]

From mid-August 1944, Morgenthau and the pro-Soviet White were vigorously advocating the dismemberment and de-industrialization of Germany. They rejected the belief that European prosperity was dependent on German industry.[388] During the Quebec conference in mid-September, Roosevelt and Morgenthau promoted the Morgenthau Plan and, perhaps to smooth the way on Lend-Lease, Churchill accepted it.[389] In October 1944, while expressing considerable sympathy for parts of the Plan, Keynes criticized as absurd Morgenthau's proposal for the de-industrialization of the Ruhr and other parts of Germany.[390] 'There is not the faintest indication of how the large population of this extensive area is to be kept alive.' In August–September 1944, Keynes evidently favoured dismembering Germany.[391] White told Morgenthau that Keynes 'seems to be in our corner'.[392] With Lend-Lease Stage II negotiations underway, Keynes did not wish to be seen by Morgenthau as an opponent.[393] But the Morgenthau Plan was widely opposed, including by such Americans as Stimson, Hull, Marshall, and Acheson.[394] By the end of September, Roosevelt had backed away from it.[395]

Although he had played with the idea that Germany be dismembered for a twenty year period, then given her freedom to reunify, Keynes was by December 1944 a strong opponent of dismemberment.[396] In February 1945, foreseeing the partitioning of Germany between Soviet and western zones, he described having a direct frontier between Soviet and Western European spheres of influence as 'very dangerous compared with the alternative of a

---

[386] Vol. 26, p. 368; see also pp. 341–2.

[387] See M. Keynes, *Essays*, pp. 194–6.

[388] 'Is European Prosperity Dependent upon German Industry?', 7 Sept. 1944, item 22e, box 7, HDWP.

[389] See, e.g. R. Dallek, *Franklin D. Roosevelt and American Foreign Policy, 1932–1945* (New York, 1979), p. 472 ff; W. S. Churchill, *The Second World War*, vi, *Triumph and Tragedy* (London, 1954), pp. 138–9; vol. 24, p. 126 ff; Moggridge, *Biography*, pp. 771–8; Skidelsky, *Fighting*, p. 363.

[390] Vol. 26, pp. 380–2; cf. Harrod, *Life*, p. 695.

[391] Vol. 26, pp. 374–5. Keynes also said he was 'tempted' by 20 years 'break-up of Germany': Keynes to Lippmann, 13 Aug. 1944, box 82, folder 1217, Lippmann papers, LOC; PP/45/187, 35–6, KP.

[392] Moggridge, *Biography*, pp. 771–2; vol. 24, p. 128 n.

[393] Vol. 24, pp. 130–5.

[394] Vol. 24, pp. 133–4; Hull, *Memoirs*, p. 1613 ff; Stimson to Marshall, 2 May 1947; Acheson to Marshall, 28 May 1947, box 86, folder 16, GCMP; Marshall to Stimson, 28 Apr. and 30 May 1947, box 137, folder 51, GCMP.

[395] Dallek, *Roosevelt*, pp. 477–8.   [396] Vol. 26, p. 382.

buffer state in the shape of a unitary Germany'. He feared the suction of the western sectors into a 'German U.S.S.R.', and highlighted the 'manifest incompatibility' between dismemberment and reparations.[397]

In discussions of reparations following Yalta, Keynes again argued against putting an aggregate global figure on them.[398] British policy followed Keynes's approach.[399] He opposed the actual de-industrialization policy pursued immediately after the war.[400] British officials involved in Allied Control Council discussions in early 1946 sought the highest levels of production in Germany. One of them, Alec Cairncross, wrote in February 1946 that

> at the end of the last war, Lord Keynes familiarized us with the truth, which experience is now reiterating, that Germany was the hub of the entire European economy and that upon her prosperity the prosperity of Europe in large measure depends.... The lower the level of industrial activity, the less rapidly will Germany gravitate either towards the west, with which her industrial links will be feebler, or towards democracy, which will appear more of a luxury.[401]

As 'the majority share my views', Keynes declined to repeat *The Economic Consequences*.[402] His approach was ultimately to prevail in the policies of the western occupying powers, between which there were, however, significant differences on the questions of levels of industry, dismantling, reparations, and the Ruhr.[403]

6.7 KEYNES'S VISION: 'THE SPIRIT OF BURKE AND ADAM SMITH' REVISITED

Keynes's vision for the post-war order was evident early in the war, especially in his 1940 Proposals to Counter the German 'New Order' and in the early CU drafts. Through long negotiations in which he sought to put them into effect, the basic ideas were unchanged until his death. On 27 November 1941, D. H. Robertson wrote to Keynes that he had read his revised CU proposals 'with great excitement,—a growing hope that the spirit of Burke and Adam Smith is on earth again...'[404] Robertson, 'an old Free Trader',[405] believed that Keynes's scheme offered hope for liberal internationalism in the place of

---

[397] Vol. 26, pp. 384–5.   [398] Vol. 26, p. 391; see also p. 394.

[399] Vol. 26, p. 398.   [400] Vol. 26, p. 400; see vol. 27, p. 479.

[401] Quoted from A. Deighton, *The Impossible Peace* (Oxford, 1990), p. 56.

[402] Vol. 26, p. 401.

[403] On the course of events, see, e.g. Deighton, *Impossible Peace, passim*; A. S. Milward, *The Reconstruction of Western Europe, 1945–51* (London, 1984), ch. 4, pp. 369–71, 383–5.

[404] Vol. 25, p. 67; see Harrod, *Life*, pp. 627–8.

[405] Robertson, *Britain in the World Economy*, p. 83.

economic nationalism. Keynes was not reverting to the free trade evangelism of his youth, or the belief that free trade unaided promoted peace. But, as we have seen, he was seeking institutions and policies to make a high degree of freedom of trade compatible with domestic order and international peace.

Keynes continued to believe, as he said in 1944, that 'it will be the role of this country to develop a middle way of economic life which will preserve the liberty, the initiative and (what we are so rich in) the idiosyncrasy of the individual in a framework serving the public good and seeking equality of contentment amongst all'.[406] His work on post-war international plans aimed to create the international context in which this was possible. Keynes's goals remained, as they long had been, full employment; interest rates set, free from interference from international capital movements, as low as necessary for that goal; and an exchange rate, predictable in the short-term, but adjustable in the long, to enable balance of payments equilibrium at full employment, without deflation imposed from outside.[407]

Keynes recognized the wartime planning as based on idealism; he sought to engage the idealism of US officials,[408] and applauded their idealism as the plans were maturing.[409] Underlying all his own work was a powerful optimism. This fundamental optimism was evident even in the face of great difficulties and stresses, for example when he was deeply apprehensive about Britain's post-war balance of payments. He was optimistic that mass unemployment would be avoided post-war.[410] He looked forward (as he had in 'Economic Possibilities for Our Grandchildren' during the Depression)[411] to a 'golden age' of 'increased leisure, more holidays (which are a wonderfully good way of getting rid of money) and shorter hours'.[412] In April 1942, he said of building projects, that in 'the long run almost anything is possible.'[413] He repeatedly argued that, especially when the future is so uncertain,[414] 'the best policy is to act on the optimistic hypothesis until it has been proved wrong'.[415]

6.7.1 An Economic Basis for Peace

Keynes's proposals for international economic cooperation were, to a significant extent, motivated by the belief that such cooperation was necessary to overcome economic causes of war, and to lay the economic basis for lasting

---

[406] Vol. 27, p. 369; see also, e.g. pp. 385–8.
[407] See, e.g. vol. 26, p. 16; Robinson, 'Keynes', p. 45.   [408] Vol. 25, pp. 43, 70, 110.
[409] For example, vol. 25, p. 356 (White).
[410] For example, vol. 27, pp. 302, 335–6; cf. p. 381.
[411] Vol. 9, pp. 321–32.
[412] Vol. 27, p. 323; see also, e.g. Penrose, *Economic Planning*, p. 320 n.
[413] Vol. 27, p. 268.   [414] For example, vol. 24, p. 275.   [415] Vol. 27, p. 446.

peace. Before we discuss Keynes's ideas, we should recognize that it was very common to see economic causes of war and the need for economic measures to promote peace. For example, Morgenthau's opening address at Bretton Woods said currency disorders in the 1930s had generated unemployment, producing the 'bewilderment and bitterness' which became 'the breeders of fascism, and, finally, of war'. 'Economic aggression can have no other offspring than war.'[416] Gardner wrote that, 'profoundly influenced by the writings of Keynes and others', US post-war planners 'believed the Versailles settlement had collapsed because of its inadequate... economic underpinning', and were determined not to repeat that mistake.[417] In 1945, Bernard Baruch wrote to Eugene Meyer (who was to be the first President of the IBRD): 'After the last war, if Wilson had been returned, you would have been head of the Reparations Commission and we would not have had this war.'[418] The widespread acceptance that there needed to be an economic basis for enduring peace was reflected in the opening words of the Washington proposals on trade and employment in December 1945:[419]

Collective measures to safeguard the peoples of the world against threats to peace and to reach just settlements of disputes among nations must be based not only on international machinery to deal directly with disputes and to prevent aggression, but also on economic co-operation among nations with the object of preventing and removing economic and social maladjustments, of achieving fairness and equity in economic relations between states, and of raising the level of economic well-being among all peoples.

The proposals referred to the important contributions already made toward the attainment of these objectives by creating the Food and Agriculture Organization, the IMF, and the IBRD. The proposals depicted an ITO as contributing 'to the creation of economic conditions conducive to the maintenance of world peace.'[420]

Clearly, the economic planning aimed to create an 'economic basis of a durable peace'[421] to accompany the political framework being created in the United Nations Organization and through other steps: this is how the US Administration, as well as many others, including Keynes, presented it. The Charter of the UN itself declared that, with 'a view to the creation of conditions of stability and well-being which are necessary for peaceful and

---

[416] Quoted from Cmd. 6597, p. 5; see also pp. 3, 8.
[417] M. Keynes, *Essays*, pp. 203–4; see vol. 25, pp. 137, 194.
[418] Baruch to Meyer, 9 Sept. 1945, box 9, Meyer papers, LOC.
[419] Cmd. 6709, p. 2.   [420] Cmd. 6709, p. 4; see also pp. 2, 3.
[421] M. Keynes, *Essays*, p. 203. *The Economic Basis of a Durable Peace* was a book by Meade (London, 1940).

friendly relations among nations', the UN 'shall promote... higher standards of living, full employment, and conditions of economic and social progress and development'.[422] While some writers have recognized the peace purpose of the economic plans,[423] studies of wartime planning for the UN frequently fail to acknowledge that an economic pillar of post-war peace was also being constructed.[424]

What, then, of Keynes's own views? We have seen that he believed that the Treaty of Versailles had contributed to causing the Second World War.[425] His draft statement to counter the German New Order began: 'The authors of the Peace Treaty of Versailles made the mistake of neglecting the economic reconstruction of Europe in their preoccupation with political frontiers and safeguards. Much misfortune to all of us has followed from this neglect.'[426] Keynes stressed the necessity not to repeat it.[427] Through policies of economic reconstruction, peace could be promoted. There is strong continuity between Keynes's approach to European reconstruction after both world wars, including his belief, as he put it in 1940, in the necessity for 'an economically reconstructed Germany', which 'will necessarily resume leadership': Keynes identified the choice for Eastern Europe as between German or Russian 'leadership'. As in 1919, Keynes opposed using 'starvation and unemployment as an instrument for enforcing our political settlement' when the war was over. But he placed greater emphasis on political and military measures to restrain Germany than he had in 1919: economic reconstruction with emphasis on social security was 'compatible with any desired degree of severity in respect of political and military conditions', which 'will be sufficiently strict to make Germany's economic and social recovery safe and beneficial to her neighbours.'[428]

It would seem from Keynes's hostility in 1941 to 'nineteenth century' laissez-faire ideas on trade that he did not believe that free or non-discriminatory trade of itself, in existing circumstances, promoted peace. He subsequently set out to create the conditions in which such trade could be restored. He clearly believed that this would be compatible with peace: in the words of *The General Theory*, there would be no 'important economic forces' setting 'the interest of one country against that of its neighbours'. Moreover, trade liberalization was more likely to be associated with international harmony than was the alternative. In advocating the Anglo-American package in

---

[422] Charter of the United Nations, Art. 55.

[423] For example, Van Dormael, *Bretton Woods* (e.g. Prologue); Gardner, *Sterling–Dollar*, pp. 4, 8, and *passim*.

[424] For example, Hilderbrand, *Dumbarton Oaks*, p. 67. Divine, *Second Chance*.

[425] See ch. 5, this volume.   [426] Vol. 25, p. 11.

[427] For example, vol. 25, p. 15; see also, e.g. p. 137.   [428] Vol. 25, pp. 9–10, 15.

December 1945, Keynes contrasted multilateral, non-discriminatory trade and currency arrangements with the creation of separate economic blocs:[429]

The separate economic blocs and all the friction and loss of friendship they must bring with them are expedients to which one may be driven in a hostile world, where trade has ceased over wide areas to be co-operative and peaceful and where are forgotten the healthy rules of mutual advantage and equal treatment. But it is surely crazy to prefer that.

Making 'trade truly international' and avoiding 'economic blocs which limit and restrict commercial intercourse outside them' was essential to 'the world's best hope, an Anglo-American understanding', creating international institutions of great potential. The institutions sought to organize 'international order out of the chaos of war in a way which will not interfere with the diversity of national policy yet will minimize the causes of friction and ill will between nations'.

That exclusive economic blocs promote international friction was one of the classical liberal arguments as to how free trade, the antithesis of exclusionism, promotes peace. In reasserting this argument, however, Keynes saw the need, if economic internationalism were to work, for states to be able to pursue national policies, especially for full employment. This required the right international institutional context for their policies. He was, thus, expounding a form of liberal institutionalism.

This study has previously identified various economic factors which Keynes believed could cause war, including impoverishment, population pressure, penetration of foreign capital, and the competitive struggle for markets. The first of these is clear in Keynes's wartime thinking; the fourth may have been present. After 1937, Keynes said very little about population questions.[430] His ideas on foreign capital, as we shall see, reflected those of *The General Theory*.

In wartime planning, Keynes referred to two economic causes of war. First, he referred to fluctuations in economic conditions—in effect, impoverishment—as endangering peace. The April 1943 CU White Paper expressed the hope that economic measures and institutions 'may help the world to control the ebb and flow of the tides of economic activity which have, in the past, destroyed security of livelihood and endangered international peace'.[431] Second, and more specifically, Keynes's September 1941 draft on the CU began by saying that failure to solve the 'problem of maintaining equilibrium in the balance of payments between countries' had long 'been a major cause of impoverishment and social discontent and even of wars and revolutions'.[432]

---

[429] Vol. 24, pp. 607–8, 623–4.   [430] See ch. 5, this volume.
[431] Vol. 25, p. 234; see also, e.g. p. 137. (Cmd. 6437, p. 20.)   [432] Vol. 25, p. 21.

This arose especially because, the onus being on debtor countries to adjust, 'it has been an inherent characteristic of the automatic international metallic currency (apart from special circumstances) to force adjustments in the direction most disruptive of social order, and to throw the burden on the countries least able to support it, making the poor poorer'.[433] As we have seen, *The General Theory* had depicted the gold standard as causing war by giving no alternative means to counter unemployment than the competitive struggle for markets. In his wartime comments, Keynes seems simply to have meant that it resulted in impoverishment and social discontent, implying that these in turn had caused wars and revolutions.

The lesson he found in 1941 for 'architects of a successful international system' was that the 'object of the new system must be to require the chief initiative from the creditor countries, whilst maintaining enough discipline in the debtor countries to prevent them from exploiting the new ease allowed them in living profligately beyond their means'.[434] In recommending the scarce currency clause in May 1944, Keynes told the Lords that the USA had 'offered us a far-reaching formula of protection against a recurrence of the main cause of deflation during the inter-war years, namely the draining of reserves out of the rest of the world to pay a country which was obstinately borrowing and exporting on a scale immensely greater than it was lending and importing'. Between the wars, that 'did more than any other single factor to destroy the world's economic balance and to prepare a seed-bed for foul growths'.[435]

The General Theory, in discussing the economic causes of war, had argued that 'if nations can learn to provide themselves with full employment by their domestic policy..., there need be no important economic forces calculated to set the interest of one country against that of its neighbours'.[436] It depicted the international monetary system as determining whether domestic policies for full employment were possible.[437] On the analysis of *The General Theory*, the following elements of post-war arrangements could be seen as promoting peace: (*a*) adoption by countries of Keynesian policies for full employment, and international agreement (envisaged in the Washington proposals) to full employment policies; (*b*) an international monetary system that, by allowing exchange rate changes and giving assistance during balance of payments adversity, enabled countries to pursue expansionary policies; (*c*) any pressure the new monetary system exerted on countries with large surpluses to adjust, so relieving those with deficits of some of the burden; and (*d*) any expansionary influence this system exerted directly (e.g. through financing

---

[433] Vol. 25, pp. 27–31, at p. 29.   [434] Vol. 25, p. 30.
[435] Vol. 26, p. 14; see also, e.g. p. 280.   [436] Vol. 7, p. 382.   [437] Vol. 7, pp. 348–9.

international development, as envisaged in the CU plan, and achieved in the IBRD). There was also a more direct way in which the CU could contribute to 'the preservation of peace':[438] through the account for an international police force, and the provision for financial blockades.

We have seen that in the inter-war years Keynes believed that penetration of an economy by foreign capital could engender animosities, and that *The General Theory* had depicted laissez-faire in international lending as hostile to peace.[439] During the Second World War, Keynes regarded it as important that there continue to be controls on capital movements after the war. He justified these as necessary to retaining the power to control the domestic rate of interest so as to secure cheap money, 'without interference from the ebb and flow of international capital movements or flights of hot money'.[440] That is, capital controls would make it possible, or at least easier, to pursue the full employment policies that were conducive to peace. We have also seen Keynes's desire that debts left by the war (which meant especially Britain's debts) not be such as to create friction and estrangement in international relations.[441] He rejected any analogy between the US loan and 'last time's war debts',[442] which had caused friction.

6.7.2 'New Modes of International Government in Economic Affairs'[443]

Keynes's hopes for international cooperation after the war were, like those of many other idealists, highly ambitious. He referred in 1943 to 'the new democracy of nations which after this war will come into existence, heaven helping, to conduct with amity and good sense the common concerns of mankind'.[444] We have seen that, for example, he favoured an international police force. Central to this vision was international economic cooperation. In recommending the CU and Stabilization Fund to the Lords in 1943, he said: 'So ill did we fare...between the wars for lack of such an instrument of international government as this' that the resulting 'frustration of men's efforts and distortion of their life pattern have played no small part in preparing the soiled atmosphere in which the Nazis could thrive'.[445] Minutes of a meeting with the Board of Trade on 1 December 1941 to discuss the Keynes Plan quote him as having it 'in his mind that there would be a new League of Nations under Anglo-American direction; that the Bank would act

---

[438] Vol. 25, p. 94.   [439] Vol. 7, pp. 348–9; see ch. 5, this volume.
[440] Vol. 26, pp. 16–17.   [441] See, e.g. vol. 23, p. 25.
[442] Vol. 24, p. 616; vol. 28, p. 218.   [443] Vol. 25, p. 280.   [444] Vol. 25, pp. 270–1.
[445] Vol. 25, pp. 279–80.

in cooperation with that League and under its direction in regard to matters of international politics'.[446]

Keynes's aspirations for international government greatly exceeded what was achieved. We have seen how he wished a CU created, and to work in collaboration with other international institutions for 'such general world purposes as (a) post-war relief and reconstruction; (b) international T.V.A.; (c) the finance of commodity agreements; (d) the preservation of peace; (e) the control of the trade cycle and the stabilisation of prices, and, generally (f) the maintenance of active employment everywhere'.[447] In his December 1941 CU draft, Keynes wrote:

It is capable of arousing enthusiasm because it makes a beginning at the construction of the future government of the world between nations and 'the winning of the peace', in a sphere not the least important because the conditions and the atmosphere are thereby created in which much else is made easier.[448]

In the January 1942 plan, this became 'a beginning at the future economic ordering of the world between nations'.[449] In discussion with European allies about the CU plan in February 1943, Keynes said that 'this scheme might become the linchpin of a general international economic system of a far more ambitious kind than we ever contemplated before the war'.[450] Throughout his CU drafts, Keynes asserted that 'a greater readiness to accept super-national arrangements must be required in the post-war world than has been shown hitherto'. Keynes described his proposed 'measure of financial disarmament' as 'very mild in comparison with the measures of military disarmament which, it is to be hoped, the world will be asked to accept'.[451]

While Keynes said that his 'scheme may seem in its entirety to make the beginning of an entirely new stage in the economic organisation of the world',[452] he also depicted it as recapturing certain advantages of the nineteenth century economy. The CU proposal

differs in one important respect from the existing state of affairs by putting some part of the responsibility for adjustment on the creditor country, as well as on the debtor. This is an attempt to recover the advantages which were enjoyed in the nineteenth century when a favourable balance in favour of London and Paris, which were the main creditor centres, immediately produced an expansionist pressure [and increased foreign lending[453]] in those markets, but which have been lost since New York succeeded to the position of main creditor, this change being aggravated by the break down of international borrowing credit and by the flight of loose funds from

---

[446] T247/116, PRO.   [447] Vol. 25, pp. 94, 138–9; cf. pp. 58–60.
[448] Vol. 25, p. 94.   [449] Vol. 25, pp. 139, 195.   [450] Vol. 25, p. 214.
[451] Vol. 25, p. 89; see also, e.g. p. 57 (slightly different wording).
[452] Vol. 25, p. 103.   [453] Vol. 25, p. 179.

one depository to another. The point is that the creditor should not be allowed to remain entirely passive. For if he is, an impossible task may be laid on the debtor country, which is for that very reason in the weaker position, so that the evils with which we are familiar are likely to ensue.[454]

Keynes was thus again seeking to overcome the effects of that shift of financial power which he discussed in the *Treatise*, and which, through American (and French) behaviour, produced strong contractionist pressures in the inter-war years. He proposed now to achieve by multilateral cooperation what British leadership of the international economy had once done. Stressing the analogy between the CU and a national banking system, Keynes wrote:[455]

Just as the development of national banking systems served to offset a deflationary pressure which would have prevented otherwise the development of modern industry, so by extending the same principle into the international field we may hope to offset the contractionist pressure which might otherwise overwhelm in social disorder and disappointment the good hopes of our modern world.

In January 1942, in discussing criticisms of his Clearing Bank plan, Keynes acknowledged a dilemma between 'giving the plan a long-term expansionist bias, and, on the other hand, the risk of inflationary conditions in the immediate post-war period'. Britain's need for expansionism weighed against overcaution. Keynes sought the avoidance of inflation through the continuance of the sort of controls over raw materials and other supplies which had been developed during the war.[456] But the fear of inflation was one of the reasons why Keynes's 'utopian' scheme was not accepted by the USA.

6.7.3 Anglo-American Cooperation

Throughout the war, Keynes saw Anglo-American cooperation as the only workable basis for international economic cooperation. His draft statement countering the German New Order in late 1940 said that Britain, 'acting in friendly collaboration with the United States, and we alone, will be in a position to implement' a policy of 'social security' for all European countries after the war. 'Europe will end this war starved and bankrupt of all the foods and raw materials, for supplies of which she was accustomed to depend on the rest of the world. She will have no means, unaided, of breaking the vicious cycle'.[457] Keynes was thus reiterating a theme of 1919: European reconstruction needed American assistance.

[454] Vol. 25, p. 78; cf. pp. 30, 49, 117, 179–80, 451; see p. 99.
[455] Vol. 25, pp. 113, 177; cf. pp. 44–8, 75, 209–10.
[456] Vol. 25, pp. 104–5; see also pp. 193, 324–5.   [457] Vol. 25, p. 11.

Increasingly, Keynes also saw Anglo-American cooperation as essential for Britain itself. In the first instance, this was for help in the war effort. We have seen that, although it embodied ideas he had long advocated, Keynes's CU plan was devised specifically as a way of meeting the requirements of the draft Article 7 of the Mutual Aid Agreement. In CU drafts in late 1941 and early 1942, he envisaged that at the end of the war, 'however hard-up we may be', Britain, as victor and 'one of the two or three masters of the future', would not appear to the USA 'the most suitable claimant' of their help.[458] It was therefore necessary to seek such help indirectly, as 'a consequence of setting the world as a whole on its feet and of laying the foundations of a sounder political economy between all nations'. An 'ambitious plan of an international complexion, suitable to serve the interests of others besides ourselves' might attract 'idealistic and internationally-minded Americans' in a way that '*our* problems' could not. Hence the CU proposals. Keynes, like many others, viewed international cooperation as necessary for the promotion and protection of national interests in an interdependent world.[459]

Keynes was clearly aware that American universalism could stand in the way of specifically Anglo-American cooperation; and that this could be compounded by American suspicions of Britain.[460] By the end of the Stage II negotiations in December 1944, probably in part influenced by Walter Lippmann,[461] Keynes believed that all responsible Americans were increasingly convinced that a strong Britain after the war was indispensable to America. This was in part because the US had no alternative, reliable and strong friends outside the Commonwealth: 'Further acquaintance with Russia does not increase intimacy or confidence. The illusion of China has faded....' (Many others, both in Washington and London, remained more hopeful for longer of post-war cooperation with the Soviet Union.) Keynes urged what would later commonly be called 'the special relationship'. If sources of mutual irritations could be avoided, 'the only brotherhood by which civilisation can be held together, already sealed in blood, will become in due time a decent, commonplace, workaday affair, which is taken for granted'. On no grounds should Britain 'stray, even in thought or hypothesis, along another path than this'. To help make possible 'the right sort of workaday relationship', Keynes

---

[458] Vol. 25, pp. 43, 69–70, 108–10; see vol. 26, p. 316.

[459] For this view at Bretton Woods, see Cmd. 6597, esp. pp. 3 (FDR message), 7–8 (Morgenthau), 15–16 (Theunis).

[460] Vol. 25, p. 152; see Gardner, *Sterling–Dollar*, pp. 6–7.

[461] Keynes to Lippmann, 13 Aug. 1944, discusses a book by Lippmann. Keynes was 'fully convinced' by Lippmann on 'the Atlantic community': box 82, folder 1217, Lippmann papers, LOC; PP/45/187/35–6, KP; see W. Lippmann, *U.S. Foreign Policy* (London, 1943) ch. 7.

insisted that 'financial independence of the United States at the earliest possible opportunity should be a major aim of British policy'.[462]

Not least from his experience during and after the First World War, Keynes realized that the course of Anglo-American cooperation was unlikely to run smooth. His late 1941 and early 1942 CU drafts all began: 'The practical difficulties in the way of Anglo-American economic co-operation after the war should not dissuade us from attaching the highest importance to it'.[463] Practical difficulties—'quarrels of intimacy'[464]—were not few over subsequent years: for example, American pressure on Britain to keep down its dollar balance,[465] and the distressing negotiations of the US loan in 1945. We have seen that, though some thought his manner exacerbated some difficulties, Keynes was deeply conscious of the need to monitor and cultivate American public and Congressional opinion as well as Administration officials. He said that the Americans negotiating the US loan intensely desired that there 'be no break in Anglo-American intimacy'; they were 'doing their damnedest all through to give us as good a deal as their own perfectly frightful local politics would permit'.[466] Despite the difficulties and irritations, Keynes wrote on 4 April 1946: 'Judging both by the progress of the British Loan and also American intentions, as they appeared during the Savannah Conference, one can say that for the time being at least America is safely set on the course of trying to make a good job of international co-operation, on the economic as well as on the political side.' Though there were American critics of that approach, 'never in my experience of the country has there been less responsible support for any brand of isolationism'. Though 'their methods will constantly irritate us', and there would be much 'good reason for complaint', American goodwill was real and reliable, and it would 'be fatal for us to stand aside or be too sceptical or critical'.[467] In seeking to win British support for the Anglo-American arrangements (especially the US loan), he found it necessary to interpret the American view to his British audience: 'How differently things appear in Washington than in London, and how easy it is to misunderstand one another's difficulties and the real purpose which lies behind each one's way of solving them.'[468]

In the inter-war years, Keynes had identified the creditor position of the USA (especially her drawing in capital on top of a trade surplus) as a major cause of international economic problems; and his wartime plans sought a solution to this. In April 1941, Keynes saw it as a necessary condition of a

---

[462] Vol. 24, pp. 220–3.   [463] Vol. 25, pp. 42, 69, 108.
[464] The phrase is Parker's: *Struggle*, p. 248.   [465] For example, vol. 23, pp. 286–315.
[466] Vol. 28, p. 219; see also vol. 24, pp. 608–9, 914.
[467] Vol. 27, p. 484; see also, e.g. vol. 24, p. 570.   [468] Vol. 24, pp. 606, 610.

return to free exchanges that the USA should find some permanent remedy for its unbalanced creditor position. He was not optimistic of this happening quickly after the war: hence the possibility of post-war discrimination against the USA if she persisted in maintaining an unbalanced creditor position.[469] With the US draft of Article 7 ruling out discrimination, Keynes tried in his CU proposals to create a general obligation on 'the countries whoever they may turn out to be, which are for the time being in the creditor position... not to allow this credit balance... to exercise a contractionist pressure against [the] world economy and, by repercussion, against the economy of the creditor country itself'.[470] Keynes clearly still had the USA in mind. We have seen that the obligation on creditors was a central issue in the negotiations leading to creation of the IMF. By June 1943, Keynes thought it quite uncertain whether the USA was 'going to run after the war an enormous credit balance after having allowed for long-term capital movements'.[471] By early 1946, he was optimistic that 'the chances of the dollar becoming dangerously scarce in the course of the next five to ten years are not very high'.[472]

In his CU plans and subsequent negotiations, Keynes sought a privileged position for the USA and Britain as joint founders of the proposed institutions.[473] Other countries which conformed to certain general principles and standards of international economic conduct could be admitted. Keynes conceived of the management and the effective voting power in the Clearing Bank as being 'permanently Anglo-American'. The special powers envisaged for the two founder states included the power to change the value of bancor in terms of gold.[474] Some Ministers were concerned that the importance of Soviet Russia was not being adequately recognized.[475] Under influence from South African, Indian, and other interlocutors,[476] and given the growing realization of the possibility of American dominance (especially under the White proposals), the provision for founder states was gradually weakened, and tactfully eliminated from the White Paper published in April 1943.[477] Indeed, the White Paper said that the 'management of the institution must be genuinely international without preponderant power of veto or enforcement to any country or group; and the rights and privileges of the smaller countries

---

[469] Vol. 25, pp. 19, 17.   [470] Vol. 25, pp. 114–15.   [471] Vol. 25, p. 325.
[472] Vol. 25, p. 444.
[473] Vol. 25, p. 88; see also pp. 45, 60–1, 92, 134.
[474] Vol. 25, pp. 86, 129.
[475] For example, War Cabinet Committee on Reconstruction Problems, 31 Mar. 1942: CAB/87/2, PRO.
[476] For example, Report on 'Post-War Economic Talks', p. 13, RG19, vol. 3989, file T-2–9–2, PAC.
[477] Cf. vol. 25, pp. 171, 449, 453, 459.

must be safeguarded'.[478] The USA was less interested in sharing power with the UK, and sought at times to dilute the British role in negotiations by consulting more widely.[479]

Increasingly, Keynes advocated Anglo-American cooperation as the deliberate and conscious alternative to focus on the Empire. In late 1941 and early 1942, he counselled that promoting 'proposals for an increased solidarity and significance for the British Commonwealth or the sterling area in isolation from the rest of the world' would arouse American prejudice and suspicion. Keynes then found such schemes the most attractive alternative to his international scheme; but they ran 'the risk of isolating ourselves from the United States and the rest of the world without real security that we had constructed a reliable economic union within the Empire'. 'Such proposals must be ancillary to, and part of, a more general international scheme.'[480] Schemes for Empire-based trading and monetary arrangements, promoted by such figures as Leo Amery and Lord Beaverbrook and within the Bank of England,[481] emerged increasingly sharply as the alternative to the international schemes based on Anglo-American cooperation which Keynes was promoting, and he opposed them with vigour and scorn.[482] He said in May 1944 that Britain could not 'on those terms remain a great power and the mother of a Commonwealth'.[483] Just as it was necessary for Keynes and others to persuade many Americans of the importance of international action based on Anglo-American cooperation, so it was necessary to persuade many in Britain. The battle was hard fought and at times, such as during the hostile reaction to the US loan, seemed close to being lost.[484]

6.8 CONCLUSION AND EPILOGUE

Chapter 5 suggested a view of Keynes's approach to trade from 1936, and perhaps before, until his death: his support for unimpeded trade was contingent upon stable full employment. By the end of 1945, Keynesian ideas were widely accepted, and major trading nations were committed to full or high employment;[485] an international monetary system had been created which enabled exchange rate adjustments in the face of fundamental

---

[478] Vol. 25, pp. 234–5.   [479] For example, prior to the April 1944 Joint Statement.

[480] Vol. 25, pp. 43–4, 70–1, 109–10.

[481] See, e.g. vol. 25, pp. 409–10, 415–8; Amery, *Empire at Bay*, pp. 922–32.

[482] See also, e.g. vol. 25, pp. 445–7.   [483] Vol. 26, p. 21; see also, e.g. p. 180.

[484] For example, Robinson, 'Keynes', pp. 63–4; Skidelsky, *Fighting*, ch. 12.

[485] For optimism on American employment: vol. 27, p. 436.

disequilibrium, and provided relief from balance of payments difficulties; Britain's current payments position was being fortified by the US loan, and it appeared to Keynes that the USA was moving from its permanent creditor position which he believed had done so much harm.[486] Keynes thus believed the circumstances were safe for internationally agreed movement under the Washington proposals towards non-discrimination and reduction of trade barriers, while retaining national safeguards. That is, he supported what we have called qualified free trade.

In Jacob Viner's words, the package of post-war measures which Keynes championed was in harmony with liberal nineteenth-century doctrine, but went beyond it in requiring an active role for governments in the international economic field.[487] In our terms, it was a form of liberal institutionalism. Viner, an economic internationalist who believed that Keynes had done much damage in the inter-war years, applauded his efforts to 'promote a postwar world in which peace, freedom and plenty can all prevail'.[488]

Not all went smoothly, however. In January 1946, Keynes attacked the 'slopping away' of the US loan on Britain's overseas political commitments, and called again for greater economy.[489] The attempt to restore convertibility in July 1947 led to a run on the pound, dollars draining away at an unsustainable rate, forcing suspension of convertibility in August.[490] Britain had not sought postponement of the convertibility attempt.[491] Not least because of that premature experiment and the Reconstruction Bank's inadequate resources, the Bretton Woods institutions failed to achieve their principal purposes in the immediate post-war years.[492] The ITO was not founded. Nonetheless, a 'temporary' General Agreement on Tariffs and Trade—forerunner of the World Trade Organization which came into being in 1995—pursued some of the ITO's purposes and, in this and other ways, much of the liberal internationalist vision of Keynes and others became 'embedded'.[493]

Amongst the reasons for this was the Marshall Plan. Hansen later said that Keynes had been right to believe that post-war rehabilitation depended upon 'vast advances' by the USA. Keynes had proposed doing this through the CU; in fact it came, 'not by expansion of central bank credit, but by appropriation

---

[486] See, e.g. vol. 27, p. 429.

[487] J. Viner, 'International Finance in the Post-War World', *Lloyds Bank Review*, no. 2 (Oct. 1946), 3–4.

[488] J. Viner, review of Mantoux, *Journal of Modern History*, 19 (1947), 69–70.

[489] Vol. 27, p. 463 ff.

[490] See, e.g. Cairncross, *Recovery*, ch. 6.

[491] Harrod, *Life*, p. 717; Robbins, *Autobiography*, p. 209; cf. Cairncross, *Recovery*, pp. 138–40.

[492] See, e.g. Gardner, *Sterling–Dollar*, chs. 15–17.

[493] For example, G. J. Ikenberry, 'Rethinking the Origins of American Hegemony', *Political Science Quarterly*, 104 (1989), 397.

voted by Congress'.[494] The reasons for the US taking so different an approach to European reconstruction in 1947 compared to 1919 include, of course, the development of the cold war. But it is clear that Marshall and some, at least, of those who advised him had the experience following the First World War much in mind.[495] Bernard Baruch,[496] Herbert Hoover,[497] and John Foster Dulles,[498] all active after the First World War in encouraging American involvement in European rehabilitation, were again in 1947 urging such involvement. It is not certain what influence, if any, Keynes's past writings or activities had on the belief that major American involvement in European reconstruction was essential. A survey of papers relating to the formation of the Marshall Plan does not reveal evidence of direct reference to Keynes by Marshall or his advisers.[499] As Hervé Alphand later observed, the 'conceptions which inspired' the Marshall Plan were 'in the air' before Marshall's famous speech in June 1947.[500]

[494] A. Hansen, *The Dollar and the International Monetary System* (New York, 1965), p. 154.

[495] 'Washington Birthday Remarks', Princeton, 22 Feb. 1947, box 157, folder 7, GCMP; see also, e.g. Acheson interview, H. B. Price papers, box 3, folder 45, Marshall Research Library. For Marshall's interest in inter-war reparations: Marshall to Charles Dawes, 30 June 1939, box 63, folder 21, GCMP.

[496] Baruch to Marshall, 19 May 1947; Marshall to Baruch, 22 May, box 57, folder 18, GCMP; see also, e.g. Baruch to Marshall, 10 June 1949, box 57, file 24, GCMP. On Baruch's hostility to Keynes: Moggridge, *Biography*, p. 743; Penrose, *Economic Planning* p. 276n.

[497] See, e.g. H. L. Stimson to Truman, 26 June 1947, box 86, folder 16, GCMP.

[498] Dulles speech to Nat. Publishers Assoc. urging European unity, 17 Jan. 1947; Dulles to Marshall, 9 Feb., to P. Hutchinson, 24 June, to E. Maher, 22 Nov., box 32, JFDP.

[499] The key papers are at the George C. Marshall Research Library, Lexington, Virginia.

[500] Alphand speech, 5 June 1967, MS 106, ERP Commem., box 1, folder 4, Marshall Research Library.

7

Conclusion

We have traced the evolution of Keynes's ideas through four phases: first, when he adhered to the classical liberal doctrine on free trade and peace; second, after the First World War, when he combined this view with the belief that international action was needed to restart the European economy and to manage interdependence to ensure stability, an approach we have described as early liberal institutionalism; third, when he espoused greater national self-sufficiency in the early 1930s in the belief that this would promote peace; and fourth, when he expounded the mature liberal institutionalism of *The General Theory* and beyond, believing that the achievement of full employment through coordinated domestic policies, within a suitable international monetary framework, would eliminate the principal economic cause of war, allow trade to be again unimpeded, and so enhance the prospects of peace.

These ideas underpinned Keynes's approach to reconstruction after both world wars. There are strong parallels in his approaches to the two periods of reconstruction. After both wars, he wished to remove or avoid the 'paper bonds' of war debts and excessive reparation demands which would shackle the international economy; to ensure immediate and adequate post-war relief to prevent starvation and anarchy; and to mobilize sufficient finance—especially US lending—to restart the European economy. In both cases, he urged the re-incorporation of the defeated enemy in an interdependent international economy, rather than the destruction of its economic base—indeed, accepting that it would need to resume a leadership role. He wished after both wars to construct a new international monetary system, and to have a high (though in 1945, qualified) degree of freedom of trade, with appropriate domestic policies in individual states.

Keynes's economics after the First World War were classical, stressing sound finance to defeat inflation; after the Second World War, his economics were Keynesian, and while he wished to avoid inflation, he especially sought to ensure full, or at least high, employment. Keynes's publications after the First World War (less radical than his more private advocacy) set out an essentially restorative programme; during the Second World War, he worked to prevent a return to the *status quo ante*, and to create instead a new international economic order based on elaborate international organization. He gave more attention then to the political aspects of maintaining international order than he had after the First World War. The policies of the western powers during and after the Second World War were much more along the lines he advocated than had been the case after the First World War.

Throughout his adult life, while seeking to defend British interests, Keynes was an advocate of close Anglo-American relations, seeing this closeness and the economic and political leadership of Britain and the USA as vital for broader international harmony. Both world wars saw major shifts of financial and therefore political power from Britain to the USA. Keynes watched those shifts with some anguish, and worked hard to minimize them. In both cases, he looked to the USA, on whose power so much depended, to implement his post-war visions. After the First World War, appeals from him and others for American leadership and generosity went unheeded. During and after the Second World War, despite difficulties, Anglo-American cooperation (much influenced by Keynes's thinking) laid the basis for post-war economic internationalism.

That Keynes worked during the Second World War to give effect to the economic ideas he had developed between the wars, and thereby create an economic basis for lasting peace, reflected the fact that he was an idealist as well as a technical expert. The ideal of free trade as a policy for peace, to which Keynes had adhered from his youth until the start of the 1930s, and to which he later partially reverted, had been a central tenet of nineteenth and early-twentieth century liberal idealism in international relations. Keynes's idealism was evident in the inter-war years in his support for the project of creating a rule of law in international politics through the League of Nations, as well as in his advocacy of international economic organization as a means both to prosperity and to greater international harmony.

A central element of Keynes's idealism was the view that there are important economic causes of conflict between states, but that these could be remedied. He also believed at times, not only that the economic causes of conflict could be eliminated, but that certain economic measures, such as the creation of a free trade union, might themselves actively foster political harmony. We have seen that Keynes's understanding of the economic causes of international conflict, and of the economic means to promote greater harmony, varied over time. He identified a variety of economic causes of conflict: impoverishment, or inflation, or even growing profits, generating domestic political disorder or extremism, resulting in international tension; population pressure which does the same, or leads a nation to seek to expand its living space, or (as he thought in 1914 might result) to 'racial wars'; the competitive struggle for markets arising from the need to export more and import less in order to overcome unemployment in the face of a tight balance of payments constraint; entanglements of finance, of large-scale debts creating friction, and their forgiveness encouraging solidarity, and the danger of capital flight constraining the capacity of states to maintain the high employment on which domestic and international order depend. Keynes sometimes advocated free, or at least non-discriminatory, trade—for example, in 1903 and again in 1945—because the alternative, exclusionist economic blocs, would cause friction and animosity. Sometimes it was the role of free trade in maintaining living standards, and hence domestic political order, that Keynes stressed; sometimes the creation by trade of vested interests in peace; and sometimes a more nebulous hint that trade promoted international solidarity.

At Bretton Woods in July 1944, Keynes seconded a motion from the Belgian delegate, Georges Theunis, on the creation of the IBRD. Keynes recalled that just days before the Armistice in 1918, he and Theunis 'travelled together through Belgium behind the retreating German Armies to form an immediate personal impression of the needs of reconstruction in his country after that war. No such Bank as that which we now hope to create was in prospect.'[1]

Keynes continued:

After the last war the most dreadful mistakes were made. It is with some emotion that I find myself today collaborating with my old friend to try to bring to birth an institution which may play a major part in restoring the devastation of a second war, and in bringing back to a life of peace and abundant fruitfulness those great European and Asiatic parents of civilisation to which all the world owes so much.

In April 1945, Felix Frankfurter wrote to Keynes that, sharing his 'feeling of the awfulness of the tasks that lie ahead once organized German resistance is over', he doubted if there were 'an adequate realization of the nature of those tasks and the demands their solution will make of wisdom, generosity and patience'.

On the other hand, I find one very important factor favoring a more decent unfolding of world affairs that was wholly absent when you and I had our heartaches twenty-five years ago in Paris. A much more permeating and informed realization exists of the extraordinary difficulties of peacefully evolving a decent world order.[2]

To that realization, there is little doubt that Keynes contributed much.

---

[1] Vol. 26, pp. 100–1.
[2] Frankfurter to Keynes, 3 Apr. 1945, box 72 (reel 44), Frankfurter papers, LOC.

Select Bibliography

At present a bibliographer takes pride in numerous entries; but he would be a more useful fellow, and the labours of research would be lightened, if he could practise deletion and bring into existence an accredited *Index Expurgatorius*. But this can only be accomplished by the slow mills of the collective judgment of the learned ...

J. M. Keynes, *A Treatise on Probability*[1]

Unpublished papers

(a) UK

Bodleian Library, Oxford (H. H. Asquith; R. H. Brand; Lord Bryce; Gilbert Murray; Sir John Simon; Sir Alfred Zimmern; miscellaneous).

British Library, London (Sir William Ashley; A. J. Balfour).

Cambridge University Library (J. N. Keynes incidentals).

King's College Library, Cambridge (J. M. Keynes papers, some previously at Marshall Library, Cambridge; *Keynes's Lecture Notes by Robert B. Bryce*, transcribed by T. K. Rymes).

Public Record Office (now the National Archives), Kew, London (Cabinet Office; Ministry of Reconstruction; Treasury).

(b) USA

Beinecke Library, Yale (*The Yale Review*).

Columbia University Library, New York (J. M. Clark; E. R. A. Seligman; miscellaneous).

Franklin D. Roosevelt Library, Hyde Park, NY (President's Personal and Official Files; A. A. Berle; Henry Morgenthau Diaries; John G. Winant; incidentals).

George C. Marshall Research Library, Lexington, Va. (George C. Marshall; interviews by Harry B. Price with Marshall, Kennan, et al.; European Recovery Plan Commemoratives).

Hoover Institution Archives, Stanford (American Relief Administration, Paris; Herbert Hoover; Inter-Allied Food Council; James A. Logan; Louis Loucheur; incidentals).

Houghton Library, Harvard (Corinne Roosevelt Robinson; miscellaneous).

Library of Congress, Washington, DC (T. H. Bliss; W. E. Borah; Bainbridge Colby; Oscar Crosby; Norman Davis; Herbert Feis; Felix Frankfurter; Emanuel Goldenweiser; Harold Ickes; Robert Lansing; Eugene Meyer; Leo Pasvolsky; Henry White; miscellaneous).

---

[1] Vol. 8, pp. 472–3.

Massachusetts Historical Society, Boston (Henry Cabot Lodge).

Seeley G. Mudd Library, Princeton (Hamilton Fish Armstrong; Bernard Baruch; Arthur Bullard; Clifford Carver; John Foster Dulles, including oral history transcripts; Raymond B. Fosdick; Charles Homer Haskins; Fred I. Kent; Robert Lansing; Jacob Viner; Harry Dexter White; miscellaneous).

Sterling Memorial Library, Yale (Gordon Auchinloss; John W. Davis; Irving Fisher; Colonel E. M. House; R. C. Leffingwell; Walter Lippmann; Vance McCormick; Charles Seymour; Paul M. Warburg; miscellaneous).

University of Virginia, Charlottesville (Carter Glass; E. R. Stettinius, Snr; E. R. Stettinius, Jnr; David McCord Wright; miscellaneous).

(c) Canada

Public Archives of Canada, Ottawa (economic discussions during the Second World War).

(d) Australia

Reserve Bank of Australia, Sydney (economic discussions during the Second World War).

National Library of Australia, Canberra (Novar papers).

Published papers

(a) The Collected Writings of John Maynard Keynes (London and Basingstoke, 1971–89)

Vol. 1 *Indian Currency and Finance* (1913).

Vol. 2 *The Economic Consequences of the Peace* (1919).

Vol. 3 *A Revision of the Treaty* (1922).

Vol. 4 *A Tract on Monetary Reform* (1923).

Vol. 5 *A Treatise on Money*, i, *The Pure Theory of Money* (1930).

Vol. 6 *A Treatise on Money*, ii, *The Applied Theory of Money* (1930).

Vol. 7 *The General Theory of Employment, Interest and Money* (1936).

Vol. 8 *A Treatise on Probability* (1921).

Vol. 9 *Essays in Persuasion* (with additional essays) (1931).

Vol. 10 *Essays in Biography* (with additional writings) (1933).

Vol. 11 *Economic Articles and Correspondence: Academic.*

Vol. 12 *Economic Articles and Correspondence: Investment and Editorial.*

Vol. 13 *The General Theory and After: Part I, Preparation.*

Vol. 14 *The General Theory and After: Part II, Defence and Development.*

Vol. 15 *Activities 1906–14: India and Cambridge.*

Vol. 16 *Activities 1914–19: The Treasury and Versailles.*

Vol. 17 *Activities 1920–2: Treaty Revision and Reconstruction.*

Vol. 18 *Activities 1922–32: The End of Reparations.*

Vol. 19 *Activities 1922–9: The Return to Gold and Industrial Policy.*

Vol. 20 *Activities 1929–31: Rethinking Employment and Unemployment Policies.*

Vol. 21 *Activities 1931–9: World Crises and Policies in Britain and America.*
Vol. 22 *Activities 1939–45: Internal War Finance.*
Vol. 23 *Activities 1940–3: External War Finance.*
Vol. 24 *Activities 1944–6: The Transition to Peace.*
Vol. 25 *Activities 1940–4: Shaping the Post-War World: The Clearing Union.*
Vol. 26 *Activities 1941–6: Shaping the Post-War World: Bretton Woods and Reparations.*
Vol. 27 *Activities 1940–6: Shaping the Post-War World: Employment and Commodities.*
Vol. 28 *Social, Political and Literary Writings.*
Vol. 29 *The General Theory and After: A Supplement.*
Vol. 30 *Bibliography and Index* (with some additional material).

(b) Others

Dept. of State, *Foreign Relations of the United States (FRUS)* (Washington, DC, various dates).
Cmd. 6437: *Proposals for an International Clearing Union* (London, 1943).
Cmd. 6597: *United Nations Monetary and Financial Conference [Bretton Woods, 1944], Documents Supplementary to the Final Act* (London, 1945).
Cmd. 6708: *Financial Agreement between The Governments of the United States and the United Kingdom* (London, 1945).
Cmd. 6709: *Proposals for Consideration by an International Conference on Trade and Employment* (London, 1945).
Documents Relating to the United Nations Monetary and Financial Conference (Canberra, 1944).
Economic Conditions in Central Europe (1), Misc. Series No. 1, Despatch from Sir William Goode (Parliamentary paper, London, 1920).
A. Marshall, *Memorandum on the Fiscal Policy of International Trade*, Aug. 1903, revised Aug. 1908 (Parliamentary paper, London, 11 Nov. 1908).

Interviews

H. W. Arndt, D. G. Badger, T. J. Bartley, Judy Butlin, H. C. Coombs, Ernest Eyers, J. M. Garland, Lord Kahn, J. B. Kirkwood, Sir James Meade, Sir Leslie Melville, Sir John Philips, Lady Philips, Louis Rasminsky, W. B. Reddaway, Sir Frederick Wheeler.

Serials

The Annual Register (AR)
The Economic Journal (EJ)
The Manchester Guardian
New Statesman and Nation (NS)
Survey of International Affairs
The Times

Theses

Brose, E., 'Adam Smith's View of International Relations', M.Phil. thesis (Oxford, 1983).

Hufton, N., 'The World Economic Conference, 1933: Signpost or Turning Point?', M.Phil. thesis (Oxford, 1987).

Mansfield, L. P., 'The Origins of the International Monetary Fund', Ph.D. thesis (University of North Carolina, 1960).

May, A. C., 'The Round Table, 1910–66', D.Phil. thesis (Oxford, 1995).

Mumpers, J. R., 'Keynes at the Paris Peace Conference', MA thesis (University of Virginia, 1961).

Articles and Books

Acheson, D., *Sketches from Life* (London, 1961).

—— *Present at the Creation* (New York, 1970).

Ambrosius, L. E., *Woodrow Wilson and the American Diplomatic Tradition: The Treaty Fight in Perspective* (Cambridge, 1987).

Amery, L., *The Empire at Bay: The Leo Amery Diaries, 1929–1945*, ed. J. Barnes and D. Nicholson (London, 1988).

Angell, N., *The Great Illusion* (3rd edn., London, 1911).

—— *The Foundations of International Polity* (London, 1914).

—— *The Peace Treaty and the Economic Chaos of Europe* (London, 1919).

—— *The Economic Functions of the League* (London, 1920).

—— *The Fruits of Victory: A Sequel to 'The Great Illusion'* (London, 1921).

—— *Human Nature and the Peace Problem* (London, 1925).

—— 'The New John Bull', *Political Quarterly*, 7 (1936), 311–29.

—— *The Great Illusion—Now* (London, 1938).

—— *After All* (London, 1951).

Arndt, H. W., *The Economic Lessons of the 1930s* (London, 1972).

Ashworth, L. M., *Creating International Studies: Angell, Mitrany and the Liberal Tradition* (Aldershot, 1999).

Ayer, A. J., *Russell and Moore: The Analytical Heritage* (London, 1971).

Baldwin, D., *Economic Statecraft* (Princeton, 1985).

Balogh, T., *Unequal Partners*, ii (Oxford, 1963).

—— and Graham, A., 'The Transfer Problem Revisited: Analogies between the Reparations Payments of the 1920s and the Problem of the OPEC Surpluses', *Oxford Bulletin of Economics and Statistics*, 41 (1979), 183–9.

Barnett, C., *The Collapse of British Power* (New York, 1972).

Bateman, B. W., and Davis, J. B. (eds.), *Keynes and Philosophy* (Aldershot, 1991).

Bell, C., *Civilisation* (London, 1928).

—— *Old Friends: Personal Recollections* (London, 1956).

Best, J., 'Hollowing out Keynesian Norms: How the Search for a Technical Fix Undermined the Bretton Woods Regime', *Review of International Studies*, 30 (2004), 383–404.

Beveridge, W. H., *Full Employment in a Free Society* (London, 1944).

—— *The Price of Peace* (London, 1945).

—— et al., *Tariffs: The Case Examined* (London, 1931).

Bird, G., *The International Monetary System and the Less Developed Countries* (London and Basingstoke, 1982).

Bishop, E., *A Virginia Woolf Chronology* (Basingstoke and London, 1989).

Blum, J. M., *From the Morgenthau Diaries: Years of Urgency, 1938–1941* (Boston, 1965).

Boemeke, M. F., Feldman, G. D., and Glaser, E. (eds.), *The Treaty of Versailles: A Reassessment after 75 Years* (Washington, DC, and Cambridge, UK, 1998).

Bolton, G., 'Where Critics are as Wrong as Keynes was', *The Banker*, 122 (1972), 1385–7.

Bonar, J., *Malthus and His Work* (London, 1885).

Brailsford, H. N., *The War of Steel and Gold* (London, 1914).

—— *Property or Peace?* (London, 1934).

—— *Why Capitalism Means War* (London, 1938).

—— *The Life-Work of J. A. Hobson* (London, 1948).

—— , Hobson, J. A., Creech Jones, A., and Wise, E. F., *The Living Wage* (London, 1926).

[Brand, R. H.], 'Lombard Street and War', *The Round Table*, 2 (1912), 246–84.

Brandon, L. G., *J. M. Keynes* (London, 1972).

Brinton, H. (ed.), *Does Capitalism Cause War?* (London, 1935).

Bull, H., 'Richard Cobden and International Relations', seminar paper, LSE, 1956.

—— *Strategic Arms Limitation: The Precedent of the Washington and London Naval Treaties* (Chicago, 1971).

—— 'The Theory of International Politics, 1919–1969', in Porter, B. (ed.), *The Aberystwyth Papers* (London, 1972).

—— *The Anarchical Society* (London and Basingstoke, 1977).

—— and Watson, A. (eds.), *The Expansion of International Society* (Oxford, 1984).

Burk, K., 'J. M. Keynes and the Exchange Rate Crisis of July 1917', *Economic History Review*, 32 (1979), 405–16.

—— (ed.), *War and the State: The Transformation of British Government, 1914–1919* (London, 1982).

—— *Britain, America and the Sinews of War, 1914–1918* (Boston, 1985).

—— *Morgan Grenfell, 1838–1988: The Biography of a Merchant Bank* (Oxford, 1989).

Burke, E., *The Works of the Right Honourable Edmund Burke*, iii (London, 1815).

Burns, J. McG., *Roosevelt: The Soldier of Freedom, 1940–1945* (London, 1971).

Cairncross, A., *Years of Recovery: British Economic Policy, 1945–51* (London, 1985).

—— *Austin Robinson: The Life of an Economic Adviser* (Basingstoke and London, 1993).

—— 'John Maynard Keynes', *Oxford Dictionary of National Biography*, vol. 31 (Oxford, 2004), pp. 483–98.

Cairncross, A., and Watts, N., *The Economic Section, 1939–1961: A Study in Economic Advising* (London and New York, 1989).

Campbell, J., 'The Renewal of Liberalism: Liberalism without the Liberals', in Peele, G., and Cook, C. (eds.), *The Politics of Reappraisal* (London and Basingstoke, 1975).

Carr, E. H., *The Conditions of Peace* (London, 1942).

—— *The Twenty Years' Crisis* (2nd edn. 1946; London and Basingstoke, 1983).

Carr-Saunders, A. M., *World Population* (Oxford, 1936).

Ceadel, M. E., *Pacifism in Britain, 1914–1945* (Oxford, 1980).

—— *Thinking about Peace and War* (Oxford, 1987).

—— *Semi-Detached Idealists: the British Peace Movement and International Relations, 1854–1945* (Oxford, 2000).

Chandavarkar, A., *Keynes and India* (London, 1989).

Churchill, W. S., *The Second World War*, i, *The Gathering Storm* (London, 1949).

—— *The Second World War*, vi, *Triumph and Tragedy* (London, 1954).

Clarke, P., *Liberals and Social Democrats* (Cambridge, 1978).

—— *The Keynesian Revolution in the Making, 1924–1936* (Oxford, 1988).

Clarke, R., *Anglo-American Economic Collaboration in War and Peace, 1942–1949*, ed. A. Cairncross (Oxford, 1982).

Cooper, R. N., *The Economics of Interdependence* (New York, 1968).

Crabtree, D., and Thirlwall, A. P. (eds.), *Keynes and the Bloomsbury Group* (London and Basingstoke, 1980).

Crozier, A., *Appeasement and Germany's Last Bid for Colonies* (London and Basingstoke, 1988).

Dallek, R., *Franklin Roosevelt and American Foreign Policy, 1932–1945* (New York, 1979).

Dalton, H., *High Tide and After* (London, 1962).

Davies, D., *The Problem of the Twentieth Century* (London, 1930).

Deighton, A., *The Impossible Peace: Britain, the Division of Germany, and the Origins of the Cold War* (Oxford, 1990).

Dickinson, G. L., *The Choice Before Us* (London, 1918 [1917]).

—— *The International Anarchy, 1904–1914* (London, 1937 [1926]).

—— *The Autobiography of Goldsworthy Lowes Dickinson*, ed. D. Proctor (London, 1973).

Dillard, D., *The Economics of John Maynard Keynes* (London, 1958).

Divine, R. A., *Second Chance: The Triumph of Internationalism in America During World War II* (New York, 1971).

Dobb, M., review of J. Strachey's *The Nature of Capitalist Crisis*, *Political Quarterly*, 6 (1935), 441–3.

Drinkwater, D., *Sir Harold Nicolson and International Relations: The Practitioner as Theorist* (Oxford, 2005).

Dulles, J. F., 'The Reparation Problem', *The New Republic*, 30 Mar. 1921.

—— 'The Reparation Problem', *The Literary Review*, 6 Aug. 1921.

Eden, A., *Memoirs, The Reckoning* (London, 1965).

Fawcett, H., *Free Trade and Protection* (4th edn., London, 1881).

—— *Manual of Political Economy* (6th edn., London, 1883).

Ferguson, N., *Paper and Iron: Hamburg business and German politics in the era of inflation, 1897–1927* (Cambridge, 1995).

—— 'Let Germany Keep Its Nerve', *The Spectator*, 22 Apr. 1995, 21–3.

—— 'Keynes and German Inflation', *English Historical Review*, 110 (1995), 368–91.

—— *The Pity of War* (London, 1998).

Fitzgibbons, A., *Keynes's Vision: A New Political Economy* (Oxford, 1988).

Forster, E. M., *Goldsworthy Lowes Dickinson* (London, 1962 [1934]).

Fosdick, R. B., *Letters on the League of Nations* (Princeton, 1966).

Freeden, M., *Liberalism Divided: A Study in British Political Thought, 1914–1939* (Oxford, 1986).

Furniss, H. Sanderson, review of N. Angell's *The Peace Treaty and the Economic Chaos of Europe*, *EJ*, 30 (1920), 84–5.

Gannon, F. R., *The British Press and Germany, 1936–1939* (Oxford, 1971).

Gardner, R., *Sterling–Dollar Diplomacy in Current Perspective* (New York, 1980).

Garvin, J. L., *The Economic Foundations of Peace* (London, 1919).

Gide, C., *Principles of Political Economy* (London, 1909 [English, 1899]).

Glass, D. V. (ed.), *Introduction to Malthus* (London, 1959).

Gray, J., *Liberalism* (Milton Keynes, 1986).

Hall, P. A. (ed.), *The Political Power of Economic Ideas: Keynesianism Across Nations* (Princeton, 1989).

Hamouda, O. F., and Smithin, J. N. (eds.), *Keynes and Public Policy After Fifty Years*, i, *Economics and Policy* (Aldershot, 1988).

Hancock, W. K., and Gowing, M. M., *British War Economy* (London, 1949).

Hansen, A., *A Guide to Keynes* (New York, 1953).

—— *The Dollar and the International Monetary System* (New York, 1965).

Harris, J., *William Beveridge: A Biography* (Oxford, 1977).

Harris, S. E. (ed.), *The New Economics* (London, 1948).

—— *John Maynard Keynes: Economist and Policy Maker* (New York, 1955).

Harrod, R. F., *The Life of John Maynard Keynes* (London, 1972 [1951]).

—— 'Clive Bell on Keynes', *EJ*, 67 (1957), 692–9.

—— 'A Comment', *EJ*, 70 (1960), 166–7.

—— *Reforming the World's Money* (London, 1965).

—— and Robinson, E. A. G., 'John Maynard Keynes', *EJ*, 56 (1946), 171.

Hayek, F. A., *The Road to Serfdom* (London, 1944).

Headlam-Morley, J., *A Memoir of the Paris Peace Conference, 1919*, ed. A. Headlam-Morley, R. Bryant, and A. Cienciala (London, 1972).

Heckscher, E., *Mercantilism* (2 vols. London, 1935).

Hession, C. H., *John Maynard Keynes: A Personal Biography* (New York, 1984).

Hilderbrand, R. C., *Dumbarton Oaks: The Origins of the United Nations and the Search for Postwar Security* (Chapel Hill and London, 1990).

Hill, P., and Keynes, R. (eds.), *Lydia and Maynard* (London, 1989).

Hinsley, F. H., *Power and the Pursuit of Peace* (Cambridge, 1967).

Hobson, J. A., *Imperialism* (3rd edn., London, 1938 [1902]).

Hobson, J. A., *Democracy After the War* (London, 1917).

—— *Free Thought in the Social Sciences* (London, 1926).

—— *Confessions of an Economic Heretic* (London, 1938).

Holborn, L. (ed.), *War and Peace Aims of the United Nations, September 1, 1939–December 31, 1942* (Boston, 1943).

Horsefield, J. K., *The International Monetary Fund, 1945–1965*, i (Washington, 1969).

Howard, M., *War and the Liberal Conscience* (Oxford, 1981).

Howson, S., and Winch, D., *The Economic Advisory Council, 1930–1939* (Cambridge, 1977).

—— and Moggridge, D. E. (eds.), *The Wartime Diaries of Lionel Robbins and James Meade, 1943–45* (Basingstoke and London, 1990).

Hull, C., *Memoirs* (2 vols. London, 1948).

Hutchison, T. W., *Keynes versus the 'Keynesians'...?* (London, 1977).

Hyams, E., *The New Statesman* (London, 1963).

Ikenberry, G. J., 'Rethinking the Origins of American Hegemony', *Political Science Quarterly*, 104 (1989), 375–400.

Johnson, E. S., 'Keynes' Attitude to Compulsory Military Service', *EJ*, 70 (1960), 160–5.

—— and Johnson, H. G., *The Shadow of Keynes* (Oxford, 1978).

Johnson, H. G., 'The Classical Transfer Problem: An Alternative Formulation', *Economica*, 42 (1975), 20–31.

Kadish, A., *Historians, Economists, and Economic History* (London, 1989).

Kahn, R. F., *The Making of Keynes' General Theory* (Cambridge, 1984).

Kent, B., *The Spoils of War: The Politics, Economics, and Diplomacy of Reparations 1918–1932* (Oxford, 1989).

Keohane, R., *After Hegemony* (Princeton, 1984).

—— 'International Liberalism Reconsidered', in Dunn, J. (ed.), *The Economic Limits to Modern Politics* (Cambridge, 1990).

—— and Nye, J., *Power and Interdependence* (Boston, 1977).

Keynes, G., *The Gates of Memory* (Oxford, 1983).

Keynes, J. N., *The Scope and Method of Political Economy* (3rd edn., London, 1904).

Keynes, M. (ed.), *Essays on John Maynard Keynes* (Cambridge, 1975).

Kindleberger, C. P., *The World in Depression, 1929–39* (Berkeley, 1973).

King's College, Cambridge, *John Maynard Keynes, 1883–1946, Fellow and Bursar*, A Memoir prepared by direction of the Council of King's College (Cambridge, 1949).

Klein, L. R., *The Keynesian Revolution* (2nd edn., London and Basingstoke, 1968).

Kramnick, I., and Sheerman, B., *Harold Laski: A Life on the Left* (London, 1993).

Langer, W. L., and Gleason, S. E., *The Undeclared War, 1940–1941* (Gloucester, MA., 1968).

League of Nations, *International Credits: The 'Ter Meulen' scheme* (London, n.d.: 1921?).

—— *Ten Years of World Cooperation* (no place given, 1930).

Lekachman, R., *The Age of Keynes* (New York, 1968).

Levin, N. G., *Woodrow Wilson and World Politics* (Oxford, 1968).

Lippmann, W., *U.S. Foreign Policy* (London, 1943).

Littleboy, B., 'Keynes versus Leijonhufvud', Economic Society of Australia and New Zealand conference paper, 1980.

—— *On Interpreting Keynes: A Study in Reconciliation* (London and New York, 1990).

Lloyd George, D., *The Truth About the Peace Treaties* (London, 1938).

Lodge, H. C., *The Senate and the League of Nations* (New York, 1925).

Long, D., 'J. A. Hobson and Idealism in International Relations', *Review of International Studies*, 17 (1991), 285–304.

—— *Towards a New Liberal Internationalism: The International Theory of J. A. Hobson* (Cambridge, 1996).

—— and Wilson, P. (eds.), *Thinkers of the Twenty Years Crisis* (Oxford, 1995).

McFadyean, A., *Reparation Revisited* (London, 1930).

McIntosh, D. C., 'Mantoux versus Keynes: A Note on German Income and the Reparation Controversy', *EJ*, 87 (1977), 765–7.

Macmillan, H., *Reconstruction* (London, 1933).

—— *The Middle Way* (London, 1938).

MacMillan, M., *Peacemakers: The Paris Conference of 1919 and Its Attempt to End War* (London, 2001).

Mantoux, É., *The Carthaginian Peace, or the Economic Consequences of Mr. Keynes* (London, 1946).

Mantoux, P., *The Deliberations of the Council of Four (Mar. 24–June 28, 1919): Notes of the Official Interpreter*, ed. A. S. Link (2 vols. Princeton, 1992).

Markowitz, N. D., *The Rise and Fall of the People's Century: Henry A. Wallace and American Liberalism, 1941–1948* (New York, 1973).

Markwell, D. J., *Keynes and Australia* (Sydney, 2000).

—— 'Sir Alfred Zimmern Revisited: Fifty Years on', *Review of International Studies*, 12 (1986), 279–92.

—— 'British Social Science and Humanities', in T. B. Millar (ed.), *The Australian Contribution to Britain* (London, 1988).

Marshall, A., *Principles of Economics* (5th edn., London, 1907).

—— *Industry and Trade* (London, 1919).

Martin, K., *Editor* (London, 1968).

Mayer, A. J., *Politics and Diplomacy of Peacemaking: Containment and Counterrevolution at Versailles, 1918–1919* (London, 1968).

Meade, J. E., *An Introduction to Economic Analysis and Policy* (Oxford, 1936).

—— *The Economic Basis of a Durable Peace* (London, 1940).

Mehta, G., *The Structure of the Keynesian Revolution* (London, 1977).

Meltzer, A. H., *Keynes's Monetary Theory: A Different Interpretation* (Cambridge, 1988).

Mill, J. S., *Principles of Political Economy* (Toronto, 1965 [1848]).

—— *On Liberty* (London, 1974 [1859]).

Miller, D. H., *My Diary at the Conference of Paris*, i, xvii (privately printed, New York, 1924).

Miller, J. D. B., *Norman Angell and the Futility of War* (London, 1986).

Milward, A. S., *War, Economy and Society, 1939–1945* (London, 1977).

—— *The Reconstruction of Western Europe, 1945–51* (London, 1984).

Minsky, H. P., *John Maynard Keynes* (New York, 1975).

Moggridge, D. E. (ed.), *Keynes: Aspects of the Man and His Work* (London, 1974).

—— *Keynes* (2nd edn., London and Basingstoke, 1980).

—— 'Keynes and the International Monetary System, 1909–46', in Cohen, J. S., and Harcourt, G. C. (eds.), *International Monetary Problems and Supply-Side Economics* (Basingstoke and London, 1986).

—— *Maynard Keynes: An Economist's Biography* (London and New York, 1992).

—— and Howson, S., 'Keynes on Monetary Policy, 1910–1946', *Oxford Economic Papers*, 26 (1974), 226–47.

Nathan, H. L., *Free Trade To-Day* (London, 1929).

Navari C., 'The Great Illusion Revisited: The International Theory of Norman Angell', *Review of International Studies*, 15 (1989), 341–58.

Newman, F. W., *Lectures on Political Economy* (London, 1851).

Nicholas, H. G. (ed.), *Washington Despatches, 1941–1945* (London, 1981).

Nicholson, J. S., *Principles of Political Economy*, iii (London, 1901 and 1908).

Nicolson, H., *Peacemaking 1919* (London, 1934 [1933]).

Nowell-Smith, S. (ed.), *Edwardian England, 1901–1914* (London, 1964).

O'Donnell, R. M., *Keynes: Philosophy, Economics and Politics: The Philosophical Foundations of Keynes's Thought and Their Influence on his Economics and Politics* (Basingstoke and London, 1989).

Ohlin, B., 'The Reparation problem: A Discusson: Transfer Difficulties, Real and Imagined', *EJ*, 39 (1929), 172–8.

—— 'Mr Keynes' Views on the Transfer Problem: A rejoinder', *EJ*, 39 (1929), 440–4.

Osiander, A., 'Rereading Early Twentieth-Century IR Theory: Idealism Revisited', *International Studies Quarterly*, 42 (1998), 409–32.

Parker, A., 'Mantoux v. Keynes', *Lloyds Bank Review*, no. 3 (Jan. 1947), 1–20.

Parker, R. A. C., 'Economics, Rearmament and Foreign Policy: The United Kingdom before 1939—A Preliminary Survey', *Journal of Contemporary History*, 10 (1975), 637–47.

—— 'British rearmament 1936–9: Treasury, Trade Unions and Skilled Labour', *English Historical Review*, 96 (1981), 306–43.

—— 'The Pound Sterling, the American Treasury and British Preparations for War, 1938–1939', *English Historical Review*, 98 (1983), 261–79.

—— *Struggle for Survival: The History of the Second World War* (Oxford, 1990).

—— *Chamberlain and Appeasement* (Basingstoke and London, 1993).

Patinkin, D., *Keynes's Monetary Thought* (Durham, NC, 1976).

—— *Anticipations of the General Theory?* (Oxford, 1982).

—— and Leith, J. C. (eds.), *Keynes, Cambridge and 'The General Theory'* (London and Basingstoke, 1977).

Peden, G. C., *British Rearmament and the Treasury, 1932–1939* (Edinburgh, 1979).

—— *Keynes, The Treasury and British Economic Policy* (Basingstoke and London, 1988).

Penrose, E. F., *Economic Planning for the Peace* (Princeton, 1953).

Perris, G. H., *A Short History of War and Peace* (London, n.d.: 1911?).

—— *Our Foreign Policy and Sir Edward Grey's Failure* (London, 1912).

—— *The War Traders: An Exposure* (London, 1913).

Pigou, A. C., *The Riddle of the Tariff* (London, 1903).

—— *Protective and Preferential Import Duties* (London, 1906).

Pollock, F., 'The League of Nations and the Coming Rule of Law', in Lord Grey et al., *The League of Nations* (Oxford, 1919).

Porter, B., 'David Davies: A Hunter After Peace', *Review of International Studies*, 15 (1989), 27–36.

Pressnell, L. S., *External Economic Policy Since the War*, i, *The Post-War Financial Settlement* (London, 1986).

Prior, J., *Memoir of the Life and Character of the Right Hon. Edmund Burke*, i (London, 1826).

Renouvin, P., and Duroselle, J-B., *Introduction to the History of International Relations* (London, 1968).

'Reparations Calendar', *Journal of the American Bankers Association*, Mar. 1923, 595–7.

Robbins, L., *Economic Planning and International Order* (London, 1937).

—— *The Economic Causes of War* (London, 1939).

—— *Autobiography of an Economist* (London and Basingstoke, 1971).

—— *Money, Trade and International Relations* (London, 1971).

Robertson, D. H., review of J. M. Keynes's *The Economic Consequences of the Peace*, *EJ*, 30 (1920), 77–84.

—— *Britain in the World Economy* (London, 1954).

Robinson, E. A. G., 'John Maynard Keynes, 1883–1946', *EJ*, 57 (1947), 1–68.

Robinson, J., review of J. Strachey's *The Nature of Capitalist Crisis*, *EJ*, 46 (1936), 298–302.

—— *Economic Philosophy* (London, 1964).

Roll, E., *A History of Economic Thought* (4th edn., London, 1973).

Rolph, C. H., *Kingsley* (London, 1973).

Rothwell, V., *Britain and the Cold War, 1941–1947* (London, 1982).

Rowse, A. L., *Mr. Keynes and the Labour Movement* (London, 1936).

Rueff, J., 'Mr Keynes' Views on the Transfer Problem: A Criticism', *EJ*, 39 (1929), 388–99.

Russell, B., *The Autobiography of Bertrand Russell*, i, *1872–1914* (London, 1967).

—— and Russell, D., *The Prospects of Industrial Civilization* (London, 1923).

Ryan, A., *Bertrand Russell: A Political Life* (New York, 1988).

Rymes, T. K., *Keynes's Lectures, 1932–35: Notes of a Representative Student* (Basingstoke and London, 1989).

Salter, A., *Personality in Politics* (London, 1947).

Samuelson, P., 'The Transfer Problem and Transport Costs: The Terms of Trade When Impediments Are Absent', *EJ*, 62 (1952), 278–304.

Sayers, R. S., *Financial Policy, 1939–45* (London, 1956).

—— 'The Young Keynes', *EJ*, 82 (1972), 591–9.

Schmidt, B. C., 'Lessons from the Past: Reassessing the Interwar Disciplinary History of International Relations', *International Studies Quarterly*, 42 (1998), 433–59.

Schmidt, G., *The Politics and Economics of Appeasement* (Leamington Spa, 1986).

Schumpeter, J. A., *Ten Great Economists* (London, 1952).

Shackle, G. L. S., 'Keynes and Today's Establishment in Economic Theory: A View', *Journal of Economic Literature*, 11 (1973), 516–19.

Shay, R. P., *British Rearmament in the Thirties* (Princeton, 1977).

Sidgwick, H., *The Elements of Politics* (London, 1891).

—— *The Principles of Political Economy* (London, 1891; and 3rd edn., 1901).

Siepmann, H. A., 'The International Financial Conference at Brussels', *EJ*, 30 (1920), 436 ff.

Silberner, E., *The Problem of War in Nineteenth Century Economic Thought* (Princeton, 1946).

Skidelsky, R., *John Maynard Keynes*, i, *Hopes Betrayed, 1883–1920* (London, 1983).

—— *John Maynard Keynes*, ii, *The Economist as Saviour, 1920–1937* (London, 1992).

—— *John Maynard Keynes*, iii, *Fighting for Britain, 1937–1946* (London, 2000).

—— (ed.), *The End of the Keynesian Era* (London, 1977).

Smith, A., *The Wealth of Nations* (ed. E. Cannan, London, 1904).

Staley, E., *War and the Private Investor* (Chicago, 1935).

Steiner, Z., *The Lights that Failed: European International History, 1919–1933* (Oxford, 2005).

Stevenson, D., *The First World War and International Politics* (Oxford, 1988).

Stone, R. A. (ed.), *Wilson and the League of Nations: Why America's Rejection?* (New York, 1967).

—— *The Irreconcilables* (New York, 1973).

Strachey, E. J. St L., *Revolution by Reason* (London, 1925).

—— *The Coming Struggle for Power* (London, 1932).

—— *The Menace of Fascism* (London, 1933).

—— *The Nature of Capitalist Crisis* (London, 1935).

—— *A Programme for Progress* (London, 1940).

Sykes, A., *Tariff Reform in British Politics, 1903–1913* (Oxford, 1979).

Sylvest, C., 'Continuity and Change in British Liberal Internationalism, *c.*1900–1930', *Review of International Studies*, 31 (2005), 263–83.

Taylor, A. J. P., *The Origins of the Second World War* (London, 1973 [1961]).

Thirlwall, A. P. (ed), *Keynes and International Monetary Relations* (London and Basingstoke, 1976).

—— (ed.), *Keynes and Laissez-Faire* (London and Basingstoke, 1978).

—— (ed.), *Keynes as a Policy Adviser* (London and Basingstoke, 1982).

Thomas, H., *John Strachey* (London, 1973).

Thompson, W. S., *Population Problems* (4th edn., New York, 1953).

Thomson, D. (with G. Warner), *England in the Twentieth Century* (London, 1991).

Thorne, C., *The Approach of War, 1938–1939* (London, 1967).

Tillman, S. P., *Anglo-American Relations at the Paris Peace Conference of 1919* (Princeton, 1961).

Toye, J., 'Keynes on Population and Economic Growth', *Cambridge Journal of Economics*, 21 (1997), 1–26.

—— *Keynes on Population* (Oxford, 2000).

Trevelyan, G. M., *Grey of Fallodon* (London, 1937).

Van Dormael, A., *Bretton Woods* (London and Basingstoke, 1979).

Van Zeeland, P., *A View of Europe, 1932: An Interpretative Essay on Some Workings of Economic Nationalism* (Baltimore, 1933).

Vicarelli, F., *Keynes: The Instability of Capitalism* (London, 1984).

Viner, J., 'International Finance in the Post-War World', *Lloyds Bank Review*, no. 2 (Oct. 1946), 3–17.

—— review of É. Mantoux's *The Carthaginian Peace*, *Journal of Modern History*, 19 (1947), 69–70.

—— *International Economics* (Glencoe, Ill., 1951).

Vines, D., 'John Maynard Keynes 1937–1946: The Creation of International Macroeconomics', *EJ*, 113 (2003), 338–61.

Walker, J. S., *Henry A. Wallace and American Foreign Policy* (Westport, CT 1976).

Waltz, K., *Man, the State and War* (New York, 1959).

Ward, B., *The Ideal Worlds of Economics* (London and Basingstoke, 1979).

Wells, H. G., *A Modern Utopia* (London, 1905).

West, F., *Gilbert Murray: A Life* (London and Canberra, 1984).

Wight, M., *Power Politics* (London, 1979).

Williams, J. H., *Postwar Monetary Plans* (3rd edn., New York, 1947).

Wilson, D., *Gilbert Murray OM, 1866–1957* (Oxford, 1987).

Wilson, P., 'The Myth of the "First Great Debate" ', *Review of International Studies*, 24 (1998) special issue, 1–15.

—— *The International Theory of Leonard Woolf: A Study in Twentieth Century Idealism* (New York and Basingstoke, 2003).

Wilson, T., *The Myriad Faces of War: Britain and the Great War, 1914–1918* (Cambridge, 1986).

Winch, D., *Adam Smith's Politics* (Cambridge, 1978).

Wittgenstein, L., *Letters to Russell, Keynes and Moore*, ed. G. H. von Wright (Oxford, 1974).

Woods, R. B., *A Changing of the Guard: Anglo-American Relations, 1941–1946* (Chapel Hill and London, 1990).

Woodward, L., *Great Britain and the War of 1914–1918* (London, 1967).

Woolf, Leonard, *Barbarians at the Gate* (London, 1939).

Zimmern, A. E., *Nationality and Government* (London, 1918).

—— *Europe in Convalescence* (London, 1922).

—— *The Third British Empire* (London, 1926).

—— *The League of Nations and the Rule of Law* (London, 1936).

Index